MAKE
WORK
HEALTHY

MAKE
WORK
HEALTHY

Create a Sustainable Organization
with
High-Performing Employees

JOHN S. RYAN AND MICHAEL J. BURCHELL

Published by John Wiley & Sons, Inc., Hoboken, New Jersey.
Published simultaneously in Canada.

For general information on our other products and services or for technical support, please contact our Customer Care Department within the United States at (800) 762-2974, outside the United States at (317) 572-3993 or fax (317) 572-4002.

Wiley also publishes its books in a variety of electronic formats. Some content that appears in print may not be available in electronic formats. For more information about Wiley products, visit our web site at www.wiley.com.

Library of Congress Cataloging-in-Publication Data

Names: Ryan, John S., author. | Burchell, Michael J., author.
Title: Make Work healthy: create a sustainable organization with high-performing employees / John S. Ryan and Michael J. Burchell.
Description: First edition. | Hoboken, NJ : Wiley, [2023] | Includes bibliographical references and index.
Identifiers: LCCN 2022054050 (print) | LCCN 2022054051 (ebook) | ISBN 9781119989806 (cloth) | ISBN 9781119989820 (adobe pdf) | ISBN 9781119989813 (epub)
Subjects: LCSH: Personnel management. | Employee health promotion. | Work environment. | Organizational effectiveness.
Classification: LCC HF5549 .R93 2023 (print) | LCC HF5549 (ebook) | DDC 658.3—dc23/eng/20221215
LC record available at https://lccn.loc.gov/2022054050
LC ebook record available at https://lccn.loc.gov/2022054051

Cover Design: Wiley
Cover Image: © VectorMine/Shutterstock
Printed and bound by CPI Group (UK) Ltd, Croydon, CR0 4YY

C004821_100223

Dedicated to the managers and leaders championing healthy workplaces. We hope you will see this book as an inspiration as to what is possible when you put well-being at the center of your people strategy and an invitation to connect with others so that all of us widen our understanding of what healthy workplaces are and can be.

Contents

PART II

Introduction: A Critical Moment

In April of 2014, Stanford professor Jeffrey Pfeffer took the stage in New Orleans and dramatically announced that workplaces were killing people. His shocking slides showed data for suicides, heart attacks, cancers, and many other diseases that could be correlated to unhealthy workplaces. He shared the astonishing fact that in Japan, because death by overworking is so prevalent, they have a name for it: *karoshi*.

And if that wasn't bad enough, he told his engrossed listeners that nobody cared!

Sitting in the audience, we immediately thought that he was exaggerating the situation for effect. But as we listened intently, the data he shared grew increasingly shocking. It seemed that work had become a dangerous thing to do, the workplace a dangerous place to be.

Having spent the previous 25 years working with organizations in a range of industries, from big pharma to high tech, retail to finance, professional services to the public sector, we thought that we'd seen it all and knew just about everything there was to know about work and the workplace. We had consulted with hundreds of organizations on their transformation journeys, guiding them from low-performance to higher-performance workplaces. We had witnessed the positive and negative effects of leaders, those who were trusted and those who were despised. We were sure that we knew the key factors that mattered, believing that organizational culture was paramount to performance and that trust was the secret sauce to unlock discretionary effort, inspire collaboration and innovation, and drive productivity, creating the much-envied agile workplace of the future.

Sitting through Pfeffer's presentation, we began to question if we'd gotten it all wrong.

Pfeffer's presentation evolved into his book *Dying for a Paycheck*, which was published in 2018. We consider it a critical moment, a catalyst that has inspired a movement that is spreading across the world. His presentation inspired John to set up the organization Healthy Place to Work, and it has become a North Star for Michael since leaving Great Place to Work in the US. We believe it has helped set a new aspirational standard for organizations.

Since that transformational moment in New Orleans, we have uncovered an important gap in our knowledge and experience. We have identified a critical factor that is a true game changer for organizations chasing the ultimate high-performance workplace. It brings together all the elusive elements that are necessary in addressing the complex issues in today's zeitgeist, from individual and corporate purpose to sustainability, mental health to gender equality, from diversity, equity, and inclusion to the creation of a safe place of belonging that is free from racism and discrimination.

It's HEALTH!

It has become clear to us that workforce/workplace health is the biggest predictor of organizational performance. However, most organizations are getting it completely wrong and are wasting huge amounts of money and resources in the process.

First, they are using an outdated definition, which focuses on a pathogenic approach to health, meaning they view health as the avoidance of disease. Instead, they should be taking a salutogenic approach, focusing on the elements that will make workers healthier and more resilient in the face of today's difficult living and working challenges. In addition, the tactical, event-based, tick-the-box approach to the issue of health is deeply flawed. A strategic, evidence-based, and data-driven approach is required.

THE PROBLEM WITH LEADERS

It also became abundantly clear that the leaders of many organizations are the biggest obstacle to workplace health. Employees need role models, and the leaders were modeling the worst behaviors. In many cases leaders had knowingly sacrificed their own health in the pursuit of power and profit. They operate in a toxic, politically driven culture focused on winning at all costs. Quarter-by-quarter reporting has created a pressure cooker that has resulted in employees being viewed as replaceable resources rather than unique individuals with personalized needs.

Most leaders, speaking confidentially, admit to being worn out, at their wit's end and close to burnout. They are working long hours, experiencing extreme pressure and stress, and attempting to achieve the impossible art of running a business in a pandemic while also being there for their families and friends.

"Things were tough anyway and then the COVID came to town," remarked one exhausted leader we interviewed. Another questioned the trade-off he had made in pursuit of career progression and a great pension; "This is why they pay me the big bucks" was his resentful comment. Some admitted to thinking twice about attracting others to take the same career route, but like a Ponzi scheme, it needed more newbies so the others could check out with the goodies.

When the COVID-19 pandemic hit, the pace of work life was already manic, the challenges significant. Leaders were juggling too many balls, hoping not to drop any important ones that could be catastrophic to the business. That was the game they all played.

And as the coronavirus lingered and mutated, in addition to worrying about their own health and safety as well as their family's and employees', leaders were confronted with a tight labor market and growing expectations around the employee experience. Heap on to those complex challenges ambitious targets around diversity and inclusion, the need to address the gender pay gap, demands for a racist-free, LGBTQ+-friendly workplace, and employee demands that companies make serious commitments to fight climate change, and you have a tinderbox of stressed-out leaders and competing priorities. There was no playbook for CEOs and executive teams who are desperately trying to navigate this new terrain.

The pandemic highlighted the fact that the system was broken. It gave people time to think. Employees realized that work simply wasn't working and in many cases was damaging their health and their relationships, and robbing them of treasured moments with friends and family members.

So is work the enemy of health? Well, not quite.

While bad work and poor workplaces can be lethal to your health, life without work is also harmful. The statistics around retirement are a bit frightening. When you remove the purpose for getting up every morning and a feeling that you are contributing to the world with your skills and talents, health declines at a significant rate. Think twice before you make retirement your life's ambition!

While it is clear that work can make you sick, it can also be the best part of your life. Work that matches your ambitions, plays on your strengths rather than exploiting your weaknesses, work that allows your talents to shine, enabling you to feel successful—that kind of work can make you the healthiest you have ever been.

WHAT YOU CAN EXPECT FROM THIS BOOK

Our intention for this book is to provide you with the theoretical and practical understanding of what healthy workplaces are and how you can create one in your organization—regardless of its size or industry or location. We begin by doing a deeper dive into why work isn't working but also why work is also (paradoxically) the answer. It's important to understand the problem clearly but also what the promise holds for leaders and managers willing to lean in and create salutogenic-focused organizations: organizations that center health as a business strategy and organizing principle.

In the pages that follow, we will share insights from experts including Jeffrey Pfeffer, Ron Goetzel, David Ulrich, Jim Loehr, and many more. You will also learn from the firsthand accounts of leaders around the globe as we relay their journeys. These brave leaders recovered from missteps and navigated dead ends as they transformed their companies into healthy organizations.

We will also share some important theoretical and historical elements as well as practical frameworks to assist you in this journey. We think that doing this will be helpful to you as a reader to understand not only how we got to where we are but will also point the way for how to think about and measure health. As you know based on your leadership experience, what is measured gets managed.

We then will pivot to examining the journey toward creating and sustaining a healthy workplace. We'll examine the symbiotic relationship between workforce and workplace health and how that informs the "lens" with which you can understand the dynamics in your own organization. We will highlight the lessons we've learned about where most organizations get it wrong and how you can accelerate progress.

For those of you with high-minded motives, that is to actually make a significant impact on the lives of the people you work with every day and the lives of those they come in contact with, their friends and family, we hope you will find answers and inspiration.

Importantly, we hope you will see and use this book as an ongoing resource. We hope you will turn to this book again and again to explore the tools, resources, helpful tips, and voice of inspiration as you take on one of the greatest opportunities to make a meaningful impact on your organization's people and its performance.

MAKE WORK HEALTHY

PART

I

CHAPTER 1

The Ultimate Driver of Organizational Performance

How healthy are you? How healthy are your people? How healthy is your organization?

These are vitally important questions—the answers to which determine the limits of your life, your team's effectiveness, and your organization's success. These questions are interrelated. Your team and your organization have a direct impact on your own health and well-being. And your organization's performance and success are dependent on the health of its people. This symbiotic relationship between your people's health and your organization's health and performance may seem like a no-brainer. You might be thinking, "Of course that would be the case." But in our research and experience in working with organizations over several decades, we find that very few organizations act on this understanding. If they do make some effort, we find that employees are typically offered some sort of wellness or workplace well-being program. These might be useful, necessary even, but not sufficient. And more importantly, they fail to address the organization's strategic opportunity in organizing itself and developing more ways of working that actually promote and support employee health.

What if leaders seriously entertained the idea that higher performance is a result of businesses organizing around their people rather than people having to organize around the business? We have taken as fact that the way to increase productivity and profit is through an absolute adherence to Taylorism, the management theory made popular by Frederick Taylor that is characterized by standards, being mechanistic, inflexible, and precise. These ideas have made a significant contribution to our understanding of organizations and productivity; they have their place. However, the wholesale shift to this organizational mindset has its limits and isn't without cost. We find that an adherence to old ways of working and relating results in a decreased sense of personal purpose and accomplishment, less role and strategic clarity, and disconnection and lack of control over one's work environment. It's unfortunate, as organizations then

3

must invest in programs and interventions just to address the problems that this mindset created in the first place!

A people-centered workplace might seem like a tough shift to make. If you're a leader, manager, or small business owner and looking to realize increased effectiveness with your people or productivity and financial results, reimagining how to organize your business and its culture seems like a bigger project than you might have the appetite for. The usual way of managing and leading may be tempting, but if you have picked up this book, we imagine that you're open to making a shift in mental mindset and aligning your behaviors to achieve outsized business gains and, concurrently, have a more authentic and fulfilling experience as a leader. In other words, it's worth the investment of creating a healthy place to work, and the energy you put into this will yield significant returns. This book aims to equip leaders with a road map and tools to make a demonstrable impact with their people and their organization. We argue here that rather than work and the workplace being the cause of disease, dysfunction, and limited performance, a healthy workplace is the key to unlocking the full value of your people and your organization.

When we ask the question, "How healthy is your organization?" we often hear from our clients' employees that it's not or maybe it's "sort of." Rarely do we hear that they work in a consistently and reliably healthy workplace. Employees at all levels will describe how it is difficult to balance competing demands at work or that their contributions aren't fully valued or that they don't feel like they belong. Sometimes their manager takes credit for their ideas, or they are given unachievable deadlines within a regular workweek, or there is little role or strategic clarity. One leader shared with us, "I'm wiped out and exhausted by the end of the week, and so I need the weekend to recharge, but that's difficult to do because I have family responsibilities on the weekend too."

DEFINING "HEALTHY WORKPLACE"

A healthy workplace is one that incorporates a strong sense of alignment to organizational values and purpose. The leaders and managers in healthy workplaces role-model a supportive and healthy workplace culture. They also support people in being the best version of themselves. They give employees opportunities to contribute their best and create an inclusive and just workplace. Employees in these workplaces feel like they have a strong supply of productive energy. They operate in an energizing physical environment, and they have a similar level of energy at the end of the day as when they started. They can attend to the demands of work and their families and communities with equitable attention. They also have healthy relationships at work, and they often feel like their work just flows.

You'll notice that this expanded definition is more than just physical health. Quite often, leaders think *health* is equivalent to *physical health*. In reality, that is just the beginning. When we look at healthy organizations, we find there is a clear sense of purpose. There is a way in which employees are aligned with the organization, both in terms of values and how their work contributes to the larger whole. *Health* is also made manifest in how the organization bolsters employees' mental resilience. The organization encourages a learning mindset and encourages employees to grow and expand their contributions. Work requirements are manageable, and employees have control over how they work. Healthy workplaces encourage connection. Employees feel like they belong and can develop authentic, productive relationships. Beyond inclusion, healthy workplaces do not tolerate racist or sexist behaviors or ways of engaging that are oppressive or unjust. These and other aspects of a healthy workplace will be explored further later in this book, but you'll note that we are taking a much larger lens when we think of *health*.

Key to understanding all of this is that our work affects our health, and in turn, our health affects our work. In some organizations, this reciprocal relationship creates a virtuous cycle whereas in other organizations, the relationship creates a vicious cycle. The symbiotic nature between worker health and organizational performance is something that will be explored throughout this book.

For managers and leaders who understand that the biggest driver of organizational performance is developing and maintaining a healthy workplace, decreasing whatever organizational friction exists and increasing employee well-being yields a powerful flywheel effect. The upside value to business can be substantial in terms of increased worker productivity, decreased sickness absences, reduced health care costs, and a compelling employer brand that attracts and retains talent (see www.hsph.harvard.edu/ecpe/the-business-benefits-of-a-healthy-workforce/). Research into the business benefits points out that healthy workplace cultures are 1.9 times more likely to innovate effectively and 2.8 times more likely to adapt well to change. (See https://joshbersin .com/2021/10/the-healthy-organization-the-next-big-thing-in-employee-wellbeing/.)

KNOWING VERSUS DOING

We find that many managers and leaders *think* they see how this works, and yet our experience is that they *act* counter to their understanding. Perhaps it is because leaders are looking at this problem entirely the wrong way. It may be an issue of awareness and knowledge of what health really is and understanding the individual and collective impact on organizational success. We'll discuss the science of well-being in Chapter 13 and what we've learned about this area; it is broader and deeper than most people think. We'll also differentiate this idea from the current wellness, well-being, and lifestyle trends that we see. They're related but not the same.

Perhaps, however, it is something more intransigent than knowing what to do. Perhaps the disconnect between "if we provide a gym and a mindfulness app, we've covered our bases" and then sending out an email at 10:00 p.m. at night is more of a "knowing-doing gap" as Jeffrey Pfeffer and Robert Sutton call it (see www.gsb.stanford.edu/insights/knowing-doing-gap). As leaders and managers, we know that our actions have both intentional and unintentional consequences and that how we integrate an understanding of health into our own personal models of leadership needs to be refined and sharpened. The bigger issue is how we act or execute on our understanding—in real time—to support employees' mental, emotional, financial, and physical health. Perhaps, though, our organizational systems are intentionally designed to be unhealthy. Our business processes, policies, procedures, and practices—our workplace culture—aim to support the opposite of employee health and well-being. This is a tougher problem to solve, for sure, but it is vitally important for leaders and managers that this be examined and addressed. You can't be healthy in an unhealthy and toxic work environment. At the same time, an organization can't be healthy (and all the tangible value that brings) with a workforce that isn't healthy. It doesn't work that way.

If the goal of leaders is to enhance organizational capabilities and performance and not simply decrease "unnecessary costs," then focusing on creating and sustaining workplace health is a useful core strategy and organizing principle. Creating an organization that is healthy and employees who are healthy is good for people and good for business (see www.hsph.harvard.edu/ecpe/the-business-benefits-of-a-healthy-workforce/). While we haven't experienced healthy workplaces with unhealthy employees in our consulting work, such workplaces could theoretically exist. Employees might have life circumstances or face other issues that produce unhealthy habits and behaviors. More often the case, we see healthy employees in unhealthy workplaces. Over time, however, employees experience negative health outcomes, disengage, or—if they are resilient—leave the organization for someplace less toxic and more supportive. A lot of our work, unfortunately, is focused on unhealthy workplaces that have unhealthy employees. Not only are individual health outcomes low but organizational performance is not as strong as it might otherwise be. Even if the financial results are solid in the short term, longer term the organization will have to address the problematic voluntary turnover of key talent, diminished ability to innovate, and the inability to move with agility to support new business opportunities. (For more information, see https://hbr.org/2020/06/times-up-for-toxic-workplaces and https://business.kaiserpermanente.org/insights/mental-health-workplace/workplace-stress-business-problem-getting-worse.)

The purpose of this book is to equip leaders with a road map or playbook of sorts—one in which you can center creating and sustaining workplace health as a core strategy and reap the benefits by enhanced organizational capacity and performance.

MODELING THE HEALTHY WAY

"Your health is your wealth," as the saying goes. Do you start work each day refreshed and ready to jump in? Do you get sufficient rest, and do you have good energy throughout the day? Are your relationships at home, at work, and with friends generative and nurturing? Do you have the opportunity to bring the best of you to work? Are you encouraged and recognized for doing so? Do you believe you can manage home and work demands and pressures in a fulsome, integrated, and healthy way? We find that most of us aren't able to give an emphatic "yes" to all of these questions. While this book is not about individual health and well-being per se, one item in our research has an outsized effect on whether employees experience their organization as healthy: senior leaders demonstrate healthy behaviors.

The significance of role-modeling the right behaviors is hard to understate as employees observe what is important and what is encouraged. We unconsciously and consciously mirror individuals and groups around us. Leaders and managers are uniquely positioned to influence behavior, given their inherent power and authority. Beyond their authority, elements of rational, social, or emotional techniques (Bacon 2011) can be learned and utilized by managers and leaders to influence employees in living healthier, connected lives. Leaders and managers can also improve workplace health by nudging employees toward certain decision choices that promote a wellness culture.

While the vast majority of adults self-report that they feel healthy or lead a healthy lifestyle, a recent study indicated that only 3% of Americans actually live a healthy lifestyle. And a "healthy lifestyle" was defined as moderate exercise, having body fat of less than 20% if you're a man or 30% if you're a woman, a good score on the Healthy Eating Index, and not smoking. Europeans didn't fare much better. A similar study indicated that only about 6% of adults across

20 countries had a healthy lifestyle (see https://research.unl.pt/ws/portalfiles/portal/11656704/Marques_Am_J_Hea_Prom_2018_1.pdf). The bar is not particularly high, and yet most of us are failing to address basic issues of physical health. But our overall health is simply not a function of our physical health.

If we turn to include mental and emotional health, we find that most of us struggle with varying levels of stress and anxiety (42% of women and 35% of men report feeling burned out often or almost always; see https://time.com/6101751/burnout-women-in-the-workplace-2021/). A more recent study by job aggregator Indeed (www.indeed.com/lead/preventing-employee-burnout-report) found that 52% of respondents experienced burnout, partially owing to the stresses of the recent COVID-19 pandemic.

A culture of overwork, stress, and burnout is not limited to North American and European workers. It is a global phenomenon. In East Asia, for example, Japanese workers have been working 60-plus-hour workweeks for decades. "Death by overwork" is actually a term in East Asia: *karoshi* in Japan, *guolaosi* in China, and *gwarosa* in South Korea. A 2016 Japanese paper on karoshi by Kamesaka and Tamura found that working more than 60 hours per week significantly increases the risk of karoshi for males, while the threshold for females is about 45 hours. Because Japanese women tend to bear more of the burden of housework, when housework is added to working time, women face a serious risk of karoshi. Thus, a fuller picture of our own health suggests that we are more likely to be stressed out, tired, anxious, and physically unhealthy than not, and it can lead to devastating consequences.

With the recent COVID-19 pandemic, our lives were upended. Many of us couldn't work from home. Instead, we had to physically show up for work somewhere, putting at risk our own lives, our families, and our co-workers. This created a different level of fear and stress that scientists are still trying to understand the effects of. For those who could work from home, that brought with it a different set of challenges. Isolation and loss of connection coupled with an "always on" expectation that was more constant than pre-pandemic created new mental health challenges. Many of us juggled being a parent with children learning from home, while attending to the demands of a changed work environment and workday. Millions of people around the world lost their jobs and incomes and were worried about how to pay the rent or mortgage and put food on the table. And, of course, millions of people lost their lives.

To be sure, our lives weren't stress-free nor were most of us engaged in a physically healthy lifestyle before the pandemic. In the Western world, the push and pull of our daily lives, unrelenting social media and social pressure, political tensions, economic changes, and so on have resulted in increasingly poor health outcomes. Layer in disparate health outcomes based on gender, race, and socioeconomic status, and the complexity and challenges just increase. And for many of us in other parts of the world, struggling economies and political upheaval bring with it another level of health challenges. In short, the pandemic just enhanced the already existing dread and burnout many people were facing.

All of this is cumulative, both for us individually but also collectively. If we step back and examine the impact at a macro level, we find that although people are living longer (today most people in the world can expect to live as long as those in the very richest countries in 1950; see https://ourworldindata.org/life-expectancy), we are living with and managing an increasing range of diseases. The world's biggest killer is cardiovascular disease, making up a total of 27% of global deaths (see www.who.int/news-room/fact-sheets/detail/cardiovascular-diseases-(cvds)). Not only is cardiovascular disease the number one killer in the world, but it is also the most expensive disease, costing governments, business, and individuals billions of dollars annually. That cardiovascular disease is largely preventable suggests that there is a significant opportunity to significantly improve health outcomes.

It is broader than cardiovascular disease, however. There exists a great body of research that an enormous percentage of health care costs stem from chronic disease, which also includes diabetes, circulatory disease, and hypertension. And research also underscores how much of that is caused by stress. McKinsey research (www.mckinsey.com/mgi/overview/in-the-news/good-health-is-good-business) highlights that poor health costs around 15% of global GDP from premature death and lost productive potential. The cost to business is tremendous. Role-modeling the way is the first step toward creating a healthy organization.

DEMONSTRATING CARE AS LEADERS

Besides role-modeling healthy behaviors, the other distinguishing feature we see from the healthiest workplaces are managers and leaders demonstrating caring behaviors for the well-being of their employees. This demonstration goes beyond the occasional check-in or spending the extra 60 seconds to invite a conversation on how employees are doing, but making an intentional effort to increase the level of trust and connection that you have with your people. It requires active listening and creative problem solving. In the healthiest workplaces, it means putting aside the rules of "this is what is available" in order to fashion a meaningful solution that centers on an employee's well-being. It means thinking through how to fit work around the person rather than the person around their work.

In most organizations today, leaders typically are stretched such that pausing to really consider the impact and implications of work demands on employee well-being is rarely an option. Leaders don't feel like they have the time given the push and pull demands of their role. For some leaders, asking these broader and deeper questions of their people, and then finding solutions that work for them, hasn't been a part of their repertoire. One senior manager confided to us, "I don't even know where I'd begin." For some leaders, the thought that this would even be a consideration doesn't really compute. Individual lives and needs that are not directly related to work product is outside work—a variation on "address your personal problems on your own time." However, leaders who are on the cutting edge of cultivating healthy workplace cultures understand that the personal affects the business and vice versa. Our lives can't be segmented and the boundaries defined so clearly.

The other issue that we find in our work is that most of this "caring stuff" has become the province of human resources. This is primarily how wellness or well-being programs were delegated (or relegated) to HR to begin with. It allows managers to redirect employees to the employee assistance program (EAP) or human resources department. And human resources, to manage a large population, creates rules, guidelines, boundaries, and policies that work for most but not for all. It's important for managers and leaders to understand the capacity of the organizational system to support employee health and well-being (and their own health and well-being). Without adding to labor costs, most organizations can expand beyond their present boundaries—akin to a balloon that can usually take in more air and expand a bit further. The challenge is equipping managers and leaders to engage employees in conversations that matter.

Aaron Antonovsky was a sociologist whose work concerned the relationship between stress, health, and well-being. He coined the term *salutogenesis* based on research of how Holocaust survivors coped with the stress they experienced. Despite going through the dramatic tragedy of the Holocaust, some survivors were able to thrive later in life. The discovery that there must be powerful health-causing factors led to the development of salutogenesis. For our purposes here, it's important to note that the workplace has the potential to be salutogenic or pathogenic. It's not "all or nothing" because the workplace is not free from tension or stress, and there is going to be conflict as goals and resources are contested. There are always going to be fewer resources than the need for resources. And that's not really the issue here. Managers and leaders can go a long way in creating "shock absorbers" so that people know how to cope with what the typical workplace throws at them. And managers and leaders can help better answer the question that Antonovksy asked: "How can this person be helped to move toward greater health?" When we do that, we leverage one of the biggest influencers of employee health and performance.

WHY TALK ABOUT HEALTH NOW?

Workplace health has long been an issue. In fact, historians trace workplace wellness back to Italian physician Bernardino Ramazzini (1633–1714), who is believed to be one of the first to write about the effects of work exposure on workers and was interested in the possibilities of taking preventative measures (Gainer 2008). Dr. Michael Rucker notes that workplace wellness was generally an afterthought for most organizations up until the 1950s, when employee assistance programs (EAPs) started to be offered in many organizations to address alcoholism and mental health issues (https://michaelrucker.com/well-being/the-history-of-workplace-wellness/). Certainly, EAPs have helped a great many people, but again, EAPs are an organizational intervention to address a symptom for which the organization itself is sometimes the cause. Jennifer Reardon (1998) notes that in the 1970s, workplace wellness programs were developed as the financial responsibility for health care, at least in the United States, moved from the government to businesses. These programs were largely seen as a way of maintaining or decreasing costs. It also coincided with the occupational health and safety movement, both in North America and many Western European countries.

In the early 2000s, smoking cessation programs, stress management, and nutrition programs became more commonplace in organizations. The idea here was to target high-risk groups, again in an effort to reduce health care costs. Leaders thought this was a beneficial use of resources, but many of these programs were unsuccessful in achieving the goal of reduced costs. This ushered in a change in approach from targeting specific groups to offering all employees wellness programs. The target of the intervention was still on employees and less on changing the organizational culture or how leaders led. More recently, organizations and government agencies have increased the number of disease management programs, corporate wellness programs, stress reduction and management, and health promotion programs. While all of this has been helpful, it has largely been insufficient to the task at hand. The current state can largely be summed up by Robert Chapman, CEO of Barry-Wehmiller, who reportedly stood in front of 1,000 other CEOs and said, "You are the cause of the health care crisis."

Given this, a new approach to workplace health is required—one that centers employee health and well-being as a business strategy, not an HR program. It comes at an opportune time. The recent COVID-19 pandemic has exacerbated several trends that were already in place. The first is the desire for employees to have more control over their work lives—how, when, and where work gets done. And a recent McKinsey study (www.mckinsey. com/featured-insights/future-of-work/the-future-of-work-after-covid-19) highlighted that upward of 25% of workforces in advanced economies could work from home between three and five days per week without a loss in productivity. The second trend has been for employees, particularly millennials and gen Z workers, to take periodic sabbaticals and exit the workforce (see www.cnbc.com/2022/05/18/what-gen-z-and-millennials-want-from-employers-amid-great-resignation.html). The third trend is a shifting psychological contract between employees and employers. The employer-employee psychological contract is the unwritten, intangible agreement between an employee and their employer that describes the informal commitments, expectations, and understandings that make up their relationship. Recent changes to this contract suggests a larger dynamic is at play.

Remember when your parent or grandparent had a job for life? They worked at one company their entire career and collected a gold watch and a pension when they were ready to retire. That was their employer-employee psychological contract. In the 1980s that contract changed dramatically after companies downsized, "right-sized," and reengineered many dedicated employees out of their jobs. Loyalty on both sides vanished, and job hopping became the norm. The psychological contract between employer and worker shifted dramatically.

Then, in the midst of the 2008 economic downturn, millions of jobs were shed again. When multinationals started to recover, they hired contract workers or temporary employees. For many people, being a part of this gig economy became the way forward. It was a win for businesses because they could moderate their staffing based on needs and requirements as well as save on worker benefits. Again, the psychological contract changed, making it less likely that a worker could rely on a business.

Now, with the COVID-19 pandemic, we once again find ourselves with millions of workers globally out of work, and for millions more, they have "had enough" and are exiting the labor force in the Great Resignation. The psychological contract is changing again, and how employees are viewing their employers is fundamentally changing. The new contract is characterized by a desire for improved work-life balance, flexibility, empathic leadership, diversity and inclusion, and matching values. (See www.hrexchangenetwork.com/employee-engagement/articles/renegotiating-the-psychological-contract-for-the-post-covid-world.)

The result of all this is that we find ourselves in a massively altered world. Most managers and leaders are struggling with how to find a foothold in this new business landscape. There are more jobs than available workers, and even if that dynamic changes, and the labor market evens out (and it likely will), and leaders can find the best talent to deliver value for the organization, employee expectations have changed. Employees expect that health and safety come first. The pandemic has put their health and the health of their families in a whole new light. Flexibility and time and the ability to work a hybrid schedule (for office employees) is more important than strict monetary benefits. And employees wanted to be treated as human, with full lives. They expect their managers to treat them with that kind of respect, rather than just assets in a transaction. Employees now see the risk to themselves and their families quite differently.

Finally, at a macro level, the big problem is that to be healthy you must be wealthy, because governments can no longer help meet the demand for services and we, therefore, need another solution to these global health crises. The next most powerful institution in society, after the government, is business. And as life expectancy continues to increase in much of the industrialized world, the responsibility and financial burden of taking care of citizens will shift to businesses and to individuals. Governments are becoming less able to finance the health and related costs of their citizens. Therefore, business leaders will need to step forward and lead on this issue. The wonderful thing is that it is in their short-term and long-term interests to encourage public health, and the ones that lead first will get the biggest benefit. Businesses can move the dial on employee health and make a real and significant difference in people's lives.

CHAPTER 2

Why Work Isn't Working

In our research for this book, one of the core themes that we kept returning to is that *work isn't working* for most people, and our goal was to offer a different approach and solution for leaders and managers to make work *work*. As we analyzed survey data and stories of employees, we identified a variety of reasons why work isn't working, and here we provide an overview of some of the consistent issues that employees experience.

PANDEMIC OVERLOAD AND OTHER EXTRAORDINARY DEMANDS

Sometimes when a workplace isn't performing well, we try to find someone to blame. But sometimes there is a system overload, a situation that is so unexpected that it demands an unprecedented response from all involved. The early days of the COVID-19 pandemic brought with it some of the worst scenes experienced by many. They were simply unprepared and overwhelmed to deal with a tsunami of illness.

> We have struggled with life-or-death cases constantly. Honestly this wasn't what I signed up for. Yes, I wanted to help people. Yes, I wanted to nurse them back to health, but now every patient was a carrier of a disease that we knew little about and it could kill us as was evidenced by the death and pain that had become a daily occurrence. You might not think death and dying should be unusual in a hospital; however, this was very different, it was my colleagues, my team members who were dying. Fit and healthy people of all ages suddenly becoming patients, struggling to breath, and dying right in front of us. We were helpless to fix the situation. We didn't know how to respond. We never received training to deal with this situation. I was terrified. It could be me next. I was absolutely exhausted. I was emotionally drained. There was nobody to turn to because everybody felt the same way. I wasn't sure if I could go on in this war zone, but there was nobody to take my place. I simply had

to soldier on and compartmentalize my feelings, hope and pray that others would discover a cure and stop this constant flow of suffering.

One of the biggest presenting issues in our workplace assessments over the last two years has been work demand. Many organizations found themselves delivering beyond their capacity, and that had a human cost. Those nurses and doctors, those transport operatives, those retail stores employees, the emergency services, frontline, backline, and many, many more were thrown into situations that were terrifying. The level of post-traumatic stress that some organizations are dealing with is simply off the charts.

However, there are organizations that run their business operations in such a way that places unfair demands on their people outside of the extraordinary events of the last 24 months. Burnout can be the result. For those in a position to leave, the exit door is the best way to escape the situation. For others not so lucky, the misery continues on a daily basis and takes its toll on them and their families. This is causing them significant health problems, and it doesn't have to be this way.

THE HORRIBLE MICROMANAGING BOSS

For others, their daily lives are miserable when they suffer under the oppression of some truly horrible bosses. They are living with a heightened stress response, which has horrific consequences on their bodies and their health. Of course, some of these bosses are particularly good at managing up, and the leaders in the organization are blissfully unaware of the impact on their people.

I feel like I'm back at school and my teacher is about to correct my homework. He watches everything I do, and at times I feel that nothing I do will be good enough. We seem to have a parent-child relationship. My daily life depends on the face that comes through the door every day. Some days the face is smiling and there is a subtle demand that everybody respond in turn and join in the hilarity of the situation, but then the next minute the face changes to a frown and everything becomes tense. Who will be picked out for admonishment today? My boss is a schizophrenic from moment to moment. Combine that with his need to control every aspect of everything, a level of micromanagement I have never experienced before. I can never relax. I am always on guard. What way will it go today?

The relationship between an employee and their manager or supervisor is critically important. Many managers are task oriented and simply want to get the job done without considering their impact on the individual employee. Some organizations now hire people and then let those individuals interview and select their managers, understanding how important the chemistry of this relationship is to the future success of the team.

NO ROOM FOR DIFFERENCE

To turn up to work each day and not be accepted for who you are is bad enough, but millions of workers around the world are hiding who they are for fear of the reaction it might provoke. That constant fear erodes confidence, ensuring those individuals will never bring their best whole selves to work. They will never be as creative or innovative as they can be because they are not operating in a psychologically safe environment.

> I'm not like them, I know that, but all I want is to be accepted, included, and treated with respect. They can't seem to get over the fact that as a Black gay woman, I'm not the norm in this organization. I was attracted to the narrative on the website which proclaimed an ambition to be more diverse, and I found the leadership's approach to be refreshing. However, the reality on the ground is very different. I suppose some people feel threatened by difference. I understand that it is easier for them to be around people who are just like them and see the world the same way they do, but do they have no room in their lives to welcome other views, other ideas, other people? I try to give the impression that it doesn't really bother me, but there are private moments where I simply lose it and cry uncontrollably. But I don't want to leave. I don't want these bullies to win with their subtle below-the-radar discrimination. I really want to fit in and belong, but I don't think I will ever be accepted for who I am. They know I'm Black, but they don't know I'm gay. Can you imagine what would happen if they discovered that? I will just have to continue hiding that part of who I am in my workplace. That is just the way life is here.

Many organizations have introduced chief diversity officers tasked with driving a more progressive approach to their diversity and inclusion (D&I) policies and practices. Many proclaim that they now welcome everybody with open arms to their companies, whereas the truth is that this new culture may often not have permeated the organization and all its layers. This can result in talent being attracted by the proclaimed employer brand communicated on their website and social media channels, but the reality on the ground can be very different. It is critical that organizations listen closely to the views of new employees to ensure that there is alignment between the real culture, the real employee experience, and the organization's recruitment messaging.

ULTIMATE BETRAYALS

In some organizations there is war being waged at the highest levels, and looking at it as a "blood sport" is not hyperbole. People pick sides and get busy undermining others. Many leaders are destroyed in the "games" that are played. We have talked to "tough men" who threw up several times before going into a board meeting because they knew they would be taken apart.

> For me everything changed that day; up to that point I counted those individuals as my friends and brought them along to family events. I thought I could rely on them if things went wrong. Little did I ever believe that they would be the perpetrators. It seemed that our interests were no longer aligned, and they felt threatened. They responded in the only way they knew, and that was to come out fighting. And when I say fighting, I mean dirty fighting. They simply wanted me out. Dante was right when he identified betrayal as the ninth circle of hell. It can be terrible. And then the power and politics start. Smiling faces were a mask, pretending to be playing by the rules while knowingly slipping a knife into my back and walking away with clean hands. Money, greed, power, ego, control, and oppression are dangerous bedfellows; that was how my ideal life suddenly changed.

In some companies it was simply "the deal." "That's why they're paid the big bucks" is a comment we would constantly hear. You were paid above the odds, but it was like a rodeo. The only question was: How long could you stay on? How much would it hurt when you were thrown off? Disregarded? With little or no concern for the social impact and community standing that a fall from grace as a senior executive can have on a family? Could you possibly last long enough to secure the financial future of your family? Many simply accept the fact that they are sacrificing their personal health to achieve this future state of financial security. Many female employees we've spoken to have simply decided that it is not worth it. The level of overworking, politicking, and back-stabbing required to make it at the top is something they are simply not willing to do.

The employees of these organizations are not blind to what goes on at the top. It seeps out. The boardroom battles are shared in dark places with hushed voices, but everybody who is anybody knows the score. Bullying, discrimination, isolation, intimidation, crazy work demands, poor managers, zero work-life balance—missing special family events, unreasonable expectations, emails at weekends or late in the evening causing sleepless nights. Others face a torturous commute simply to get to that workplace, hours added to their day, time away from families and loved ones. The frustration grows; the sense of being trapped increases. Of course, this most definitely is not a healthy place to work.

THE STRESS OF THE DAILY GRIND

One of the employees we interviewed at a well-known technology company offered the following anecdote we thought was very typical of others we heard in our research.

Honestly [the panic] probably started the night before. I had the kids finally to bed and I needed to check my email as my boss often has last-minute requests. There was an email requesting an early morning meeting. It simply said, "I need to see you in my office at 8:15; we need to talk urgently." Two thoughts surged through my mind. How am I going to get to the office by 8:15 as I have the kids' drop-off at that exact time? I'm going to have to pull in another favor from somebody, but who this time? What does she mean "we need to talk urgently"—am I going to get fired? And another thought raced through my mind: I can't afford to get fired! I'm struggling as it is financially. I really need this job.

Needless to say, my night's sleep was ruined. It was restless, to say the least. Tossing and turning, anxiety building. When the alarm sounded at 6:30 a.m. I hardly felt I had closed my eyes. I pulled myself out of bed exhausted. I had no energy. I was really worried about what my day would bring.

I arrived at the office at 8:15. There was no sign of my boss. I checked everywhere. Her phone rang off. I opened my email to read a message to say she couldn't make the meeting, but we could "catch up" next week and have a chat!

I was furious and slightly relieved at the same time. Furious because she had no idea the pain she had caused me, and being a woman, she should understand. Mind you, she can afford child care, but as a single mom I don't have that privilege. This kind of thing always happens to me. I'm a fool to let this go on, but what can I do?

That day was busy as I needed to deliver a project proposal to the senior team. I worked on this for weeks. What I'm going to present will save the company a lot of money. And then, as I'm grabbing a coffee in the canteen, I see the head of finance and am shocked when she tells me that the meeting has already happened. I wonder how this happened and whether my boss presented my work and never mentioned me. I still don't know if she has and have been too fearful to ask. And all of this happened before 11 a.m. A lot of days honestly feel like this . . .

Sometimes we need to be reminded of how the workplace is affecting people. When you have caring responsibilities, often others will subtly make you feel terrible. Many people, but particularly women, face a workplace that operates in a way that simply makes their life impossible. The sexual harassment that they face. The "jokes" about half-days. The unrealistic expectations. The complete disregard for the requests placed on a single mother. The broken systems. The fear. Being undermined, undervalued, disenfranchised. Most worrying is the fact that "I hate my job" translates into "I hate my life." The ultimate tragedy is that this woman, like many low-paid workers, feels trapped in a job for financial reasons and is suffering emotional anxiety, unsure whether she will lose her job. This is the reality for many people in many workplaces.

This gets translated into workplace "dread." Is your workplace a "dreadful" workplace? How many of your people are depressed? It is important that you know the signs. This woman's story makes it clear that she is sleeping poorly, has very little energy, is demonstrating high levels of anxiety on a constant basis, is worried and concerned about her finances, seems to be suffering from a low mood, has lost her appetite, and hates her life. These are just some of the signals of concern. If this was your employee, would you provide the professional help she needs? Would you change the culture? Would you fix the system?

Stress levels have some workers at breaking point. Is it any wonder that the American Institute of Stress maintains that job stress costs US employers more than $300 billion annually? Fifty percent of people say that they have changed jobs to escape stress. Stress kills like a cancer, and in fact the linkages are alarming. In Australia, workplace stress costs the economy about $14.8 billion a year according to one estimate, with work pressure, harassment, and bullying constituting some 75 percent of psychological injury claims. These statistics are featured in Jeffery Pfeffer's excellent book *Dying for a Paycheck*, where he also cites the number of people killed in work-related violence while at the workplace is "more than were killed by fires and explosions, getting caught in equipment or machinery and exposure to harmful substances combined." More people have heart attacks on Monday morning than at other times during the week, maybe because they are back at work after the weekend. In total, workplace environments in the United States may be responsible for 120,000 excess deaths per year—which would make workplaces the fifth leading cause of death. At least one million people in China currently die from overwork each year. As previously mentioned, they even have a word for it (*guolaosi*), and it is available as an option on a person's death certificate!

Stress itself is necessary to get people out of bed in the morning, and there is such a thing as healthy stress, the type that helps you build muscle in the gym that makes you stronger in the longer term. That is very different to the negative stress that is debilitating. That form of stress can take a physical and mental toll on your body and can lead to harmful long-term effects if not treated professionally. Often it is the consequential effects that are most dangerous. In an attempt to dull the pain or reduce the discomfort that individuals feel, they simply self-medicate, often in the form of drugs or alcohol. This in turn can damage relationships and affect the individual's ability to perform their role. This can lead to a vicious cycle.

SOCIAL POLLUTION

The health services around the world are dealing with the effects of bad workplaces every day of the week. This has led Nuria Chinchilla, professor of managing people in organizations at IESE Business School in Barcelona, to coin the phrase *social pollution*. She believes that it was only when organizations that polluted environmentally were fined that they stopped polluting, so too she believes that it is only when organizations are fined for their mistreatment of employees that it will stop. These fines will help to fund the health services that are entrusted with picking up the pieces of the lives that have been damaged by terrible organizational practices.

There has been an explosion in demand for mental health services for employees and former employees who are trying to recover from the effects of poor workplace practice. As discussed earlier in this book, societies are being unfairly asked to pay this bill, and with the dramatic demands expanding on the health services from demographic changes and increased longevity, not only can they not afford to provide the services, but they also can't meet the services with resources. There simply are not enough therapists to deal with demand.

The solution is that we must deal with the root cause rather than the symptoms. That means we have to deliver a new organizational performance model that works and achieves the high-performance outcomes that are demanded but critically without the devastating social impact on individuals' physical, mental, and emotional health.

Organizations that respond to the unrelenting pressure on their employees by providing a digital solution such as the wonderful Calm or Headspace apps, for example, are again purely dealing with the symptom rather than the root cause. Companies who roll out well-being days or give a week off to allow the whole company to recover are completely missing the point and these practices should be a red flag to potential recruits. Why have a well-being day? Should you ignore the need to be well for the other 364 days? Giving all staff a week off to recover acts as a bandage over a deep cut as they will return to the same workplace, designed the same way, with the same baked-in problems that will cause the same issues. That is simply not sustainable. We need a radical rethink of how we get work done.

Some employers are being forced to respond because of the Great Resignation, as their preferred model of just simply replacing worn-out people with new resources has floundered. The next generation is simply not buying into the deal. Sell yourself to an organization, work crazy hours under intolerable working conditions, accept unrelenting pressure as a given, agree with a "forced distribution bell curve" broken performance management system, report to a poorly trained manager, and be happy with a couple of weeks' holidays to recover annually until you retire and die. They have spotted the flaw!

Even our experience, working with executive teams, tells us that many senior leaders believe this is just a necessary by-product of getting high organizational performance and indeed a price worth paying. Even they themselves have sacrificed their own health to achieve their results and land a C-suite role. However, that is a choice, and what is not fair is when they build a system that sacrifices the health of their workforce in an effort to deliver supernormal profits.

CHAPTER **3**

How Work Can
Be the Solution

The solution for an unhealthy workplace is, counterintuitively, work. But how do we make work actually *work*?

Work is like fire.

Fire can be a very destructive force. Once fire takes hold, it can change from a flicker to a flame and turn into a raging torrent eating up everything in its way. Anyone who has witnessed a bush fire or a forest fire has seen the devastation it leaves in its wake. The human cost is horrific when people watch the place they called home simply disappear in flames and smoke. It doesn't take long to realize that their life has been irreversibly changed.

Those negative effects do not mean that fire in and of itself is a bad thing. When fire is controlled (picture a campfire), it can bring amazing benefits, such as warmth and light and s'mores. Fire is not simply good or bad. Our ability to use fire in the correct way is key to its impact.

Just like fire, work can be a force for good just as much as it can be a cause of devastation. Work can be the very worst part of our lives, causing us immense pain as articulated in Chapter 2, or it can be one of the best parts of our lives, allowing us to flourish in ways we simply could not imagine.

Organizational leaders all over the world have fought to implement a model of organizational performance that is simply not fit for purpose in the world where we live. In fact, it probably never was. The classic command-and-control approach might suit an army setting in battle, when it is life or death and orders must be followed as there is no time for discussion or input to question the wisdom of the approach being taken. But most of the time, we are not in a life-or-death position, although we still act as if we were. We still design an organization based on that philosophy. So work is not the problem, but how we arrange ourselves to work is the issue. The present approach is simply not working. We need to reassess and reimagine. The COVID-19 pandemic has provided us with a game-changing revolutionary moment where we can disassemble the architecture that has caused so must conflict, pain, and disengagement and replace it with a model that supports human endeavor collaboration, creativity, productivity, and performance. Our focus needs to change. How we think about how work gets done needs a radical overhaul, and we believe we have discovered the solution.

THINKING ABOUT WORK IN TERMS OF ENERGY

If we view an organization from an energy management perspective, it changes how we create our environment, structures, practices, and culture to be more supportive to humans delivering their best work. In physics, the first law of thermodynamics tells us that energy cannot be created or destroyed, but it can be transformed. Fundamentally that is the role of leadership and management in today's world. They need to create structures that view an organization as a complex and dynamic system of energy. The aim of the game is to transform energy from one form to another. The two forms in which energy exists are potential and kinetic (energy in motion). Everyday people (humans, employees, workers) are contracted to do a job. They arrive (in whatever form, virtually or physically) with a range of skills, competencies, knowledge, talents, and energy. The aim of an effective organizational system is to transform those inputs into energy in motion, resulting in a range of outputs. The cumulative output is the organization's performance.

In viewing the organization in this way, the leaders should now see themselves as energy convertors, transformers, and managers. If they reimagine their role in that way, their approach may be very different.

ONE OF OUR BIGGEST HEALTH DECISIONS

Because work has such a bad name, people automatically reject it as something to be avoided. Whenever people talk of their priorities on winning the lottery, escaping from work comes high up, with many already rehearsing exactly how they would break the news to their boss. However, often the problem is not your role, work, or job; instead in a lot of cases the problem is the match.

In fact, paid work takes so much of a person's life, if the average person is lucky enough to sleep eight hours a day, it leaves sixteen waking hours to live life. On an average day, half of those hours are spent completing paid work. This equates to the average person spending 90,000 hours at work over their entire lifetime! Therefore, our work has a huge opportunity to significantly affect our lives. For a large number of people, particularly women, unpaid work in the form of caring responsibilities take up a significant amount of their waking hours outside of any paid work. Again, the choice to take on such responsibilities should be made in the full knowledge of the effect it will have on them as individuals. However, rearing a family or caring for an elderly relative can be one of the most rewarding things a person can do with their energy and life.

The question often relates to how you feel at the end of the day when you finally reach your bed often exhausted and fully expended of your energy resources. Do you feel that your time and energy has been well invested, or do you feel resentful for the decisions that have led you to your current life and all that it requires and demands of you?

On a very functional level, paid work provides us financial resources to fund our lifestyle, but it also has the capacity to affect our health in incredibly positive and incredibly negative ways. As seen in Chapters 1 and 2, we are reaching an inflection point as our health needs change; governments cannot supply the suitable services to look after us, and our wealth has become our health. Because a huge part of our life is spent working, it gives businesses an opportunity to truly influence employee health and thus the health of our society. Therefore, our decision to select a job, role, and company is one of the biggest health decisions we will ever make in our lives.

FINDING A ROLE THAT HELPS YOU FLOURISH

As we have said, our work can be the best thing about our lives or the worst thing about our lives, so why do people spend so little time figuring out where they can truly flourish as individuals? Many will follow the money or a popular beaten track to "success" without ever really doing the necessary research to ensure they make a great decision. And that is just the actual work. What about the role, the career path, the boss/manager, the colleagues, the people, the leadership, the culture, the structure, the processes, the practices, the supports, the autonomy, the politics, and ultimately the fit?

Every potential employee is making a decision that affects their life. They need to take the time to make a healthy decision. Rather than prioritize salary, benefits, or flashy offices, potential employees should prioritize their health and rate every business/organization on whether it will be good for their health. If you use this lens, everything else will fall into place!

Too often we look into the deadened eyes of a frustrated soul who is living to regret a poor choice that at the time they had completely underestimated the long-terms effects it would have. Often, they are trapped and have built a lifestyle that makes it impossible to escape, or worse, their confidence has been shattered to the point that they don't believe they can succeed anywhere else and must stay. Both the organization and the individual will suffer.

Rather than sleepwalking into a role, a job, or an organization, the individual needs to dedicate a large amount of time so that they select a place where they can thrive and flourish—a place that plays on their strengths and talents and gives them purpose and meaning in what they achieve on a daily basis.

As a slight aside, often people will say to us that their job is mundane and boring, so how could they possibly find meaning in what they do? That is the role of the leader: to connect people to a greater purpose. If all you do is fix a widget on an assembly line, you may not be inspired by that work; however, it is essential that the leader explains how what you do fits into the overall goals of the organization and what it is achieving, and the critical part your role plays in that process. Sometimes there is little purpose in some roles, and in that case your community might create your purpose for coming to work each day. Often it is not until people retire or leave a role that they realize how much they underestimated the purpose it provided or just how important their relationships with their colleagues were in their lives.

The starting point is to deeply understand yourself. Our experience from witnessing many people who clearly don't fit the role they are being asked to deliver tells us that two things are at play, as we discuss in the following sections.

Getting Clarity from Your Organization

Firstly, often we see that the organization has not been clear about who will succeed in their culture and environment. They tend to want to attract everybody to their workplace and will select based on a range of factors that they determine will make the candidate a successful employee. However, the best organizations are clear. When you read their website and particularly the career section, they go to huge lengths to describe their culture and the environment along with the roles on offer. They do not try to sell it but rather have the confidence to tell it as it is. If they communicate well, they get fewer people applying, but those applying will be a much greater fit. This is not about a good and bad culture but rather just different cultures that suit some people rather than others.

Spectrums aid thinking. Often, we will ask leaders to position where they believe their organization sits on the following spectrums in no particular order.

Hierarchical	Flat
Secretive	Transparent
Homogenous	Diverse
Safe	Risky
Boring	Exciting
Calm	Chaotic

Disciplined	Creative
Supportive	Sink or swim
Quiet	Noisy
Slow	Fast-paced
Defined	Creative
Tightly managed	Empowered
Pedestrian	Dynamic
Short term	Long term
Tense	Relaxed
Serious	Fun
Individual	Collaborative
Moral	Amoral
Number focused	People focused
Rule based	Value based
Formal	Informal

It is important to realize that this is not a case of right or wrong, just different and appropriate to your organizational needs. You can choose your own words and your own spectrum. This assists you in having the conversation with potential candidates, being honest about what you are. Finding people who will naturally thrive in your culture and environment is the key and not having employees who are constantly struggling to fit in.

The problems start when we proclaim to be something we are not. We basically recruit on a lie. Those people will feel hoodwinked. Some will leave when they see the mismatch. Others will stay. Feelings of resentment will grow. It is time for organizations to be clear about who they really are and become obsessive about getting the correct people for those roles.

Once you define the culture, the next step is proclaiming it from the top. Dolly Parton once said the biggest problem about having a hit record is that everybody expected her to sing it every day for the rest of her life. It is similar with culture; once you decide the culture you want, you need to articulate it and reinforce that culture, every day in every way. As a leader, ensure that you are constantly highlighting when you see people living the culture you want and more importantly deal with people when they act in a way inconsistent with your proclaimed culture. This can be difficult, and you may need to make some difficult decisions about some popular people who may not be living consistently with that culture. But everybody needs to know that the previous ways are gone and those who can change over to the new ways of working are welcome, but those who can't change may perhaps be more successful elsewhere.

Understanding Yourself

The second part is about the individual. Most people don't have a deep understanding of who they are. Right now, there are digital companies who know *you* better than you know yourself. They see the digital footprint that you leave. They have created a map of the most valuable thing in your life—your attention. They know your patterns so well that they can predict what you will react to and what will tickle your fancy. They know your hidden secrets. They are constantly computing and analyzing your every (online) move. One of our goals in life should be to understand ourselves better than the computers and technology that is constantly tracking us.

The most important questions relate to you as an individual and your preferences. Most personality profile diagnostics focus on a number that again use a spectrum. Here is a list of a few words, again like the organization earlier with the different aspects of its culture. You can determine where you lie on this spectrum.

Open	Private
Intuitive decision maker	Analytical decision maker
High control	Low control
High need for inclusion	Low need for inclusion
Work independently	Work as a team
People focused	Task focused
Confident	Timid
Operates Fast	Slow and methodical
Creative	Rational

It is often useful to consider three areas when you think about your preferences: environments, teams, and managers.

- What are the environments and cultures that you thrive in, and which sap your energy? Where do you do your best work and why? What type of physical environments do you find energizing?
- In terms of teams, what do you look for most? What teams have you enjoyed being part of and why? Which teams that you were a part of were most suc-

cessful and why? What teams did you dislike being part of and why? Can you handle team politics? Are you a team player? How do you like to collaborate in a team?

- Finally, in terms of managers, what type of relationship would you prefer? Distance or closeness? What approach do you prefer to communication, support, appreciation, autonomy, and freedom?

These are just some of the ways an individual should have a deeper understanding of themselves, but there are others that may be even more relevant to you in your context. Consider your principles, your values, and your core beliefs.

Finding the workplace where you fit is like finding your tribe or returning home. Everything becomes natural and easy. You are completely aligned to the organization and its leadership, its mission vision values culture, and goals. You find deep purpose and meaning. You can operate naturally without trying to be something you are not, which will negatively affect your energy and your health. Finding an individual who is the perfect fit for your organization is also a great moment as they add to everything, they contribute, they perform, they shine, they hit flow, and the results follow.

TAKE THE EXPERT ASSESSMENT QUIZ

Let's do a little expert assessment of your workplace through the eyes of your employees. As a leader, please respond to the following set of statements. However, you are not simply responding in a personal capacity, but rather you are predicting what you believe the workforce would say. For the purpose of this assessment, we will use the Likert scale, which was first developed in 1932 by social scientist Rensis Likert. The scale gives respondents the opportunity to score their view/perception to the relevant statement on a scale from negative to positive, allowing them to express the intensity of their view.

1. Almost always untrue
2. Often untrue
3. Sometimes true/sometimes untrue
4. Often true
5. Almost always true

We simply want to determine what percentage of your employee population will agree with the statement posed. For example, if you believe 40% of your workforce would score a statement as a 4 or a 5, put 40% in the relevant box. As you notice, we combine the positive scores (4's and 5's) to achieve the % score, as the % score indicated that that % of your workforce responded positively to the statement.

Now it is your turn fill in the percentages that relate to what percentage of your workforce you believe will respond positively to these statements.

Statement	%
Senior leaders at my organization care about the well-being of employees.	
Senior leaders at my organization demonstrate healthy behaviors.	
This organization is competent and compassionate in dealing with mental health issues.	
My efforts are appreciated.	
The workplace is organized so that no injuries occur.	
I'm clear on what my line manager expects from me.	
I can balance competing demands.	
People are positive about their future careers.	
This organization helps me deliver on what is important to me.	
All things considered, I'd say this is a healthy place to work.	

This exercise gives you a little opportunity to predict the results. However, as a leader you may be completely out of touch with your people. The only way to find out is to survey or talk to your people and see their real responses.

What you will notice from the preceding test is that there are aspects about the organization, its leadership, its design, its culture, etc., that can have a very positive effect on the health of employees or a very negative effect. You need to have your finger on the pulse.

What we are dealing with are perceptions. In some cases, leaders say that the perceptions are not accurate, but remember that your perceptions are your reality. If you identify that employees have perceptions that are at odds with the reality, there is a communication gap that needs to be filled. As an example, if only 10% of people believe that *senior leaders at my organization care about the well-being of employees*, but you know every senior leader is truly passionate about the well-being of every team member, that message is clearly not landing. Therefore, you need to find ways to demonstrate that care and communicate that fact to all employees so that they really believe it to be true.

If, on the other hand, the perception is correct, then you simply need to address the issue head on. For example, if senior leaders don't have employee wellness on their agenda at all, they need to. If they don't measure it currently, they need to. If they don't manage it, they need to. If they don't talk about it, they need to. If they don't demonstrate it, they need to. If they don't respond to the presenting needs of the health status of the workforce, they need to.

WILMAR SCHAUFELI

Wilmar Schaufeli is professor of work and organizational psychology at Utrecht University in the Netherlands and distinguished research professor at Leuven University in Belgium. He has published over 400 scientific articles, chapters, and books.

> If you do not recover, recuperate, or replenish your energy, finally you'll burn out.

When it comes to the hot topic of burnout, few have researched it more than Wilmar Schaufeli.

Defining Burnout

Schaufeli sees a difference between how burnout is defined in the United States versus Europe. In the United States, it is often a crisis people have with their work, but in Europe it is a medical condition where you need to leave the workplace.

> There is research showing that it has to do with a lack of optimism, lack of self-esteem and self-efficacy, and an external locus of control. There is a whole set of personality characteristics that are related to burnout, but it is the result of a complex interaction between a person and their environment.

Interestingly Schaufeli believes employees' increased expectations can be a contributor.

My students want meaningful work, to contribute to society, to learn, develop themselves, which is all legitimate, of course, but when you have high expectations, there is a huge risk of failing and being disillusioned.

Successful Interventions

Interventions, according to Schaufeli, are normally focused on the individual, but he believes they are better targeted at the organizational level in terms of job design and job control.

It is easier to send people on a course for assertiveness, self-efficacy, or optimism than it is to structure your job, your work processes, or your management style in a better way.

Most large organizations have burnout on their radar, but most people work in small and medium-sized enterprises where the problem is greatest.

Important but Not Urgent

Occupational health is important but often not seen as urgent. Many organizations ignore the signs as job redesign or job enrichment programs are difficult; it is only when they hit high attrition or sickness levels that companies react.

A Culture That Supports Burnout

Burnout can be hidden as often employees don't want to hurt their promotional prospects by complaining about problems and workload.

People fear that it's bad for the promotion, for their reputation, so they hide it.

Supporting managers are critical.

Often they feel insecure in dealing with the psychological aspects of their managerial role.

Workaholism

Schaufeli see workaholism as different and describes it as an uncontrollable need to work excessively hard, but he believes it comes from a difference place.

Engaged and workaholic persons seem to be similar; they spend a lot of energy in their work. But there is a motivational difference. The engaged people are intrinsically motivated. For them, work is a kind of appetite. They have an approach motivation. Workaholics have an avoidance motivation; they want to avoid the negative emotions that are associated with non-working.

A Solution Focus

The key to address burnout is to catch it early. It starts with an open culture where employees feel comfortable talking about work issues. Next is to recognize the signs (exhaustion and fatigue, cynicism, and reduced professional efficacy) and build awareness so everybody can spot them. Increasing autonomy and control along with cultivating a more participatory approach to decision-making helps. Finally, along with developing good team working and social supports, Schaufeli believes that better clarity around tasks and responsibilities aimed at reducing conflicts reduces the levels of stress.

CHAPTER **4**

The Evolution
of Workforce Health

Well-being in the workplace has become mainstream in the last decade. As always, a few high-profile early adopters set the pace. And then, over time, more and more companies recognized their duty of care and moral obligation to support their employees' health, or they followed the trend, or they saw the productivity gains that can accrue. However, the concept of well-being and its applicability to the work setting has been recognized for centuries, and significant efforts have been made to address the issues of employee health through campaigners, philosophers, reformers, industrialists, legislators, social commentators, scientists, and physicians. In this chapter we will travel back across time to look at some of those key moments that have laid the foundations for our current ideas and concepts around good work and good workplaces.

There is a bias at play that we recognize. Many of the examples described are from Europe or North America. When we selected the examples, we felt we needed to highlight items that were the first of their kind, were seen as important to contemporaries, had an effect beyond their region/state at the time, influenced a new way of thinking, or have left a legacy. There are probably other examples that could be included, but we endeavored to select ones that had international impact.

One of the dangers in this type of study is to bestow our current conceptual models, frameworks, and paradigms on historical events or the protagonists. So as far as possible, we will try to explain the event or example from a factual perspective, acknowledging the thinking at the time would have been very different from how we in the early days of the 21st century conceive or perceive these events.

THE CONCEPT OF "A GOOD AND VIRTUOUS LIFE" IN ANCIENT TIMES

People could be forgiven for considering the recent interest and near obsession with health in general, but workplace health in particular, as a function of changes borne in the 21st century. However, to truly get a sense of the evolution of workplace well-being, you must travel back to Grecian times circa 300 BC! As with so much from that period, the work of Aristotle stands out. In his time, many would have been familiar with the concept of living a hedonic life—a basic searching out of pleasure with the consequential avoidance of pain. However, Aristotle believed that approach to life left individuals unwell and not deeply fulfilled in their lives.

In his pondering on the subject best articulated in his writing in *Nicomachean Ethics*, he introduced the concept of *eudaemonia* and contrasted it with the hedonic approach. In his view, eudaemonia was more closely aligned with a much deeper sense of well-being. Some literature translates eudaemonia as "happiness" and highlights the top ways that a person can find happiness, but that rather misses the point completely because Aristotle knew that looking to achieve happiness in itself and for itself is pointless, whereas if by living a "good and virtuous life" you achieve happiness as a by-product, that is more in keeping with his philosophical viewpoint.

"A good and virtuous life" is one where you discover and use your talents to their best possible effect, achieving true excellence in what you do and making a real contribution (finding meaning); this is in essence what we uncover when we talk about finding your purpose in life and aligning to it. This requires a degree of self-reflection and self-discovery, which many people fail to do in their lives, only to discover too late that they may have wasted their time and talents on pointless activities rather than the very thing that they could have excelled at. However, if people invest the time and energy to discover their talents and skills and develop a real contribution to their society, and if they do so with a moral compass and live their lives with virtue, capable of navigating with wisdom many of the challenges that life will present, they will achieve true well-being—at least that is what Aristotle believed.

WELL-BEING BEGINNINGS IN SPAIN AND ITALY

To get close to the first mention of workplace well-being, we need to fast-forward to 1593, when we first hear mention and get some legal support for the concept of the eight-hour day. Philip II of Spain, in the *Ordenanzas de Felipe II*, established the concept, which was preceded by many people working in excess of 12 hours, so this was quite a progressive departure and set the tone of things to come. The key aspect of this edict was the distribution of those hours as was sensible, with not all 8 hours having to be worked in a row. It introduced the concept of the siesta, allowing workers to split their 8 hours, 4 in the morning and 4 in the afternoon, so that they could avoid the maximum heat of the midday. Philip was also progressive with regard to sick pay, allowing those construction workers injured during the building of El Escorial to receive half pay while they were recovering. While these laws initially were implemented in Spain, they soon expanded across the Spanish empire and across the Americas.

Next, we move across to Italy circa 1700, to a famous Italian doctor, Bernardino Ramazzini, who was the first to write about and catalog occupational-related diseases. Ramazzini was among the first to highlight the effects of work exposure and the possibilities of taking preventative measures to advance employees' health and safety. *De Morbis Artificum Diatriba* was his main contribution, which provided a comprehensive handbook for medical practitioners to diagnose and treat a wide variety of occupational illness. Most notably he highlighted the link between repetitive movement and poor posture as being linked to work routines. In addition to prescribing treatments for these conditions, he proposed preventive steps that employers could take to avoid these conditions arising in the first instance.

DEVELOPMENTS IN GREAT BRITAIN DURING THE INDUSTRIAL REVOLUTION

Moving geographically and temporally, we journey to Great Britain in the mid-eighteen century and the dawning of the industrial revolution; over the course of the next 150 years, the nature of work in terms of both occupations and the workplace itself changed significantly. The development of the factory system and the advances in technology created a whole new series of risks to employee health and safety. While other countries around the world were experiencing the development of industrialized factories, it was Great Britain that became the path finders for those interested in finding better ways to deal with issues of employee health. The working conditions were harsh, and the working hours were long with little or no job security. Even though we will talk later in this chapter about several humane employers, the vast majority of industrialists showed very little interest in the health and well-being of their employees.

Robert Owen, a Welsh textile manufacturer, social reformer, and philanthropist, was an early example of the caring capitalist. From humble beginnings, Owen became an extremely wealthy factory owner and businessman. His strong moral values led him to actively campaign to improve the working and living conditions of factory workers. In 1800 he commenced the redevelopment of the New Lanark Mill in Scotland. Bringing in a new philosophy of genuine concern and care for the workforce outside of simple commercial motives, Owen was able to dispel the myth that a compassionate workplace could not be commercially successful. Having seen for himself the benefits of employees reducing the working day to 8 hours, he began to campaign actively throughout Great Britain to see the introduction of the said 8-hour day more universally. His interest in his employees extended beyond the factory walls; from both a moral and practical perspective, he understood that decent housing conditions enabled workers to be productive. He had knowledge of many workers who experienced cold, damp, dreary living conditions and the negative effects they had in their capacity to perform at their job and be truly productive. He invested in the building of high-quality dwellings for his employees, ensuring that they and their families had a strong base for their lives.

To our ears his style of management may not have seemed radical; however, the efforts he made to engage and support employees, building strong personal relationships and deeply connecting with them, signaled a truly progressive approach and laid the foundation for the success that New Lanark and its enlightened approach to management was to achieve.

Considered the father of occupational medicine, Charles Turner Thackrah, an English surgeon, carried on the work Bernardino Ramazzini had started in Italy. In addition to his own medical observations, Thackrah had access to various reports and statistics from local government inspectors to build a picture of the impact working conditions had, particularly on children in the mills of his native Leeds in England. His most influential publication, *The Effects of Arts, Trades and Professions on Health and Longevity*, provides an insight into harsh working conditions and the health and safety risks associated with various occupations and industries. Many of these jobs and roles were relatively new, and their short- and long-term negative effects were not fully understood. By cataloging the health and safety risks associated with the wide range of occupations, his studies influenced the regulations and legislation relating to the use of the removal of lead, fumes, and high temperatures from certain jobs. Sadly, Thackrah himself died at the young age of 38 of tuberculosis; despite his short life, his impact was felt not only in Great Britain but in other countries where industrialization was taking root and where campaigners and governments wished to introduce legislation to underpin improvements in health and safety.

Ironically in the same year that Thackrah died (1833), the Factories Act became law in Great Britain. This was really the first comprehensive piece of legislation to establish rules and regulations governing employee safety in the workplace. This was not just a window-dressing exercise, and to ensure compliance, a group of factory inspectors was established to carry out assessments to enforce adherence to the regulations. The scale of the task was enormous with some 3,000 individual factories identified across Great Britain and a team of just four inspectors. This was obviously not sustainable as an operation, and as if to prove the point, one of those appointed inspectors died within three years from overwork!

While there may have been limitations to the practical impact on the lives of most working people, the establishment of legislation governing employee well-being did create an awareness in society of the responsibility of business owners and organizations to consider the welfare of employees. Throughout the rest of the 19th century, further legislation built on the Factories Act of 1833, and gradually the working lives of most people became safer if not yet truly healthy.

Throughout the latter half of the 19th century, there was a growing sense of confidence and assertiveness among employees as they began to organize collectively and demand a whole series of further improvements, not just in terms of standard pay and conditions but also in terms of workplace safety.

Influential writers such as Karl Marx and Friedrich Engels, observing the great inequalities within society, articulated racial and revolutionary solutions at the political level. For the vast majority of workers, the opportunity to join a trade union was an important step in negotiating a more favorable set of employment terms. This dialogue between companies and unions saw gradual improvements in the working conditions across many industrialized countries.

Some employers didn't need the demands of trade unions to influence their decisions to proactively improve the working culture as well as the physical infrastructure of their workplaces, and examples can be found in most industrialized countries of caring employers. One case in point is the famous chocolate manufacturer Cadbury of Birmingham, England. When the success of their chocolate business required a more extensive manufacturing facility, the Cadbury family were intent on ensuring that the factory was not simply a functional production facility but rather a healthy, safe, natural setting for employees to live and raise their families in a community environment. By the 19th century, the Cadbury family had built over 300 cottages and homes for employees on their estate, which they called Bournville (later to become a brand name for one of their chocolate products).

The visionary behind the move from the cramped conditions of central Birmingham to the open fields of Bournville was George Cadbury. He truly believed in the connection between health and fitness and general well-being. With that in mind, he invested significant amounts in the development of sports and recreational facilities for employees and their families within the newly created village. Along with the physical infrastructure, George's commitment to his workforce can be seen in the establishment of a culture of respect, through comparatively high wages, excellent working conditions, employee representative committees, pension schemes, and a staff medical service. This was an exemplar of its day and clearly demonstrated that investing in employee well-being need not come at the cost of commercial success.

IMPROVEMENTS IN THE EARLY PART OF THE TWENTIETH CENTURY

Despite two World Wars and a Great Depression, the first half of the 20th century saw more and more improvements in the nature of work, working lives, and the workplace, with a growing emphasis on the health, safety, and welfare of employees. This was a global phenomenon and not just the preserve of rich industrialized nations. The Treaty of Versailles, which was signed at the end of World War I, included a clause establishing the International Labour Office (now the International Labour Organization), demonstrating the growing significance of the rights of employees and collective representation. The International Labour Organization's Hours of Work Convention in 1919 established guidelines and recommendations on working time and in particular the eight-hour working day, which was ratified by many industrialized countries over the following decade.

This era was also characterized by the dual factors of increasing female participation in the workforce, which was out of necessity during both World Wars, and an increasing level of automation within the workplace. This meant organizations were hiring employees with different skillsets and different career expectations. By the time the 1950s arrived, organizations were becoming more sophisticated and complex in structure, and more and more were operating at a global rather than regional scale. Management practices, driven as much by the advances in behavioral science as the growth of the multinational corporation, changed some of the preconceived philosophies of leadership, management, and the psychological contract of the employment relationship.

CHANGES IN THE UNITED STATES AFTER THE WORLD WARS

During the post-war 1950s, the USA's preeminent economy provided the fertile environment for the introduction of new concepts in organizational design, production, and the growing emphasis on employee development. With the growth of business schools investing in research and harnessing the findings, more and more recognition of the employee's value became mainstream. "People are our most important asset" became a mantra, even if the lived experience of most employees was not anything close to this tagline. However, it would be churlish to say that all organizations were just paying lip service to the employees' health and well-being. Like all new trends, there would be early adopters who would provide the example for others to follow, particularly if the practice demonstrated some competitive advantage or efficiency.

During this era, many companies moved beyond the mandated health, safety, and welfare standards and began to incorporate other support systems, such as the introduction of employee assistance programs (EAPs). While today EAPs have an extremely broad remit and are much more commonplace, the early programs tended to focus primarily on issues of alcoholism and broader mental health issues. These early programs evolved over the following decades through the Occupational Safety and Health movement and the Worksite Health Promotion movement. Again the momentum was for a greater focus on health and well-being in workplaces grounded in research, promoted by leading brands and gradually spreading to more and more organizations as they became mainstream.

One leading brand, Johnson & Johnson, introduced a program in the late 1970s called Live for Life. While there is no doubt that all over the world, smaller, less high-profile organizations were introducing similar initiatives, the comprehensiveness and scale of the J&J program was immense. Its holistic approach for workplace well-being meant it became the prototype for large corporations to emulate, and they did in droves.

Workplace well-being had emerged as the result of a coalescence of developments. The evolution of the workplace through greater employee participation or representation, the advances in understanding of organizational psychology, the changing nature and makeup of the workforce, the increasing statutory obligations, the changing concepts of management behavior, the greater levels of affluence, education, and career opportunities within society, and the case studies demonstrating that some investment in employee well-being could bring productivity improvements and efficiencies all contributed to the growing prevalence of well-being initiatives.

STUDIES AND RESEARCH FROM GOVERNMENTS AND UNIVERSITIES

Governments around the world introduced schemes and programs to encourage organizations to promote health in the workplace for the benefit of employees, employers, and society. In the United States, the Healthy People 2000 initiative of the early 1990s focused on encouraging organizations with over 50 employees to provide health promotion services to their workforce. Again in the United States, surveys were undertaken, such as the National Survey of Worksite Health Promotion Activities in 1994, to understand what activities, programs, and facilities organizations were undertaking or providing to support employee health and well-being. The results of these indicated organizations were doing quite a lot, and the fact that these surveys were occurring created a greater awareness by employers and employees of what is possible.

At the same time, in the European Union more and more directives were issued requiring member states to enact legislation covering a range of traditional health-related themes, such as working time regulations, but also other issues that would not have conventionally come under the health banner, such as discrimination and equality within the workplace.

Not only were advances being made in terms of government initiatives, but more and more evidence emerging from occupational health departments in universities also added energy and momentum to these initiatives. This included the shift away from an over-focus on mitigating health and safety risk to health promotion. An example of this is the work of Nola Pender. Pender is a Professor Emerita at the University of Michigan and designated a Living Legend of the American Academy of Nursing. Her research and work dating back to the 1970s resulted in her publishing the Health Promotion Model in the early 1980s. While the intent was to assist nurses in understanding the factors affecting health-promoting behaviors, its relevance to well-being in the workplace has been significant. Her comprehensive model provided guidance, consciously or not, for the development of almost all modern corporate wellness programs today.

With the increasing recognition, popularity, and growing acceptance of the need to incorporate some workforce well-being strategies, it was only a matter of time before rigorous research into cost-benefit analysis was undertaken. The Baicker, Cutler, and Song Harvard study of 2010 was titled "Workplace Wellness Programs Can Generate Savings" and suggested that well-being programs would be financially beneficial investments and would improve productivity. A couple of years later, the RAND Workplace Wellness Programs Study rebuked the earlier Harvard study and stated that "lifestyle" interventions have little effect on companies' bottom line.

So to summarize, the research is mixed, and the complexity of the factors affecting employee well-being, productivity, and efficiencies are such that definitive assertions will always be a challenge to prove. If the key research papers were producing contradictory results and the ensuing arguments are challenging the assumptions and methodology, the impact on organizations adopting more and more elements to their well-being programs has not abated.

Other heavyweight institutions have weighed in, including the World Health Organization (WHO) and the United Nations (UN). The WHO Healthy Workplace Model provides a holistic framework for organizations to assess their own programs against. In addition to supporting the workplace to be healthier for the benefit of the employees, the WHO, with its remit on public health, was acknowledging the role the work and the workplace can play in a range of broader aspects such as disease prevention, mental health, and obesity on society at large.

The United Nations' high-level meeting on non-communicable disease prevention and control in 2011 called on the private sector to "promote and create an enabling environment for healthy behaviors among workers, including by establishing tobacco-free workplaces and safe and healthy working environments through occupational safety and health measures, including, where appropriate, through good corporate practices, workplace wellness programs and health insurance plans." The UN's Sustainable Development Goals (SDGs) are a collection of 17 interlinked global goals designed to be a "blueprint to achieve a better and more sustainable future for all." The SDGs were set up in 2015 by the United Nations General Assembly with the intention of achievement by 2030. A number of the goals have relevance to comprehensive 21st-century workplace health and well-being programs, such as "Good Health and Wellbeing," "Gender Equality," and "Decent Work and Economic Growth."

While many of the corporate programs and government initiatives were more commonly found in developed economies, the reach and global remit of the WHO and the UN have raised the profile of employee well-being in less developed/emerging economies.

CHALLENGES IN THE TWENTY-FIRST CENTURY

The last 15 years of workplace evolution from a health perspective has been dominated by a desire to show the workplace as one that embraces difference and allows all employees to feel included and experience high levels of psychological safety.

Organizations have absorbed many of the societal campaigns with an emphasis on gender, race, and sexual orientation. #MeToo became the pivotal event signaling an end to unacceptable treatment of women in the workplace from a viewpoint of abuse, harassment, and a lack of respect. But in addition there are moves around gender equality from a pay perspective and attempts to remove barriers allowing women to progress to the very top of organizations, being viewed as equal to their male colleagues in every respect.

Black Lives Matter once more raised the issue of race and racism. While society had made moves to legislate for protection based on race, the reality for many was that they were not experiencing equality at work or in society as a whole. Organizations had to move beyond the policies and proclaimed practices to deal with the cultural reality on the ground. While many global organizations were working hard to root out racism, others had to revisit their values to ensure that institutional racism was not a reality in their corporations.

While the origins of #MeToo and BLM were in the United States, they soon spread across the globe with organizations in different continents working to ensure minority groups in their country could feel truly accepted and equal. These changes were more pronounced first in the larger corporations but soon transcended to the small organizations.

In keeping with the diversity and inclusion agenda, people's sexual orientation was another major issue of campaign. For years the fight related to discrimination, but once that hurdle had been overcome, the challenge was to drive integration and acceptance on a global basis. LGBTQ+ and pride parades became must-support events for organizations to celebrate, making the workplace feel safer and more accepting of a range of sexual orientations.

The data coming from EAP (employee assistance program) providers clearly showed an upward trend in anxiety, stress, and depression among many employee cohorts. Organizations responded with a renewed openness for people to feel comfortable to discuss their mental health struggles. "It's okay not to feel okay" became the clarion call of the mental health first aiders deployed throughout many companies, with a clear realization that governments or indeed HR departments could simply not be resourced to deal with the number of requests for help, a case made worse with the arrival of the COVID-19 pandemic.

However, this event seemed to provide a moment in time that gave all people permission to express their sense of personal struggle to handle the challenges it brought. Many turned to neuroscience for answers, with mindfulness becoming increasingly popular. The pandemic itself provided the biggest change to workplace practices in a century, with working from home (WFH), remote working, and hybrid working becoming essential for half the population who were lucky enough to be able to operate and deliver their work in that way. For others, simply going to work was a risky business. The new ways of working leveraged the possibilities already provided by technology and cloud computing, allowing many to choose a way of working that better suited their lifestyle.

Technology also entered the health world with a proliferation of digital apps to deal with a range of workplace and personal life challenges brought on by life in the 21st century. Societal issues of climate change and sustainability were weighing heavy on people's minds, with employees only choosing to work for employers who could prove their credentials on both topics.

In some ways workplaces and society have moved full circle from the start of the evolution with Aristotle's contemplation of eudaemonia as the answer to a good life being rediscovered, as employees also sought out organizations that could provide them with purpose and meaning along with a paycheck.

CHAPTER 5

Salutogenesis: A New Model for Workplace Health

This book opened in Chapter 1 with a question: How healthy are you? In answering that question, we will often consider our own health status in relation to whether we are experiencing any ailments. If we aren't suffering from a cold, flu, sore muscles, achy joints, or some more advanced form of illness, we will probably answer in the affirmative that we're feeling fairly healthy.

This is what is called a pathogenic orientation. When we have this type of orientation, we see "health" as something we have automatically, or inherently, that can be taken away from us if we experience disease or sickness of any sort. We simply see health as the absence of disease. But there's more to health than that, as you will find out in this chapter.

A PATHOGENIC ORIENTATION VERSUS A SALUTOGENIC ORIENTATION

When researching the development of our Healthy Place to Work model, we discovered the work of Professor Aaron Antonovsky, an American Israeli sociologist and academic whose work focused on the relationship between stress, health, and well-being.

Antonovsky had an alternative view to the pathogenic one described earlier. His theory was developed during his time researching women in Israel who had been in concentration camps during World War II. These women had experienced firsthand the horrors of the Nazi regime. It would be truly understandable if these women were unable to live normal lives following their release, maybe suffering higher levels of depression or anxiety or worse, considering what they had been through, but Antonovsky was intrigued to see that many (over one-third) went on to lead extraordinarily normal lives, showing no differences compared to a control group. He wanted to understand why in the face of similar stress forces, some were equipped and able to handle or absorb that stress without it having a debilitating and devastating effect on their lives moving forward. This would provide him with insight into the ability of individuals to be truly resilient in the face of hugely challenging circumstances.

While initially we will look at Antonovsky's finding from an individual perspective, we believe there are real gains to be achieved when we view this in an organizational context. Organizations by their nature create and deal with a significant amount of tension and stress, and this can have a very negative impact on individual employees. If we could extrapolate the learning from Antonovsky's work, we could provide leaders with a range of strategies that they could deploy to mitigate the negative effects of stressors on their people and in turn on their performance.

Antonovsky was interested in the origins of health rather than the origins of disease. He wanted to discover the assets people could acquire and deploy to make them healthier rather than focusing on avoiding the risk factors for diseases that would make them sick. This led Antonovsky to coin the term *salutogenesis* from the Latin and Greek languages, describing the origins of health, rather than *pathogenesis*, which is more focused on the origins of disease. This shift in orientation and focus had profound effects and began a philosophical movement that has grown and expanded through the years since his untimely death in 1994. Antonovsky also uncovered what he believed to be key attributes of people who had acquired a higher level of resistance to life stressors—that is, a "sense of coherence," which we will discuss later in this chapter.

In some ways this orientation is best exemplified by the recent COVID-19 pandemic. If you have a pathogenic orientation to COVID-19, you will hide away from the disease, staying isolated in your home, not interacting with friends, neighbors, and work colleagues, as each could bring you closer to the disease. When moving about, you will wear a mask and take many precautions to ensure you avoid the disease. It is about reducing the risk factors.

In contrast, with a salutogenic orientation to COVID-19, while people clearly understand that the disease severely affects those who already have underlying health conditions or are immunocompromised or are frail in some way, the aim is to develop a resistance to the disease. In that regard people with a salutogenic orientation may work hard to become physically, mentally, emotionally, and socially stronger, and more resourced so that if they are infected with the disease, they will be better equipped to handle its effects.

We know there are many risk factors that could negatively affect our health. We have a choice to constantly avoid these factors, which is virtually impossible, or we can take an alternative approach that is focused on building better resistance to those negative disease-forming risk factors.

THE EASE TO DIS-EASE CONTINUUM

Some view the human condition as being stable and healthy, and at certain points people face stressors. Antonovsky saw things differently; he believed that life was inherently full of stress and the moments without stress were the exception rather than the rule. For him life is a constant struggle. People face all kinds of stressors; the ultimate one, no doubt, is dealing with their own mortality. However, some can cope with those stresses better than others and function effectively while others will suffer, and their life will be negatively affected.

Antonovsky was obsessed about knowing the difference. What was it that made one person healthy and the other ill in the face of the same stressors? Antonovsky laid out his philosophy in his seminal publication *Health, Stress, and Coping* in 1979 and later added to his views with his book *Unraveling the Mystery of Health* in 1987.

Rather than seeing healthy versus sick as a binary option, Antonovsky encouraged us to view it as a continuum from ease to dis-ease. At any moment in time, we are at some point on this scale. The key is to move away from dis-ease and move toward ease.

Generalized Resistance Resources

What determines where you are on the ease to dis-ease scale? This is where Antonovsky introduced the concept of *generalized resistance resources*. While we will all be faced by stressors in our lives, the level of resistance resources we have at our disposal to mediate the stress at any time will determine the overall effect it will have on us as individuals. If we have significant resources to mitigate the stresses, they will have a lesser effect on us as individuals. Alternatively, if we have low levels of resistance resources, the stresses will have a negative impact. The key is the level of general resistance resources we can deploy.

In this regard he highlighted a number of resources at our disposal, including material ones, knowledge and intelligence, ego, identity, coping strategy, social supports, commitment continuance, cohesion, control, cultural stability, magic, religion, philosophy, and a preventative health orientation. Many of these resources may have resulted from our upbringing or the culture of our society. People who are born into poverty have fewer resources to deal with life's challenges and they often take a greater toll.

Antonovsky talked about the "river of life" to explain his concept further. Many will know the story of the man walking by a river, seeing someone drowning, who he then saves, only to see another and another. His constant attempts to save people exhaust him.

Sometimes, we seem to be constantly saving people from drowning in the river of life without ever going upstream to understand why people are ending up in the river in the first place. However, Antonovsky believed that we are all in the river, but some can swim better than others, and the resources mentioned earlier can help us stay away from the dangerous part of the river and allow us mostly to swim in calm waters. Others, not so fortunate, are swimming in polluted waters and can experience a flood where they feel out of control. The salutogenic model is about equipping people to swim and providing them with resources that allow them to experience an easier part of the river.

A Sense of Coherence

Antonovsky believed that it was pointless to try to control all the risk factors that affect us as individuals from getting sick or contracting diseases. For him a better and smarter approach was to focus on the factors that make us healthier and allow us to fight disease and handle the stressors that our environment presents to us. This constant adaptation to the environmental factors that we face defines the second concept that Antonovsky discovered and considered key to staying healthy in life. He answered his initial question as to what are the origins of health. His solution was a "sense of coherence," which he described as follows:

> A global orientation that expresses the extent to which one has a pervasive, enduring though dynamic feeling of confidence that (1) the stimuli deriving from one's internal and external environments in the course of living are structured, predictable, and explicable (comprehensibility); (2) the resources are available to one to meet the demands posed by these stimuli (manageability); and (3) these demands are challenges, worthy of investment and engagement (meaningfulness). (Antonovsky 1987)

The three key concepts are comprehensibility, manageability, and meaningfulness. When an individual is affected by a stressor, do they believe that they can put a shape on the problem and issue that they are dealing with, often seen as their ability to get their head around it? This relates to their cognitive abilities to understand all aspects of the issue that they are facing, which is causing them stress. Once they have captured the essence of the issue at play that is causing the stress, do they then believe that they have the resources at their disposal to manage the situation successfully, are they equipped to overcome the challenge they face, and finally and crucially, are they motivated to do so, is it worth the effort to fight to overcome the challenges they face? Because that fight takes energy every single day. These are all critical factors when we turn our attention to the application of Antonovsky's philosophy in the context of a workplace.

The difference between a pathogenic orientation versus a salutogenic orientation is fundamental to how we approach work, life, and our world. This book and the general Healthy Place to Work model is built on the principles of the more positive salutogenic orientation. In our model, we aim to identify the factors that make an individual healthy, particularly with a focus on their work life and all the stresses that they will face in delivering productively.

What are the factors that we can strengthen to make us more resilient? How can we create a greater level of sustainability? In workplaces and organizational terms, how can we create a system that will be resilient, sustainable, and focused on high performance, a healthy system with healthy people?

SALUTOGENESIS IN AN ORGANIZATIONAL CONTEXT

In this book we discuss the workplace as a complex system of energy. We look to the laws of thermodynamics in physics to understand how it operates. The first of those laws tells us that energy cannot be created or destroyed but only transformed. For this chapter the second law is particularly instructive; it relates to entropy. Entropy is the level of disorder within a system; if left untouched, the system will gradually move toward disorder and disintegration. The key message here is that organizations and leaders within those organizations need to be proactive to ensure that the system is working effectively to reduce stressors and increase the resistance that individuals in that system have at their disposal to deal with the negative effects of stress. It is worth noting that Antonovsky did not see all stress as bad or negative; some can act as an impetus for positive action. Entropy shows us that doing nothing is a recipe for disaster; we need to be proactive, and we need to make things happen positively if we want the system or organization to perform and sustain.

In the workplace we have a range of stressors; it can often be described as a stressor-rich environment. Many organizations are focused on risk reduction, be this related to health and safety in general. Often this is seen by a range of initiatives targeted to reduce accidents, rules about holding on to handrails, awareness about safe lifting of heavy items, advice on dealing with chemicals or other hazards, and the like. However, if we take Antonovsky's work to heart, we need to take a more broad and holistic view of the workplace and the stressors that exist and the mechanisms that can help to mitigate their negative impact.

This is not about a workplace having a pathogenetic orientation or a saluto-genic orientation; it is actually a recognition that both exist together. The work-place is full of pathogens, and the role of leaders and those involved with organizational design and tasked with ensuring an effective environment where people can do their best work and the organization can achieve its goals is to recognize those pathogens, measure and manage those pathogens, and in the best case reduce those pathogens. But that is only half the story. If they want to create an agile, resilient, and sustainable organization and workplace, they will also be clear about the salutogenic factors at play, and in the same way, they will measure and manage those factors and intervene when they recognize that they have dropped to a low level.

We must recognize that many factors can be both potentially pathogenic and salutogenic—for example, clients and customers! Many employees have been heard to mutter that it would be a great business if only they didn't have to deal with clients. The reality is that clients can be both pathogenic and salu-togenic; some can bring great stress in terms of their demands over delivery and accessibility with unfair expectations, whereas others can be a source of energy when they discuss the success they have had with the organization's products.

Managers can again be both pathogenic and salutogenic; they can place too high a demand load on individuals, or they can be a great support through coaching, advice, and navigating a way to get things done throughout a complex organization. Relationships throughout the business can be a source of conflict or a source of support. The culture of the business itself can be a source of stress in the "way things get done around here" or it can provide a great deal of stabil-ity in a fast-changing world. Policies and practices again can be positive or nega-tive, with tight rules and regulations giving little flexibility, or they can allow input in decision-making and free-flowing communication. The leadership of the business can be both a positive and a negative; they can be caught in internal power battles that play out as politicking, undermining, and bullying behaviors, or they can provide a clear vision and strategy for success. They can help make sense of the unstable environment that the organization occupies, setting a clear direction, navigating the challenges ahead. The role and job you have may have just evolved and the lack of thought or clarity around its design may cause it to be pathogenic, whereas a well-crafted role with absolute role clarity and respon-sibilities may allow you to thrive and experience success acting as truly salutary in nature.

A successful, thriving dynamic organization will provide a high degree of job security for all involved, leading to a predictable flow of income to support its employees' lifestyles, whereas an organization with an uncertain future will not provide job security, creating an environment of constant change as people leave to join other organizations with better prospects for pay, promotion, career advancement, learning, and security for their family.

Our ability, as organizational leaders, to identify all the aspects that are critical to both the individual's and organization's performance is essential so we can analyze whether they are salutogenic or pathogenic and make changes to address the challenges.

One seemingly minor factor can have a dramatic effect on performance. Consider rest and recovery for a moment. Have you ever had a bad night's sleep? Often it will negatively affect your performance on the following day. One night's poor sleep may not lead to accidents but maybe just a poor mood and irritability that could damage relationships at work and make you less effective. Now if that one night's experience became a prolonged issue, with a number of sleepless nights combining to ensure you are less creative, collaborative, productive, and energetic, we now have a performance problem. Now if you multiply that effect across your 1,000-person workforce, you will understand how just that one element has a significant impact on output and organizational performance. If you become significantly overweight, it can affect your energy levels and may affect your self-image. Now multiply that effect across the organization. We have just highlighted two physical aspects, but combine that with a range of mental, social, and emotional attributes, and you will see the incredibly destructive effect of a range of individuals attributes on their organization. Most organizations don't measure these aspects of their system. Thus, most are not in a position to manage these aspects either.

While the "sense of coherence" is normally viewed from an individual perspective, we can equally consider an organization to have a high or low sense of coherence. Using Antonovsky's three aspects of a "sense of coherence" as comprehensibility, manageability, and meaningfulness, we can see the role that organizations and leaders have in strengthening them. The ability of leaders to communicate consistently with great clarity is crucial to helping employees make sense of what is happening around them. When communication is poor and rumors abound, people find it more difficult to predict the future, and that uncertainty creates high levels of stress. Leaders who ensure that there is a strong match between the demands that are placed on a function, division, department, or team, ensuring they are matched by suitable resources, will strengthen the sense within their people that they can manage through their issues.

However, when there seems to be a constant mismatch of demand/resources, when forecasting models are poor, when recruitment fails, when resources fall by the wayside and the team or organization become overwhelmed, employees lose confidence in their ability to cope. When the organization has forgotten to remind people about the "why" of their job, their role, their function—in fact the overall organization, why it exists, why what they do is important, what is their purpose—then they lose a sense of meaning and they question why they should bother. This is opposed to leaders who constantly connect each individual and their role, even if it is just a small part of a big system; they show them and remind them that *what* they do while at times may seem pointless is, however, absolutely crucial and important. They instill people with a sense of passion that sees them through the tough moments that we all experience. Equipping them with a deep sense of meaningfulness is an essential role of managers and leaders in a high-performing organization.

Antonovsky's model is a framework for success. It shifts the focus from a negative avoidance mentality to a positive disposition. It accepts that life is tough for many, but our work can provide us with so many resources to allow us to see our lives as comprehensible, manageable, and meaningful. It moves us away from dis-ease to the ease side of the continuum. It makes us stronger and more resilient, and allows us to experience life in a more sustainable manner. It provides us with a frame to see and understand the world around us and all the challenges we face. It encourages us to measure and manage all of the important elements that allow us to live our life to the best of our abilities.

GEORG BAUER, MD, DrPH

Georg Bauer is professor and head of the Division of Public & Organizational Health, Center of Salutogenesis, Epidemiology, Biostatistics and Prevention Institute, at the University of Zurich.

> A healthy or salutogenic organization is low in producing pathogenic processes but high in producing salutogenic processes—for both its human members and the whole organization as a complex social system that vitally pursues its purpose.

Georg Bauer is extremely passionate about progressing the development of salutogenesis across the world. He is involved with three organizations dedicated to this ambition. First he leads the Center of Salutogenesis at the University of Zürich in Switzerland, second is the Global Working Group on Salutogenesis of the International Union for Health Promotion and Education (IUHPE), and finally the Society for Theory and Research on Salutogenesis (STARS).

A Handbook on Salutogenesis

The Global Working Group produced an extremely useful and comprehensive publication called *The Handbook of Salutogenesis* (Mittelmark et al. 2016), which includes 87 authors and is a mine of information. They have also made it available free of charge.

Bauer explains that during the development of the handbook on salutogenesis, there was a feeling that while the health promotion community has taken on the concept of salutogenesis as a general orientation fostering resources and capacities to promote health and well-being, there was a need to go further. In this regard they identified four key conceptual issues to be advanced: (1) the overall salutogenic model of health; (2) the SOC concept; (3) the design of salutogenic interventions and change processes in complex systems; and (4) the application of salutogenesis beyond health care.

The OHD Model

Bauer himself has written extensively on extending the salutogenic model into organizations and workplaces. Along with Gregor Jenny, he developed an Organizational Health Development model (OHD) in 2012. (See Figure 5.1.) Their model highlights the key role of job demands and job resources and the impact that they have on health (both can be positive or negative) and the resultant effect on sustainable performance. It also incorporates the effect of organizational capabilities (structure, strategy, and culture) and individual capabilities (competency, motivation, and identity) on the overall system.

Job resources in Antonovsky's view were GRRs (general resistance resources), which are useful to help individuals cope and overcome adversarial stressors; however, Bauer has omitted the resistance word in his model as he also sees them as critical for pursuing a person's own positive goals, personal growth, and thus positive health development, or as he calls it, "thriving."

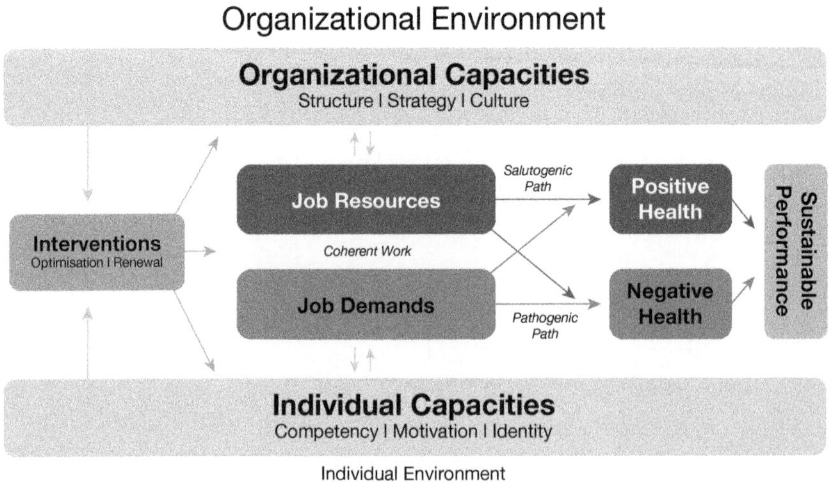

FIGURE 5.1   Organizational Health Development (OHD) model (Adapted from Bauer and Jenny 2012).

Capacity Building

Capacity building within the organization and individual are key according to Bauer. The OHD model shows that interventions should build up the individual and organizational capacities that influence the job demands, and job resources of their employees show social responsibility and sustainability. The Ottawa Charter for Health Promotion considers health as a resource for everyday life (that is, a positive concept emphasizing capacities rather than vulnerabilities) and not as the end in itself.

The Line Manager's Critical Role

Bauer also highlights the critical importance of line managers in this process. As line managers are seen as key change agents within organizations, they typically take part in a workshop where they learn to see and talk about OHD from their perspective and within the logic of their organization. During joint action planning, they self-experience how to improve their own job demands and resources and are empowered to work with their team on these issues.

A "No One Size Fits All" Approach

Adaptation is the recommended approach for organizational interventions. A one-size-fits-all set of interventions is not the answer. Interventions must be designed and adapted, applying variations based on a participatory problem-solving philosophy.

A General Organizational "Sense of Coherence"

Applying Antonovsky's Sense of Coherence (SOC) concept in an organizational context, Bauer believes that consistency in life strengthens comprehensibility, an underload-overload balance will strengthen manageability, and participation in socially valued decision-making strengthens the meaningfulness aspect of the SOC.

The Evolving Workforce

Bauer has witnessed an evolving workforce: increasingly well-educated employees demand more autonomy, self-defined flexibility, meaningful jobs supporting their self-fulfillment, opportunities for personal development, and a good life domain balance. If these requirements are met, employees are more likely to remain in working life until retirement age. This individual search for flexible and fulfilling work meets the increasing search for purpose orientation by organizations; these individual and organizational needs come together in the recent emerging concept of purpose-driven organizations.

Securing Organizational Buy-in

Organizations need to continuously self-observe and self-improve their impact on employees' health, particularly in unstable organizations with continuously changing workforce compositions. Developing such a capacity-building approach first requires a good understanding of how health continuously develops in organizations and what intervention approaches exist for targeted improvements. Promising ways to obtain the initial buy-in of organizations for such an OHD intervention might be linking the promotion of positive health to the broader corporate agendas of sustainable workability, keeping the aging workforce engaged, promoting agility and innovativeness of the organization, being perceived as an attractive employer, and the desire to show social responsibility and sustainability.

We believe that such an expanded salutogenic model of health that includes both a negative, pathogenic path of stressors leading to disease outcomes, a salutogenic coping path of GRR and specific resistance resources (SRR) helping to overcome adversarial life situations, and a direct, positive, salutogenic path from resources to positive health outcomes can cover the full human health experience and thus can be universally applied.

We propose to add direct paths of positive health development to the salutogenic model to show how GRRs and SRRs can lead to positive health. This fits with the concept of "salutary" factors mentioned by Antonovsky in his ultimate publication (1996).

PART II

CHAPTER **6**

Accelerating to Success: Where Some Get It Right and Others Get It Wrong

Firstly, we have some bad news. If you are like most organizations we observe, you are probably getting your approach to workforce health wrong. That means you are wasting valuable organizational resources, namely, time and money, but far more important than that, you are losing out on effectively managing the greatest strategic driver of organizational performance, especially if your business is people dependent.

The approach of most to workforce health in summary is tactical, ad hoc, tick-box, event based, programmatic, short term, focused in the main on building awareness, aimed at reducing illness and absenteeism, and sits under the ownership of human resources (HR). Alternatively, the few who get it right see it as strategic, long term and ongoing, data driven, evidence based, systematic, and focused on building work capacity, resilience, sustainability, and high performance; it is culturally embedded, considered as part of organization design; it is owned by the CEO, and the senior leaders are viewed as role models. Figure 6.1 shows the various elements required to move toward a more strategic implementation of health.

KNOWING WHAT SUCCESSFUL ORGANIZATIONS DO

When we have our first conversations with organizations, we ask them to explain their approach to workforce health. They normally start to list a range of initiatives that they have in place. Many will talk about implementing digital well-being through the use of platforms and apps such as Headspace and Calm. They will share photos from their well-being days. They will discuss proudly the ways in which they support international events such as women's days

THE MOVE TO A MORE STRATEGIC IMPLEMENTATION OF HEALTH IN ORGANIZATIONS

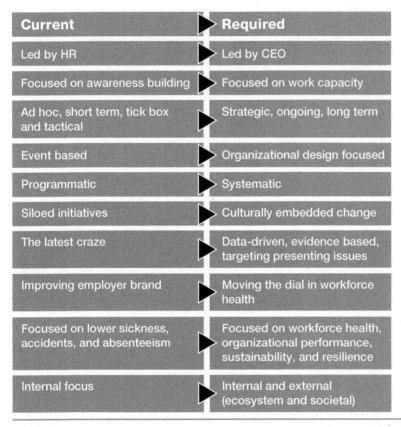

Current	Required
Led by HR	Led by CEO
Focused on awareness building	Focused on work capacity
Ad hoc, short term, tick box and tactical	Strategic, ongoing, long term
Event based	Organizational design focused
Programmatic	Systematic
Siloed initiatives	Culturally embedded change
The latest craze	Data-driven, evidence based, targeting presenting issues
Improving employer brand	Moving the dial in workforce health
Focused on lower sickness, accidents, and absenteeism	Focused on workforce health, organizational performance, sustainability, and resilience
Internal focus	Internal and external (ecosystem and societal)

FIGURE 6.1 The move to a more strategic implementation of health in organizations.

or pride. Often, they will highlight a range of talks aimed at healthy eating or managing stress. Some say they encourage employees to get regular check-ups. Yoga at work has also become popular. While these are all admirable, many are simply about building awareness or treating the symptom.

Organizations that perform well tend to take a different approach. The CEO has decided to take the lead on this topic because they are truly passionate about it and understand the critical link to overall organizational performance. They raise the issue at the board level because they want everybody to understand the importance of measuring and monitoring it because they see it as a canary in the coal mine in helping to identify future risks to performance. Often board members are inspired to bring that same passion to other organizations where they sit on boards. It is difficult to identify why some CEOs get it and others don't, but in many cases there may have been an experience that has had an impact, such as a suicide of a work colleague or a personal mental health episode, or they may have come from a background in high-performance sport and automatically understand the connections at play, especially with regard to energy management, rest, recovery, resourcing, and support.

The shift in thinking away from awareness building to building capacity is important. When you move away from the view of workforce health as simply being about keeping people fit, free from disease, and able to show up to work, you end up with a more interesting conversation around our overall capacity as individuals to live our lives and achieve our goals and how building our capacity to work plays into that approach. These types of organizations are more likely to see the workplace as a dynamic complex system of energy that needs to be monitored and managed. The focus then switches to the need to build resilience and sustainability into that system. Changing the narrative around resilience is important, moving it away from the old-fashioned idea of the corporate warrior who gets knocked down nine times and still gets up a tenth to one of building a network of resilience focused on increasing your strength in all areas of yourself, including the physical, mental, emotional, social, and spiritual. The last thing you want to do is become completely burnt out. It is about understanding what are the factors that will allow you to perform at your best in a longer time frame and sustainable way, renewing and recovering as you go by doing different activities that require different skills.

There is a mental move from seeing workforce health as a hodgepodge of initiatives and interventions related to the latest greatest trend from TikTok or some other social media platform to a more strategic, long-term developed approach that is evidence based and data driven.

The exemplars in this space have very integrated data feeds that allow them to have their finger on the performance pulse of their organization. They focus on a range of sources to inform their approach. Most start with safety. The most important thing to know is that an employee can deliver their work in a safe environment and return home without a risk of injury (physical or mental) or loss of life through accidents. They will study the data, and if it indicates that particular issues exist, they will address those issues immediately with changes to the physical infrastructures, or if the issue is more behavioral based, they will create interventions to affect change.

The next area where exemplars stand out tends to be attrition statistics. If there are high numbers of employees leaving the organization, they need to know why. Attrition in itself is not a bad thing, as it is often necessary to freshen up an organization with new skills, talent, ideas, and so on, but what you really need to know is why people are leaving. If the exit interview or survey data tells you that people are retiring or simply leaving to travel the world or maybe even for career progression, you may simply accept that your organization cannot fulfill all their needs right now. If they are leaving because the job affected their health through excess demands, poor management, bullying, and so on, then it is essential that you respond.

Absence and illness data is another source of insight, along with information from your EAP (employee assistance program) providers who will aggregate data to allow you to understand the top issues where people require support. General survey data can be useful too when broken down by demographics to assess gender, race, etc. These and other data sources will allow you to understand the factors that are at play in your organization that you need to respond to.

Moving from a programmatic approach to a more systemized approach is another trademark of exemplars in this space. For example, a survey highlighted the fact that Black and Asian members of the workforce feel that they are excluded and discriminated against. Some organizations will run programs of training courses to raise awareness, while others will take a more systematic approach to the issue, running listening sessions to deeply understand the core issues and why the BAME demographic (Black, Asian, and minority ethnic) feel the way they do. This might result in a new approach to the communication of the corporate employer brand, a change to the recruitment and selection process, a new module in the induction process and new recruit training dealing with unconscious biases, the introduction of training courses for all staff on acceptable behaviors, and building a more diverse and inclusive workforce, including training managers and leaders. It might include the introduction of monitoring systems, confidential email addresses to report behavior, and a very public process in dealing with complaints using the CEO and senior team to reinforce the message that there is no room in the organization for racism, and finally making examples of people who cross the line and ensuring they change fast or exit the organization. The difference between a program and a system change is significant; both are useful, but the latter ensures you are changing the culture and baking in the change systematically to every policy practice and behavior in the organization.

The organization is not implementing changes simply to reduce absence or improve their employer brand on Instagram but is making changes that support the development of a culture of care that has both an internal and external focus. The exemplars in this space will lobby for better, cheaper housing in the community in which they sit, because they understand how low supply leads to high prices for renters and that reduces the money the employees have to live their lives, with financial worries high on workers' lists of concerns. The organization could lobby for better, safer, cheaper transport, again realizing that they have a voice that can be useful in delivering things that are really important to employees who may have to depend on unreliable buses and trains, or dirty or unsafe transport that might result in fear of attack or assault. These are just some examples where the organization can leverage its power within society to make the lives of its workforce safer and therefore healthier.

The shift from left to right on the diagram in Figure 6.1 allows organizations to be significantly more successful in delivering a healthy place to work.

AVOIDING COMMON MISTAKES

Before you embark on the journey to creating a healthier workplace and organization, it is important to identify the mistakes that other organizations who have gone on a similar journey have made so you don't repeat them and rather learn from them in advance. This approach accelerates your journey to success.

Wrong Definitions

The organizations that have made mistakes did not, unlike you, have the benefit of reading this book. Therefore, they launch into this journey with an incorrect view of what is involved in workforce health. Often, they haven't created a shared understanding and clearly defined the factors that matter. Many overemphasize the physical attributes of being healthy and ignore many of the physiological aspects. They also do not use the holistic and salutogenic approach we detailed in Chapter 5. They ignore factors such as leadership, purpose, alignment, demands, organizational design, and relationships. It is essential to agree on a shared definition and communicate it to everybody through the organization, explaining in detail why these factors are important and why you will be measuring them. Otherwise, they may be confused when they see a survey that asks their opinion about aspects that they would consider unrelated to health and well-being.

A Lack of Data

Sometimes you can rely on your intuition, your gut, or your sense of what is happening by having a few random conversations with employees. However, that is one of the mistakes that is most common when organizations fail to create a healthy workplace. They extrapolate the views of a few to represent the many. Often it later turns out to be a very unrepresentative grouping whose issues are very sectionalized. To be effective, we need to ensure that we are getting a true representation of the issues affecting your whole workforce.

Data is your friend. Organizations that decide to make decisions and allocate resources based on poor or little data often flounder. It has never been easier to deploy technology to quickly get the views of your workforce. The annual survey in many cases has been replaced by a continuous listening approach supported by intelligent algorithms ensuring you can ask fewer questions more regularly and be able to rely on the veracity of the data that surfaces. If you ignore data and move away from an evidence-based approach, you may end up fixing the wrong problem while frustrating people even more.

The healthiest and most successful organizations use data to build a foundation for evidence using benchmarks for comparison to bring better meaning to their data. They deeply analyze the information spotting correlations, using key driver analysis to uncover trends. Predictive analysis tools allow them to identify issues before they result in absence, sickness, or attrition. This approach greatly assists them in investing resources based on the greatest needs, ensuring information collection and targeted execution are always occurring in a cyclical manner rather than a once-off event.

No Clearly Articulated Plan

Well-intentioned people can often be very busy working away trying to deal with issues relating to workforce health. Some are implementing ideas that they hope will address the needs before them. Often, they will respond to those who shout loudest, and their responses can be viewed as firefighting. Having a clear plan that is co-created with input from many and is seen to be data driven and evidence based allows the owner of workforce health to become more strategic rather than purely tactical. The plan will have a vision, clear objectives, goals, methodologies, measures, time frames, and targets. It will be communicated clearly to all staff so that they can be confident that the organization is taking a thorough and effective approach to the measurement and management of their health and clearly understand the effects that the work and workplace have on them as individuals, mitigating any potential negative outcomes.

No Impact or Success Measures

When finances become tight, well-being is an area that often takes a hit with budget cuts. This happens when senior leaders do not see a correlation between workforce health and organizational outcomes. If the owner of workforce health has failed to draw a clear line between the investments in this area and the performance of the organization, they will find it difficult to put forward a cogent argument to stop the cuts.

Measures around days lost to absence and illness, the direct and indirect costs associated to high attrition rates, health care insurance costs/premiums, litigation around workplace accidents, underperformance and costs associated with disciplinary processes and exiting individuals from the business, innovation statistics, engagement measures around collaboration, and a range of general organization financial data are essential to prove impact. Once you can show clear correlations between the areas of the organization where the employees are healthiest and the areas of high performance, you will reassure everyone, particularly the decision-makers around budgets, that the investment in this area is bringing a substantial return and should not be cut. Increasingly this is wrapped up into a measure called return on wellness, akin to the financial measure of return on investment.

Leaders Not Being Role Models

Some leaders have no realization about the tone they set from the top of the organization or indeed the shadow they cast. No amount of PR from HR can counteract a situation where human resources is encouraging employees to act in a particular manner related to their health and then those same employees witness senior leaders acting in ways inconsistent to the proclaimed message. This can be most visible when an organization has a set of values, and the leaders evidently don't believe in them and don't live them. "What you do speaks so loudly that I cannot hear what you say" is a great quote attributed to Ralph Waldo Emerson that perfectly exemplifies the situation that exists in many organizations.

When the messaging from the human resources department is about the need to balance work and home life, ensuring people do not overwork, clashes with the reality of senior leaders burning the midnight oil, working crazy hours, foregoing vacations, and sending countless emails late at night and at the weekends, it is clear to all that they are not role-modeling healthy behaviors. If employees, for example, see leaders fighting political battles, using underhanded techniques to get their way, playing favorites, acting inconsistently, behaving disrespectfully, being racist, or humiliating people in public, they will not view them as healthy role models. If leaders act in this way, they are sending a message to the organization that says if you want to get promoted, you need to be like us. That approach ensures that the organization will never be a healthy place to work for anybody.

To play their part in the development of a healthy workplace, senior leaders need to be role models. They need to embrace every aspect. They need to change their ways. They need to ensure that their actions and behaviors are consistent with their words. They must ensure that the shadow they cast is an example of healthy behaviors in action and healthy habits all day, every day. They must live it and breathe it to be consistent and authentic.

Awareness Rather Than Action

The sixth key way organizations limit their success in improving workforce health relates to their focus. Many choose to turn to their communications department to design beautiful posters that reinforce certain messages. They create and execute campaigns focused on healthy eating or others on supporting diversity within the workplace. While all these approaches are useful in and of themselves, action is what matters. From our studies, most people know what they should be doing to stay healthy, but they aren't doing it, as discussed earlier in this book. So what is wrong? If they buy the message in the poster, why don't they change their behavior?

Actions matter; offering healthy options in the canteen and removing all junk food from the workplace vending machines is very different from just talking about healthy eating. Firing employees who consistently bully others or make racist comments is much more effective and in line with a non-bullying/racist culture than posters dedicated to promoting healthy relationships. Encouraging people to avoid working too hard is a lot less useful than having a discussion about how to distribute workload or implementing more efficient work methods. A manager encouraging a direct report to be healthier versus the organization associating 25% of an employee's performance bonus to the achievement of personal development goals will probably be far more successful, as well as deeply understanding the factors that are causing a strain on people's mental health and training mental health first aiders who can provide support in the moment versus providing a lunchtime speech on stress management.

As they say, talk is cheap, and actions speak louder than words. To move the dial, you need to take bold actions, and that will require behavioral change. No matter how beautiful, smart, or witty a poster on a wall is, it is no match for a set of measures focused on dealing with the core issues that need to be resolved.

No Culture of Health

Do you have a culture of health in your organization? Are healthy behaviors endemic? Do practices and policies support every member of staff to be healthy? Are there values that relate to wellness? If people are asked to use words to describe your organization, will they talk about health and wellness? Does the career page articulate a compelling message to potential candidates that they are joining an organization that passionately believes and supports the health of their people? Have you secured independent certifications to prove you take health seriously? These are just some of the ways that an organization can prove that they have a culture that supports the health of their employees. Organizations that attempt to create a healthy workplace without first tackling their culture normally fail.

Successful organizations clearly define (or redefine in some cases) their culture so that there is absolute clarity and everybody can clearly articulate it. They develop clear values that are lived rather than just posted at reception. They co-create policies and practices that set clear rules for acceptable behaviors. They deeply embed employee health into every role, team, department, and division. They ensure that everybody feels part of a healthy place to work.

RON GOETZEL

Ron Goetzel is a senior scientist and director of the Institute for Health and Productivity Studies (IHPS) at the Johns Hopkins University Bloomberg School of Public Health. Previously he was on the faculty at Emory University and Cornell University. He is an internationally recognized and widely published expert in health and productivity management (HPM), return on investment (ROI), program evaluation, and outcomes research in the United States.

An Implementation Problem

Creating a healthy workplace with healthy people is not easy—if it were, everybody would be doing it—but Ron Goetzel has the experience to know that it requires tenacity.

> It is really hard to do it right. It's easy to do it wrong. The wrong way is basically, here's the website, here's the awareness-building materials, etc. A lot of organizations want to have a healthy workforce. They want people productive; they want people happy. They want people at their desks or their assembly line, they don't want them to worry about their health, but they just don't know how to do it. I think that is the gap. That's the mismatch between what the evidence in science tells you to do, and actually figuring out how to implement that.

Convincing CEOs to Go on the Journey

For Goetzel, making it personal is the best way to convince CEOs that this is a journey worth taking.

Asking them how their own health is or how is the health of their family is a great starting point.

He highlights four key approaches to encourage CEOs to take workforce health seriously.

1. Talk About the Cost
To make the argument compelling to a CEO, you need to show the cost. A huge range of research projects have proven beyond doubt that poor employee health costs companies more money.

A lot of diseases and disorders are caused by modifiable lifestyle factors. These things cost a business money. If somebody is obese, a smoker, doesn't exercise or eat healthy, doesn't sleep, has high blood pressure, glucose, and cholesterol, drinks a lot of alcohol, is stressed out, these people cost money. It's not just medical costs. It also includes productivity issues and accidents.

2. You Can Move the Dial
There is clear evidence that you can move population health in a workplace.

If you put in the right programs, then you can move the needle on employee health, get people to exercise, eat healthy, lose weight, quit smoking, can actually move the needle [on workforce health].

3. Costs Will Drop
You will save money if you move the dial on employee health.

If you move the needle, costs will go down eventually.

4. A Sensible Investment
Particularly in the United States, organizations are investing on average $10,000 per employee on medical care each year.

These programs are nowhere near as expensive as what it costs you to treat people. You can redeploy some of those funds into prevention, health promotion, and evidence-based programs. You get people healthier, and it doesn't cost you anything.

Prioritizing Health

Everything is affected by health. Workers themselves, and their ability to focus and concentrate and not be absent because they're sick or not worried. All of that is going to affect your performance as a company.

Making an Announcement

While you can't change culture overnight, you do need to announce your intention.

This is the culture we are trying to attain.

It needs to be emergent and palpable; you need to see it in the norms and patterns.

You need an infrastructure to support whatever you want to happen.

Deeply Embedded Well-Being

There is no quick fix. You can't outsource well-being; you need to own it.

I don't like programs that are just a flash in the pan excitement and then you never hear them again. It's really got to be a full court press, something that sticks, that people can relate to, they can identify with. It has a brand. It has leaders as champions, and it's also supported at the middle management level.

CHAPTER **7**

The Symbiotic Relationship of Workforce and Workplace Health

If we told you that a recent scientific discovery showed that small levels of carbon monoxide in your workplace could have a dramatic effect on employees' productivity and in some cases could kill them, would you install a carbon monoxide detector? Or would you decide to completely ignore the advice while you see other workplaces taking action to address the issue? Maybe you believe that you will smell the problem as you walk around because you know your workplace better than others. But what happens when employees start to leave your workplace because they don't want to expose themselves to the risk and they are unhappy that you are doing nothing to mitigate the problem?

Work and the workplace can have a very negative effect on the health of employees. But the same is true of employees; unhealthy employees can have an extremely negative effect on their workplace and organization. Our data shows clearly that if employees self-report that they are unhealthy, they will often report negatively leadership and the organization itself, whereas when they self-report strong personal health, they report more positively on leadership and the organization itself. In the latter case, we witness this positivity being played out by increased discretionary effort, greater flexibility and agility, higher productivity and creativity, stronger collaboration, and more harmony in relationships. They usually express loyalty by staying at that employer.

Equipped with this knowledge, smart employers have decided to measure and monitor the interrelationship and interdependence of the employees and their personal health and the organization and the impact it has on the health of employees. In this chapter, we highlight the key areas that an organization should focus on. First, we will begin with the individual health factors of employees, and then we move to organization factors. We wrap up this chapter by depicting the symbiotic relationship between these two categories.

INDIVIDUAL HEALTH FACTORS

In analyzing the most important factors that affect an individual's health, we believe that the factors in Figure 7.1 most affect their ability to perform. A full, more in-depth explanation is available in Chapter 13 on the science of well-being, which includes the detailed theories that drive thought leadership in this arena, but for now we will give a short summary to assist us in demonstrating why it is important to measure and monitor these factors and why the model we use is so effective in providing a lens or a frame to view this symbiotic relationship.

Energy and Rest

Without energy, we cannot perform any tasks in life. In fact, in physics energy is often described as the ability to do work. Our ability to develop and maintain strong energy levels will define us as individuals and what we can achieve with our lives. Critical to this energy level is our ability to recover, rest, and renew.

Physical Fitness

General fitness is not only related to our aerobic capability (cardiovascular) and ability to recover fast from exercise but also factors around flexibility and movement, our overall strength and endurance, and finally body composition.

Energy and Rest,
Physical Fitness, Diet,
Flow and Gratitude,
Financial Well-being,
Congruence, Work Control,
Self-Efficacy (Job and Career),
Belonging, Peer Support,
Self-Efficacy (Health),
Emotional Expression,
Relationships

FIGURE 7.1   Individual health factors.

Diet

Eating a balanced diet is important to any individual. However, there are differing views on what a healthy diet is, and this can be affected by cultural considerations. In addition, your gender and age also have an impact. According to the World Health organization (WHO), a healthy diet will balance energy intake with energy expenditure and control the intake of saturated fats (should be less than 10% of total energy intake, with trans fats less than 1%). Sugar intake should be targeted at between 5% and 10% of total energy intake, with salt levels of less than 5 grams a day. All this advice is aimed at reducing diabetes, heart disease, stroke, and cancers.

Congruence

If a person is living a life that is in perfect harmony with their beliefs, values, talents, skills, etc., they will experience high levels of congruence. The opposite would be disharmony and conflict. When, for example, our view of our ideal self is in daily contradiction to our lived reality, we will experience low congruence. This misalignment can lead to us experiencing feelings of dissonance and can lead to disease. Feeling our daily work suits us and aligns to who we are is an important factor in living with high congruence.

Flow and Gratitude

The concept of flow was first described by psychologist Mihaly Csikszentmihalyi. We experience flow when our work offers us the appropriate level of challenge that allows us to demonstrate our mastery of the skill required. If we "lose" ourselves in our work to the degree that we lose our sense of time, it is a good example of being in flow, which is the ultimate state of high performance.

Gratitude has also been strongly linked to well-being. When we focus and are thankful for the best things about our lives, our health, our family and friends, our skills and talents, and the ability to use them successfully, we experience high levels of gratitude.

Work Control

For some individuals more than others, their personal need for autonomy is an important driver of life satisfaction. If they feel that others are taking control or making all the decisions, they will experience high levels of frustration. Self-determination to many is an essential part of their personal well-being. In this book we talk about the need to give employees as much input and say in decisions that affect them. This can be seen particularly in organizations who allow high levels of job crafting. The opposite, micromanagement, can be soul destroying to an individual who desires high levels of work control.

Financial Well-Being

While health is more important than money, when you have money concerns, they can very negatively affect your health. These concerns can weigh heavily on you and can greatly affect your cognitive capacity to deliver your work to the required level. Organizations can have resources and supports that can alleviate problems and allow an individual who is in a financial crisis a way out. Many very intelligent people are simply not good at personal finances and can benefit from support in terms of coaching.

Relationships

If your relationships are broken, you can also be broken. Personal health can be affected when people choose to respond to relationship challenges by turning to drugs or alcohol to remove the pain and discomfort they are experiencing. These relationship difficulties can be work related or personal in nature. Skills developed in managing those relationships effectively are very transferrable. Workplaces are becoming more diverse, and in some cases, people struggle to relate to those who see the world differently from the way they do. This can lead to conflict. The ability to manage rich and diverse views and achieve harmonious relationships is critical to successfully operating in the world of work today.

Self-Efficacy (Health, Job, and Career)

Psychologist Albert Bandura brought the concept of self-efficacy to the world. When you exhibit low levels of self-efficacy, you deem yourself to have very little personal effect on the situation or context you find yourself in and, for that reason, are at the mercy of forces outside your control. The corollary finds that people who have high levels of self-efficacy believe they have personal agency in most situations. Self-efficacy is highly correlated to well-being. This is true particularly with regard to the decisions you make involving your personal health, the job and role you choose to deliver, and the choices you make to further your career.

Belonging

As a basic human need, belonging is one of the most important. When we find people who we believe are our "tribe," we want to connect and feel part of that group. In work terms this belonging is often demonstrated by support when you feel you can rely on those individuals in your work group. More recently, with people working in remote locations because of the COVID-19 pandemic, they have experienced low levels of belonging coupled with high levels of isolation.

Peer Support

The knowledge that the members of your work team, department, or division will be there if you need their help and assistance is reassuring. It means that a person has access to others' ideas, thoughts, insight, and support when they face a challenge or an obstacle that they are struggling to overcome. When peer support is high, you feel you fit in; when it is low, you feel excluded.

Emotional Expression

Psychological safety is important in any relationship and supports our well-being, particularly our mental health. The ability to feel comfortable in expressing how we feel at any given time on any given topic is fundamental. It means that an individual can be authentic. When they do not feel that level of safety, they hold back or hide who they really are. That reluctance to share their deepest feelings acts as a block of their contribution to their team or workgroup and reduces their performance.

ORGANIZATIONAL HEALTH FACTORS

The following sections discuss organizational health factors. See Figure 7.2 for a summary of these factors.

Wellness Culture,
Organizational Values,
Manager Support
Work Environment and Safety,
Work Demands,
Diversity and Inclusion,
Social Well-being,
Learning

FIGURE 7.2   Organizational health factors.

Wellness Culture

When employees experience an environment where it is easier to be healthy than not be healthy, then they are most probably in a strong wellness culture. This does not happen by accident. The architects of that culture have worked to ensure behaviors, habits, routines, and ways of working are all designed to support the development of a healthy environment.

Organizational Values

The culture of an organization is often best viewed by the way people act when they are delivering their daily work, making decisions, and interacting with colleagues and clients. These set of principles are often codified by a set of words that exemplify the ways that the leadership wish people to behave. Dissonance can happen when employees and leaders act in ways that are inconsistent with the articulated values of the organization. Examples of organizational values within healthy organizations are healthy (no surprise there!), kaizen-focused (based on a Japanese philosophy of constant improvement), supportive relationships, disciplined, fun, and always learning.

Manager Support

One of the biggest drivers of a person's health is their relationship with their manager. However, one of the lowest scores in many organizations is the manager's support. The role of the manager in a remote working environment is even more important as often they are the sole touchpoint for the organization. They need to provide support and be aware of the challenges that employees face in the new world of work. They need to spot the signs of poor health, mental challenges, and struggle, and address them with exceptional support.

Work Environment and Safety

One of our basic human needs is to feel safety. Unfortunately, across the world many employees and workers lose their lives in workplace accidents every year. Added to that the significant numbers who are injured physically, mentally, and emotionally at work, and you understand why it is so important to measure and monitor safety in the workplace. It is essential that leaders inculcate a philosophy of safety into their company's culture. This can include regular reporting on accidents as well as awareness building through training, coaching, posters, videos, inclusion in company communication, and speeches by the CEO.

Work Demands

As individuals, we are personally and professionally resourced to deliver work to a certain capacity. If we are operating below capacity, we can often become bored and disinterested and indeed make mistakes, but on the other hand, if our demands are too great, we may become overwhelmed. The key is getting the balance right. This is facilitated by a strong relationship between a manager and a direct report. They have absolute clarity about the person's capability and capacity to deliver on a particular task and match the work demands to those. In some cases they may test the individual by exposing them to demands a little beyond their present capability to see if they can grow through the experience.

Diversity and Inclusion

More recently organizations have embraced diversity. They have profiled and analyzed their organization to see if it is diverse and particularly that it reflects the community it sits in geographically and reflects the customers they serve daily. While great strides have been made in addressing diversity, inclusion measures have been less successful. It is essential that no matter your gender, racial or ethnic identity, sexual orientation, religious beliefs, disabilities, or cognitive difference that you are accepted and feel you fit into your team, department, and organization.

Social Well-Being

Our ability to support others in society has a tremendously beneficial effect on our level of well-being. Volunteering allows individuals to give back to society. This can involve support for charities or becoming involved in social justice campaigns. When we do work for selfless causes, it boosts our self-image. It is also an opportunity to experience the lives of people who are less fortunate than we are and, in that respect, allows us to view our problems from a different perspective.

Learning Mindset

Change is everywhere. Some people fear change because they don't believe they will be agile enough to adapt and thrive. In that case, the only way the individual can respond is to fight the change. That fight often results in conflict. Constant negative conflict is bad for your health. The answer is to have a learning mindset. To be a healthy individual, we should be constantly learning and growing, and equipping ourselves with useful skills and talents, ensuring that we will always be in demand. That will feed into our level of self-esteem.

PUTTING IT ALL TOGETHER

Figure 7.3 combines the individual health measures and the organizational health measures. Each individual health indicator is represented by a dot in the individual health circle. This relates to the response an employee gave to a survey statement indicating whether they agreed with it and the intensity to which they did or did not agree using the Likert scale. Here we convert the Likert responses into a 0–100% scale. For example, the score for energy and rest is 51%. You will see all the dots representing the scores for each of the indicators on the right. The ambition is to move the dots to the right as that indicates a more positive perception for the employee.

Individual Health Indicators

Energy and Rest	Belonging	
Physical Fitness	Peer Support	
Diet	Self-Efficacy (Health)	
Flow and Gratitude	Emotional Expression	
Financial Well-being	Relationships	
Congruence		
Work Control		
Self-efficacy (Job and Career)		

Organizational Health Indicators

Wellness Culture
Organizational Values
Manager Support
Work Environment and Safety
Work Demands
Diversity and Inclusion
Social Well-being
Learning

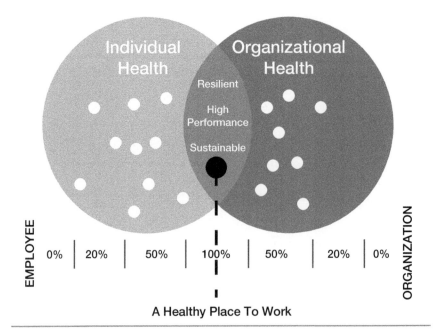

FIGURE 7.3   The Healthy Place to Work lens.

Now moving to the right-hand side of the diagram, we see a list of the organizational health factors. Again, the dots in the blue circle represent the scores given by employees in the survey. For example, the sense that there is a culture of wellness in this organization only has a score of 31%. The aim here is to move the dots from right to left.

You will notice that both circles overlap in the center with percentage scores around 70%. The ambition of any organization should be for all dots to be within the area of overlap. Our experience tells us that the people in organizations with scores in the overlap areas tend to be more resilient, exhibit greater levels of sustainability, and perform better.

These intersecting circles act as an informative lens for an organization to understand where they stand in terms of how healthy their people are and to understand what issues and challenges they may be facing at any particular time. It also gives them a clear view of the factors that are under the control of the organization that are affecting employees and thus their health status.

The area of intersection is also the point at which we will certify an organization as a healthy place to work.

Having the data represented in such a simple way allows all leaders to quickly understand where they are and can represent a team, department, division, set of roles, or particular geographical location. It also works for the comparison to several relevant benchmarks so an organization can assimilate quickly where they stand compared to the population as a whole or their industry.

The key point when using this process is to appreciate that many of the items on the left of Figure 7.3 (the individual health indicators) are the responsibility of the individual. However, if the organization chooses to support the individual in improving a presenting issue and in doing so improves their health status, it will often reap the benefits as the employee will be healthier and will reciprocate with appreciation through better and more dedication to work and show increased loyalty. As an example, if financial well-being is identified as a presenting issue from the diagnostic, the organization, using many tools such as semi-structured interviews or focus groups, can get a qualitative view of the quantitative issue represented earlier. It may be discovered that many employees have resorted to using money lenders to overcome difficult times in their financial lives and are struggling to pay back the loans as they have extremely high interest rates. Those money lenders may be putting the employees under pressure to pay the money back. The organization may decide to extend loans to the individual to remove them from the grip of the money lenders, and they may organize a series of financial education seminars equipping the employees with the knowledge they need so they do not find themselves in a similar situation again. Other less caring organizations might simply say that it is not their responsibility and the employee needs to resolve the situation.

With the items on the right-hand side, these are clearly the responsibility of the organization to resolve, and they possess the agency and control to fix them. In some cases, they will need to influence the employees to achieve movement. For example, if the organization wishes to improve the wellness culture in the organization, the employees have a significant part to play. It is important to realize the dual roles many fulfill. Even the CEO, senior leaders, managers, and supervisors are also employees too!

To be successful at creating a healthy workplace with healthy workers, leaders must appreciate the symbiotic relationship at play. The organization, through leadership, culture, practices, policies, and behaviors, has a huge impact on the health of employees. Leaders have the responsibility and control to change many things. However, the employees also have a significant impact on the organization, particularly in how they turn up, perform, and contribute to and support the culture. They have responsibility for many of their own personal health indicators; however, while the organization does not have responsibility for those indicators, it can have influence, agency, and capability even beyond its present knowledge to assist in resolving issues that may lead to healthier employees.

It is by recognizing the symbiotic relationship and working together that they can achieve a healthy place to work.

CHAPTER **8**

The Development Scale: Where Is Your Organization?

In the previous chapters, we explained why we believe measuring and managing the health of your workforce is essential if you want to deliver exceptional organizational performance. We have shared our view that work can be a very negative force in the lives of many people. It can also be a force for good if the organization and the leadership create the right environment, culture, and practices. Critical to this is the need to ensure that HR recruits and selects employees who fit the culture and are matched to the work so they can deliver their objectives in a way that doesn't negatively affect their own health but rather provides many of the resources to allow them to live a full and purposeful life. We have shared with you the science and theories that support our model and framework so you understand why it is important to measure the aspects and perceptions of your employees' experience of your workplace and how it affects their lives and health.

By now you are hopefully inspired to set out on the journey to transform your organization and workplace into a healthy place to work.

Here we introduce two constructs that we believe will help you on your journey:

- The first looks at the stages an organization can go through as its awareness and commitment increases toward being a healthier place.
- The second is a representation of the data that we captured while assessing the personal health perception of employees (based on the four pillars in the science of well-being covered in Chapter 13) and their perceptions, beliefs, and experiences of their workplace, culture, and leadership. This lens allows us to see where we are right now in a simple way and the destination to which we need to travel. Viewing the data in this way allows everybody to see their part in the journey.

That lens and framework perfectly demonstrates the symbiotic relationship between employees' individual health and organizational health and the fact that both have an important impact on each other, as we discuss in Chapter 7. It is our belief that you can't be a healthy organization if you are full of unhealthy individuals, and equally you can't be a healthy individual if you are working in an unhealthy organization. The aim should be the creation of a healthy organization with healthy individuals. That is the sweet spot of resilience, sustainability, and high performance.

When the workforce is healthy, there is a high probability that the organization will be healthy, and if the organization is healthy, there is a greater probability that high performance will follow. There will always be some exceptions to this rule; however, it is our clear experience over the last six years that this is the correlation we have observed. When you achieve this mix of healthy individuals in a healthy organization, you will experience greater agility, collaboration, creativity, productivity, and thus overall performance.

Leaders of healthy organizations do not view health and well-being as a separate area within the business, but rather they see it deeply embedded into every aspect of the business. Figure 8.1 presents the various stages we have observed that organizations go through when moving to finally becoming a healthy place. There are seven aspects worth highlighting, which assist us in seeing their impact. The model allows us in a very simple way to get a sense of where we are as an organization and the factors that we need to change to move along through the stages.

LEADERSHIP

As you will see, leadership is the first factor to focus on. In some organizations leaders have little or no interest in the health and well-being of their people; it just simply is not on the radar. They are merely a means to an end. As we pass through the stages shown in Figure 8.1, you will see that leaders begin to take an interest in the need to create a healthy workplace, and a key aspect of this is workforce health.

At the early stages, they don't really value the impact of this on the organization's ability to deliver its outcome. At stage three (adopter), a eureka moment happens where finally the leaders realize the link between business outcomes and the overall health of the system with its component parts (people) and the impact it has on organizational performance. In stage four (expert), leadership moves from understanding to a deeper level of commitment as they have fully appreciated the connection between the system and performance.

Stage five (black belt) is a realization that this is their most important role as a leader, not only because it directly affects performance but because it is the right thing to do. In this stage the leader is a passionate advocate and becomes extremely vocal reading up on the subject, reflecting on their own roles in their

DEVELOPMENT SCALE
WHERE IS YOUR ORGANIZATION

	Stage One **Beginner**	Stage Two **Initiator**	Stage Three **Adopter**	Stage Four **Expert**	Stage Five **Black Belt**
Leadership	No real interest	Passing interest, no relationship to business outcomes	Get it: Supportive, some relationship to business outcomes	Committed, clear relationship to business outcomes	Absolutely passionate, data lead – evidence-based role models
Ownership	No one	Health & safety officer	HR + (Well-being champions)	HR + dedicated team	CEO + (everybody feels they do)
Investment	No budget	Health and safety budget related to risk minimization	Budget related to activities	Significant budget	Large ring-fenced budget
Approach	No plan	Tactical: Ad hoc	Event based programmatic	Integrated systematic	Collaborative plan organizational
Interventions	Health & safety legislation	Health & safety legislation Wellness Day	Calendar of well-being events	Responding to presenting needs	Cohort based
Shows up as...	Accident data	Absence data	Attrition data	Strong employer brand	Individualized interventions
Employer perception of employees	Replaceable resources	The workforce	Team members	Human beings	Valuable individuals

FIGURE 8.1 Development scale for organizational health.

career and how they were affected by good and bad workplaces and good and bad bosses. Often, we see stage five leaders promoting these ideas externally at corporate business events as they are seen as visionary and that this humanistic approach is not only the right thing to do but the smart thing to do. These leaders suddenly realize that they can't just speak the words; they need to live them. They need to be authentic. They take their position as a role model very seriously, especially when it comes to healthy behaviors. This becomes a regular topic at senior leadership meetings. The senior leaders demand data points so that they can manage this critical aspect of the business and will place it at the top of the agenda as they realize that it is the best predictor of future performance and helps identify potential future risks down the road.

OWNERSHIP

Who owns workplace health in your organization? In some organizations no one owns it because it is not on anyone's agenda. No one has responsibility for this item. It is not built into an individual's performance objectives. No one is reporting on this item because it is not seen as important. At stage two (initiator), we see the focus becomes a baseline health and safety issue; therefore, it becomes the responsibility of the health and safety officer. In some industries with little protection for employees and few standards in place, this can mean a significant improvement in work practices.

In stage three you will see the human resource department is tasked with the responsibility to monitor, measure, and own workplace health. It is one of a range of items that a busy HR department needs to deliver, and therefore they recruit people throughout the organization who seem to have a passion for this type of work. These health champions take on this role on a voluntary basis, but it is additional to their role, and they don't have any formal training or sometimes understanding of the factors at play.

Stage four is where HR develops and trains a dedicated team of experts to drive a range of initiatives and deliver on the strategy required to move the dial. In stage five HR delivers the strategy to the CEO, who takes personal responsibility for the health of the organization and its people because they passionately believe it is important and their ownership gives it the platform and focus it deserves.

INVESTMENT

Budget time in organizations is often a time where real priorities get crystalized as we see the resource allocation matching the commitment that the senior team have for delivering the overall strategy. In stage one (beginner), there is simply no separate budget for workplace health as it is not on the radar, not a priority, not seen as important. In stage two we see a small budget allocation focused on the funding of health and safety initiatives. This normally relates to the organization attempting to reduce its exposure to being sued or insurance claims for accidents. This budget will fund clearly identifiable risk minimization measures.

Stage three sees the need to fund activities that have been proposed by the well-being champions and the HR department. Often this is related to events to drive awareness on areas that are seen to need a push. At stage four there is a different approach; workplace health is seen as a strategic driver of performance and now needs a significant budget to measure, monitor, assess, analyze, and respond to presenting issues. The budget funds the development and delivery of a strategic plan. Stage five is a full commitment to a large, ring-fenced budget that will not be cut if there is a round of cost minimizations proposed. It is seen as essential to the delivery of the strategy and organizational performance.

APPROACH

What approach does your organization have to workplace health? At stage one leadership has no interest. It has no owner and no budget. It will probably not shock you to know that it normally has absolutely no plan and therefore no measures. Effectively it is ignored as an area of importance for the organization or its leadership. Stage two sees a little improvement. At this point it has been raised as an issue with a particular emphasis on health and safety, so we start to see some initiatives. However, everything is reactive, ad hoc, and tactical without any sense of an overarching strategy in place. In the more cynical organizations, this stage could be signified by a tick-box approach, which may support a general cynicism about the value it delivers.

At stage three we witness an improvement; the cynicism has been replaced with a clear belief that a focus is needed and will bring value. However, rather than a detailed plan being created and executed, this stage is more associated with a series of events. Well-being is delivered in a very programmatic way, with a series of individual non-connected events. Awareness building can still be a feature of this level of maturity.

At stage four we have the commitment of the leadership, the ownership of HR with a dedicated team, a significant budget, and now the emergence of a plan. At this point we witness a move away from a series of disparate events delivered in a very programmatic way to a much more integrated approach.

Here the focus has markedly changed from symptom management to root cause analysis and the integration of systemic change to address the presenting issues. This approach continues into stage five, where the corporate health and well-being development plan is an essential organizational bible. A significant amount of time and resources have been expended on a co-created plan that is truly collaborative and reflects the needs of all areas, divisions, levels, and geographies of the business. It brings together factors such as diversity, equity, inclusion, engagement, sustainability, gender equality, mental health, and finally wellness as an overarching measure. As we will discuss later in this book, this is a development plan for the business with a clear vision and with goals and objectives, measures, and targets. This approach ensures that workplace health is deeply embedded into the culture of the organization.

INTERVENTIONS

Stage one interventions are normally associated with health and safety legislation. The only reason there are any interventions is related to the legal requirement associated with the employment of individuals and ensuring that you avoid getting sued as an employer. In stage two this extends to include such interventions as "well-being days" and "burnout weeks." Both interventions are really focused on symptom management rather than any level of dealing with the root cause issues. The idea of having a wellness day does not compute to a company that focuses on building a sustainable working model. Employees should be well every day, not a special one day in the year. Burnout weeks again have become popular with organizations requiring a complete company-wide shutdown to facilitate recovery. In fact, to many potential employees they see these as red flags of an employer whose organizational structure and design is not based on sustainable performance but rather a dysfunctional approach. This type of employer approach to work demands seems to require interventions that allow employees recover from the negative effects of their working life, which does not signal a wonderful employer brand.

Stage three will often see a programmatic approach with a range and calendar of events ensuring that they are seen to provide a series of interventions that employees can select from, a type of à la carte well-being menu of options and events. In many cases these are useful interventions; however, there is little in the form of impact measurement or dedicated follow-up to individual areas of concern. They can be quite generic offerings from a range of external providers. That is what really separates stage four interventions. They are very focused on the results of a diagnostic. They directly relate to the presenting needs of the workforce in a prioritized way.

Stage five is significant because it builds on the stage four approach to presenting needs, but rather than dealing with the workforce in its entirety, this drills down to particular cohorts who may have very specific issues. This approach facilitates very targeted actions. Cohorts may relate to generations, racial or ethnic minority groups, gender identity, LBGTQ+, a grouping in a particular role or job family, or a grouping in a geographical area. The aim here is to address very specific issues and design new processes and practices. Leadership approaches that ensure the negative issues are overcome and the health status of the individuals improves.

SHOWS UP AS: HOW MANAGERS THINK ABOUT ORGANIZATIONAL HEALTH

Stage one is often signified by accident data as a driver of injuries and the required response for a reduction in numbers. Stage two is more concerned about general absence and illness data affecting the ability of the organization to deliver, ensuring that high absence rates are not pervasive with the knock-on effect of work demand overload on other employees trying to shoulder the extra responsibilities of their sick colleagues.

Attrition is often a greater concern in stage three with regard to the ongoing cost of losing talent and the need and cost of constant recruitment to simply replace and stand still. The results of exit interviews are used to inform decision-making. The focus at stage four moves to the talent pipeline and the desire for improvement and perfection of the company's employer brand, desiring to be seen as an employer of choice within their industry or geography. These types of organizations realize that particularly the new generations are not willing to accept substandard conditions, toxic work cultures, and poor leadership, and have prioritized their own health and well-being and will choose an employer that will support their desire to be healthy on a more consistent basis.

Stage five brings the individualization of the workplace employee experience to a new level. This most definitely is about making work *work* for you and your life rather than changing your life to facilitate your work. Organizations were resistant to this approach because it is difficult to deliver. It is much easier to have everybody working in the same way, on the same equipment, at the same time, in the same location, with the same benefits, etc., whereas the COVID-19 pandemic has shown that when push comes to shove, it is possible to be flexible, and that does not just mean working from home. It is about breaking down all the component parts of your workplace engagement and responsibilities and implementing design thinking to enable an individual employee to job craft (that is, to decide what work they will deliver, how they will deliver it, where they will deliver it, with whom they will work, etc.). Obviously this is done in consultation with the employer, but you can create a role delivery system that works for both sides but is clearly tailored to the specific and individual needs of the employee in their context. Maybe that means working from Bali and split shifts to facilitate caring duties. Maybe that means working on a project for 12 hours a day for a straight two weeks with a team of ten people off site. In stage five everything is up for grabs; the objective of the employer is to show extreme (radical) flexibility to facilitate the requirements of the employee to ensure they can maximize their capacity and minimize any negative impacts that the work might place on them.

EMPLOYER PERCEPTION OF EMPLOYEES

The last but really important area relates to how the employer perceives their employees. In stage one there is a view of dispensability; some employers simply view workers as a replaceable resource. When an employer doesn't need you, they fire you, having very little concern for the effects that decision will have on you, your health, and your family. To their mind you are a generic replaceable resource. The only problem is the cost impact that decision has on the organization from the need to recruit and train replacements. Stage two organizations tend to view the employees as a collective and deem them to be "the workforce." In some cases, they may make collective agreements through negotiations with unions, but there is very little room to engage as an individual. It improves a little at stage three; at least at this point employees are seen as team members with specific role requirements rather than a total collective. There can be room for specific arrangements to be facilitated.

It improves even further at stage four when the employees are seen as human beings with specific needs. This might seem bizarre, but many people who currently have this work experience take it for granted. In many parts of the world, employees do not feel like they are treated like human beings but rather a means to an end for an employer to get work done at the lowest possible cost. When you engage with employees as human beings, you understand that this is not just a method of production and a tool of productivity. When you view employees as human beings, you see them in a broader context—not as a person doing a job or role but as a person who will have multiple roles in life (son, daughter, wife, husband, father). You build a much bigger relationship and a deeper understanding of who they are and what is important to them, their hopes and desires, their strengths and weaknesses, their aspirations, what they are trying to achieve with their life, and their responsibilities. It is not unusual for work colleagues to meet and see their partner and children for the very first time, after 40 years of working together, on the day the person is retiring; this is often the time that their colleagues find out about the person's passions, interests, hobbies, etc. At stage four there is an attempt to get to know the whole person and not simply put them in a box or identify them as their name and role; "John the senior engineer" does not really tell the whole story about John.

Stage five takes this one step further and endeavors to unearth the talents within the individual, giving them opportunities to grow and contribute in new and diverse ways. At this stage the employees feel heard and valued, feel recognized for who they are, feel loved and respected, feel included, and truly belong. Those individuals then see their work and their workplace as a source of true health.

PETER CHEESE

Peter Cheese

Chief executive of the Chartered Institute of Personnel and Development (CIPD) in the UK, which is the main professional body to accredit and award professional human resource qualifications. Formerly Peter was global managing director of Accenture and is author of *The New World of Work*.

> "Well-being has to be the central construct of business."

Finger on the Pulse

Having written his book on the new world of work during the recent pandemic, Peter Cheese has thought deeply about the way work is delivered today. His clear conclusion and advice to business leaders is to prioritize the health and well-being of their people if they want to achieve organizational success.

He believes the problem is about execution. Business leaders know it is important but struggle to figure out the best approach.

> "One of the most important constructs is well-being. It must be seen as one of the central constructs of business and yet it isn't, Business has to play its part in creating healthier societies."

Peter encourages HR professionals to provide the data to their leaders because they respond to numbers.

"The language of business is very much the language of numbers. Now those numbers can be quantitative as well as qualitative. But we've got to get a lot better at measuring. Then we can raise awareness amongst the business."

Standards and Frameworks

According to Peter Cheese the whole well-being space has exploded; however, there is a need for clear, consistent frameworks and standards that organizations can rely on. As the marketplace has evolved to understand health beyond the physical aspects encompassing social, emotional, and mental aspects, there is a need to bring an increased level of professionalism to bear in this arena.

Profit versus Purpose

Cheese is extremely critical of the Milton Friedman philosophy, also called "shareholder theory," which posits that the sole responsibility of a business is simply to make profits. He says this outdated approach has been replaced by a view that there are multiple stakeholders to an organization, and good businesses will ensure that they are delivering for society. The number one way they can do so is by ensuring their employees are holistically healthy. A critical part of that is a focus on purpose rather than profit and creating good work for their employees.

In fact, Peter sees clear evidence that employees' expectations are changing. No longer are employees solely focused on pay and promotion. They want to be part of an organization that has a purpose—something they can align with and feel that they are contributing to—and they want to feel they are making the world a better place.

Bring Humanity Back to Work

Businesses and organizations who treat employees as human beings will win, while those that view them as disposable and replaceable assets will flounder.

"For many decades, we have almost dehumanized work, the 'human' is just there as a working asset; indeed, we've used that language, human resource, or human capital. The future work has got to be human."

The Most Important Part of ESG

Business leaders are finally taking the UN sustainability goals seriously, and ESG reporting is a critical element. Cheese believes that the "S" in ESG, standing for social, is the most important measure but also the hardest.

> "What's really interesting in the ESG debate is the growing view from some very influential people that well-being should be perhaps one of the most central measures."

He believes that organizations need to provide evidence to prove they are taking ESG seriously.

> "With the growth of ESG we are getting serious about these things, there's got to be more organizational transparency. It's not good enough for organizations just to write some narrative saying, oh, yeah, we're doing this great stuff for environment or we're looking after our people. Where's your evidence?

According to Cheese, companies need to provide data around the makeup of their workforce ensuring they are delivering on diversity and sharing how they are investing in their people and how they are measuring and managing their culture.

Reskilling Is the Key

The costs associated with constantly recruiting new skills into the workplace are prohibitive; therefore, the successful organizations will be those with a deep capacity to reskill and upskill their current workforce providing education, training, and lifelong learning.

Well-being is the Future

Peter urges organizations to take workforce health and well-being seriously.

> "The evolution of humanity should be anchored around the construct of well-being that we are creating happier and healthier people. That is a societal construct. It's an individual construct. But of course, it's also an organizational one all linked to good work."

The best business will be seen to put their people at the heart of their business agenda.

> "We've got to understand our people, see them holistically as front and center of our business agendas. Well-being is the construct that can perhaps best help us really understand what it means to put human beings at the heart of our business."

CHAPTER 9

A New Lens: Individual and Organizational Measures

In Chapter 7 we introduced the range of the individual health factors and the range of organizational health factors at play in any organization. It is only when we measure these factors that we can truly manage them, and when people witness measuring and managing these factors, they understand that the health of the organization and the people in it really matters to the senior leaders. In this chapter we discuss the measurement in more detail.

The concept is best presented considering an organization and a workplace as a dynamic system of energy where work is completed. Within any system it is important to identify and measure the component parts and the factors that affect its operational efficiency. People-dependent organizations can increase their capacity to deliver by focusing attention on the health and well-being of their workforce and the environment where they operate, ensuring maximum performance can be achieved.

To illustrate, the branch of physics known as thermodynamics focuses on how energy works within a system. There are three main laws in thermodynamics:

- The first law of thermodynamics, also known as the law of conservation of energy, states that energy can neither be created nor destroyed but it can only be transferred or changed from one form to another (potential energy becomes kinetic energy, which is energy in motion).
- The second law of thermodynamics says that the entropy of any isolated system always increases (entropy is a state of disorder, confusion, and disorganization); therefore, entropy is the gradual decline to disorder.
- The third law of thermodynamics tells us that the entropy of a system at absolute zero is typically zero; however, that is almost impossible to achieve.

The preceding comparison of the workplace as a dynamic system of energy is very much in line with this new definition of health in the workplace.

UNHEALTHY TO HEALTHY: AN OVERVIEW OF THE JOURNEY

> You can't be a healthy organization if you are full of
> unhealthy individuals, and you can't be a healthy indi-
> vidual if you work in an unhealthy organization.

The ambition of any leader who signs up to go on this journey is to believe that the goal is to create a healthy organization full of holistically healthy people.

The healthy workplace matrix (see Figure 9.1) clearly identifies this ambition: to end up in quadrant 4 as an organization with high organizational health and high levels of individual health. This is where resilience, sustainability, and the elusive organizational performance lives.

So where is your organization right now? Maybe you are experiencing poor performance because you are presiding over an organization with low organizational health and the individuals in that system are experiencing resultant poor health themselves (quadrant 1). This has a negative cycle effect, and one makes the other worse. Maybe you are experiencing high individual health but low organizational health (quadrant 2); often this is the experience of a new start-up where people arrive bright-eyed and ready to go with energy to burn, but slowly

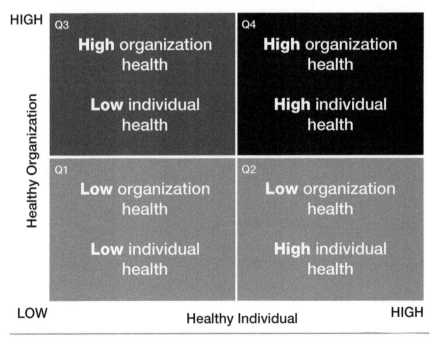

FIGURE 9.1 The healthy workplace matrix.

they start to experience the energy-sapping structures and politics of an ill-designed system that constantly frustrates their desire to create or move with pace. Invariably, an organization like that will soon move from quadrant 2 into quadrant 1.

What about quadrant 3, the unusual case where you have high organizational health but with low individual health? This can often exist where the organization may have strong leadership and a great culture with policies and practices to support its ambitions, but somewhere along the line the individual behaviors have become a problem. Selection and recruitment may lead to people entering the business who don't share the values or may be misaligned to its vision; these individuals start to infiltrate the structure and the system and cause chaos affecting the work environment and the recent concept of the "employee experience." There are two futures for this business:

- They lose the employees who are clearly not a fit for the business and put clear structures in place around the acceptable behaviors, focusing a large amount of attention on the managers' skill sets to support this approach and transfer to quadrant 4 (high organizational health and high individual health).
- They don't deal with their problems, those behaviors become pervasive, and eventually they end in quadrant 1.

As discussed earlier, we have identified the two important components of success or failure: organizational health and individual health. We now need to dig deeper to get a better understanding of what exactly we are talking about when we use those terms because that will determine what indicators we should be measuring to identify where we are and the starting point of our journey. The destination of the journey is clear: we want to create a healthy organization full of healthy people.

We have yet to meet an employee who goes to work every day into an unhealthy organization and is in some miraculous way able to insulate themselves in a way that the dysfunctionality of the organization is not affecting them. It is true that some individuals are more affected by it than others. This is in no way putting forward a proposition that some people are tougher than others and "can take it" or have "got on board" and "go with the flow" of the frustrations that they experience daily. This should not be seen as a character trait required to work in a job. "You need to be really resilient to work here!" We were talking to one recent recruit who was told he would need to flex a lot and work on his own initiative because there is a lot of uncertainty, a lot of change happening at short notice, and he would come up against some people with challenging behaviors. These are all indicators and signs that the organization is unhealthy or sick. That fact rubs off on you.

Some people are not as exposed as others to the effects of the organization's dysfunctionality. By virtue of their role, some can operate in a cocoon. They may have very few interactions that would see them get annoyed by systems failures, poor decision-making, or bad interpersonal relationships. They may be able to rely on their close employee friends and colleagues to support them through the tough times and insulate them from the rough and tumble of a manic workplace.

Others will be, metaphorically speaking, tearing their hair out trying to get things done. They hit roadblocks and obstacles every which way they turn. Systems and processes are broken, others are bypassed and not observed, decisions get made differently every day, and there is no level of consistency in application. Nerves get frayed, relationships get tested, conflict erupts, and sides get taken and suddenly "I can't breathe"; it gets to you and the stress affects you. You are on edge; your mind has shifted from open and inventive, creative and risk taking to closed tight, obsessed with not making a mistake or being blamed, to a "head down and get my work done" approach.

Likewise, you can have a healthy organization with a clear vision mission and values developed with a lot of thought and time. The organization design is in place to deliver on what is required. The policies and practices have been developed with care and communicated with expertise. The role has been defined, clear job descriptions are in place, remuneration systems are fair, and recognition has become part of a clearly defined culture that sets the framework for acceptable behaviors. But then the employees enter the equation; while new to this organization they are not new to organization life, and they arrive with many preconceptions and views of leaders, having very critical eyes to systems that would have let them down before. Their lives outside of work are challenging, and they bring those failures into their workplace. The conflict-filled relationships at home flow into the work colleagues.

THE CRUCIAL STEPS TO BECOMING A HEALTHY WORKPLACE

There is a lot going on in workplaces. They are dynamic and complex systems that need to be managed. High performance doesn't just happen; it's not about looks. It needs thoughtful design. It needs care and attention and constant monitoring and measurement.

Here we have set out what we believe are the steps you need to follow if you want to become a healthy workplace:

- Step 1: Committed leadership;
- Step 2: A new definition of "healthy";

- Step 3: Create a culture of health;
- Step 4: Measurement of baseline data;
- Step 5: Analysis and interpretation;
- Step 6: Create a shared understanding;
- Step 7: Develop and execute the plan;
- Step 8: Constant evaluation and celebration of success.

Step 1: Committed Leadership

All the research (and indeed our personal experience) tells us that if the leadership of the organization is not fully behind the philosophy of becoming a healthy workplace and truly believe that it is the ticket to overall organizational high performance, then most initiatives are dead in the water. We have seen countless organizations where the leaders have paid lip service to the concept and are happy to make a supportive speech extoling the benefits, hoping that HR will lead and awareness will follow and that the employer brand will improve and talent will be attracted but don't really care if the employees, who they see as expendable resources, are truly healthy individuals. Few are convinced that a firm commitment to the health of the organization and its workforce is the secret fuel that drives high performance, but they should be.

How many boards start by asking for the monthly figures for workforce health? Well, if they really want the best indicator of future performance and to highlight potential risks ahead, they should analyze that data first. The boards that do can then be seen to be taking organizational sustainability seriously. A healthy place to work is a philosophy. Either people believe in it and think it is important or they don't. If shareholders care, they will insist on getting annual reports that include nonfinancial measures such as workforce health statistics. In many parts of the world, this is a requirement, particularly for large organizations. Shareholders should be very concerned about the sustainability of the organization that they have invested in.

ESG (environmental, social, and governance) reporting has become popular in many enterprises, and that is something to be welcomed. ESG reporting is the future. Environmental includes climate change, waste management, and energy use. Social responsibility includes diversity and inclusion, human rights, and employee rights. Governance covers compliance, business ethics, procedures, and controls. Many will be cognizant of the framework provided by the United Nations and their 17 published sustainability goals. Two of those goals relate to work and well-being; goal 3 relates to good health and well-being, and goal 8 has measures related to decent work and economic growth.

It is not enough for the CEO or C-suite executives to make the right noises in this regard; they must be seen as role models. In fact, truth be known from our decades of being involved in organizational assessment that some of the unhealthiest people are in the C-suite, and in some cases, it is killing them and they don't realize it. The stress of an organization bubbles up to the top, the decisions to make at that level are tough, the power and political interplay gets more vicious, the fall from grace is harder the higher you get, and sometimes it is really hard to walk away from the lifestyle you and your family have created.

So a healthy workplace starts with a firm commitment from the board, CEO, and C-suite that they are going to understand the process, show real commitment to it in terms of time and energy resources, and be ready to become role models for health within the organization. In fact, the more dramatic the conversion, the better as the organization is watching closely. More than ever people are watching for inauthentic leadership. In one organization employees took great pleasure in showing us the CEO's car parked in the disabled parking bay, highlighting the fact that the CEO had made a big deal of removing the C-suite reserved parking spots as a demonstration of a more equal approach to all employees, but he had been found out and his true colors shown through. Get ready to be real and authentic, or don't bother even starting the journey.

Step 2: A New Definition of "Healthy"

As has been described earlier in this book, we need to work with a new definition of "healthy." At our organization, Healthy Place to Work, we describe a healthy person as an individual with the vitality to flourish at work and beyond. We describe a healthy organization as one that enables its human capital (its people) to sustainably deliver on its objectives. These two definitions are crucial to understanding the interplay between the individual and the organization and the fact that one hugely affects the other. If individuals do not have the vitality (effectively energy) to flourish at both work and in their home life, they will not be able to deliver sustainably for their organizations.

However, when you mention health and well-being to employees and organizations, their minds default to an old-world view of what that means, mainly physical health with some mental health layered on top; few consider a more holistic view of the multitude of factors that affect their health and play a part in keeping themselves mentally strong and resilient and in the space of high performance.

Therefore, a key aspect of creating a healthy workplace is educating the employee population about the holistic and salutogenic model that will define success (see Chapter 5 for an introduction to salutogenesis).

It is about educating everybody in your organization with the knowledge they need to travel on this journey. Our experience tells us that they too will probably have a very narrow understanding of the drivers of individual health. At this stage we need to help them explore this whole area. This is not about simply presenting them with information but rather inviting them to learn about a more holistic way to view their health. Often the leader of the organization may wish to share their own personal journey that has taken them to the point of being passionate about the importance of workforce health, explaining their previous mindset about the topic and the process by which they reached the realization that there could be a different approach and that work, the work-place, and the organization can be real drivers to support a new approach.

Organizations have used speeches, interactive workshops, exploration training sessions, group discussions, webinars, book sharing, and so forth, to begin this conversation. Remember, not everybody will necessarily be jump-ing on board at this stage. They may be cynical. Many will have been through organizational change programs or transformations before and may have seen them fail. Some may wonder what is in it for the organization and why the organization has suddenly taken an interest in their employees' health. For this very reason the organization should set out clearly from the start their motives and be very clear that a successful journey destination—a healthy place to work—will have huge benefits for everybody involved, including the organization, but that is not the biggest driver or motivation of the company. However, a strong, resilient, sustainable, high-performing organization should be in the interests of all involved.

It is important that those leading this movement can articulate the why and the why now so that this is seen as a real priority. It is important to understand who the influencers in your organization are and get them on board.

This is about creating and assessing whether your employees all have a shared understanding of the journey ahead. You can map out what this journey *might* look like, but in truth nobody knows what the road ahead will look like in detail. Each organization's journey will be different because they are made up of different individuals at different stages of their lives and careers. It can be useful to share the journey that other organizations have gone through in creat-ing their own healthy place to work. This can act as a great motivation, whereby those organizations can explain their previous expectations when starting the journey and compare those with the reality of the process they went through. They can talk about the bumps on the road and the obstacles that they faced and overcame. They can talk about the destination. Being officially certified as a healthy place to work is a destination and one that many are very proud to achieve; however, the journey does not end at that point. This is a never-ending journey. You can go backward as well as forward.

At this stage it is worth assessing how many employees are up for the journey, usually through the use of a survey. This is important because this is *their* journey. It is their journey as individuals and their own personal health journey, but also it is the combined workforce's journey of which they are an important part.

Some will be very passionate about this arena for many different reasons, others less so. It is important to channel the energy and enthusiasm of those passionate employees. Often this might mean letting them set up "Healthy Place to Work" teams in their division, department, state, country, or region. These can be the individuals who can keep the motivation strong for the changes that will be needed. They can drive forward strategies and localize initiatives. They can provide feedback as to how changes are being received and what is working well. Stories are important during any change program, and channeling these success stories back so they can reach a wider audience is essential. This feedback is crucial because this cannot be seen as a top-down process but rather bottom-up. Therefore, if some changes are not working, they need to be adapted, altered, tweaked, or in some cases potentially abandoned.

Everybody needs to believe that their voice is heard and, importantly, valued.

Step 3: Create a Culture of Health

Much has been written about culture and its importance in organizational performance. It is impossible to become a healthy workplace if the culture simply does not support it. There are innumerable ways to look at culture and countless definitions. Personally, we were extremely fortunate to meet and chat to Ed Schein, who wrote the seminal book *Organizational Culture and Leadership*. His model clearly demonstrates all the intricate parts to a culture and the importance leadership plays in creating that culture. You need to know the component parts that make up your company culture and be ready to change the parts that are not consistent with creating a healthy workplace. Often, this can be a person or persons with a set of behaviors that are making life miserable and unhealthy for others. These individuals can be high performers. A situation like this is often the acid test for organizations: Will they make a long-term decision and have the conversation that may lead to the individual or individuals exiting the organization, or will they simply focus on short-term priorities and stick with the status quo?

Culture has often been described as the air in an organization; it is there, but you can't see it. Culture is also described as "the way we do things around here." The question is, do you do things that are supporting people's health or causing people to get sick? How are decisions made? Where does the power lie; what is the informal organization influence structure?

From our experience, some organizations don't actually own their culture, but the best definitely do and place a high priority on getting it right. Owning your culture means defining it and deciding what it is going to be. What are the most important things? This often starts with defining your values. This is not the creation of a set of PR values that look good and "cool" to outsiders and new recruits. It is about having a deep conversation about the things that will drive the organization forward. In too many organizations, we have asked employees to articulate their values, and suddenly they want to run downstairs to reception to be reminded what they are. Values must be embedded in the policies, practices, and desired behaviors of the organization. They must be reinforced. For example, your recognition practices must recognize people who have lived the values, not just those who reached a target or KPI. Recognition should also focus on *how* something is achieved.

Moments define. Many organizations muddle through the whole culture thing, but then a defining moment comes along and the real culture steps forward. A decision must be made; maybe it's a choice around reducing headcount or reducing profits, maybe it's handling a situation with someone's mental health, maybe it's the treatment of a bully. This decision really matters and defines the leadership for years to come. People have told us stories as if the event happened last week, even though it emerges that it was 10 years ago. Moments matter.

Creating a culture that supports health is crucial to creating a healthy workplace. Prioritizing people over profit matters; assessing that the demands placed on employees are just right to stretch them to high performance but not overwhelm to illness or underwhelm to boredom; giving people control over their work, their projects, their roles, allowing them to job-craft, reducing their stress by increasing their control and autonomy. These things matter.

Step 4: Measurement of Baseline Data

One of our favorite things to do when we run a program with an organization is to get them to predict their starting point or baseline. Everybody has a view. But it is fascinating to see how far or near that view is to the reality of the situation. This is not a case of a leader giving their view of their own experience but rather them predicting what they believe will be the overall result for the total workforce. There is a risk involved, and for that reason many are only comfortable to do this with us on a confidential basis, while others are very happy for all to know their views. It can often be the case that when we return with the real results, there can be some shocks, and it can become clear that many were unaware of the situation in their organization.

There is a concept called STABS. When asked questions, people use words like "It **S**eems to me," or "I **T**hink," or "I **A**ssume," or maybe "I **B**elieve." Once you have conducted a survey and received a statistically significant level of responses, you will no longer be relying on your intuition or a gut feeling as to the state of play in your organization. Now you will know exactly what the number is for your workforce health.

Individual Health

In Chapter 7, we identified several areas that we need to define to determine what elements we should measure to get a clear indication of our individual health. As discussed earlier, many people have a very narrow view of the factors that make them healthy, but we are following Aaron Antonovsky's lead and taking a more holistic and salutogenic approach (see Chapter 5).

From a healthy individual's perspective, we have identified 21 key elements that drive health outcomes. Physical fitness, nutrition, energy levels, safety and security, robust thinking, stress levels, personal agency, learning mindset, financial well-being, relationships, sense of community, emotions, inclusion, authenticity, purpose, alignment, appreciation, flow, and passion are just some of the indicators that we ask individuals to self-report on using a number of tested and benchmarked statements. This results in a view through a lens of everyone in an organization. For confidentially reasons we would never share individual results, but this is a simple demonstration of how we build up an effective model to measure whether an organization is a healthy place to work. See Figure 9.2.

At this stage we not only look at an individual, but we combine all individual results for the total workforce population, say 5,000 employees. As you will see, the results for a particular individual are slightly different from the total data set for the full workforce. Therefore, it is important to survey a full workforce initially so you can get a strong baseline measure; for some organizations a statistical sample can be used with good reliability that the results could be replicated if the survey was rerun. We see in the example in Figure 9.3 that the results of the full workforce are slightly more positive when reporting on its own health status.

Organizational Health and the Healthy Place Lens

Next, we turn to the perceptions of the employees of the health of the organization. We introduced organizational health factors in Chapter 7.

To be a healthy organization, research points to the fact that you must have a culture that supports health and wellness, and as discussed earlier, the leadership of the organization is crucial to the development and sustaining of that

INDIVIDUAL HEALTH STATUS

Health Indicators

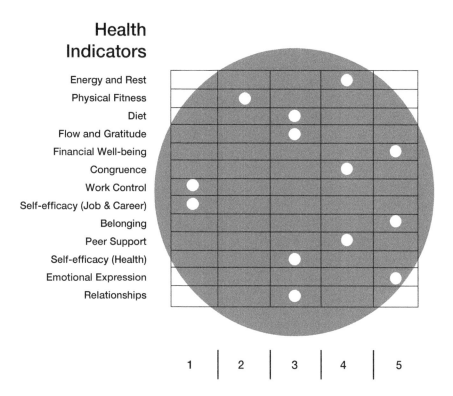

FIGURE 9.2   Individual health indicators.

culture and organizational climate. We have also learned that the relationship between employees and the manager population is central to feelings of well-being. The managers are closest to the individual employees, and they need to understand the interplay between matching organizational and personal resources to the demands that are being required of the workforce. They also bring the clarity that is required in so many areas of the employee experience: clarity of expectations, clarity of roles, funneling information, and preparing the organization for change. They implement policies around recruitment, promotions, and developmental opportunities, and importantly also recognize and assess performance, which is often an area of conflict and stress in the relationship between the organization and the individual.

WORKFORCE HEALTH STATUS

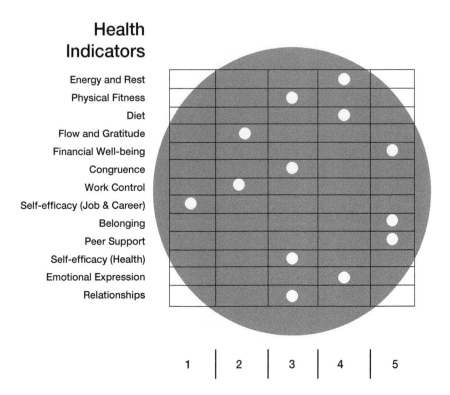

FIGURE 9.3   Workforce health indicators.

There is a range of indicators that we need to gain understanding from the workforce in order to understand the relationship between the organization and the individual. Gathering data points from individual employees who self-report on their perceptions of all these aspects of the organization and then combining these responses gives an overall assessment of the organization from a perspective of how it affects the workforce health. See Figure 9.4.

Developing the model in Figure 9.4, we now allow our two circles to overlap and become a Venn diagram. This Venn diagram is called the healthy place lens. The place of overlap is where employees have responded on average with a score of 4 (out of 5) for both the statements relating to the indicators of individual health and the statements relating to organizational health. We believe that this is an important lens for people to view any organization. It needs to be

ORGANIZATION HEALTH STATUS

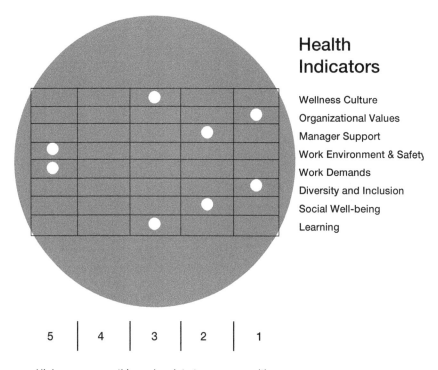

Health Indicators

Wellness Culture
Organizational Values
Manager Support
Work Environment & Safety
Work Demands
Diversity and Inclusion
Social Well-being
Learning

5   4   3   2   1

Higher scores on this scale relate to a more positive
responses related to the health indicator

FIGURE 9.4   Organizational health indicators.

understood that every data point relates to the perceptions of an employees and is valuable.

The location of overlap denotes a healthy place to work as one where employees believe themselves to be healthy using the holistic and salutogenic assessment model and where they believe the organization is supporting them in carrying out their roles to a high level and is in fact a healthy organization. This should be the aim for all organizations.

This effectively is the starting point for any organization. From this visualization you will see the task that lies ahead. Your ambition is to move the 1's, 2's, and 3's to 4's and 5's. In assessments we use statements that relate to the indicators and use a Likert scale to allow employees express how much they agree or disagree with a particular statement.

1. Almost always untrue;
2. Often untrue;
3. Sometimes true/sometimes untrue;
4. Often true;
5. Almost always true.

The visualization in Figure 9.5 is the ideal destination where the employees' feedback on their own health indicators and the organizational health indicators are all positive. The intersection between both is the sweet spot for organizational high performance, resilience, and sustainability.

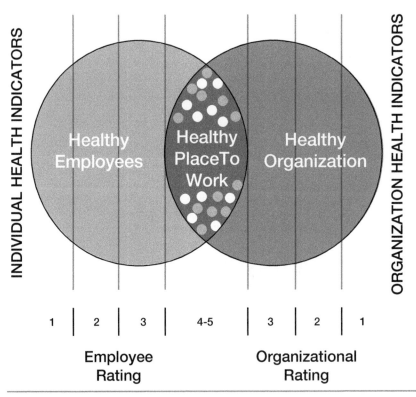

FIGURE 9.5   A simple view of the healthy place lens.

Step 5: Analysis and Interpretation

We now have a topline view of how near or far this organization is from becoming a healthy place to work.

For the purposes of this example (shown in Figures 9.2, 9.3, and 9.4), we have given quite a simplistic view of this model. The deeper analysis of the topline data can uncover real insights and a better understanding of what is driving the results. Firstly, we investigate the demographics and slice the data by age, gender, roles, geographies, hours worked, general view of their own health, and so forth. Next it is useful to identify correlations in the data—for example, maybe age plays a significant role in the results about financial worries, with younger employees less concerned but middle-aged employees very concerned.

Our data clearly showed that the under-25-year-old cohort were worst affected by the COVID-19 pandemic; working from home for them was no fun, some living with their parents, others living in studio apartments, most wishing they could spend more time in a vibrant workplace where they could learn and get mentored, grow and develop, and find friends and maybe life partners. It also became clear that when we combined several statement responses, many were struggling with their mental health. In some organizations employees were working long hours, which in itself may not be a problem because many can do so out of choice, building a career and getting a lot of enjoyment when they find meaning and purpose in their work; however, when correlated with a sense that they received little real recognition for their efforts and had little control or autonomy, it is probably no surprise that they were open to moving to another company if paid even slightly more.

Using a multitude of data analytical tools, we can interrogate the data deeper and better uncover the meaning behind the data points. For example, regression analysis allows us to understand the relationship between two variables, and sentiment analysis allows us to effectively capture the views of employees as articulated through their responses to open-ended questions.

Finally, benchmarking allows us to compare an individual set of results against a range of combined results of a country, geographic region, industry, or sector. This is very useful as some data points may look low until you compare them to a relevant benchmark and suddenly it changes how you interpret the results. For example, the statement that asks individuals whether they worry about their finances may surprise you when you see a low score until you realize that this is one of the lowest-scoring statements in our model.

Data scientists can bring their expertise to bear in turning unstructured data into actionable insight, giving organizations an evidence base to allow for strategic decision-making. Their work often facilitates organizations to target resources where they are needed most. It is often useful for an organization starting this journey to obtain some outside-in perspective and support on data analysis and planning, if your organization doesn't already have such resources. As a manager, you can conduct a micro-targeted approach utilizing some of the constructs in this chapter to gain a fact base and determine the implications of your data.

Step 6: Create a Shared Understanding

Often, we have seen CEOs jump into action mode and want HR to develop a list of 50 actions with owners and dates to deliver a cascade intervention. This rushed approach can often be flawed. Others take a little time to sit with their results and let them sink in.

It is interesting that the time taken to mull over a set of results can be invaluable and perspective kicks in and so does establishing what is possible and the best approaches that could be considered to respond.

Once a full analysis has been undertaken and the organization has interpreted their results correctly, they need to feed back the results to the full workforce. This is a critical point as it ensures a shared understanding between all players as to the starting point of the journey that they are taking together. While there are many ways to communicate and feed back these results to employees, our experience tells us that town hall meetings, quickly followed by small-group or department meetings to debrief and make sense of the key messages, can be very useful here. Remember that involvement results in investment, and to get employees invested in this effort, it is useful to get them involved in the feedback process.

Step 7: Develop and Execute the Plan

Right now, you have your baseline results. You have sliced and diced them, the data scientists have completed their magic, and you feel you have deep insight into the health of your workforce and the health of your organization.

Often many leaders will ruminate on the challenges that are thrown up by the set of results, especially if some have come as a surprise. However, the first thing you should focus on is the positives from the results; all too often we have seen leaders skim over all the positives and jump to the areas of concern or opportunity. It is as important to recognize the areas that are working both from an individual perspective and an organizational perspective. Also, leaders should resist the temptation to take any criticisms personally. Brilliant leaders never tell the survey respondents that they are deeply disappointed with the results no matter how low the scores are. The best starting point is to thank everybody for taking the time to respond and for their openness and honesty. That is a great starting point. At least now you have a starting point.

Once you have communicated the results throughout your organization, everybody is committed to taking action. Enter the "Healthy Place to Work" development plan; Chapter 10 outlines how this action plan is created. One of the greatest temptations is to try to act on everything from your list of items that needs work. However, your first task is to start prioritizing items. Many leaders want to jump to quick wins, but that is not a good idea. We've seen cases where bullying is virtually endemic and employees also complain about the temperature of the air conditioning, and the leader starts a big discussion about how they will fix the heat and completely ignore the biggest presenting issue of bullying. Our advice is always to hit the biggest issues head on. This is really important because it builds confidence in the process and belief that change is possible and that the leadership is committed to making it happen.

As you will see in Chapter 10, the plan is about building a clear vision of what you want to achieve, being clear about the process you will implement to make that happen, and identifying how you will support the change process and how you are going to promote the various change responses that you are driving forward over the next 6 to 12 months (or whatever time period is possible in your organization).

The execution phase takes time. It is important to identify and celebrate early wins (see step 8), but we find that marshaling the right resources at the right time to enact the required changes often takes longer than initially anticipated. Active change management, whether it is at the department or division level or organization-wide, is required. Managing this kind of change requires tracking performance over the course of time and adapting actions (and being agile) to address issues that go "sideways" or taking advantage of unexpected opportunities. More about executing the plan is in Chapter 10.

Step 8: Constant Evaluation and Celebration of Success

Creating and sustaining a healthy place to work is a never-ending journey. Realizing that fact, it becomes clear to most that employees need a constant flow of information that will allow them to understand what is happening in their organization and respond to issues when they are identified. Continuous listening is useful for larger organizations, who utilize statement rotation algorithms surveying their people with a few questions weekly or monthly; this allow them a constant flow of data.

Crucially we will clearly identify a destination in this journey where you can celebrate when you arrive. That celebration is important because it is life enhancing for all. This is a journey that the leadership alone can't deliver. It can only be achieved by all employees, in all departments, at all levels, in all geographies if they can deliver on their part. Every employee has to play their part in making it a healthy place to work for everybody else.

DAVE ULRICH

Known as the father of modern HR and the creator of the hugely influential Ulrich HR model, Dave Ulrich has published over 30 books on leadership, organization, and human resources. He has consulted with over half of the Fortune 200 and worked in over 80 countries. Currently, he is the Rensis Likert Professor at Ross School of Business, University of Michigan, and partner in the RBL Group.

Customer Focus and Employee Well-Being: Two Sides of the Same Coin

Getting a message across in a distracted world can be tough, so expert communicators use a technique of repetition. If you have been lucky enough to be in conversation with Dave Ulrich, you may miss it at the time but later discover that he finds innumerable different ways to reinforce and repeat his overarching message. His message is clear: if you are in business, everything you do should focus on serving the customer, because if you don't, you may not have a business to focus on. If your company does not succeed in the marketplace, there is no workplace. So too, when it comes to employee health and well-being, he believes that leaders need to connect the dots between investments in workforce health with the impact on the bottom line. Healthy employees have the capacity to deliver brilliant front-line customer care, and that type of customer care keeps customers coming back again and again.

Leaders Failing to Connect Mental Health to Organizational Success

For Ulrich, leaders too often fail to link the mental health of their workforce with their future organizational success with customers and investors, but he believes this is essential. If everybody understands that improving the mental health of employees will drive organizational success, then people will take it more seriously; if they don't make that connection, then they won't put the required effort into measuring and managing mental health in their workplace. Ulrich's research proves that a 10% change in employee experience results in a 5% change in customer experience.

Leadership Self-Care

Leadership is not a role but rather a relationship, according to Ulrich, who adds self-care to the five behaviors of successful leaders, along with setting and executing strategy and managing people today and into the future. The ability to manage their own mental health along with the mental health of their team will define the leaders who will deliver customer success.

Three Major Themes of the Future of Work

Personalization, uncertainty, and the navigation of the tension of paradoxes will be the major themes of the future of work, and each requires a focus on health. For employees to perform at their best, they need to be able to create a way of working that suits their personal circumstances. This is in keeping with our desire for employers to allow employees to deliver their work within the needs of their life. To deal with an uncertain world, Ulrich recommends refocusing on the aspects of your world that you are certain about, with learning and adaptation being key. Navigating a range of competing and seemingly conflicting demands or paradoxes is a real challenge, with the ultimate balance being the tension between success in the marketplace and care and compassion for your workforce.

Psychological Safety: The Bedrock of Success

Ulrich's repeated mantra (along, of course, with customer focus) is the three B's of believe, become, and belong. *Believe* relates to connecting and aligning every employee to the purpose of the organization, *become* is focused on growth through learning and participation, and finally *belong* is concerned with building a sense of community and loyalty. The foundation for all three is a fourth B: be safe physically, emotionally, and psychologically.

Hybrid Working? The Wrong Question

Ulrich passionately believes the debate about hybrid work (where and how you work) will be overtaken with a stronger focus on why people work and what people work on. Identifying work that gives you purpose and meaning should be a person's ultimate goal, because you will be healthier if you're doing something that gives you deep satisfaction. Ulrich believes that if you have a strong why and what, where and how disappear into the background and become secondary.

The Power of Taxonomy

It is no surprise that Ulrich's PhD was on taxonomy, the classification of living things or, as he puts it, the "science of simplicity." It is clear that he has taken a systems approach to reach many of his conclusions about the most effective ways to combine people and organizations to reach superior levels of performance. It was a joy to listen to his conclusions.

JEFFREY PFEFFER

Jeffrey Pfeffer is the Thomas D. Dee II Professor of Organizational Behavior at the Graduate School of Business, Stanford University, where he has taught since 1979. He is the author or co-author of 16 books. Pfeffer received his BS and MS degrees from Carnegie Mellon University and his PhD from Stanford.

Measure behavioral and workplace health regularly, and use employee-centered job design.

As stated already in this book, Jeffrey Pfeffer was the inspiration for our organization, Healthy Place to Work, and continues to inspire us today. He is truly uncompromising in advocating for a change to how work is designed and workplaces operate so that they don't damage employees' health.

Advice for Success

Pfeffer's best advice for organizations who want to achieve success through their people is to measure their health constantly and use design thinking to improve every role.

1. Measure

Information is crucial if you want to understand what is happening in your organization. Pfeffer believes the starting point for success is to have a constant measure in place for the health of your people.

If you don't measure behavioral health, you won't know if everything is okay. If you don't measure workforce health, you can't tell if it's getting better or worse.

Measurement comes first, and then it is about prioritization and accountability.

I would certainly put in a compensation system that paid people not just on their individual performance, but on the well-being and welfare of the whole.

2. Design Thinking

For Pfeffer, many of the issues in our current workplaces are a result of poor design. He believes we need to implement the many techniques of design thinking to create roles and jobs that work better for those who deliver them daily.

Design thinking in terms of everything, not only the work, but the tools that I give people.

No Quick Fix

The desire for many to search for quick fixes greatly frustrates Pfeffer, who wants those in control to focus on the root cause of problems.

I see yoga, mental health apps, a nap pod, a meditation app. But I don't see enough organizations still to this day saying, "I'm going to get at the root cause of the problem, how work is designed and how much autonomy people have. And do I really have policies that give people the flexibility that they need and the support in dealing with their family situation?" I see palliatives; I don't see much fundamental change.

Prevention Is Better Than a Cure

In behavioral health, mental health, and physical health, prevention is much more effective and much more cost effective than remediation.

It is much cheaper and more effective to prevent it than it is to treat it. That is also true for mental health. It is easier to prevent people from being stressed and depressed than it is to try to get you the mental health that you need once you are stressed and depressed.

Stewardship Is Important

According to Pfeffer, it comes down to the values of the leaders in the organization.

> Leaders need to recognize that they are responsible; they are ultimately in control of both their impact on the physical environment and their impact on the human environment.
> Leaders can be either good or bad stewards. Most would prefer to be good stewards; this comes down to values.

> Boards also have a critical role to play.

> This should be part of the governance and oversight. This is a basic, important part of the ESG. If the boards are concerned about the performance of the organization, they should have more oversight, but they have typically not been very concerned with human resource issues.

Change Is Coming

Sometimes you feel that Jeffrey Pfeffer is pessimistic about the future of workforce health until he proclaims that change is coming simply because the current trajectory is literally not sustainable.

CHAPTER 10

From Unhealthy to Healthy: A Plan for Success

Healthy organizations are made, not born. They are crafted, cultivated, worked, and reworked toward greater health. It requires intentionality and careful planning. Even if your organization is a complete start-up, organizational health and a focus on employee well-being are not a given. Health needs to be a central organizing principle in how you, as a leader, design the business, its policies, practices, and programs, and how its strategy is executed. However, most of us are not starting a business from scratch. Instead, we will find ourselves in existing organizations, and so the task of transforming the business toward greater health requires greater energy, attention, resources, and commitment. But the potential payback to you, your colleagues, and the business' bottom line is worth it.

If you are a senior leader in an organization, there are specific things that you can do to support the development of a healthy organization. If you are a manager in an organization but are not necessarily in a role that can affect organization-wide change, creating a plan for how you can effect change in your own sphere of influence is still very important. This chapter will help address some of those considerations as well. And if you're an employee, you still have a role and responsibility to play in supporting the planning process and thinking about how to create a healthy organization. This chapter will support you as well in that context.

CHARACTERISTICS OF EFFECTIVE CHANGE

As consultants, both of us have advised organizations in the process of making sustainable culture change. This is no easy task. A McKinsey study (2021) highlights a durable statistic: only 30% of transformation efforts succeed in achieving their intended goals. We say that it is durable because McKinsey, in addition to other firms, has conducted this same or similar research and have seen similar results over time. In other words, most change efforts fail to deliver on their intended value. We find that when organizational changes fail to take root, it is because the culture incentivizes other or conflicting behaviors. An organization's strategy cannot achieve what the culture fails to support.

In our experience, most organizations have viewed organizational health and wellness as ancillary or disconnected to the framework of how work gets done. Quite often these efforts are still viewed as "risk mitigation" and a "good thing to do" for employees. If there are efforts, they are episodic or programmatic, and are usually driven by and housed within the human resources function. Human resources plays a vital role, of course, but unless senior leaders and managers are accountable for delivering on performance tied to organizational health, the results will be reduced. As a result, organizational health and wellness doesn't deliver the performance impact that it might otherwise have.

In the previous chapter, we discussed the crucial steps in becoming a healthy workplace. Step 7 is to develop a robust plan and execute it. Managing the change process can be complicated and nuanced. Successful organizational changes we have observed share several common characteristics:

- First, there is a clear vision of what success looks like, and leaders at all levels are aligned to that vision.
- Second, managers at all levels actively role-model the required behaviors for the change effort.
- Third, there are multiple communication vehicles and feedback mechanisms.
- Fourth, various stakeholders are engaged in promoting the desired change rather than the effort being delegated to human resources.
- Fifth, organizational practices are reconfigured, created, or removed in order to support the required changes. As an example, hybrid work and flexibility policies change to support the needs of individual employees.
- Sixth, the right resources are set against the change effort. This includes time, mind share, and money.
- And seventh, successful organizations that embrace wellness and organizational health are also learning organizations. They celebrate successes, examine and correct for failures or misses, and incorporate feedback as they progress. They are constantly learning and refining their approaches to organizational health.

1. A Clear Vision

Successful organizational health and well-being change efforts begin with a compelling vision. What does "well-being" really look like in your organization? How are people involved? To what end or how will health ultimately benefit the organization? Is there a clear connection between this broad change effort and the purpose or mission of the organization? Is the change story compelling, and is it meaningful to the various audiences and stakeholder groups?

Employees and managers in healthy workplaces have clarity about why these efforts are important and how they drive real value for the organization. Importantly, employees can see themselves, their families, and their colleagues in the story. There is room for them, and they are encouraged to align their efforts to the overall vision of creating a healthy organization.

2. Role Modeling

Role modeling the behavior the organization wishes to see and have reinforced is essential to creating a vibrant, healthy workplace. If your manager sends emails at all hours of the night, what message does this send? If the key influencers and people in your department that you view as "successful" always eat at their desk or are perpetually "busy," what do you take from this?

There is a lot of research on the impact of role modeling. Bandura (1979) contends that social behavior is primarily learned by observing and modeling others' behaviors and is further shaped by positive and negative reinforcements. While leaders are uniquely positioned to influence the behavior of employees, everyone has the power to influence. One need only look at the "watercooler" effect—the process by which rumors spread in an organization (DiFonzo 2008)—to understand how we influence and shape the conversation on a team or in an organization.

3. Communication and Feedback

In organizations that have made tremendous strides in creating healthy workplaces, we find many different communication vehicles and feedback loops. This is connected to the promulgation of "vision" we highlighted earlier. However, this success characteristic is focused on utilizing communications to frame organizational health and help employees and managers connect the dots. Is workplace health part of the dashboard leaders track? Is it incorporated into town hall meetings (and is more than just safety statistics)? Are messages incorporated into "meetings in a box" for managers so they understand what is important to convey during team huddles or one-on-ones? Does the organization take a pause to review progress, draw various stakeholders into the conversation, and utilize the feedback to sharpen the programs, policies, and structures that enable a healthy workplace?

A robust communications strategy is essential for any change program, and especially for a program aimed at reimagining the employee experience and each moment of truth the organization has with its employees.

4. Making a Shift

In Chapter 5, we discussed the salutogenic orientation to organizational life, or an approach that seeks health rather than the avoidance of disease. It's a profound paradigm shift for organizations to make, and it doesn't happen by relegating the change effort to one function or department. Stakeholders from across the organization (and outside the organization as well) need to be engaged in making this mindset shift. We find that when we work with a broad cross-section of stakeholder groups in an organization, the speed and impact of change is greatly enhanced (Buchanan 2005).

Creating a healthy workplace is impossible unless you can gain the support of most of the employees. First, employees will want to understand what being a healthy workplace will mean for them. They will probably be cynical about the reasons why the company and leadership might launch such an initiative, believing that it will fundamentally benefit the shareholders only. It is easier when trust is high, but even when trust isn't where you wish it were, your approach to explaining the "why" is crucial. Once employees understand the concept, they can become part of creating the infrastructure that is needed for it to be a success. They can become ambassadors.

It is clear that there is usually no shortage of people who are willing to come forward and take on roles and activities as they see a huge payoff in terms of the health of themselves and their colleagues. It is wonderful when you see the energy and enthusiasm that is brought to bear and to ensure that there is successful implementation. It is all about ensuring everybody has their say and feels part of the journey. This is not something that you simply mandate people to do. You need to build a coalition among your people so that they are committed to the journey ahead.

5. Aligning Systems with the Vision

The fifth success characteristic addresses systems alignment. We have not experienced a successful change effort that doesn't fundamentally integrate key processes and systems, particularly in relation to talent management. How are the moments of truth in the employee experience (or customer or vendor experience) reimagined to promote health and well-being? These moments include the hiring and onboarding process, performance management, career development, benefits and compensation, and so on. If the systems and incentives are not aligned with the vision, then the change effort will be stunted and anemic at best. Refer to our case study at Centiro in Chapter 12 as a terrific example of changing the fundamental design of the organization to achieve certain purposes. Too often, we reward A while hoping for B behaviors and outcomes, and this simply doesn't work if you're trying to change your organization.

6. The Right Kind and Level of Resources

A corollary to changing the system is also ensuring that the right level of resources are set against the change process. If a pathogenic orientation is default in the Western world, then it takes intention and attention to move toward a salutogenic model of organizations. It requires time and energy and, quite often, some level of financial investment. The important thing is that investing in this change lever supports an organizational "flywheel effect" (the idea was made popular by author Jim Collins). The flywheel happens when small wins in enhancing organizational health build on each other over time and eventually gain so much momentum that growth seems to happen on its own. Without the right level and kind of resources, the focus by stakeholders will not be there and the flywheel effect won't take hold.

What is the right level and kind of resources to support organizational health and well-being? This is highly dependent on the type and size of your organization, but we find that it always takes more than expected. And realize that this may not necessarily be monetary/financial resources but technology or creativity or knowledge development or time.

7. Constant Learning

Finally, healthy organizations are also learning organizations. They consistently take stock of how they are doing and celebrate wins and examine failures. Celebrating the wins gives energy to the organizations and supports that fly-wheel effect. Celebrating wins also underscores what health looks like in the organization. We borrow the concept of appreciative inquiry, an organizational development methodology, which is a strengths-based, positive approach to change. Taking an appreciative inquiry approach uncovers valuable lessons and unlocks opportunities of what an organization can do more of and grow into. Learning organizations also take time to pause and reflect on what has been learned and to codify those lessons. They work to uncover what doesn't work and why so that it can be changed or reframed. We find that introducing a number of experiments—short change projects that are evaluated in real time with lessons incorporated into the ongoing redesign—creates an agile approach to enhancing organizational health and well-being.

CORE CONSIDERATIONS FOR A HEALTHY PLAN

No doubt that if you have come this far in reading this book, you are interested and perhaps committed to the idea of creating a healthy organization. In the rest of this chapter, we will examine the core considerations for developing a framework for thinking about a healthy organizational plan and what you may need to do to move this work forward. There are many great resources on action planning and overall change management, so our intent is not to recreate that wheel but, more specifically, help you think through how an "organizational health action plan" may be different than other types of organizational and culture-based action plans and how you might approach that task.

Consideration #1: Create a Vision That Is Broad and Inclusive

Every organization that we have interviewed or worked with in order to make this book has started with a clear vision for what a healthy organization looks like. The vision is big enough and bold enough to capture the hearts and minds of stakeholders throughout the organization. It answers the "why" of organizational health and well-being. A vision provides a "north star" for your organization's work but should also be pragmatic enough that employees can see themselves in the vision. Create a participatory approach to the development of the vision that includes the voices of stakeholders throughout the organization.

Questions to consider as you develop your vision:

- What would it look like if the people in our organization were physically well (physical fitness, energy, diet, rest, safety)?
- What would it look like if the people in our organization lived and worked with a strong sense of purpose (people worked with a sense of flow and there were congruence and gratitude)?
- What would it look like if the people in our organization had a strong sense of connection and belonging (they felt included and appreciated for who they are; there were strong relationships between team members and between managers and team members)?
- What would it look like if the people in our organization had strong mental resilience (there were financial well-being, an ability to manage stress, self-efficacy, and a learning mindset)?
- What behaviors would you see employees exhibit? What about managers? What behaviors would you see senior leaders exhibit?
- How would behaviors change over time? In one year or three or five years?
- What would it look like to have the vision be the guiding document for how you engage with each other, support each other, manage talent, and evolve culture?
- How do the values of the organization align with the vision?
- What type of organizational capacity, opportunity, and creativity would you see as a result of this?

You need not "boil the ocean" with this vision statement, and you don't want employees or other stakeholders to confuse this with the organization's purpose. But it is helpful to consider how you can go from having no vision or having it be the vision of the "wellness committee" to having this vision be the cornerstone of your employer brand or organizational culture statement.

Consideration #2: Take an Honest Look at Your Current State

An important consideration at the outset is to conduct an audit of your current organizational health and your organization's capacity and capability to change. These two different but related tasks will equip you and other organizational leaders in the process of establishing a plan. The task of conducting an organizational audit is centered on obtaining a solid fact base. Consider the following as your collect information for your fact base:

- What is the baseline upon which you will measure progress over time?
- What data do you have? Earlier in this book, we provided a series of measures to give you a better understanding of what elements constitute a healthy workplace. Use a more robust survey process to engage employees in understanding the current state.
- How is well-being manifested in how you recruit, hire, onboard, develop, support, manage, and make decisions? Engage in some cultural due diligence around your people policies, processes, and procedures.
- How are people currently behaving? What data do you have about employees' current levels of engagement? Use of sick time or absenteeism? Are there reported safety issues? What does EAP or, if possible, insurance data suggest? What are typical medical or stress-related issues people in your organization are experiencing?
- What mindsets might inform the behaviors that you currently see? What do employees believe about the nature of collaboration, flexibility, and support from managers?
- Do your managers and leaders lead by example? What are the inconsistent messages that employees might be receiving (for example, "By all means take care of yourself, but please have this report complete before you leave for the day.")?
- What can you learn from scanning the external environment and conducting a benchmarking activity?

Establishing a robust fact base will support your effort in identifying the most important leverage points in your improvement or action plan. Establishing this fact base will also provide you a baseline so you can track changes over time and see what progress has been made and where improvement is still crucial.

Consideration #3: Ensure a Governance Structure

Embarking on this change journey toward a healthy workplace requires good governance in much the same way that your organizational operations does. It may seem obvious that establishing good governance management is important for a change initiative to be successful, but unfortunately this is a step that is often skipped in the rush to get started. You might also experience senior leaders uncertain as to whether having a governance structure is crucial. According to Dr. Anderson (2016), setting up a change initiative without effective change governance can radically slow progress. Without governance management, delays may be caused by the resulting confusion about who is in charge of what, political in-fighting, and backtracking on decisions made. People may fail to take action if they are unclear about who is authorized to make decisions or who should be getting informed about key issues.

Here are some best practices for establishing good governance (Davidson and Buchel 2011; Zbrodoff 2012):

- Define the scope and objectives. Clearly determine what is being tested and expected impact for each pillar or experiment or initiative.
- Define success criteria and metrics. Specify individual criteria across categories. Each measurement description should include a target metric and an acceptable range of values.
- Establish methods of tracking and sharing progress. Develop processes and methods to learn and track progress to inform a scalable plan.
- Designate an overall project manager. In pilot projects, it's crucial that someone be appointed to oversee pilot measurement, timelines, reporting, and to help teams remove barriers and coordinate with the central task force. In many cases, pilot programs have dedicated resources for each pilot group, solely focused on helping implement and track pilot objectives.

Consideration #4: Develop an Agile Plan

We recommend developing a plan that is agile and evolving. The idea of "agile" refers to having an agile mindset or agile thinking. Characteristics of having an agile mindset are as follows:

- It embraces an iterative approach over perfection, so that a team can iterate over time based on feedback from key stakeholders (improvement and not perfection as the goal).
- It focuses on just-in-time readiness so that stakeholders get what they need when they need it and the team doesn't wait to release everything all at once—doing so would slow down the change process.

- It breaks larger goals into more manageable chunks.
- It continually gathers data and insights that allow the team to refine their experiment or process and plan to better meet stakeholder needs.
- And it focuses on co-creation and collaboration, such as new ways of working or use of technology.

Your plan should incorporate what you have learned from your assessment and what will be required to move the organization toward your vision of organizational health. A solid and robust plan is characterized by the following:

- The use of "SMART" goals (specific, measurable, achievable, relevant, time-based);
- Evidence of support from executive level managers within your company and commitments to allocating resources for the changes;
- Organization-wide communications demonstrating commitment and integration between business objectives and health outcomes;
- Reference to risk assessments and reflection;
- Inclusion of a governance team with a clearly defined set of tasks and activities; and
- Integration of a health approach into your talent management processes, employer brand strategy, and/or culture.

As you go about developing an agile plan, consider the following questions:

- What will be your organization's approach to health?
- What is the relationship between your health plan and your organization's overall strategy?
- Is the plan clear in how its implementation will help deliver competitive parity and/or advantage?
- What role will leaders and managers take on to support, encourage, and hold accountable organizational efforts for creating a healthy workplace?
- What key performance indicators (KPIs) can you use that will demonstrate links between your organization's approach to health and individual high performance?
- How does your approach clearly define where individual and organizational responsibilities lie?
- How does your plan cater for high-risk or various groups?
- How does your plan address the needs of a multicultural, multiracial employee population?
- Is there a clear cascade of the overall plan to reach each area of the organization?

Consideration #5: Your Organization's Health Journey Requires Ongoing Active Engagement

Having a solid plan to assist you in navigating your organization's health journey is 90% of the battle. The other 90% is executing against it. Many management books have been written on the challenge of execution. The execution phase is where good plans go to die. As a result, we ask you to carefully consider how your organization's health journey will be advanced and how you will engage the hearts, minds, and hands of people across your organization (or department or function). Our experience in helping organizations navigate this journey offers up a few useful lessons to take into account as you execute your plan:

- First, be aware of the "knowing-doing gap."
- Second, integrate the efforts into where the work happens.
- And third, adapt the journey for employees at all levels of the organization.

The "knowing-doing gap" was made popular by a book of the same title published in 2000 by Jeffrey Pfeffer and Robert I. Sutton (Jeffrey Pfeffer is featured in Chapter 9). It refers to the problem in most organizations of failing to turn talk into action. Indeed, many organizations are designed for inaction and their policies and rewards reinforce the status quo. Humans are wired to avoid inconsistency and ambiguity, and this can create a gap between what we know and what we do. And in the context of health, most of us know what to do to increase our health and resilience, but our habits reinforce the status quo.

Execution falters when organizations fail to integrate health efforts into where the work happens. For example, how is health incorporated into the process of interviewing candidates, onboarding new employees, making promotion decisions, providing feedback to a colleague, conducting team meetings, or evaluating employees? How is health embedded into regular people processes such as performance management and talent development? More broadly, do the work conditions and work environment (workstations, environment, technology, etc.) support the promulgation of employee health?

Powerful change occurs when the transformation journey is adapted for employees at all levels, locations, and functions in the organization. What aspects of the health vision and story resonate and are important for different audiences? How might health need to show up for mid-level managers versus call center employees or plant workers in the United States versus software developers in South Africa? The organization, after all, is not engaged in a single health journey but the number of journeys equivalent to the number of employees (contracts, partners, etc.) in the organization.

Consideration #6: Measure What Matters

One of the authors, John, has a mantra that he likes to repeat in working with organizations. The health journey, he says, must be "data-driven, evidence-based" or the effort will not be successful. Consideration #1 was to begin with the end in mind by having a clear vision of the future. Consideration #6 is to have clear metrics, KPIs, and a way to gather data and evidence so that you know when you have moved the needle.

Some questions to consider as you make evidence-based decisions:

- How is your organization promoting health?
- What measures does your organization use to identify where it will get the best return from its efforts and investment?
- What is the relationship between the measures used and the priorities identified in your promotional plan?
- How do you promote and measure health awareness?
- How do you promote and measure healthy behaviors?
- How do you promote and measure a healthy culture?

And here are some questions to consider in evaluating your progress:

- How is your organization matching the supports it provides to the needs of the employees and the demands placed by your organization?
- What resources does your organization invest in to support your employees' physical well-being?
- What resources does your organization invest in to support your employees' mental well-being?
- What resources does your organization invest in to support your employees' emotional well-being?
- What steps has your organization taken to align employee outcomes with your organizational outcomes?
- Does the plan meet the real needs and issues of employees along their journey with the organization?
- How does your organization measure the impact of its investment across each of these domains?
- What has gone better than expected? Worse than expected? How might you incorporate those lessons as you revise and renew your plan?

Consideration #7: Embed the Changes

The last consideration as you develop your road map or blueprint for the health change journey is to consider how to embed the changes you make. We believe that programs change and some fade away. New leaders and new priorities and changes to a company's resources result in programs and initiatives ending and others take over. Your organization will stand a better chance of seeing permanent gains in workplace health if your changes are embedded in the organization's culture and institutionalized. Embedding change into the organization prepares the company for the transition from "how we do things now" to "how we will do things in the future."

Aguirre, Brown, and Harshak (2010) suggest that change leaders "often declare victory too soon, diverting leadership, commitment, and focus from the ongoing effort. To embed the change and ensure that it sticks, you should acknowledge the lessons learned. You also should investigate how to engage and involve employees over the long term and how to institutionalize best practices to capture the full benefit of this change and any future changes."

They suggest that the human resources function can play a critical role in this process. They advise that "to enable lasting change, all HR systems, structures, processes, and incentives must be aligned and consistent with the goals of the transformation. You need to articulate clearly the various people-oriented elements of the future organization—not just its structure, but also employee value propositions and individual and team roles, as well as required competencies, skills, and behaviors. Things like performance management, learning and development, workforce strategy, and retention programs are key enablers of the change program."

MAPPING THE TERRAIN

Our work with clients had led us to understand that organizations go through a series of stages toward developing and sustaining a healthy workplace. In Chapter 8, we outlined the various stages we see organizations move through as they create healthy workplaces. Here we suggest some specific interventions to help organizations move from one stage to another.

Moving from Level 1 (Beginner) to Level 2 (Initiator)

It starts with data. Find a way to collect data on organizational and employee health. Often this is the "canary in the coal mine" that will help move an organization to act, particularly if the organization's main focus is on managing risk. An employee survey can be an efficient intervention in the organization. You might also choose instead to have focus groups or other data collection methods. But start with establishing the fact base we discussed earlier.

A good rule of thumb for any stage of the journey but in particular as your move through the first levels of creating a healthy place to work is: be focused on attending to the vital few initiatives that will deliver the biggest impact. Don't take on too much. Show evidence of success (or learning if the program or experiment didn't succeed in the way you expected).

Early on in your journey, vetting the plan and getting buy-in and support from as many stakeholders as possible will help to solidify institutional support. Get buy-in first from friendly managers and then engage in more people to pressure-test and refine your plan. Engage in those conversations before presenting the plan to senior managers.

Look for quick wins as you begin the process. For example, you may wish to focus on easily implemented programs such as wellness checks or activity/movement challenges or stress reduction workshops or financial wellness seminars in order to get employees thinking differently about their own health and wellness.

Moving from Level 2 to Level 3 (Adopter)

Securing the right resources for long-term, sustainable change is a challenge and opportunity at each phase of growth and development. As the organization sees the value and benefit of focusing on health, the investment of resources will increase. It's important to understand that if you are still early in the journey, the likelihood of securing funding for wellness coaches for every employee isn't likely. But determine what the organization can invest, and then invest wisely. Show a return on that investment, and track it to the KPIs you have established.

To be sure, communication is essential at every level, but active, two-way communication is especially advantageous as you enact a broad employee engagement plan. The journey should include a lot of communication channels. Excellent communication yields a high level of impact on change efforts.

Early on in your journey, it is useful to understand how to manage resistance. Who are the likely "blockers"? Why might they be resistant? Understanding how to address managerial and organizational resistance is an important part of the change process and thinking through the most likely scenarios can be useful in the beginning.

Moving from Level 3 to Level 4 (Expert)

Build the case. The healthy organization doesn't manage by being reactionary and putting out fires. Healthy organizations, in our experience, take a long view of things and have deep, core values that guide them. They often have a core sense of purpose, and leaders see the inherent value of well-being and health. However, most organizations don't completely grasp the value of health, at least initially, and so the task of building the business case is an important step in moving your organization forward. Using internal HR data and external benchmarking can be useful in this process.

Gathering passionate champions will accelerate the change process and help to cascade key messages and initiatives throughout the organization. Many clients we have worked with have established local chapters with local leaders that have accountability (and are paid) to hold the role of health facilitator.

At some point, typically as you move from level 3 to level 4, creating a healthy workplace and actively creating a healthy organization requires that you manage the change journey. Change experts such as John Kotter, Richard Beckhard, and William Bridges all point to some common hallmarks of effective organizational transformations:

- They are data driven.
- There is a high level of communication with a focus on highly visible actions.
- There is significant role modeling by leaders and managers.
- Action planning is across the organization and not just within HR.
- There are clear accountability models to ensure action.
- The right resourcing is in place (and this includes talent, money, and time).
- The change is baked into systems and processes (such as performance management).
- Knowledge and training is provided during the change process so people know how and where to fit in and what steps they can take action on.

Find opportunities to engage in storytelling. While storytelling is an important component of communication overall, we highlight it here on its own because stories of individual and team health journeys can be powerful energizers for the organization.

To the degree that you are able, work to align and reinforce the business strategy as you create a healthy workplace. Reinforcing linkages to the business strategy will make all the difference. Note the expert spotlight of Dave Ulrich (see Chapter 9) that underscores the relationship between healthy employees and customer service. Look for and make clear those links in your organization.

Moving from Level 4 to Level 5 (Black Belt)

When executive leaders get it, it can make all the difference in the world. Having leaders connect with other executives from other organizations that are further down the path can be very powerful. Short training, presentations, or videos from subject-matter experts can go a long way. We engage with leadership teams on a regular basis to provide the latest thinking and facilitate a process to shift executives' thinking on this issue. Get someone who might have that influence with your senior leaders.

Training and education is an important lever across the journey, and a focused learning intervention for managers on understanding what a health-focused manager does can have a tremendous impact on the success of your journey. A health-focused manager understands how to incorporate a saluto-genic approach to team meetings, performance conversations, results calls, communications, and so on.

Measuring progress against KPIs is the surest way to move from stage four to stage five. Look at data and artificial intelligence (AI) or people analytics to engage in more focused interventions, demonstrate impact, and problem solve more intractable challenges.

Invest in engaging in "lens agility." Lens agility is the moving from indi-vidual to organization to individual. An example of this is to focus on employee-focused wellness or fitness goals, and then shift gears to consider how the organization supports physical wellness, and then eventually pivot back to the individual level, but this time get focused on individual solutions rather than the one-size-fits-all programs. Also consider not just programs but redesigning individual jobs and eliminating workplace practices that con-tribute to stress at the individual level.

One of the most important issues to address to move from level 4 to level 5 is the performance management and talent management systems. What are managers rewarded for in relationship to organizational health? And are manag-ers provided the flexibility and guidance to challenge and support individual employees in cultivating healthy work habits?

THE JOURNEY CONTINUES

The transformation journey is not linear. It evolves over time and often seems to be winding and circular. It can feel frustrating as if you are trying to push a carpet up a staircase. Managing resistance, evaluating change efforts, address-ing incorrect planning, tracking project health, and demonstrating impact can seem overly challenging. However, the value of creating a healthy workplace is tremendous, and it is important to hang on to that idea. As employees move toward a salutogenic way of living and working and the organization becomes healthier and more productive, resilience increases and individual and organi-zational capacity increases.

We have had the privilege of accompanying leaders and organizations in this journey, some of whom are detailed in case studies and examples in this book. We know that longer-term benefit outweighs the shorter-term costs. We hope that some of the process points and tips outlined in this chapter will assist you as you create and act on the right health journey for your organization.

PAUL LITCHFIELD

Paul Litchfield CBE is the Independent Chief Medical Adviser to ITV and to Compass Group plc, and from 2001 to 2018 he was the Chief Medical Officer for BT. He has pioneered a "whole person approach" balancing the needs of individuals, employers, and wider society. From 2015 to 2021, he was the founding Chair of the UK "What Works Centre for Wellbeing." Paul is renowned for his progressive work in the arena of mental health, well-being, sickness absence, hazard control, and ethics in occupational health.

> Be authentic. Be yourself. Be compassionate in the way that you deal with others, and be compassionate to yourself because the most senior people are usually hardest on themselves, and if you're too hard on yourself, you're probably going to be too hard.

The Pandemic Impact

Reflecting on the COVID-19 pandemic, Litchfield feels that it has simply accelerated trends that were already happening around hybrid/remote working. He also believes that the pandemic restrictions on globalization and migration has affected both the supply of labor and the dynamics between employers and employees—giving more power to the employees. With inflation rising and organizations limited in the level of pay rises they can give in response, Litchfield believes companies have been forced to turn to nonfinancial benefits and thus the elevation of workforce health and well-being in the EVP (employee value proposition).

Changing the Priorities of Employees

Litchfield sees major changes to the workplace as organizations attempt to convince employees to return to their offices. Investments in design to create environments that are more attractive and geared to personal interaction will be a first step. Reducing fear is also important—not just the fear of infectious disease but also the growing fears around financial security in a cost-of-living crisis. In keeping with his focus on the "whole person approach," Litchfield believes organizations will need to focus on the areas affecting an employee's personal life as much as those affecting their life within the workplace as both are clearly interrelated. Finally, he sees an increasing desire by employees to focus on eudaemonia (see Chapter 5)—namely they want their leaders to demonstrate the purpose and meaning in the work their people do on a daily basis.

The Challenge Ahead

According to Litchfield's research, the desire to work from home is often influenced by age, with younger workers more eager to return as they seek to advance their careers and escape what can be unsatisfactory home working environments. The second reason driving this desire is social. From a social viewpoint, the workplace is often where people build their network of friends and relationships. Organizations will not be able to provide a one-size-fits-all approach but rather will need to deliver a more flexible approach. But as Litchfield points out, flexibility is a two-way street, and achieving a solution that works for both the employee and employer is proving to be challenging.

Mental Health and Leadership

Mental health is not some short-term fad. Organizations have now realized that it is critical to business performance and outcomes.

> Mental health in the workplace has matured over the last 40 years; it's more evolution rather than revolution.

Litchfield believes it can't be just associated with the leader but must be cultural and embedded in the organization.

> It's how we do things around here.

The relationship with your manager is critical; hybrid working has made this more difficult, especially when things are not going right with an employee's performance. Litchfield's advice is to meet in person at least once a month—virtual meetings rarely allow for the social exchanges that can indicate how people are really feeling and body language is harder to assess. Line managers also need training to spot the signs of when things are going wrong.

It's not about training people to be psychologists but rather heightening their awareness to spot a problem early and signposting the person on to professional help.

Litchfield believes the biggest challenge for leadership in delivering a healthy workplace is the middle manager population. He puts it brilliantly:

Their job is to translate chaos. They take the "good ideas!" from the people in the C-Suite, which may well be barking mad, and try and turn them into what's going to work in the real world. Often against push-back from those they're trying to manage. Line managers and middle managers are in a really difficult position.

This is where organizations need to focus attention to ensure success.

Anxiety at Work?

I don't think that the incidence or prevalence of mental health disorders has changed significantly, I think what has changed is people's willingness to talk about it.

Litchfield believes we are getting our approach wrong on two counts. Firstly, by medicalizing normal human reactions when things in our lives are going wrong—inappropriate prescriptions for drugs can delay the natural recovery process. Secondly, the development of a victim culture; sometimes it's nobody's fault, and often the answer is in the person's own hands. He does not believe it is healthy for people to abdicate that responsibility.

Designing for Success

One of the keys to success is organizational design. Organizational justice is the top priority; people need to believe that decisions are being made for the right reasons. We need a more sophisticated approach to organizational design rather than one based on a simple mathematical review of spans and layers. The key is to give people what they need in terms of job satisfaction while making it work for the business.

Fundamentally it's about good values, and I don't mean the five things written up on the wall that I never remember, but fundamentally good values and a good culture. And then I think that translates into people being happier and healthier within the organization.

SUSIE ELLIS

Susie Ellis, CEO

Global Wellness Institute (GWI)

A nonprofit organization with a mission to empower wellness worldwide by educating public and private sectors about preventative health and wellness:

"A world free of preventable diseases"

Workplace Health

In its 16 years in operation, the Global Wellness Institute has published multiple reports, policy documents, and information on current and future trends within the wellness industry, which they say is worth $4.4 trillion US dollars. These data offer valuable insights into this relatively young sector. One of the key surprising facts is how small the proportion of spend that workforce and workplace health accounts for compared to many of the other segments in the wellness industry.

A Clear Business Case

Susie Ellis is very clear as to why there has been very little comparative attention paid to this area by CEOs across the globe. She believes there has been a lack of proof about the impact of investments. She believes more and more CEOs are requesting evidential proof of return, ROW (return on wellness), before they will commit significant budgets. To date, those championing workforce health have had to rely on short-term metrics around absence, illness, and attrition to secure necessary funding. Case studies with clear proof points and data demonstrating the link workforce/workplace investments has on organizational performance will be necessary to convince a large majority of business leaders to make significant, targeted, and strategic investments on a multi-annual basis.

Preventative Approach

According to the Global Wellness Institute's latest report, "Defining Wellness Policy," they believe that the widespread adoption of preventative approaches and the promotion of healthy lifestyles are essential if the global community is to address the mounting global health crises and spiraling economic costs associated with health care. They believe that public policy supported by employers is key. In fact, they have statistics to prove that 70% of health care costs are related to preventable diseases.

Moon Shot

GWI has set an ambitious moon shot to achieve a world free of preventable diseases. According to Susie, prevention is no longer optional to global wellness—it is mission critical. Lifestyle-related diseases and the continuously skyrocketing costs of health care are creating a global crisis affecting both mental and physical health.

"According to the World Economic Forum the global cost of largely preventable chronic diseases could reach $47 trillion by 2030. The time has come to pool our resources—knowledge, access, funding—and use our collective megaphone on the world stage to work towards a world free of these preventable diseases."

We support Susie and the Global Wellness Institute in their ambition.

Culture from the Top

Finally, Susie believes that the key is to bring leaders on board on the mission to make workplaces healthier. In that regard she is very clear that it is not a raft of health care programs that will move the dial but an obsession around creating a health-focused culture for every organization.

"It's not a matter of programs, it is all about leadership and culture."

CHAPTER **11**

Healthy Interventions

Throughout this book, we have endeavored to include the voices of experts in the field and organizations that have made a solid effort in becoming healthier places to work. Hopefully their voices and their examples illuminate, educate, and inspire. As we indicated in Chapter 10, each organization will come to its own plan of action. Organizations differ in terms of culture and context, how they are structured, and how they operate. As a leader or manager, you may wonder about some practical ways of intervening to create a healthy place to work. This chapter attempts to provide some useful interventions based on the model we discussed in Chapter 7, with particular attention to issues of equity in the workplace and some other typical issues we see in organizations we work with.

MOVING FROM "NORMAL" TO AN EQUITY LENS

One of the biggest barriers to creating and sustaining a healthy workplace for all employees is management's focus on "normal" or "average." This mindset frames our organizational life: performance expectations, hiring criteria, culture fit, employee compensation and benefits, and yes, well-being. The term "normal" entered the English language in the 1840s, and its first use was related to statistics and geometry, not people. Adolphe Quetelet, a Flemish mathematician, made the jump from astronomy and math to people. Quetelet claimed that every one of us is a flawed version of some sort of cosmic template for human beings. He dubbed this template the "Average Man." And that thinking persists today. Today's BMI, or body mass index, which is a value derived from the height and weight of a person, is the modern version of the original Quetelet Index.

As author and speaker Jonathan Mooney points out in his book *Normal Sucks: How to Live, Learn, and Thrive Outside the Lines*, in the mid-1800s, the academic disciplines of comparative anatomy and physiology had started to use the word "normal," and by the 19th century, "normal state" was widely used to describe bodies and organs that were ideal or perfect and to judge an organ as healthy. This was Quetelet's contribution. Importantly, academics never defined what was a normal state, however; instead, they studied the opposite of that. They defined normal as what is not abnormal. But normal isn't just what is *not* abnormal. It begins to shape how we think of an "average" body, person, family, community, worker, and so on. What is average is often called normal, and what people call normal becomes the expected norm.

This has material implications for us as leaders in considering how to create a healthy workplace because most of our efforts are targeted toward that broad middle of the bell curve, or "average." And in organizations that have historically, at least in Western Europe and North America, hired and managed a largely white, male, straight, able-bodied workforce, people policies and practices have been designed with those "norms" in mind. And those norms are so ingrained that we rarely scrutinize and interrogate them—unless, of course, we are a part of an underrepresented group. In that case, our experience of the organization, its culture, its policies, and its practices may be harder to understand, access, engage with, or utilize.

It's important to note that Quetelet's "Average Man" describes, in fact, no one. As leaders, our task in creating a healthy workplace requires us to consider how our approach may "normalize" and reify ways of being, knowing, and working that are not equitable or inclusive. When we make a decision to enact a policy to support our team or the organization, it is likely to have a disparate impact based on the unique life circumstances of a team member. And as we consider a broad range of evolving needs and issues, such as hybrid and virtual work environments or how we address mental health, we need to consider the ways in which identity and culture affect employee well-being. This may seem a bit overwhelming. Surely, you might think, there is no way to address the unique individual needs of every employee. That is a recipe for chaos and unmanageable! A healthy workplace, however, puts the employee at the center and asks a different question: How best do we apply our policy or program to set this employee up for success?

As a leader, if you "de-center" what is considered average or normal and work to address the needs and issues of employees from an equity lens, it is likely that you will improve the work experience for *all* employees. For example, addressing flexibility scheduling, parental leave, or floating holidays benefits everyone, not just a specific population. One could argue that by approaching the well-being needs of women, people of color, differently abled, LGBTQ+ employees, "pink," "gray," and "blue collar" workers, and other underrepresented groups with an inclusive mindset, this will positively affect the experience of *all employees*. Thus, an important determinant of whether your organization is really a healthy place to work is based on how effectively your organization addresses the presenting needs and concerns of a broader group of employees than what organizations tend to typically focus on.

The phrase "canary in the coal mine" is used to describe an early warning signal for danger. The canary played an important role in both American and British mining history. Coal miners took caged canaries into the mines with them to monitor for toxic gases. When the canary showed signs of distress, miners took this as a signal to promptly leave the mine to avoid asphyxiation. While the practice was discontinued in 1986, the phrase is often used as it relates to well-being, burnout, and toxic workplaces. In today's modern workplace, there are a range of indicators that are "canaries" such as burnout, stress, absenteeism, microaggressions, and discrimination. And underrepresented populations are often the first to experience unhealthy practices in the workplace and experience them most severely. For example, as a result of the COVID-19 pandemic, millions of women left the workforce, many of them leaving to take care of children at home. As of this book's publication, women have yet to return to work in the numbers from pre-pandemic times; that impact has negative consequences for organizational growth and social well-being as well as family and societal implications.

Women's Health

Gallup's 2021 State of the Global Workplace report found record levels of stress—and nowhere in the world are female workers less stressed than men. On average, 46% of working women in 2020 reported stress "a lot of the day yesterday," as did 42% of working men. In the United States and Canada, it's 62% and 52%, respectively. Meanwhile, well-being is declining among employed women, whether or not they have children, faster than among working men. (See www .gallup.com/workplace/352529/wellbeing-stats-women-workplace-show-need-change.aspx?version=print.) Well-being in Europe and South Asia was hit hard in 2021 by COVID-19 waves. Both Europe and South Asia (which includes India) dropped 5 percentage points in well-being in 2021, with South Asia having the lowest well-being in the world at 11%. Workers in these regions not only felt like their current life was worse than it had previously been, but their hope in the future also dropped. Women, in all instances, fare worse than their male counterparts.

The list of challenges affecting women is long. Inequities at work, including unequal pay, unconscious bias, lack of sponsorship and advancement, and harassment or outright discrimination, continue to persist. Physical and emotional caregiving roles—as daughters, mothers, colleagues, and even leaders—result in heavier burdens. Women are twice as likely to experience depression, generalized anxicty disorder, and PTSD and much more likely to deal with eating disorders then men. Caregiving responsibilities tend to fall to women more than men, even when both are working full-time outside the home.

Moreover, during child-rearing years, the "unemployment penalty" for women is longer. This means that when women take longer leaves, they have a much harder time getting rehired.

A recent McKinsey study (www.mckinsey.com/featured-insights/diversity-and-inclusion/women-in-the-workplace) highlighted how the pandemic continues to take a toll on employees, and especially women. Women are more burned out now than they were pre-pandemic, and burnout is escalating much faster among women than among men. One in three women say that they have considered downshifting their career or leaving the workforce, compared with one in four who said this only a few months into the pandemic. Additionally, four in ten women have considered leaving their company or switching jobs—and high employee turnover throughout 2022 suggests that many of them are following through. This trend will most certainly persist as women and their families make calculations about the costs of a lack of well-being in the workplace.

Now, layer into all of this the additional challenges of navigating "double only" status as a woman of color or member of the LGBTQ+ community. Often, women having to navigate their "double only" (or triple-only) status are left isolated since there are fewer of them. They might have to fight impostor syndrome. Feeling like an impostor can cause some women to hide their true selves or downplay their backgrounds to fit in with the dominant culture at an organization—also called "code-switching." Changing how you speak, look, and act to conform can be exhausting. Moreover, they may have to contend with being seen as too _____ (fill in the blank, e.g. angry or distant) in the workplace. This happens when they have to work through white or straight normative expectations. And all of this can be exhausting at best and stressful or debilitating at worst. Since many of these challenges are largely invisible, women may be reluctant to discuss them at all, much less at work.

The research on the value of gender diversity in the workplace is clear: women matter. Across every metric—team performance, innovation, driving economic growth, profitability, and meeting market demands—having a gender diverse and representative organization returns better than expected results. Conversely, not proactively and forthrightly addressing well-being in the workplace for women reduces organizational capacity and capability. Globally, the lack of gender parity shaves upward of $12 trillion (USD) in global growth. (See https://www.mckinsey.com/~/media/mckinsey/industries/public%20and%20social%20sector/our%20insights/how%20advancing%20womens%20equality%20can%20add%2012%20trillion%20to%20global%20growth/mgi%20power%20of%20parity_full%20report_september%202015.pdf.)

Some interventions to address women's well-being in the workplace include the following:

- Provide greater flexibility and time off, including alternative schedules, hybrid or remote work, four-day workweeks, and job-sharing.
- Increase caregiving leave policies.
- Include return-to-work support for new mothers, including phased reentry, breastfeeding support, and maternal health programs.
- Provide reproductive health care support.
- Launch a women's employee resource group (ERG) for recruitment and development.
- Offer childcare or elder care support.
- Provide equal pay. Where gender pay gaps have been identified, a clear action plan is required to redress the balance.

Diversity and Inclusion

Beyond the well-being of women, a broader look at the equity of well-being requires us to consider the impact of workplace policies and practices on people of color, people with health conditions or impairments or who are neurodiverse, LGBTQ+ individuals, and other underrepresented groups. It requires us to consider the well-being of people based on generational or religious differences as well. Well-being and diversity travel together.

Research has documented the importance of diversity, equity, and inclusion (DEI) for business. We know that organizations with diverse workforces enjoy increased financial performance, innovation, and creativity, and decreased attrition and related costs. But efforts to address DEI in the workplace are typically disconnected from those aimed at supporting employee health and wellness. Research shows police killings in the United States contribute to 1.7 additional poor mental health days for Black Americans. Compared to their white counterparts, American Indian or Alaska Native (AIAN) people are more than twice as likely to be uninsured, leaving many without access to health care. Consequently, AIAN people have a higher prevalence of many chronic health conditions than those from any other racial or ethnic group.

Taking a more global perspective:

- While 43% of Americans face discrimination at work, 36% of employees in Germany, 34% in the United Kingdom, and 32% in France also experience discrimination at work.
- People of Southeast Asian origin have a higher risk of developing type 2 diabetes (https://www.diabetes.co.uk/south-asian/).

- People of Irish descent are at increased risk of developing dangerously high iron levels, or hemochromatosis (https://www.bbc.com/news/uk-northern-ireland-43245267).
- Black women are twice as likely to be diagnosed with advanced breast cancer (www.thetimes.co.uk/article/black-women-more-likely-to-have-advanced-cancer-diagnosed-wt7mhkfvt).
- LGBTQ+ folks are 2.5 times more likely to experience depression, anxiety, and substance misuse than non-LGBTQ+ individuals, yet they face significant discrimination in health care that leads them to avoid care, putting their health at risk. (See https://hbr.org/2022/03/supporting-the-well-being-of-your-underrepresented-employees and https://eightfold.ai/blog/workplace-discrimination/.)

Altogether, these challenges complicate our efforts at increasing equity of well-being in the workplace.

As highlighted earlier, increased stress relates to things such as microaggressions in the workplace, and experiences with discrimination can lead to physical concerns such as headaches, high blood pressure, and difficulties with sleep, which of course affect mood as well. Beyond microaggressions, employees from underrepresented communities may also experience "micro-insults" (as when someone was hired or promoted or included because of their social identity) or "micro-invalidations" (as when someone is asked where they are from, assuming they are from another country, or when someone says, "I don't see color," which invalidates another's experience).

Different generations in the workplace also face challenges as it relates to well-being. Millennials are more likely to struggle with financial wellness resulting from student loans or being in jobs that are entry-level. Gen X individuals may also be struggling with financial wellness, but the causes are perhaps related to raising a family and caring for aging parents. Baby boomers may wish to retire, but rising health care costs or lack of a pension or retirement savings may affect their ability to finish out their careers. Other aspects of wellness and well-being also affect different generations in various ways, such as how different generations engage in exercise, nutrition, and sleep and manage energy and social connections. In all of these ways, a sophisticated approach to well-being across generational differences is required by leaders and managers.

A 2021 study by Mind Share Partners, Qualtrics, and ServiceNow found that LGBTQ+ workers were more likely to experience mental health challenges such as anxiety, depression, and burnout. Study participants also indicated that their work or work environment had a negative impact on their mental health.

They found that LGBTQ+ workers were more than twice as likely to report having ever voluntarily left a previous role due at least in part to mental health reasons. (See https://hbr.org/2022/07/supporting-lgbtq-workers-mental-health.)

Transgendered people face related but different challenges. The National Center for Transgender Equality in the United States notes that "more than one in four transgender people have lost a job due to bias, and more than three-fourths have experienced some form of workplace discrimination. Refusal to hire, privacy violations, harassment, and even physical and sexual violence on the job are common occurrences and are experienced at an even higher rate by transgender people of color. Many people report changing jobs to avoid discrimination or the risk of discrimination" (see https://transequality.org/issues/employment).

To improve well-being in the workplace and make work healthy, leaders need to examine and address diversity and inclusion issues. Organizations need well-being strategies that are equitable and inclusive of diverse employees, as well as comprehensive DEI initiatives that deliver a consistent employee experience for everyone. At the same time, leaders need to recognize that employees' experiences and needs related to well-being can differ dramatically based on their identity. Therefore, diversity is an important consideration or presenting issue for leaders and managers committed to creating a healthy place to work.

Interventions that support diversity and well-being include the following:

- Create a well-being centered ERG;
- Connect employees with culturally sensitive resources, such as mental health, medical, and financial, that meet the unique needs and concerns of diverse populations;
- Provide insurance and resources for gender-affirming care;
- Upskill managers on working with diverse populations;
- Conduct a diversity facilities audit (how accessible are your facilities?); and
- Assign wellness coaches to your ERGs or diversity networks.

Mental Health

In 2019, employers were just starting to grasp the prevalence of mental health challenges in the workplace and its link to diversity and inclusion. Fast-forward a few years; with the collective trauma of COVID-19 and more local or regional challenges such as the war in Ukraine, economic upheavals, racial violence in the United States and other countries, and technological disruptions, there is a greater awareness by leaders of the factors that contribute to mental health issues in the workplace and also how those issues intersect with diversity and inclusion. *Corporate Wellness Magazine* notes that in 2022 "more employees dealt with mental health challenges over the past year, from stress and burnout to anxiety, depression, post-traumatic stress disorder (PTSD), and substance use problems...the employee mental health crisis is worsening." They continue, "Mental health issues like burnout have contributed to many workers' decisions to leave their jobs, if not the workforce entirely." (See www.corporatewellnessmagazine.com/article/the-2022-state-of-workforce-mental-health.)

It is important to understand that mental health is more than the absence of mental illness. One can have poor mental health without having an illness, and conversely, you can have good mental health with a mental illness. Anyone can experience poor mental health, and because of this, mental health is both a presenting issue when thinking about well-being and an equity of well-being concern.

In the past two years, employers identified stress and burnout as a major threat for their workforces, according to survey results released in January by consultancy WTW (formerly Willis Towers Watson). The firm's 2021 well-being report, conducted in October, asked 322 US employers with 100 or more employees about their expectations for 2022 (see www.shrm.org/resourcesandtools/hr-topics/benefits/pages/employers-identify-workforce-mental-health-priorities-for-2022.aspx). Among the findings:

- 86 percent of employers said mental health, stress, and burnout were still a priority;
- 49 percent, however, had not formally articulated a well-being strategy for their workforce; and
- 26 percent had adopted a well-being strategy.

While stress and distraction levels are lower in the healthiest of workplaces, rates of stress and distraction remain high across all workplaces. Eighty percent of employees agree that the stress from work affects their relationships with friends, family, and co-workers. Seventy-one percent of employees find it difficult to concentrate at work, compared to 65% in 2021 and 46% in 2018 (see www.mhanational.org/mind-workplace). And another study by McKinsey found that one of every three employees say their return to the workplace has had a negative impact on their mental health, and they're feeling anxious and depressed. A total of 59 percent of Americans are feeling isolated since the start of the COVID-19 pandemic despite the fact that 75 percent are living with someone, and a third are more depressed. (See www.mckinsey.com/industries/healthcare-systems-and-services/our-insights/returning-to-work-keys-to-a-psychologically-safer-workplace.) A 2022 KPMG study found that 94 percent of employees are stressed because of the pandemic, suggesting that mental health issues will increase as we reach an endemic stage with COVID-19. (See www.forbes.com/sites/benjaminlaker/2021/05/04/the-future-world-of-work-is-fascinating-reveals-new-research-from-kpmg/?sh=177090c6865c.)

Signs of burnout or exhaustion may signify mental health issues. There may be other signs as well. Changes to appearance, mood swings or erratic behavior changes, needing to take a lot of time off, a decrease in productivity, and confusion with tasks can also be warning signs of potential mental health issues. Beyond episodic mental health issues that any employee might experience, it is also important to be able to identify and appropriately intervene when there are signs of deeper mental health issues such as anxiety disorders, major depressive disorders, eating disorders, or substance abuse. As a leader or manager, you can play a supportive role in helping employees obtain the assistance they need to become or remain productive team members. Having an "equity of well-being" mindset will support that effort.

Several interventions you can take to support mental well-being include these:

- Encourage the utilization of EAP programs;
- Provide screenings for depression, sleeping disorders, etc.;
- Offer free or subsidized mental health coaches;
- Provide relaxation spaces; and
- Educate managers and employees on mental health issues and how to access support.

HEALTHY INTERVENTIONS BASED ON THE DATA

Along with taking an equity lens when considering well-being, our research based on our surveys with organizations from around the world suggests that there are four typical issues facing employers in creating a culture of well-being. Here we present some useful interventions in each of those areas.

Physical Health and Fitness

Employees often report that their physical health is lacking. Scientific evidence backs this up. Many of us do not get enough physical activity, drink enough water, manage our diet, and so on. When data points to this as a presenting issue, organizational leaders can do the following:

- Name it. There is power in clearly stating that this is an issue for employees and therefore the organization.
- Start a conversation. Do people see a lack of physical exercise as okay? If so, maybe the organization needs to build awareness of the benefits of fitness.
- Run focus groups and/or semi-structured interviews to get beneath the reasons why people are not exercising. In a few organizations, it is a lack of time rather than will. Understanding the "why" is important to determining the best solutions.
- Leaders will need to role-model this behavior. One CEO takes his colleagues on a run, regardless of the office he visits.
- Help employees set targets/goals. Many organizations now have "health coaches" who support employees in this process.
- Your organization could gamify its approach, such as step challenges or introducing treadmills near workstations. In fact, there are now "walking desks" where a treadmill and desk are combined.
- Introduce other activity practices such as walking meetings.
- And, of course, make it fun and celebrate successes.

Obesity and Overweight

Obesity and overweight are major health challenges in most developed and developing countries. In the workplace, obese individuals have substantially increased rates of absenteeism. Leaders can do the following when this is a presenting issue:

- Like the issue of fitness, it is important to name it.
- Assess the workplace and see if healthy options are available.
- Have a focus on healthy foods: canteen/cafeteria menu, replacement of sugary drinks in vending machines, free cold water fountains, and so on.
- Offer people the opportunity to take a programmatic approach through motivation weight loss such as Weight Watchers.
- Have lunchtime lectures about healthy eating.
- Teach people to cook.
- Get creative; for example, start a "Biggest Loser" campaign.
- For education, invite families to join their employee-family member, such as Thursday dinners.
- Subsidize healthy foods to make them a cheaper option.

Leaders Who Are Not Role Models for Healthy Behaviors

One of the most common presenting issues that we find in our data is that leaders do not role-model the kinds of behaviors necessary for promoting a healthy organization. Often it is "do as I say, not as I do," which sends a mixed message. Consider the following actions:

- Share feedback with leaders.
- Educate the senior leaders on their impact.
- Convince them about the tone they set and what healthy is, and educate them about being holistic.
- Employ a health coach who will watch behaviors and provide feedback.
- Ask employees for examples of times when leaders have not been healthy role models.
- Help leaders build healthy habits, such as not overworking and not sending emails during holidays/weekends.
- Get an annual health checkup and publicize that fact.

Financial Well-Being

While perks and benefits are important, baseline compensation that provides for a livable wage is essential. Your organization should align itself to solid compensation practices and communicate those to employees. Further, even when compensation is good, employers can support employees in making good financial decisions (most people do not learn about financial health as young people). Consider the following:

- Understand the issues, such as challenges employees face with student loan debt or credit card management, or saving/investing in a home, or saving for retirement.
- Offer one-on-one coaching to get personal finances back on track.
- Offer tax clinics to help employees claim their entitlements/tax efficiency.
- Educate broadly on tips and tricks about using financial resources well.
- Train on big purchases such as mortgages and how to get the best value.
- Implement discounts schemes from local shops.
- Arrange concessionary discounts if employees sign up to one particular health care scheme.
- Offer a loan scheme so that employees don't have to have credit card debt.
- Sign up to early salary payment schemes.
- Use Christmas or holiday savings schemes and company matches.

In this chapter, we identified several presenting issues that require an equity lens to effectively address the opportunity. We also identified a series of issues that routinely present themselves when we work with organizations and conduct a survey or audit. There are many creative interventions that can assist leaders and managers in cultivating a healthy organization and supporting increased health and well-being among employees. In Chapter 12, we provide a number of examples of organizations that have worked to create a healthy place to work. In these examples, we believe you will find a lot of great illustrations of interventions and ways of addressing health opportunities.

CHAPTER **12**

Stories of Healthy Success

In this book so far, we have explained why leaders, managers, and companies in general should prioritize the development of a healthy workforce and a healthy organization. We have shared models and methodologies, getting very specific about what needs to be measured and managed.

In this chapter, we want to share some ways in which companies are implementing change and attempting to make their workplaces healthier. We look at some like Centiro and Futurice who implement different organizational structures, giving individual employees more control and intentionally attracting work that is focused to a greater extent on their people's natural talents and skills.

We take inspiration from cashew nut supplier Amendoas and pharmaceutical company P&G in South America, who create cultures of health and use deep analytics to create very specific health score cards that drive focused responses to improve organizational health.

We look at a healthy approach to leadership both at the top of enterprises and throughout at the manager population levels at Takeda Plasma, Deloitte, Kingston Council, and Cohesive, supporting the workforce to make work *work*.

We learn about PwC's new approach to development, how Concentrix is implementing a range of flexible options, and how it increases their ability to recruit faster. US-based SAS Institute talked to us about the importance of recruiting people who have an orientation to be naturally caring and supportive and the impact that has on creating a strong healthy culture.

We discuss diversity with IIS, trauma support with the Royal Society for the prevention of cruelty to animals, and how SAP has developed a program around neurodiversity that makes people with autism succeed.

Dubai Police helped us understand their approach to keeping their people physically fit while Aviva in the United Kingdom demonstrate how they are making work a net positive activity, and we learn how Thames Water keeps its finger on the pulse of their people by focusing on health data.

Is there a better way to structure our workweeks? Well, Danish company IIH Nordic believes so and have found success by implementing a four-day week. Danske Bank tells us how a simply weekly podcast can inspire their people to healthier habits and how Leek United Building Society have moved healthy to a strategic driver of performance, and we end with a four-year case study as European IT company Version 1 details their own journey to creating a healthy place to work.

We would like to thank each of these organizations for taking the time to discuss in detail their innovative approaches to making work and the workplace healthier for everybody.

CENTIRO, SWEDEN, ORGANIZATIONAL DESIGN

centiro®|GROUP

Centiro is an innovative global leader and tech company that connects, empowers, and makes delivery networks available and smarter for marquee brands. Centiro is a fast grower with 600+ employees in eight countries. All types of goods get delivered on time in over 175 countries thanks to Centiro technology. In December 2021 they were awarded the top Swedish accolade for quality.

In this interview, Niklas Hedin, founder and CEO, challenges our views on organizational design, communications, sustainability, presence, and success, all with a cup of coffee!

The Healthy Alternative to Hierarchy

English band Blur claimed, "There's no other way" in their 1991 hit song, and many organizations and their leadership teams may believe there is no alternative to hierarchy as an effective organizational design. However, they will hit a problem when they meet Niklas Hedin, CEO of Centiro. He is a passionate proponent of holocracy, which he describes as a system that removes all unnecessary levels of bureaucracy, removing friction and obstacles so people can succeed, ensuring that teams and individuals are trusted to make decisions closer to where their effect will be experienced. It requires trust and transparency but brings empowerment and agility.

For Niklas and the team at Centiro, it is all about value creation. Short decision paths, short distances for information to travel, and a lack of blame culture create the right environment for success. Many leaders who are high on a need for control and who love power will not be attracted as both are reduced in this approach.

One might think this self-organizing teams approach will only work in small companies, but Centiro is now passing through 600 employees on a continued rapid growth journey and has proven the model is effective with productivity, profitability, and business success as a by-product but not the most important goal.

A Healthy and Sustainable Working Environment

While organizational design is important, so too is physical design in Centiro's approach. Their headquarters is a shining example of their commitment to a sustainable future but also integral to setting employees up for success: creating and maintaining a safe, healthy, and functional workplace is part of their sustainability credentials; efficiently using and reusing energy (solar panels for self-sufficient energy supply), water, and other resources; and reducing waste, pollution, and environmental degradation required an investment, but those actions speak louder than words according to Hedin.

Healthy Communication Is Critical

One of the greatest frustrations employees express is not knowing what is going on in their organization. With remote working, this has been made more difficult, especially if you recognize that sending an email or simply giving people information is not effective communication. For Centiro every Friday at 1 p.m. Hedin goes live across all their locations with a fun interactive session, where any employees can pose any question anonymously and he will answer. His promise to employees is that they will hear the company news first, positive or negative, and he will answer any question. The sessions also include guests and can be fun and quirky, keeping people really engaged with authentic content. "Relaxed seriousness" is how staff at Centiro explains their overall approach.

The Secret Ingredient: A Cup of Coffee!

Simply offering a coffee when someone arrives is part of a welcoming ritual that sets the tone for an introduction to Centiro. Again, a coffee break (or whatever you choose to drink) where everyone stops work, leaves their desk, and socializes is a very Swedish practice called Fika, but it ensures that relationships are built and become stronger. And if anybody does not clear up their coffee cups, it provides an opportunity to discuss the need to take ownership and responsibility; leading by example is key!

The Power of Digital Presence

According to Hedin, leading in a remote/hybrid world of work is more difficult because face-to-face communication is more engaging, and that is why the focus at Centiro is all about being truly present when communicating digitally. They are working hard to ensure they don't lose collaboration and creativity by creating engaging workspaces, attracting employees to make the effort to commute to their closest office. Short-term efficiency rises when working from home (or as Hedin calls it, "living at work!"), but interorganizational connectivity suffers along with innovation and your problem-solving network.

Who Succeeds at Centiro?

For Centiro, the organization must succeed! People need to put the needs of the organization equal to their individual needs because if it succeeds, everybody's future is more secure and the opportunities expand. However, unlike other organizations, if you have built your individual success at the expense of someone else, they would prefer if you don't join them because they do not see that way of working as healthy. Collaboration and winning together and enjoying every moment of the journey is the signature of success at Centiro.

Advice to Other Leaders

Let go and trust people. If you believe in people, 95% won't let you down, and it seems crazy to have rules, regulations, and controls for all when only 5% require them. At Centiro they have no budgets, they don't check for deviations, and they don't do formal performance appraisals. Sometimes mistakes happen, but Centiro is a fan of the Japanese aesthetic concept of wabi-sabi, which celebrates imperfection; instead constantly learning and improving is the way forward (they also have nine ISO certifications), and based on their success so far, who are we to argue?

THAMES WATER COMPANY, UNITED KINGDOM, WORKFORCE ANALYTICS

The Thames Water Company is a water utility that serves 15 million customers across London and the Thames Valley in the United Kingdom. It delivers and removes over 7 billion liters of water and wastewater every day. It employs circa 7,000 people in a range of roles from operational, management, and call center. Aimee Cain is the Occupational Health and Well-Being Manager.

> We have a whole fleet of vans working for Thames Water, you'll see them on the road all the time, we MOT them every year, because we are legally required to. Our people are a much bigger asset than our vans, so we should assess them annually too.
>
>   (*MOT: Ministry of Transport Test for vehicles in the UK)

A Preventative Approach

Proactivity is a word that describes Thames Water's approach to the health of their workforce. Ten years ago, while they had a health team, it was a very reactive clinic health team who responded when someone became ill. That changed with the appointment of a health and safety lead, and the focus became more about building a culture around health and safety. The occupational health and well-being service became more proactive. They expanded the team of nurses and had more trained staff. Seventy-five percent of all referrals to occupational are now from people within the workplace rather than people who are off work ill.

A Personal Medical Assessment

Thames Water invested in a personal medical assessment for each employee, which included blood pressure, diabetes, cholesterol, cardiovascular risk, height, weight, BMI, respiratory assessment, and for men over 50 a prostate specific antigen test. (They have already identified 20 cases of prostate cancer with undiagnosed symptoms.)

A Direct Line to the CEO

The Health and Safety lead was given direct access to the CEO. That was a clear signal to the employees that the leadership viewed workforce health as a priority.

Workforce Health Requires a Strategy

Organizations often introduce initiatives such as mental health first aiders without a clear supporting strategy. Thames Water introduced a range of measures to support the mental health of their people. They launched a communications strategy to support a range of interventions encouraging Mental Health Awareness Week, World Mental Health Day, supporting their mental health first aiders. All first aiders get a green lanyard, so they are easily identifiable, which they wear with pride, and they also have a little emblem that they insert on their email signature. The strategy also included the development of a power app available online or on phones, allowing employees access to their nearest mental health first aider no matter where they are geographically located.

> You can't just introduce an initiative and think that's it, job done, tick the box, you've changed well-being because you haven't.

Thames Water measure the number of contacts to their mental health first aiders monthly and report the data back to their board to demonstrate the true value of their mental health strategy, and they use that data (trigger) to respond to the presenting issues.

> We understand what the trigger is to somebody's mental health worries and use that knowledge to promote messaging across our business focused on that issue.

VR Technology Supporting Mental Health

Aimee explains the application of virtual reality technology at Thames Water, which made a real difference in building awareness of mental health and is so popular there is a three-year waiting list!

> We developed some VR technology footage. You put the headset on, and you become the person suffering from stress and depression. You are sitting in your car, not wanting to get out of the car to go into work or you are sitting at your desk, crisp and sweet wrappers everywhere,

and you can't remember your password to get into your computer. Then you overhear people talking about how work hasn't been completed. It brings a bigger picture of how someone's health can decline. No one has asked how that individual is.

The Disability Network

The Disability Network is just one of a large range of support groups throughout Thames Water. Inclusion cards are used to increase the awareness of disability and how it affects the person with the disability.

After picking an inclusion card, the employee steps into the world of the person with a particular disability, how it makes them feel and how they need to resolve the challenges they face daily. It also acts as a great training for managers.

A Major Impact

Building a link between physical health and mental health has been a game changer for Thames Water to build a resilient organization.

It's changed from people going to the gym to exercise, to now exercising to build personal resilience, increase your ability to cope with family life and your ability to be productive at work.

Data-Driven Decisions

Aimee explains how data drives her actions to deal with the presenting issues of the workforce.

Some well-being leads introduce initiatives based on the UK well-being calendar; blood pressure awareness day, diabetes awareness day, etc., but I need the data to understand what health issues are impacting our employees the most. I know through my data that occupational health referrals and our sickness absence are highest for mental health conditions. Second is musculoskeletal conditions, back pain, neck pain, similarly with our physio referrals, I know these are the biggest health issues we have in our business. Any initiative that I want to introduce needs to directly influence both of those. My priority as a clinical well-being lead is to look at our clinical data and understand what our main health issues are amongst our employees and introduce initiatives and support services to address those.

The support that the team at Thames Water facilitates the employees to make better decisions around their own health.

DELOITTE, UNITED STATES, HEALTHY SPONSORSHIP

Jennifer Fisher is the chief well-being officer in the United States at Deloitte Services LP and drives the strategy and innovation around work-life, health, and wellness to empower Deloitte's people to be well so they can perform at their best in both their professional and personal lives.

Widespread Burnout

Eight years ago, Jennifer Fisher suffered burnout. Back then most people didn't use the term. Now everybody knows about burnout.

> I think it is a double-edged sword. It's wonderful that we're talking about it now. But it's also awful that we're talking about it now because it's way too prevalent.

According to Jennifer, burnout is not an overnight event; you know what you are doing is not sustainable, but you keep doing it. But it is top of the agenda for organizations right now.

> With the Great Resignation we now have the attention of the organization.

Time to Redesign Work

Deloitte is clear that aspects of work are never going to be easy, and sometimes you'll find yourself in the middle of a project with a deadline, but you need to find time to recover. Jennifer created her role as chief well-being officer after her own experience with burnout and needing to take a leave of absence because work wasn't working for her; now her focus is on making the workplace work for everybody.

> The Great Resignation is a sign that the way we're working isn't working, we need people to engage and be involved with the redesign of work, that includes everyone, the C-suite, the middle managers, and that includes the person that started yesterday. We all have a role to play.

Work life is often not going to light us up and bring us joy day in and day out, but in the main it should be a positive experience.

> I think that requires a complete redefining of the way that we look at organizational metrics and what we measure and how we measure them and what types of metrics actually make it into the talent experience because I think that many organizations, Deloitte included, kind of mix operational metrics with talent or HR. Operational metrics are important, but they don't really have a place or a role in talent based metrics.

Managers' Accountability

Deloitte believe that managers need to be accountable for the health and well-being of their team members. It needs to be a key metric of leadership across the board. It needs to be seen as a core skill and competency of every manager.

> Just like we hold leaders and country business leaders or service-offering leaders accountable to other metrics, there needs to be a human metric. The question to be answered: Are your humans thriving?
> The role of a manager needs to evolve. We should incentivize and reward managers who build a healthy team. It starts from onboarding and is built into the culture of the business.

The Role of the C-Suite

Research undertaken by Deloitte is stark when it comes to the role of the C-suite in creating a healthier organization. The C-suite need to be role models for healthy behaviors.

89% of the C-suite say that improving their well-being is a top priority for them this year.

81% of the C-suite say that improving their well-being is more important than advancing their career, but 73% of the C-suite reported that they aren't able to take time off and disconnect.

The vast majority of the C-suite (95%) agree that executives should be responsible for employees' well-being. 68% also admitted that they're not taking enough action to safeguard employee and stakeholder health.

There is a major disconnect: 73% of the C-suite say they're transparent about their well-being, but only 22% of employees agree. For Jennifer, the C-Suite's role is crucial, and their behaviors are key.

> It is not just talking; leaders truly need to walk the talk in a very visible and verbal open way.

Eighty-four percent agree that when executives are healthy, their workers are more likely to be healthy too.

This is definitely a team sport as the vast majority of C-suite respondents say that it's important for them to see other leaders taking care of their well-being (84%) and that seeing this would motivate them to improve their own well-being (82%).

It is clear we need to redesign work to make it healthier. The managers and C-suite have a key role to play based on their commitment to place their own health and the health of their teams as a number one business priority.

AVIVA, UNITED KINGDOM, NET POSITIVE WORK

Headquartered in London, England, Aviva plc is a multinational insurance company with over 18 million customers in the United Kingdom, Ireland, and Canada employing over 22,000 people. Debbie Bullock is the Wellbeing Lead at Aviva UK.

If you want your people to perform well, they have to be well.

If you don't make time for wellness, you need to make time for illness.

Our People Are Our Product

Aviva doesn't sell a tangible product; they sell a service. In a service industry your people are your product. Our client interactions with our people are better when people feel well. If our people work in an environment that is supportive, where they've got a supportive leader, where they've got a role with purpose, and clear accountabilities, they perform better. That is why our people's well-being is a strategic priority of the business.

The Conscience of the Business

It is critical that someone is appointed who can always represent the well-being of the workforce. They share how business decisions may affect the well-being of employees.

Senior stakeholders and leaders can be reminded about the impact the decisions they make may have on colleagues' well-being, whether it is positive or negative, factoring it within a commercial lens.

Aviva is clear about the value of investments they make around mental health and mental fitness.

From a mental well-being perspective alone, data has shown that every pound you invest results in a five-pound return in terms of reduced absenteeism and presenteeism.

A Net Positive Work Impact

According to Bullock, work should be net positive on your overall well-being.

Having a purpose, something to get out of bed for on a morning, being able to earn an income, making connections and collaborations, all these have a positive impact on your overall well-being. The role work plays in supporting people to stay net positive from a well-being perspective needs to be embedded in what we do as a sustainable business.

Well-Being for Leaders

Aviva recognizes that employees have a greater expectation than ever from their managers and leaders. Those leaders need to provide time to listen and care for their people. Aviva now provides strong training and support for managers around signposting of services and the setting of boundaries. The virtual nature of the workplace, not just remote working, but managing teams across multiple locations, provides a real challenge for managers today. It is easier to spot when people are struggling when you see them face-to-face. Aviva want to support managers who support their teams.

Overcoming Isolation

Aviva has spotted that sometimes employees may feel isolated, and for that reason they are driving connections by setting up online Yammer groups, direct support groups (for example, menopausal support), Aviva Connections (online chat tools), and the introduction of "happy to chat" benches within their offices. They have redesigned their office space to drive collaboration, with team desks, flexible drop-in areas, focused work areas, and collaboration zones.

Healthy Job Redesigning

Debbie works closely with the organizational design team and the business architecture team to create healthy roles. She describes the four components as follows:

A role with purpose, clear accountabilities, empowerment, and a generally sustainable workload.

Inclusion at the Heart of Employee Resource Groups

Aviva has six Employee Resource Groups: Balance, focusing on gender parity; Pride, LGBTQ+ group; Generations, dealing with age-related issues; Abilities, supporting people with visible and invisible disabilities; Caregivers, for those looking after someone, for example childcare or elder care; and finally Aviva Origins, which is about race, ethnicity, social mobility, and religion all ensuring that the organization is inclusive.

A Workplace Adjustment Passport

People work best when accommodations can be made to facilitate their personal situations; in line with that approach Aviva has introduced a Workplace Adjustment Passport that allows an individual employee to share accommodations that help them work better, which they can discuss with their leader to work collaboratively on what can be done to help. One of the benefits is the employee doesn't have to have a detailed conversation about their ways of working every time they join a new team but rather the new manager can read the information in their passport.

The Power of Advocates

Debbie highlighted a program in Aviva that focuses on career development, progression, and succession. Having advocates, mentors, or allies is useful to support other people; this is also important when it comes to people's well-being and inclusion. Having a person who is not your manager but will advocate for you is powerful, championing your work or making sure that you get the credit for a project you have contributed to.

Finding Others Not Like You

An interesting approach used in Aviva is to encourage people to find others and engage with people who don't think like you, speak like you, look like you, and the newest one, work like you; this has been very successful at breaking down barriers and supporting their inclusive culture.

Senior Leaders as Role Models

Senior leaders at Aviva are encouraged to use every opportunity to call out inappropriate behaviors and encourage people to live the organization's values. Debbie gave many examples, like two senior directors job sharing; often people said job sharing couldn't happen at that level, but they proved it can. Leaving loudly was another, where rather than leaving quietly slightly embarrassed to be leaving to get to the gym or attend your child's school play, you actually make a point of telling people that you are doing it; this is especially important for senior leaders. The last example was the chairman of Aviva, who very publicly told shareholders that some of their comments during their annual general meeting about the gender of the CEO were misogynistic and were therefore not in keeping with the values of the organization. Now that is role modeling from the very top.

IIH NORDIC, DENMARK, FOUR-DAY WORKWEEK

Recently there has been intense interest in the four-day workweek approach. But this is nothing new. Danish company IIH Nordic implemented it in 2017, and it still operates today. Not only do employees only need to work four days but they get paid for five. It seems too good to be true. But can you really squeeze five days' work into four days? IIH Nordic CEO Henrik Stenmann explains how they did it.

> It's about working smarter, not longer, experimenting with tools and optimizing workflows.

The Pomodoro Technique

First, they changed how they worked, implementing the Pomodoro technique, developed by Italian Professor Francesco Cirilo. Pomodoro means tomato in Italian. But this relates more to a tomato as a timer than as a fruit. Using the Pomodoro technique IIH Nordic broke all work into 25-minute work sprints after which they would take a five-minute break. Importantly once a person was in a work sprint nobody could interrupt them, and they could work in flow. To signify that they were in a work sprint each employee had a red/green light on their desk. (Now it's online.) They could complete three to five work sprints and then take a longer break.

To make it more fun IIH Nordic introduced a platform with a Pomodoro leader board to share what people were working on and to encourage more sprints. When in a sprint they wore headphones, which played music especially selected by neuroscientists to aid concentration.

> There's better energy distribution, focused attention, timeboxing task, and more organized workload.

Maximizing Meetings

IIH Nordic realized a lot of time was wasted in meetings. They changed how meetings operated. No more 30/60 minute meetings, they were reduced to 20/45 minutes. To allow this reduction all meetings required an agenda setting out the purpose and expected decisions. To keep attendees focused all meetings operate with a timer counting the minutes. Meetings are scheduled in the afternoon because their data showed employees were more productive in the morning.

Virtual Assistants and Tools

In an effort to ensure that employees utilized their time on higher value tasks, IIH Nordic carried out a full assessment of tasks categorizing them A, B, and C from least to most challenging. The least challenging tasks were then outsourced to virtual assistants in the Philippines. These virtual assistants attended a comprehensive induction program to ensure a seamless transition.

> We use Google Workspace for internal communication. For workflow we use Asana as a task management tool. That creates a full overview about the tasks, deadlines, resources, and workload. Task management tools also ensures that nobody in the organization has too heavy a workload. E.g., if we see an employee has too many tasks and shows stress symptoms, we just remove her or his task away or change the deadline where it is possible.

And What About Friday?

The bonus of working efficiently and effectively for four days is a Friday for yourself. Well, IIH Nordic have asked employees to use some of that time on Friday for self-development, but for most that time is used to catch up with friends, rest and recover, and do household chores, leaving time at the weekend to spend with family. Every last Friday in the month is now called LIF, "Learning Innovation Friday". This concept was generated from employee feedback.

TAKEDA, SWITZERLAND, RESPONDING TO PRESENTING NEEDS

Takeda is a Japanese research-based global pharmaceutical company. The Plasma Operating Unit (OpU) is one of the operating units within Takeda's global manufacturing and supply organization. Paul Creedon is the head of human resources at Plasma OpU. In this interview Paul explains how they focused their attention on their senior team in response to Healthy Place to Work survey data.

The Critical Importance of Senior Leadership

We were aware from the start how important our senior leaders were in setting the tone in the organization. The previous 24 months with the pandemic had been extremely demanding on all parts of our business and we knew that this was significant for our people, including of course, our senior leaders. The data we received from our survey wasn't a huge surprise, but it did act as a lightning rod for action.

Paul explains the main concerns for the senior leaders and how they set about addressing those concerns.

Workload

The main issues related to the level of demand that the leadership teams were experiencing. We wanted to ensure that our teams could get the support they needed to balance their workload effectively. We took a range of actions and a few prioritized and focused initiatives to provide our teams the necessary support.

Managing Change

The second issue was around managing the change process and the level of anxiety that is naturally experienced by leaders when leading and managing change.

Always On

We also knew from the results the ways of working currently in place were causing an issue for managers in terms of their overall well-being with regards to energy, and their inability to switch off. This needed a cultural change in terms of how to best integrate well-being into "how" we work.

Responding to Presenting Issues

At this stage the issues were clear, now it was about responding correctly. For Takeda Plasma it started with their strategy planning process.

In looking to respond to the concerns of our managers, we needed to realign the organization. This meant we needed to have our proposed responses built into our strategy plan so we could ensure success. We wanted to prioritize the health and well-being of our workforce, so we delegated power in that regard to our teams in sites throughout our organization, setting up well-being councils in each geographic location, as there were several site-specific issues that needed a local and tailored response.

Prioritization Was Key

However, globally we were aware that we needed to revisit our priorities. There was a feeling that with often competing priorities, demand on the business was increasing. We had open conversations and included all our leaders in that process. There was broad agreement that the well-being of our workforce needed to be a top priority.

Changing How They Do Change

Change is a constant in organizations today so that they are constantly responding and adapting to changes in their environments, but managing that change effectively is the key to success.

We are a fast-moving business, and we naturally strive for high performance. Change is a constant, but we were now being challenged by our manager population to get better at implementing change to also better account for and manage the impact on people. This included the assessment of change initiatives, crystalizing in advance the impact they would have. Communication was also critical, in terms of bringing people with us on the change journey, understanding why the particular change was required and how it would be implemented, and so on. Engaging with our people along every step of the way was essential.

Setting Up People for Success

While many organizations were implementing hybrid approaches to work, a manufacturing business requires more thought.

> The final area of focus was "how" the work got done. In a manufacturing context working from home would clearly not always be possible; however, there were opportunities to allow more flexibility. Implementing hybrid working and introducing more flexible approaches was key. Running a global business across multiple time zones could lead to managers working extremely long days and being "always on." We introduced a range of new protocols and actions, including some simple ones around meetings, which seemed to be one of the biggest challenges for our people, soaking up a lot of their time resources.

Building a Healthy Workforce from the Top Down

Many organizations like the idea of creating a culture of well-being, but for that to be successful it is essential to ensure the senior leaders are part of the process and become role models for healthy behaviors.

> We know our leaders need to be healthy role models if we want healthy behaviors to cascade down through our organization. Implementing new ways of working and ensuring they are implemented consistently on a global basis is difficult but necessary if you want to achieve success. This isn't about implementing a few programs or events; this is a about making systematic changes to how you go about your work, this is about creating a culture of well-being in our business. Health is our business so making our business healthy makes absolute sense.

COHESIVE, THE NETHERLANDS, HEALTHY MANAGER CONVERSATIONS

Cohesive

Henri Snijders is the chief transformation officer for Cohesive, a global organization with approximately 500 employees, all with very specialized and diverse skills across different locations, sectors, and disciplines. Cohesive works with organizations to maximize benefits from data, technology, people, and processes by designing and delivering transformational outcomes for their clients, assets, and the environment in which they operate.

It Starts with Relationships

Strong relationships are at the core of most successful businesses. At Cohesive they are passionate about emotions. They understand that each day both their employees and clients are in a range of emotional states. They believe that this should be the starting point of their conversations.

When you enter the Cohesive workplace, you will notice posters and cards everywhere highlighting an emotional scale/ladder. This acts as a trigger to start a conversation about emotions. The emotional ladder was developed by Edith van den Anker from High Vibration People.

How Is the Emotional Ladder Used?

Cohesive uses it with their leadership team and managers, and each manager uses it with their individual team members. Rather than jumping into the agenda for their meeting (the default is usually business results or project updates), they start by asking each participant where they are right now on the emotional ladder. This ensures that people have an opportunity to honestly express how they currently feel. If you ignore those feelings, the meeting will not be as effective as it might be.

> We have so many meetings, so why not spend them wisely, make sure that these meetings create people that are happy, that are more effective, that they trust each other more.

Henri explains the impact when they realize that certain employees are at the low end of the scale.

> The lowest frequency that you bring into the room is when you have fear, sadness, regret. When people are in that state you really need to pay attention, because that's not something that you can just fix in a two-minute session, there is something deeper there.

They find that a number of people at a meeting are feeling miserable, and often they will simply cancel the meeting.

There may be factors outside of the workplace that are affecting people's mood, and the team need to be cognizant of those factors and support those individuals.

The Initial Reaction

Initially when this approach was introduced in Cohesive people were cynical and a little uncomfortable in discussing their emotional state, particularly when it came to the higher levels of the scale around gratitude and love, but now people have become more open and transparent, and it has become part of their culture.

Training Was Key to Success

Cohesive ran a range of training courses to prepare people to use this tool so that they could become more effective in their communication. It was also about learning how to give and receive feedback.

> How do we respond to each other? Are we open for feedback? Do we want to receive it? Do we dare to give feedback?

According to Henri it was essential that employees realized that this tool was not just for the workplace but could be just as useful in their home life context.

The Virtual World

This has been even more important now that many employees are working remotely or hybrid. In this situation you miss meeting the individual face-to-face and picking up all the nonverbal signals that will give you a clue as to their emotional state. Now when they meet on Teams or Zoom the energy scale is in the background, and that ensures that every conversation starts from that point.

Self-Reflection and Impact

This tool has allowed everybody to become more self-reflective, understanding that their mood state has an impact on the energy level of others.

> Sometimes I bring a mood into the company and start smashing the door in the morning, because I'm not happy or just being grumpy. People see that and it affects the output of the team; that's a big influence. Alternatively, it's nice when people say, you were so energetic, and it also helps us deliver.

As a leader it is so important that you realize the impact you have and the tone you set in the organization.

Overall, the employees have become more emotionally literate. They have a language that lets them discuss their emotional state. It makes mood, emotions, and energy state more tangible for all involved and leads to more effective results.

P&G, LATIN AMERICA, INCENTIVIZING HEALTHY BEHAVIORS

P&G has operations in more than 80 countries, and its nearly 300 brands are sold in more than 160 countries. Operations in Latin America are spread across 14 countries, including 19 manufacturing sites, nine general offices, 12 distribution centers, and a service center. P&G's largest markets are in Mexico, Brazil, Venezuela, and Argentina. Dr. Jorge A. Morales Camino is the *director médico, Latinoamérica*.

Branding Wellness

P&G in Latin America provide a host of supports in the field of workforce health. To ensure all employees know what is available, they have branded all activities under the "Vibrant Living Framework," including meaningful "heart," happy "mind," and healthy "body."

Communicating what is available is a critical step, and so too is ensuring consistency across the region. Even the medical division of P&G is branded with the strapline "healthy people healthy business," reinforcing the relationship between the two.

Well-Being Supports

There is a wide range of supports for employees, including activity pauses in work for movement, mindfulness, meditation, and nap pods, sleeping supports, telehealth, on-site medical and psychiatric support, wellness assessments, environmental circles, storytelling, family days, yoga, walking circles, community support (habitat for humanity), and focused training sessions in response to presenting issues around stress, anxiety, and depression.

Site Certification

Based on their Vibrant Living Framework, they have created a certification process that each site must be assessed against. Every region has a Vibrant Living Council who ensure that health is top of the agenda. They also use health coaches and "champions" to ensure success. Inter-site sporting competitions are used to drive fun and to reinforce the importance of physical activity into the process.

> We have interplant tournaments, Olympic Games, every single plant is represented from the football team to the basketball team, the volleyball team, to the runners, even people playing chess.

Health Scorecards

Lifestyle factors (alcohol consumption, smoking, diet, exercise, weight) combined with psychological factors (personal stress, depression, sleep and fatigue, and finances) plus organizational stress are tracked along with other measures and data points to create health scorecards, which act as a springboard to change.

At Risk and Ready to Change

Having data is one thing, using that information to improve the health of your workforce is another. P&G is focused on improvement. Their scorecard identifies the cohorts who are at risk but also identifies those who self-report as ready to change. They have a range of activities across a broad spectrum and have identified a linear correlation between the number attended and the improvements registered in individual well-being; this is a measure of success that is used to reassure leadership that investments in this space make sense.

Total Productivity Impact

P&G has taken a scientific approach to the measurement of their investments in workforce health. They analyze the impact that poor health has on the ability of employees to perform their role. The demands include mental personal (concentration), time management (work schedule/pace), output (workload), and physical (sitting or standing). They also measure workplace stress, the level of control versus demand, and effort versus reward employees face, combined with an assessment of respect and support they receive from managers resulting in a total productivity impact measure where job satisfaction beats the stress level required to complete the role.

Healthy Payback

In recent years employees at P&G are required to make a small contribution to their health insurance costs; however, the organization has devised a way that they can avoid this charge. If the employees undergo a medical assessment and check-up and based on the finding agree and achieve a personal health goal, the company picks up the cost. This approach has resulted in health improvements across the workforce.

> I'm very happy that in the last year, we have only 4,000 people partici-pating in the health assessment program. And the last year we have 7,000 of the 15,000 population.

Real Impact

Dr. Morales gets very excited when he shares a story about one employee that clearly explains why he is so passionate about making P&G a healthy business with healthy people.

> He was a diabetic person. He was very overweight, actually obese. After participating in the Vibrant Living, he lost around 44 kilograms, and the most important thing is that his two children were obese as well and they also are now the right weight. He doesn't use any medica-tion anymore. Wow!

Wow indeed!

SAP, IRELAND, NEURODIVERSITY

SAP SE is a German multinational software corporation headquartered in Walldorf, Baden-Württemberg. It develops enterprise software to manage business operations and customer relations.

Starting the "Autism at Work" Program

Autism is a collection of behaviors that indicate a different way of experiencing the world.

It is often seen as an invisible disability. It is a neurodivergent condition that exists on a spectrum. Unfortunately, a significant majority of people with autism are unemployed.

A healthy place to work is an inclusive place that positions itself to make space for a range of different types of people and personalities. The inclusion of neurodiverse people has often been a challenge for many organizations, but German multinational software company SAP has led the way—specifically for individuals who are on the autism spectrum.

The Dreaded Interview

Historically, the interview has been the greatest obstacle for people with autism, as often they simply do not conform to normal expectations and are rejected at the very first hurdle.

SAP realized that they were missing out on wonderfully talented people and set about creating a practice called "Autism at Work." Its ambition was to make SAP autism friendly. They engaged a recruitment company founded by Thorkil Sonne from Denmark called Specialisterne, which specializes in recruiting and onboarding talented individuals with autism.

Education Is Key

Firstly, Specialisterne prepare the candidates for the interview process. They also train the internal recruiters not to assess all people in the same way, as people with autism often react differently in an interview situation. A simple example is that many people with autism may fail to make eye contact during an interview or can choose extremely bright clothing, which they might consider usual, but the recruiters are encouraged to see past those aspects and focus on the skills and talents.

Managers across the organization were provided with special training to understand how to manage people who had autism. In addition, organization-wide training was delivered using inventive techniques to create a greater awareness of what autism is and how it felt to have autism. On one occasion staff were welcomed to a buffet lunch that included some disguised hot dishes with chilis; the moment they realized they had eaten something hot they reacted in panic, only to be informed that what they were now experiencing was how someone with autism might feel in a particularly uncomfortable situation. A second technique used had staff wear headphones with music playing only for a sudden piercing high tone to be played, again helping them build awareness for the sudden feeling that people with autism might experience in a given situation.

Employees at SAP now appreciate the differences that autism brings such as misunderstanding social cues, misinterpreting body language, or being too literal, and they make allowances in their interactions.

Special Talents

It became clear to SAP that employees with autism were extremely talented, especially in roles that required intense focus or deep analytical skills such as coding. While it was great for SAP to be seen as autism-friendly they are very clear that this is not seen as a CSR (corporate social responsibility) initiative, but rather diversity is a critical aspect of building a high-performance organization and widens their talent pool. People with autism often see things from a different perspective, bringing innovative new ideas and fresh thinking critical to a company like SAP.

Spectacular Results and Advice for Success

The "Autism at Work" program has worked for both SAP and the many individuals now employed. Some have taken on managerial roles and are dealing with clients at the highest level, building increasing confidence in their own value and ability.

For other organizations considering implementing a program similar to the one in SAP the advice is to ensure there is sponsorship from the top and to include people with passion to ensure its success. It is also useful to partner with expert organizations such as Specialisterne.

RSPCA, UNITED KINGDOM, TRAUMA SUPPORT

The Royal Society for the Prevention of Cruelty to Animals (RSPCA) is the old-est animal welfare charity in the world. Established in 1824, its primary focus is on rescuing, rehabilitating, and rehoming animals across England and Wales in the United Kingdom.

The RSPCA has over 1400 employees and 6000 volunteers in the National Society and over 140 branches. Their people are extremely passionate about animal welfare, and like many people whose work and passions intersect, they often become deeply and emotionally invested in their role. Unfortunately, their work can expose them to some terrible situations of incredible cruelty in many cases, which can lead to staff suffering mental health issues and in some cases post-traumatic stress disorder (PTSD). This led the RSPCA to introduce TRiM, a peer-to-peer support program. Jeremy Gautrey-Jones is the assistant director, employee experience.

What Is TRiM?

TRiM stands for trauma risk management. It was first used by the British Army. It complies with the National Institute for Health and Clinical Excellence (NICE) guideline 26 in the UK.

Who Uses TRiM?

This is deployed in workplaces where employees may witness extremely upset-ting events or may be exposed to trauma. Often, they experience initial shock from the event. This can lead to a range of symptoms, such as anxiety, feeling of fear, and sleep disturbances. For many these will subside with time, but for oth-ers they will get worse. Several emergency services, such as the police or fire service, implement this practice in their workplaces.

How Does TRiM Work?

In the case of the RSPCA, 20 employees were selected from a number who volunteered. These were selected based on their natural skills of being good listeners, strongly empathetic, and who were themselves very resilient.

These individuals received training from TRiM experts. These experts also provide ongoing support for the volunteers themselves (now known as TRiM practitioners). Four TRiM managers monitor the referrals and look after the TRiM practitioners. These managers have an elevated level of training.

The service is available to anyone in the organization who needs to talk or who is struggling after witnessing a difficult event. People can raise their hand and call for help, or the organization can offer it to individuals. This is particularly relevant when they know there is an upcoming operation: they will offer the service in the pre-briefing and again in the post-briefing. Other staff can also make a referral to the TRiM coordinator if they witness a colleague struggling. The service is confidential, and there is no reporting back to line managers.

Combining Peer-to-Peer and Professional Support

The TRiM practitioner will make a risk assessment of the situation, quickly determining whether the individual will require further professional help and support to overcome the trauma they are experiencing (signposting) or whether they believe their own support will be sufficient. In the event that they require further support, the TRiM practitioner arranges everything.

Feedback and Advice

Jeremy Gautrey-Jones of RSPCA says that while initially employees were skeptical, the feedback has been great. Everybody wishes they had introduced it earlier as many had previously suffered in silence. The key is to respond quickly as there is a moment when an intervention can ensure the person's mental health does not suffer. Jeremy also advises anyone considering introducing TRiM in their organization to first contact others who have used it as a successful intervention.

CONCENTRIX, GLOBAL, FLEXIBLE WORKING

Headquartered in Newark, California, Concentrix is a leading global provider of customer experience (CX) solutions and technology, improving business performance for the world's best brands. They presently employ more than 290,000 people. Sarah McKay is the vice president of service delivery.

For most organizations the decision to go remote or hybrid or return fully back to the office post pandemic is theirs and theirs alone; however, for Concentrix that decision is taken in consultation with their clients, who get to decide what form of working location is acceptable for the delivery of their business.

Prior to the COVID-19 pandemic Concentrix had 8,000 employees working remotely out of a global staff of 290,000. During the Pandemic 96% of their employees switched to working from home. What does the future hold?

A Complexity Matrix

While many organizations have struggled to decide which deployment model to go with, Concentrix turns to the data and brings science into the mix. They created a complexity matrix. They analyzed the pre-pandemic data from 2019 and compared it to 2020 and 2021. The key question they needed to answer was what approach worked best.

Sarah McKay is surprised that so many organizations called it early without analyzing the data because for her the insight from the data was informative. Concentrix analyzed every work type, the industry sector, where regulation played a part, the experience level of the employees, language mix, shift work, and so forth, and overlaid that with performance data such as customer satisfaction metrics, speed to answer, security considerations, and sales.

Hybrid and Remote Win Out

The analysis was clear: in almost all cases some form of remote or hybrid work engagement was preferable and better for overall performance. However, some roles, particularly those with first-time entrants to the workplace or those returning to the workplace, needed an environment with high support to hit performance goals. The delivery of government services in particular suited the remote model while media and communications was an example where a workplace was preferable to deliver first-line tech support, intense working environments, and roles that required shift work. Some sales roles were also delivered better in a team environment as the isolation of home working could lead to demotivation of team members. Initial concerns around privacy and security were quickly overcome based on the data. Concentrix were able to reassure clients that their work could be as effectively delivered off-site as on-site.

Bricks and Mortar Limit Recruitment

Again, Concentrix turned to the data to prove to clients that talent prefers flexible work options. They analyzed their recruitment campaigns over a 30-day period and discovered that advertisements for similar jobs attracted 70% more applications if remote working was offered.

Social Media Sentiment Analysis

Over 25 million social media posts were analyzed for sentiment in relation to remote working/working from home. It was clear that the biggest driver was a desire for choice. No amount of workplace enhancements around free lunches, entertainment, or medical facilities would make a difference. Even COVID safety concerns were trumped by a lack of commuting, boosted productivity, and improved work-life balance.

Evidence-Based Decisions

Sarah believes that leaders need data to back up their decisions, or otherwise they risk losing current talent and struggling to attract new recruits.

> When it suits some companies, they were happy to have working from home, but now for their own reasons, which many can't articulate, they want their people back in the workplace.

Support Required to Make WFH a Success

Concentrix has discovered that for a working from home model to be successful, managers need to manage differently, with a lot more consistency around check-ins. Training is also a key part of the jigsaw puzzle, which required a major revamp to be effective in a virtual world. It is not simply a matter of delivering the same content over Zoom or Teams. It all has to be re-created using gamification, for example, to keep the attention of the learners. Concentrix is also exploring the Metaverse, giving employees avatars, allowing them to meet other colleagues online in a new social setting and access a range of online supports in a fun virtual environment.

Virtual Onboarding

The toughest challenge has been virtually onboarding new recruits, helping them to understand the culture of the business. In some cases, they are deploying personality assessments to see which employees might be more successful in a remote environment.

Corporate Wellness

Concentrix has recognized the importance of the health and well-being of their employees and has invested in tools, training, and support for managers. They provide a wellness guide for all managers, realizing how crucial their role is in a virtual world. The guide gives equal billing to the performance of the team from a metrics viewpoint and the mental well-being of the team.

Remote Working Here to Stay?

Concentrix will keep tracking the performance data and will listen carefully to the views of present and future employees, but for the moment remote is the way to go for their business, heavily supported by workforce well-being.

If you look after your front-end staff, everything else will look after itself.

FUTURICE, FINLAND, HEALTHY CLIENTS

futurice

Headquartered in Helsinki, Finland, with offices in Tampere, Berlin, Munich, Stuttgart, London, and Stockholm, employing 800 people, Futurice is a digital engineering company. Tuomas Syrjänen is a board member.

> We started asking people to think instead of following rules. We started getting rid of artificial approvals, using transparency and responsibility. Transparency is actually a really effective control.

The Ambition: To Maximize Energy

In 2008 Futurice experienced growing pains in their attempts to scale the company. The ways of operating as a sub-50 employee company were no longer fit for purpose. All the advice pointed toward the development of a hierarchical organizational design structure with control at the core; however, they resisted and created something quite different.

Tuomas Syrjänen, the then CEO, asked a simple question.

> Do we build an organization to deal with the control needs of our senior management or do we build an organization that maximizes the energy of our people?

They chose the latter, and the rest is history.

Trust and Transparency Drive a Healthy Culture

In line with their Nordic culture the starting point was trust. They decided to trust their people. This was best exemplified by their decision to issue everyone with a company credit card and then not to check the bills. The most effective control for them was transparency. All the bills were posted internally on their intranet (including the CEO's) for all to see and anybody could query any charge.

> The community became the control.

Interestingly the monthly bills went down!

While other companies were tying themselves in knots with policies and rules for every eventuality, Futurice just asked their people to use good judgment.

Do you ruin it for the 95% because of the 5% who might misuse, or do you just deal with them separately?

Futurice also introduced salary transparency so there were no side deals, everything was out in the open, a particular benefit to highlight any gender pay issues. New hires were shocked at the level of responsibility they were given, but they stepped up and owned it.

Clients Impact Employee Health

Critically Futurice realized that their clients could have a huge negative impact on the health of their workforce with increasing expectations, access requirements, and high demands. To ensure that this didn't happen they sat with new clients and explained the rules that operated and what behaviors they wanted from clients. The clients agreed and admired that approach with many of their own employees wishing they operated in the same way.

Client onboarding comes to mind. There is a kind of shared code of conduct. So how do we treat each other in this kind of relationship as consultants and as clients? What do we expect from each other? And how do we make this work?

Pitching for Meaningful Work

They also recognized that employees preferred some types of work over others. They profiled each employee and understood the work that they preferred and actively pitched for that type of work in the marketplace. They didn't want to just accept any work that would pay the bills, but they wanted to bring work and projects that their employees would enjoy and that would give them a sense of meaning and purpose.

Understanding the individual is critical, what is meaningful for a person, because of course there is no one size fits all.

Job rotations and project rotations were implemented regularly to keep everybody moving and learning and not getting bored.

This work/project selection also extended to their clients. They decided to say no to work from potential customers because they didn't feel their client's business had a positive social impact but rather a very negative one. They simply wanted to work for clients whose businesses were good for society.

SAS INSTITUTE, UNITED STATES, RECRUIT WELL-BEING

SAS is a global leader in analytics software based in Cary, North Carolina. Through innovative software and services, SAS empowers and inspires customers around the world to transform data into intelligence. SAS has ranked among the best workplaces worldwide, receiving recognition for its commitment to work/life integration and diversity, equity, and inclusion, including being a "Best Company to Work For" in Fortune's annual rankings each year since the list's inception in 1997. The company was used as a model for workplace perks at Google and is taught as a case study in management seminars at Stanford and Harvard.

A Culture of Care

Since the founding of SAS, employees have been at the heart of its business model. Jim Goodnight, the co-founder and CEO of SAS, has long maintained that "if you treat employees as if they make a difference, they will" and has ensured people and their well-being are a top priority. Being a developer himself, he also understood that creativity doesn't happen on command and that knowledge workers need to feel nurtured to innovate.

SAS nurtures their employees' holistic health and well-being and helps employees do their best work by providing programs and resources that reduce stress and distraction. Creating a culture of care was not a single decision but a series of thoughtful and intentional cultural and business decisions spanning more than three decades.

SAS launched a health center on its campus back in 1994, one of the first companies to do so. To the executive team, it was good for its employees and also made good economic sense. Today, it is a full-service, primary care health center with MDs, nutritionists, disease management, wellness, and related services, which translates to fewer sick days, more productive employees, and less costly turnover. SAS offices in other geographical locations are offered in-kind types of programs and services.

Beyond the health centers, however, SAS provides onsite fitness centers, daycare centers, and even hair salons and pharmacies. SAS brings work-life integration into employees' day-to-day experience so they can be their best selves. And while SAS has previously invested heavily in their physical spaces, the pandemic and resulting emergence of a hybrid work model has focused SAS on providing employees with choice with more flexibility and virtual offerings.

Different Needs Require Different Solutions

While all of the employee perks and benefits may seem to grab headlines, there is something more fundamental at play. SAS recognizes that employees are unique and have different needs. And so SAS ensures that they don't have just one sweet spot and supports all dimensions of employees' well-being—physical, emotional, social, community, career, and financial. In focusing on emotional well-being, SAS works to create a safe place for employees to be creative and innovative and effectively manage stress and mental health. For employees' physical well-being they provide programs and benefits that focus on physical health such as various medical plans, movement, and nutrition.

For employees' social well-being, they focus on creating a sense of community within their organization, such as grassroots-driven and employee-led inclusion groups. For financial well-being, they go beyond appropriate compensation and look for opportunities to educate, develop a retirement plan, or manage student debt. The culture of care extends in all of these ways, helping employees navigate their own well-being journey at SAS.

As the CEO notes, "Because we eliminate unnecessary distractions and help relieve everyday stress, our employees are happier, healthier, and proud of the difference their work makes."

It Starts with Talent

While SAS provides a variety of resources for employees and supports managers in aligning and advancing a culture of care, for SAS it starts with their managers. Leaders are given the support needed to engage, support, and grow their teams. Jennifer Mann, SAS's executive vice president and CHRO, puts it this way: "We are grooming from within the organization so that people get a feel for what the culture is and can see what's expected of them. The majority of our leadership positions are filled internally." And their development programs "reinforce this holistic approach so that they can feel it and see it." Beyond this, she notes that employees will often "boomerang" back if they leave: "And what they say is, 'Oh my gosh, I missed the people.' Those are the words they use and the data shows this. [For those that left recently because of the Great Resignation] they were thrown ridiculous financial packages, but they're calling back, and saying 'What did I do?'

Because, in the end, those work environments don't have the same caring aspect to the company's culture. For us, our value is being a company that cares."

Importantly, SAS hires top talent, but they also ensure that their hires are committed to the culture of care that SAS has developed. In this way, the culture of care is mutually reinforcing. Leaders set the tone, managers lead by example and connect employees to resources and opportunities, and employees support one another and ensure that they take care of themselves, their families, and their communities. For over 40 years, SAS has proven that a culture of care works and results in solid business growth.

AMÊNDOAS DO BRASIL, BRAZIL, A CULTURE OF WELL-BEING

Founded in 1992 and located in Fortaleza, Ceará, Amêndoas do Brasil is one of the world's most respected cashew nut suppliers. Sandra Oliveira is the Head of HR.

A Community of Well-being

Imagine achieving annual employee satisfaction ratings of over 99% and a staff attrition rate of less than 1% among the firm's almost 600 employees. Amêndoas do Brasil, based in Fortaleza, is one of the world's leading suppliers of cashew nuts.

Since its founding in 1992, it has been crystal clear that it is part of a community comprising the employees and their families and the surrounding community. Like many organizations its values include trust, respect, and the development of people. Unlike many it incorporates these values into programs designed to support the communities it serves. Central to the Amêndoas culture is a dedication to the creation of an organization focused on the education, health, and well-being of their employees. This commitment to its employees is role-modeled from the top down and interestingly, shows how effective measures need not cost the earth if they are implemented with genuineness and consistency. They believe so much in their health-centric approach that they are happy to share their experience and practices with other organizations to maximize health and well-being in the broader community.

Practices Makes Perfect

So, what practices do they implement? At the most basic level, the company ensures it is in the vanguard in implementing international standards across all aspects of the organization's operations and particularly regarding health and safety standards. In the sphere of more conventional health and well-being, Amêndoas do Brasil provide healthy eating options for staff along with providing exercise and fitness classes. But even here they go further, providing access to company medical staff, a psychologist, a nutritionist, a physiotherapist, and a massage therapist. They provide support for staff with diabetes and hypertension. For employees or spouses who are pregnant there are obstetrics and gynecological services, and during the pandemic the company provided vaccination programs for their workforce community well in advance of the rollout of the national health care service vaccination scheme. They also provide advice and information services and even programs on domestic violence. The company provides health insurance for staff.

This care and concern for the health and well-being for the workforce through the provision of support and services is the tangible expression of the company's values and beliefs, with echoes of those enlightened nineteenth-century employers such as the Cadburys who believed the organization had a moral obligation to its workforce beyond just the transactional payment for work.

Humanity at Work

Amêndoas do Brasil recognizes that health is much broader than just these traditional practices and supports of physical and mental health mentioned above. The culture of the workplace plays an enormous role in the well-being of employees and the company truly believes in the criticality of humanity in workplace relations. Interpersonal relations are supported by education and a focus through various incentives to foster relationships through mutual support, developing friendships, practicing forgiveness, showing gratitude, valuing diversity and inclusiveness, and inspiring each other to be better through positive psychology.

Learning to Be Healthy

Amêndoas do Brasil also recognizes that learning and development is not just about equipping employees with skills to improve efficiency. Of course, it does that, but continuous learning, building employees' belief that they are important and that the organization values them and their development, is an important, if often ignored, aspect of a corporate health strategy. It gives people a sense of optimism and hope as well as reducing stress emanating from not having all the skills and confidence to deal with their workload. Learning and development is used to prevent mental health difficulties and to promote well-being through providing a higher sense of self-efficacy in terms of their job and career.

Managing "with" People

Managers are required to strengthen team culture, to listen to ideas and facilitate both feedback and feedforward. Encourage a sense of participation and to not "manage people" but to "manage with people." This sense of shared ownership is also evidenced by schemes such as the profit-share program in place, which helps employees' financial well-being. This sense of connection and collegial friendships supports all staff in feeling that the challenges of normal day-to-day work and deadlines will not be exacerbated by unhealthy, energy-sapping, and emotionally damaging interpersonal relationships. This enormously helps employee health but also advances productivity, efficiency, effectiveness, and high performance at work.

The Foundation of a Healthy Community

Recognizing their role in the external community is also a hallmark of Amêndoas do Brasil. From its foundation it has supported a range of local charitable programs directly through financial donations and also through encouraging staff volunteering in education, rehoming animals, reducing food waste, and environmental protection. This has demonstrated to staff that the company rhetoric about community is not some marketing slogan but highlights a company genuinely believing that acting as good corporate citizen is beneficial to society and bolsters the pride employees feel in saying they work in Amêndoas do Brasil.

LEEK UNITED BUILDING SOCIETY, UNITED KINGDOM, HEALTHY STRATEGY

Leek United Building Society in the United Kingdom is a great example of the combination of leadership and strategy to fundamentally change the health and general well-being of a workforce and deliver on business outcomes. Rob Longmore is the HR director.

People Agenda Front and Center

Andrew Healy joined in 2019 as CEO. As a fellow of the UK's Chartered Institute of Personnel Development he had a deep focus on people. One of the first things he did was expand the senior leadership team to include HR, bringing the people agenda front and center for the organization. It also sent a clear message to the other members of the executive team. There was no doubt that it was going to be a people-first organization with a priority for the health and well-being of all staff.

The Starting Point

At that time the survey results showed plenty of areas that could be improved, but the turnaround since has been remarkable.

- 28% said the internal communication was good.
- 40% of staff said the senior managers were visible and approachable.
- 40% said performance management effectiveness was really low.
- 47% felt the organizations culture got in the way of being successful business.

A Culture of Openness and Tone from the Top

A leader who is authentic and transparent sets a clear tone for any organization. In this case Andrew was willing to share personal information about his own health challenges, creating a culture of openness and making others in the organization feel comfortable and psychologically safe to share their own stories. In fact, Andrew himself recorded interviews with those brave employees who were willing to talk about their own experiences. Those recordings were shared with all staff and sent out a clear message that it is "all right not to feel all right."

A Plan for Transformation

Previously the people agenda only had minimal visibility within the corporate plan, but now there was a stand-alone people strategy for the organization. As Rob Longmore, HR director, says:

> The corporate plan was about business, products, and financials; the people element didn't get the focus it deserved.

Understanding what is to be achieved and linking decisions back to these clear objectives is the approach that is routinely focused on by Andrew and the leadership team.

> Once you figure out that, everything else falls into place. By nailing down the objectives and goals all the actions become common sense.

It was clear that to change the negative survey metrics, change employee perceptions, and improve business performance Leek Building Society needed to support their people, and that is why they launched their employee support program (ESP) to respond to presenting needs. It dealt with four priority areas:

- In-house support: Including mental health first aiders, domestic abuse support champions, and a range of health and well-being policies.
- Third-party support: Partnered with the Togetherall mental health digital platform where individuals support each other anonymously through difficulties providing a safe place for them to talk about their problems. Initial engagement was very strong.
- Line manager support: Guidance was rolled out to line managers as they are such a crucial link between the organizations and the individual employees. The training focused on check-in conversations equipping managers with the skills to spot the signs that people might be struggling so they could direct them to support. This acted as a real preventative care from the managers.
- Annual health screening: Available to all employees. Not only do the society pay for health screening, but they also use the anonymized data to identify broad areas of concern and target future well-being initiatives, ensuring their focus is evidence-based and outcome-focused.

Additionally, as a response to the anxiety that employees were feeling with regard to their personal finances, Leek United launched a comprehensive package of financial supports for employees. This package included an innovative savings scheme for employees, commitment to the living wage, cost of living increases, pension and retirement planning, occupational sick pay scheme improvements, and increased maternity, paternity, and adoptive leave and payments.

A Physical Space Upgrade

The society has invested in better facilities in its branch network and customer service center, understanding the link between a positive energizing work environment and performance. This work also incorporated improved accessibility for people with varying degrees of disability.

Assessing the Impact

The society has seen a significant fall in absence and illness rates. It has also achieved lower staff turnover levels compared to its industry average. They have experienced limited attrition with the achievement of a green rating from their auditors with respect to the society's culture (the highest possible grade). In a recent survey, 88% of staff agreed with the statement "The Society has prioritized my health and well-being during the pandemic."

Of the wider business benefits, staff efficiency has improved significantly in terms of business volumes versus cost of delivery—for 2020, costs as a proportion of total loans and advances reduced by 1.3% against 2019 and by 5.2% against 2018.

Rob Longmore says it clearly shows that investments in employee health go hand in hand with better business performance.

ISS, DENMARK, DIVERSITY AT ITS CORE

ISS (International Service System) is a Danish workplace experience and facility management services company founded in 1901. Employing more than 350,000 people, it provides a range of services including food, cleaning, technical services, and security across Europe, North America, Asia-Pacific, and Latin America. Margot Slattery is the global group head of diversity and inclusion.

A Healthy Approach to Diversity and Inclusion

The first thing I would say about ISS, and many other organizations in the same industry, is that the frontline is very diverse. But as you go up to the organization, that's not quite as diverse, particularly around nationality, gender, and age.

ISS provides many people with their entry job to the workplace. Often these are low-paid roles that attract migrants or refugees who often won't speak the language. The organization prides itself on providing people a pathway to progress.

The industry is not the highest payer, it's not going to be the most glamorous work, but the work is guaranteed and they are treated fairly. And you have the chance to move up the chain and start on a new career path within the organization.

ISS provides permanent jobs and schedules people fairly so they can plan their lives. The COVID-19 pandemic has changed many people's views of frontline workers for the better.

Diversity Data

Diversity starts with data for ISS. The ability to have transparency around the numbers ensures that everybody knows how the organization is performing. Having the facts is crucial to start the conversation because you can spot the gaps.

The next stage is identifying the blockers, particularly the things that stop people progressing through the organization.

A Global Company of Belonging

ISS has an ambition to be seen as the global company of belonging. However, belonging and inclusion are more difficult to measure. Inclusion is a very intangible part of the jigsaw puzzle.

A clear strategy around DEI is essential and one that every person in the organization relates to and understands. A willingness to have the uncomfortable conversation is essential, which is made much easier when you have support at the top.

> We were very lucky. We have a CEO called Jacob Aarup-Andersen; Jacob just gets it.

Diversity and inclusion doesn't just happen; they have to be backed up by training, development, and awareness building.

The Talent Pipeline

The next most important area to investigate is the talent pipeline as it gives a sense of what the higher levels of the organizations will look like in time.

> If the succession plan isn't answering some of the lack of diversity needs, then you've obviously got a lack of awareness.

It needs clear targets that everybody owns and is responsible and accountable for.

> Everybody had to bring a plan on their gender balance, because it's a target we have for 2025, the only big target that we've publicly stated.

Frontline Managers Are Key

Margot explains how crucial the front-line managers are in achieving this cultural transformation.

> We've put a percentage of bonuses for leaders and for managers around actually demonstrating that change. And that's been measured.

Front-line leaders are the biggest accelerators of change both positive and negative, so it is crucial to get them on board. For Margot it is important not to come from a politically correct viewpoint but rather to connect people with stories of how people felt when they were treated unfairly or excluded. ISS has invested heavily in awareness training as they could see that many people were fearful about saying or doing the wrong thing particularly around race.

> We provide conversation guides so people can sit down and look something up without being embarrassed, we want to make it easy. Everybody is learning in this space.

At its core, ISS wants to create a culture of psychological safety. They constantly encourage everybody to speak up when things happen that are clearly not right.

Advice for Others

The board of the organization needs to be engaged on this topic and they need to support the executives to make change happen. It also needs investment; appointing one person to tick a box is pointless. According to Margot, the whole diversity and inclusion agenda needs to move out of HR and be owed by everybody across the business.

> Don't approach this with policies alone, you must engage with people because we are dealing with humans, and we need to be flexible and adaptive to learn and make progress; we need to appeal to people's hearts and minds.

From social mobility programs in India, to Finnish refugee recruitment, from opportunities for Indigenous groups in Australia to the Valuable 500 global business collective working together to promote disability inclusion through mentoring, ISS is working hard to drive the D&I agenda and the creation of a "place to be you."

PwC, BUILDING A VERY PERSONALIZED LEARNING FUTURE

PricewaterhouseCoopers is a worldwide network of firms providing professional services, operating as partnerships under the PwC brand. It employs more than 320,000 people. Here we talk to Kathryn Kavanagh, managing director and global learning and development leader; Sarah Lindsell, global chief learning strategist; Sajan Samuel, network partner key talent and development lead; and David Buglass, director for global learning services.

Accounting for a Very Personalized Learning Future

Many may not immediately make the connection between learning and health, but in a world of fast-paced change for both individuals and organizations, the ability to adapt and respond fast is essential. When people struggle to adapt, it can cause great stress and anxiety, undermining the health status of both the organization and the individual.

> Put me in the heart of my development experience, and let me explore, give me a really personalized, tailored experience, so that I can be truly successful, and show up to work in my best way.
>
> —Sarah Lindsell

A Growth Platform

Five years ago, PwC introduced a state-of-the-art learning and development platform to meet the needs of its people around the world. Today it is refreshing that platform to deliver a new user experience, AI enabled, allowing the learners to set their own agenda, putting them in the driver seat for their own learning journey. They call this their growth platform.

> One of the things our people were telling us is that they were wasting too much of their valuable time trying to go in and out of multiple different systems to find the development that they need and want—to match development with their career goals.
>
> —Sarah Lindsell

Their new platform has that intuitive capability, with user recommendations to speed up the access to relevant information and reduce overload. They have combined a user-led self-service training approach with an immersive learning experience.

> We could see what apps people were searching for at a moment in real time and respond to those needs by populating new content.
>
> —Sarah Lindsell

The change has been significant. It became clear that employees wanted a fresh repository of content that was relevant exactly to what they were doing when they were doing it. Providing that healthy learning ecosystem has been the role of the learning and development (L&D) department who take that challenge seriously.

Data and Analysis at Its Core

Analysis is at the core of what PwC is great at, and that analysis has been insightful when it comes to responding to the learning needs of their people. PwC has watched carefully how those needs have changed.

> During the pandemic, our learning analytics became part of the leadership benchmark data that was provided to senior leaders around our entire network on a weekly basis. What were people searching for? How much time were they spending in the learning platform? What were they learning about? It was incredibly powerful information.
>
> —Kathryn Kavanagh

Changed Learning Needs

Learning has changed. While the days of the full-day face-to-face training courses are not dead, they have been overtaken with a requirement for an intuitive in-the-moment, answer-driven system that provides on-demand content enabling its people to solve clients' problems. Learning and development is no longer a separate activity; it is now integrated into people's daily routines, so the systems need to be integrated too. It is now about providing bite-sized, refined, and curated content that saves time and anticipates future needs.

Leading a Connected Community

When you have an internal network of 320,000+ people, the ability to find an efficient and effective way to share knowledge is critical. The COVID-19 pandemic itself has seen an explosion in social learning and sharing. This is particularly true in a fast-changing world when you have experts and thought leaders in your network of firms. The ability to share knowledge from the top and vertically is essential so it reinforces a company's competitive advantage and brand. The demands on leaders are ever increasing, and the number one requirement will be the capacity to see around corners!

> The ability to see around the corner, how do you make sense of where the world is going? What does that mean for our clients and the customers we serve?
>
> —Sajan Samuel

Immersive Learning

The ability to use technology to enhance the learning experience has helped PwC overcome the age-old challenges of keeping people engaged. Augmented reality (AR), virtual reality (VR), and immersive learning have been used to great effect, placing learners in the shoes of someone else and allowing them to see the world from others' perspective.

> It's an attention economy and what VR really allows us to do today is actually get and keep people's attention, away from all the distractions of everything else.
>
> —Sajan Samuel

The New World of Learning

PwC is a people business. Those people need to be at the cutting edge of knowledge so that they can solve clients' problem efficiently. The L&D department need to respond and support the development of the workforce to build a growth mindset with all 350,000 people to deliver in the new world of work.

> Business is evolving, people are really demanding a new type of work experience. They want work that is inspiring. They want to work for people who inspire them. Learning is a massive and critical business enabler, people want to be in a place where they actually have some agency around building and growing their career now and in the future.
>
> —Kathryn Kavanagh

A company with a strong approach to learning and developing, agility, and adaptability will ensure both the individuals and organization are healthy.

KINGSTON COUNCIL, UNITED KINGDOM, LEADING THE WAY

Kingston Council is the local authority for the Royal Borough of Kingston upon Thames in Greater London, England. It serves over 170,000 people. Ian Thomas has been its chief executive officer since December 2018. In this interview, Ian Thomas highlights what he believes are the components of healthy leadership.

Creating a Psychologically Safe Environment Should Be the Top Priority for Leaders

The key to success as a leader is the creation of a psychologically safe environment. Ian's personal experience of many leaders who he fondly remembers relates to the fact that they "gave me the wings to fly," but with that freedom comes risk of failure, and true psychological safety means knowing that "they will have your back if things go wrong."

The healthiest leaders give a combination of high challenge with high support, and this allows people to grow and develop. This growth often happens as the result of mistakes. Rather than being castigated, the best leaders see these as opportunities for their people to learn and develop.

Distributed Leadership

This growth acts as a foundation for Ian's next most important attribute, and that is the development of distributed leadership. He talks about the COVID-19 pandemic as a time that would have been much tougher had they not had that foundation in place. People were well used to stepping up and taking responsibility, so it came naturally when needed.

Self-Confidence Is Key

Both these aspects of leadership relate to a leader's own level of self-confidence. Some leaders who lack self-confidence will endeavor to control as many variables as possible. But for Ian Thomas the secret is management "by letting go." Trusting people and giving them freedom and latitude to be the best they can be develops talent throughout the organization. Confidence also plays a role in being comfortable in surrounding yourself with people who are more intelligent than yourself, people who you can learn from, and people you can help develop.

Responsibility versus Accountability

Creating a learning organization is essential to being responsive to changes in the environment where you operate. According to Ian:

> You can delegate responsibility, but you can't delegate accountability.

At the end of the day leaders need to be accountable. No organization is perfect, but the aim should focus on being best in class.

The Inclusive Leader

Leaders more than ever need to be inclusive. Kingston Council is hugely focused on ensuring their workforce reflects the community they serve. They are very proud of the inroads they have made. With staff retention moving from 82% to 92%, a reversal of the gender pay gap in favor of women, and staffing networks that span the diverse workforce, Kingston Council is definitely making progress.

An Employer of Choice

While retaining the people you have is more than half the battle, being attractive as a place to work is essential to bring new blood into the organization. Ian believes the two biggest factors in being an employer of choice are the type of work you offer and providing more options in how that work is delivered. The careers section of the Kingston Council website focuses on why it is an exciting place to be and how it is delivering projects that matter, making people excited to be part of it.

A Changing Workplace

Ways of working and flexibility are critical ingredients for talent to want to work with you today. Allowing people create roles that suit their lives is possible. Redesigning the physical workplace environment to be more in line with the needs of the organization is next up with Kingston's needs reducing by two-thirds because of remote working and changes in work practices. Ian believes everybody needs to reassess how they work but leaders in particular, because they have a huge impact in setting the tone and culture.

> I don't send emails after 7 or at the weekends unless there is a crisis. The vast majority of communications can simply wait. I don't want people to be distracted from their families, from their relaxation and their recovery.

Final Advice for Healthy Leaders

The final advice comes in three forms. Firstly, self-care tops the list, taking your annual leave, taking your breaks, and being a role model in looking after yourself is really important for everybody but even more so as a leader, because people are looking at the messages you send by your behaviors. Second is being focused on creating the working conditions that allow everybody to do their very best work, and finally becoming more adroit at managing change, because it is never ending.

DANSKE BANK, UNITED KINGDOM, PODCASTING HEALTH

Danske Bank UK introduced 30-minute "Positivi-tea" podcasts to share information on a holistic and personal approach to well-being topics, including mental and physical fitness, mindset and motivation, to practical coping strategies.

Flexibility and Interaction

They hold a podcast once a month. They avoid Mondays and Fridays and say early mornings work best (9:30 to 10). The recent topics included:

- Igniting the spark;
- Walking the walk;
- Adaptive working;
- Mindfulness;
- Physical fitness;
- Better sleep;
- Work-life balance;
- Managing loss and bereavement.

All podcasts are available on demand giving full flexibility for people to listen at a time that suits them. The benefit of attending live allows team members to pose questions, take part in polls, and interact. The presenters are a mix of internal and external experts. The platform is run on Microsoft Teams, which can take up to 1,000 participants. They don't post outside the organization.

Some Interesting Points

Positivi-Team podcasts are part of the holistic approach to well-being and supporting colleagues. Senior leaders champion well-being by walking the talk and trying to attend.

Colleagues have stepped forward and shared very personal stories to support others. The openness and vulnerability has been truly appreciated by all.

It is pull rather than push. Information is shared via a number of communication platforms. People can listen on headphones while out for a walk.

Advice for Others

Try it; you have nothing to lose and everything to gain.

Feedback is key. All topics for the year are open for registration so the most popular can be identified. It is a fluid practice, so if some topics are not "hot," they will be replaced. The team are constantly getting feedback from the people who attend and those who don't!

Shorter bite-sized sessions work best. Promotion about the podcasts is through the internal communications platform, Yammer.

Impact and Platform

Over 50% of the workforce either attend the live events or download and listen off-line, as all sessions are accessible 24-7. As previously mentioned, it's run on Microsoft Teams, which can take up to 1,000 participants. They don't post outside the organization.

DUBAI POLICE, UNITED ARAB EMIRATES, PHYSICAL READINESS

Established in 1956, the Dubai Police employs over 15,000 staff. Renowned as one of the most technologically advanced forces in the world, Dubai Police is part of the United Arab Emirates Police Force. Dr. Abduladheem Kamkar is the director of the rehabilitation and readiness enhancement centre.

The Dubai Police Health Services are highly innovative in their approach to the well-being of police and civilian employees. They can receive medical consultations and health care from the in-house center, which exclusively attends to the Force's needs in all aspects. Moreover, one step further, Dubai Police established a center dedicated to ensuring the physical readiness of all its staff.

Information and Data

Critical to their approach to the health and well-being of their workforce is information and data. Each individual employee has a body scan lasting only 20 seconds, which provides details of a range of biometrics including weight, fitness, BMI, body composition, etc. This procedure is mandatory for all military employees but optional for civilian employees. From this process, the Rehabilitation and Readiness Enhancement Centre create a database and dashboard, which gives the employees a clear view of the overall physical health. They then are provided with various interventions and support programs to respond to any issues arising across their teams and departments.

A Focus on Prevention

Based on the data from the scan tests, Dubai Police developed an educational program to address the biggest presenting issues. As an example, like many organizations across the globe, employees suffer from muscular skeletal issues often resulting in back pain. To address this health issue, Dubai Police launched a campaign to educate employees about the importance of regular stretching and strengthening exercises and adoption of an active lifestyle. The campaign has had positive outcomes. For those involved in sports activities, anterior cruciate ligament injuries were common. Dubai Police made an effort to raise awareness on preventing those ACL injuries occurring in the first place. The Rehabilitation and Readiness Enhancement Centre prioritizes the prevention of injuries. It encourages higher fitness levels by promoting regular exercise and a better diet, reducing fats, and enhancing fitness and body composition.

Rehabilitation and Readiness

The very fact of having a rehabilitation and readiness department shows the commitment that Dubai Police has to the physical fitness of their employees, which as a consequence improves their work performance.

> We see a clear connection between physical fitness and strong mental and psychological health; we invest significant resources in driving our employees to higher levels of physical fitness.

Sports-Focused Fitness

Sports play a significant role in the physical fitness of the workforce at Dubai Police. Employees are given many opportunities to do sports training. As an organization, Dubai Police entered many competitions and won many international awards in cycling, track and field, sailing, and various other sports.

Family Inclusion

At Dubai Police, the family members of employees also benefit from the health services, as the Force recognizes the importance of families as a crucial segment of society.

VERSION 1, EUROPE, A HEALTHY STRATEGY

Version 1 is a European IT service and solutions provider for both public and private sector clients with offices in India, Spain, the United Kingdom, and Ireland. Their clients include top global banks, many FTSE 100 listed organizations in the financial services, utilities, and commercial sectors in addition to a range of central and local government customers.

The Impetus for the Journey

Version 1 was competing for talent in an extremely competitive marketplace. However, unlike brands like Google, Facebook, and Twitter, they did not have unlimited resources to pay above market rates to attract talent. They needed to find new ways to provide a compelling offering to potential employees. They found success by focusing on creating a working environment, one that talent was willing to prioritize over pay.

The Start of the "Healthy Place" Journey

2017 saw the start of the journey for Version 1 to become a healthy place to work. They were very clear that their organization and clients had high delivery expectations that required employees to deliver consistent high performance in a fast-moving environment.

They realized that workforce health was crucial to deliver that performance level, so it made sense to measure and manage the health status of their people. At that time, Version 1 admit that health initiatives were singular events unconnected to an overarching business strategy. With further growth planned they set about developing a plan that would support their people's health moving forward and help to insulate them from the stresses and strains that they would experience as part of business delivery. They identified three areas that they needed to deliver immediately:

- A workforce health strategy that was aligned to the overall company strategy;
- A plan that had full leadership support;
- A plan that would be supported by a communication cascade.

The Results in the First Year

Their first diagnostic survey delivered their results in 2018 and included some surprises. Their overall health score was 68%. Their highest pillar score related to connection was 74%, highlighting the strong relationships, sense of belonging, and support experienced by employees in the organization. The mental resilience pillar was second at 70%, demonstrating a strong learning mindset, high levels of self-efficacy, optimism, and autonomy. Purpose was a close third at 69%, with employees aligned to the organizational values, showing high levels of congruence, and showing belief in leadership. Physical health was the lowest-scoring area for Version 1, coming in at 59%; it was clear there was work to be done to move the dial in this arena.

Version 1 got busy embedding their well-being strategy throughout the business with a focus on resilience, trust, and empowerment. Late 2018 saw the launch of their "My Wellbeing" model, which brought a holistic health and well-being framework into their business. Aligned to the Healthy Place to Work model it separated out financial well-being as a separate area of focus. They submitted their first "Healthy Place to Work" development plan, moving away from event-based wellness initiatives to a greater examination of their ways of working and leadership styles. They wanted to embed healthy behaviors into every aspect of the employee experience.

Improvements in the Second Year

2019 brought a 3% increase in the Version 1 overall health score hitting a high of 72%. While the order remained the same, all pillars increased in scores with connections still leading the way at 76% (up 2% points), mental resilience 73% (up 3% points), purpose 71% (up 2% points), and physical health 63% (up 7% points).

Communication was key to this success in 2019. Getting the leadership buy-in to the process, concept, and philosophy was essential, and Version 1 worked hard to make this happen. The Version 1 leadership team developed their own awareness of the factors that make an organization a healthy place to work. They became both advocates for the program and role models for the necessary behaviors. They demonstrated this through their participation in roadshows, quarterly updates, and monthly communication from their CEO.

Results, Transparency, and Competition

Securing the understanding and support of the manager population was important. In line with their philosophy of transparency, they shared all their results by team. This highlighted significant differences. The leadership encouraged the manager population to own their results. As these figures were now part of their performance dashboard, the managers quickly set about learning how to improve their team's health status. This was now a priority; previously it was simply nice to have. Often, this meant turning to their peers who had achieved better results to understand the drivers of their success.

Manager Training

Health and well-being was integrated as a core module of their managers training program (strength in balance). The workshops involved reviewing their "My Wellbeing" model and well-being strategy, as well as exploring what managers could do to allow people to stay on top of their well-being. Over 160 managers participated in the well-being module.

Quarterly Comparisons

Quarterly meetings were held to share and discuss their "healthy place to work" results. Action plans were agreed, and they launched a health and well-being champion network to drive tailored responses to presenting issues.

A new employee experience team was created to own and lead health and well-being allowing a further in-depth analysis of the "healthy place to work" data, and ways were devised to support managers and the champions.

In an effort to ensure transparency, all data and action plans were communicated openly company-wide to all employees so they could feel part of this journey.

A Digital Approach to Health in 2020—Did It Affect Results?

Yes, it is not always the case that numbers rise year on year; there can be bumps along the way, but for Version 1 2020 brought another improvement across the board, which was particularly welcome in the face of COVID-19 and everything the pandemic brought.

The overall health score rose to 79% (up 7 points). Connection now at 85% continued to lead the way with purpose moving into second place, moving a massive 10 points to 81%, mental resilience increased 7 points to 80%, with physical health still in last place but improving to 66% (up 3 points).

Now working with an increasingly diverse workforce across multiple geographies and time zones they needed to find a way that they could deliver a consistent employee experience particularly in the health arena. They further embedded a digital-first approach to well-being across their organization. They delivered 42 company-wide health and well-being events in 2020. It was extremely satisfying for them to see the increase in purpose score as this reflected the work they had conducted to increase a sense of purpose within the company, so their recognition program was a key tool in making this a success. They launched a "Callout" platform enabling peer-to-peer reward and recognition, which had an immediate impact. In addition they launched a new digital excellence award, securing over 126 submissions from across the organization.

Again 2020 saw more focus on improving overall ways of working, moving from policies to practices; according to the team at Version 1 this increased a sense of belonging for all employees. Some of the day-to-day frustrations of work were removed with the introduction of the "welltech" app, which allowed employees to deal with remote working more successfully, everything from ergonomic assessments to placing orders for new chairs. Importantly, this approach released HR personnel from administrative roles, giving them more time to focus on the employee experience.

Did COVID-19 Negatively Affect Results in 2021?

Incredibly the answer was no. Indeed, 2021 brought another increase in results, with their overall health score now reaching 81%. Connection at 87% was really important considering the reports of isolation felt by many employees in other organizations during the pandemic. Purpose at 84% continued to perform well with mental resilience at 83% close behind. Physical health at 69% was improving all the time, but more worked needed to be done in this space.

Both 2021 and the early part of 2022 saw a move away from a one-size-fits-all approach to a key emphasis on personalization and individualization. One-on-one conversations facilitated a sharing of information about the needs of the business and the needs of the employees. Allowing employees to design their jobs and how they delivered their work in a way that was acceptable to the organization allowed for the development of a workplace that worked for employees and let them build work around their life limitations. Both 2021 and 2022 also saw the introduction of the concept of "moments that matter." In our lives we can experience moments of crisis. If these are handled well by the organization, it will strengthen the relationship to the employee and build loyalty. Training was rolled out to ensure that all those moments were positive for all involved.

The Correlation to Business Results

While the participation in health and well-being events showed that these events were focused on presenting needs and delivering real value to employees, it was the correlation to business performance metrics that was most striking with headcount increasing, the ability to recruit talent getting easier, and revenues surging ahead.

Key Takeaways

Moving from awareness to accountability, from tactical to strategic, from one-size-fits-all to a highly personalized approach focused on each employee's own personal situation, and moving away from top-line numbers to a data driven, deeply analytical, evidence-based path have all been key to their success.

Internal bootstrapping along with external benchmarking, devolving ownership to the managers, building team charters, embedding a structured yet agile approach, have all facilitated a truly holistically healthy performance by Version 1.

CHAPTER **13**

A Deep Dive into the Science of Well-being

The Healthy Place to Work model consists of four broad pillars of well-being, each of which comprises a number of elements. The pillars are as follows:

- Purpose;
- Mental resilience;
- Connection;
- Physical health.

The model implicitly recognizes that mental and physical health are inter-related. It maps to the *biopsychosocial model* of health, which was first formulated by the American psychiatrist George Engel in 1977 and which is widely used by health care professionals. This model states that our biological health can be affected by psychological and social factors and vice versa.

The first two pillars look at our internal psychological environment. *Purpose* looks at the things we consider important in our personal and work lives and the extent to which there is alignment between the two. A sense of purpose helps individuals be mentally resilient and foster connections both inside and outside the workplace. *Mental resilience* measures aspects of our mental toolkit such as our beliefs about our self-efficacy and our orientation for personal growth, which give us mental strength. It also measures some factors that can have a big impact on our mental health such as workplace and financial pressures.

Connection recognizes that we operate in a social environment and assesses key aspects of our relationships both inside and outside of the workplace. The extent to which we feel connected to other people, whether in the workplace or outside in wider society, affects our mental health. A strong feeling of connection can help strengthen our mental resilience and reinforce our purpose.

The final pillar, *physical health*, covers the visible and tangible aspects of biological health such as diet, exercise, and the physical working environment. The demographic section of the Healthy Place to Work survey also includes a number of indicators of health, and these mainly inform the physical health pillar.

Each pillar and its associated elements are described in more detail in this chapter.

PURPOSE

Ancient Greek philosophers understood that a sense of purpose is important for well-being. In the fifth century BC, Socrates described *eudaemonia* (literally "human flourishing"—that is, "life purpose" or personal fulfilment) as being important for happiness and well-being. Life purpose can include personal growth through learning and discovery or raising a family. Such eudaemonic happiness is distinct from hedonic happiness, which is the short-term pleasure gained from, say, a drink with friends.

When we have a strong sense of purpose, whether in work or in life, this gives us *intrinsic motivation* to do what we enjoy doing and contributes to our eudaemonic happiness. Extrinsic motivators such as pay and incentive plans only have limited effectiveness as motivators.

Edward Deci and Richard Ryan's self-determination theory (1985) is one of the most influential theories in the psychology of motivation. They argued that we have a need for what they call "relatedness." By this they meant that we need to understand how our role or the project we are working on contributes to something bigger than ourselves such as organizational goals or societal benefits—in other words, our purpose.

The elements of purpose are covered in the following sections.

Organization and Values

This element measures whether an organization walks the talk. The organization's values need to be lived throughout the organization and not merely empty slogans on a wall or web page. This is particularly important for anyone in a leadership role. Senior leaders above all need to be seen to be role-modeling values. They need to demonstrate clear alignment and exhibit healthy behaviors consistently.

This element also assesses whether employees feel that the organization will act on employee feedback such as the Healthy Place to Work survey. If employees give feedback but the organization does not acknowledge that it has heard or acted on the feedback, then they may become more disengaged and will certainly be less inclined to give feedback in the future. Declining scores on this statement are a leading indicator of declining survey response rates and probable declines in employee engagement and well-being.

Congruence

In a healthy workplace, our individual purpose at work will align with the overall aims of the organization. This alignment also includes the opportunity to use our strengths and do what we do best. As individuals, we want to be in the role and organization to which we are most suited. In psychology this is known as *person-organization fit.*

Congruence can therefore be described as "the degree to which my current self and my ideal self are aligned with my organization." Significant misalignment can lead to lack of purpose, ill health, and possibly depression. People who do not feel they fit are much more likely to leave their organization and will not be in a position to do their best work.

Flow and Gratitude

When we do something that we really enjoy and are passionate about—whether an aspect of our job or a hobby—we can get into a state of mind called *flow* where we lose track of time. This concept was described by psychologist Mihaly Csikszentmihalyi in his 1990 book *Flow: The Psychology of Optimal Experience.* Flow expands your mental and physical skills and is fundamental to your well-being and life satisfaction.

Work that can put us into flow is at a sweet spot where it is neither too easy to bore us, nor too difficult or challenging to motivate us. It should have enough challenge to be enjoyable and where we are demonstrating our mastery of the skill and/or learning something new. A job and an organization that is designed to allow you spend more of your time in flow is most definitely a healthy place to work.

As individuals we are often tempted to look toward our weaknesses and our deficiencies. This can lead to very negative feelings about our self-worth and general self-esteem. A healthy individual in contrast will always seek to focus on things they have and things that are important. Each day they will be thankful for their health, friends/family, and skills and talents that allow them to navigate the world around them. There is a strong correlation between people who exhibit this level of gratitude and their general feelings of well-being.

Wellness Culture

Culture is key to ensuring the creation of a healthy organization with healthy individuals. Employees need to believe that their organization and its leadership truly and authentically cares about them. They need to experience an environment that has been thoughtfully designed to be conducive to healthy behaviors, healthy ways of working, and one where it is easier to be healthy than not. This element assesses whether employees consider that the organization does actually care for workplace health and whether they participate in workplace health programs when they are available.

A key aspect is that senior leaders walk the talk—in other words, they don't just talk about workplace health, but they actively role-model healthy behaviors. A workplace in which senior leaders work late in the office, thus fostering a culture of presenteeism, and one where there is an ongoing expectation that emails will be answered out of hours, is highly unlikely to be a healthy workplace.

This element obtains the employee's overall perception using the statement: "All things considered, I would say this is a healthy place to work."

MENTAL RESILIENCE

Resilience is the ability to learn and bounce back from difficulties or problems. This improves our ability to deal with future challenges. Resilient people are better at dealing with uncertainty as they are constantly learning and better able to adapt. As a result, resilient people tend to have better mental health.

The good news is that one can develop one's resilience by changing one's mindset. Our thinking is critically important and can have a significant impact on our health—we think all the time—but often we don't think about the type of thinkers we are. How you think affects how you feel. For example, resilient people are likely to be optimists.

Optimism is defined as an inclination to put the most favorable construction upon actions and events or anticipate the best possible outcome. Martin Seligman, professor of psychology at the University of Pennsylvania and one of the founders of the positive psychology movement, contrasts two types of thinking and their effects on us as humans in his 1990 book *Learned Optimism*. Seligman invites us to view life events through the frame of an optimistic thinker versus a pessimistic thinker using three key aspects—namely, permanence, pervasiveness, and personalization.

- Looking at the first aspect, permanence: optimistic people believe negative events are more temporary in nature, unlike pessimists, who believe they have a more permanent nature.
- Next is pervasiveness: pessimists believe failure in one area of life will move to failure in a range of other areas, while in contrast optimists tend to compartmentalize the negative event.
- Thirdly, personalization: optimists attribute bad events to forces outside themselves and good events to forces within themselves, while pessimists do the exact opposite. Therefore, optimists see a bad event as situational and unlucky, not permanent in nature and just specific to the context.

The mental resilience pillar consists of six elements. Three elements assess part of our mental toolkit—our learning orientation and our beliefs about our self-efficacy, which help strengthen our armor. This is echoed by the European Council, which recognized "personal, social and learning to learn competence" as one of its eight key competencies for lifelong learning in 2018. The definition includes "the ability to reflect upon oneself . . . remain resilient and manage one's own learning and career. It includes the ability to cope with uncertainty and complexity, learn to learn . . . and to be able to lead a . . . future-oriented life, empathize and manage conflict in an inclusive and supportive context."

The three remaining elements of mental resilience assess some of the biggest factors that influence our mental state: our work pressures, the amount of control we have over how we do our work, and the extent to which we are affected by personal financial pressures.

Purpose and connection support our mental resilience by helping develop our mental "armor," which helps protect us when times get tough. The elements of mental resilience are covered in the following sections.

A Learning Mindset

One of the most important developments of the positive psychology movement is the recognition of the need to keep learning. The psychologist Carol Dweck first articulated this with her concept of the *growth mindset* in her 2006 book *Mindset: The New Psychology of Success*. She argued that people who have a fixed view of their own abilities were more likely to stop when faced with a difficult task. However, people with a growth orientation were more likely to keep going and figure out a solution. She discovered that people can be encouraged to develop a growth mindset by praising effort put in ("Well done, you worked very hard!") more than apparent ability ("Well done, you are very clever!")

Closely related to a growth mindset is the ability to keep going after failure, and to pick oneself up and try again. Psychologist Angela Duckworth described this resilience in her 2016 book *Grit: The Power of Passion and Perseverance*. She found that an individual's *grittiness* can be a better predictor of success than their ability as measured by, say, academic achievement.

Self-Efficacy: Job and Career

This element concerns our self-beliefs. Fundamentally, many in life believe that their own personal decisions matter little as there are forces much stronger than they are that will determine the results that will be achieved. However, people with high levels of self-efficacy believe that their decisions are crucial and highly correlated to the success or otherwise that they experience. High levels of self-efficacy in ourselves and our context enables us to do our best work. When we believe that we are capable, we are most able to be at our best and accomplish great things. This element looks at whether we believe we are actually in an environment that enables us to be at our best, and whether our role and/or work tasks make the best use of our talents both now and in the future. It can be stressful if we perceive a mismatch between the role we are in and our capabilities such as being out of our depth.

Stanford psychologist Albert Bandura developed social cognitive theory (1986), which states that the self-efficacy beliefs we have about ourselves often predict behavior better than our actual capabilities: "I'm not very good at something, so I won't give it a go." Our perceptions of self-efficacy affect how we use our knowledge and capabilities and how much discretionary effort we are willing to put in. Supportive line managers who adopt the correct management and leadership style can help develop our self-efficacy beliefs.

Deci and Ryan's self-determination theory (1985) is also important to this element. They argued that we all have a basic need for what they called competence, by which they meant that we need to feel competent enough to control the outcome and demonstrate mastery of the task or skill at hand. They found that unexpected positive feedback increases our intrinsic motivation to complete a task because such feedback supports our self-perceptions of competence. Negative feedback has the opposite effect. Achieving mastery is important because we are most likely to be able to get into flow when we are good at something and striving to become even better.

Self-Efficacy: Health

Our self-efficacy beliefs also affect the extent to which we are motivated to take responsibility for looking after our own health and well-being. Sometimes knowing where and how to start can itself be a challenge, and organizations can help us understand what we need to do to improve our own individual physical and mental health. This includes taking time out for reflection and putting things into perspective.

This element also helps inform the organization where its health promotion efforts need to focus and whether they will be viewed as credible. Healthy workplaces give people the tools that help them manage their well-being as well as providing a supportive environment. This particularly applies to mental health, where organizations need to provide a supportive framework for mental health such as employee assistance programs and mental health first aiders. Healthy workplaces have leaders who are compassionate in dealing with mental health issues of their direct reports and can direct them toward support, as well as being open about their own mental health issues.

Work Demands

One of the biggest stressors many people face at work is a heavy workload. A certain amount of pressure for a short period, such as completing a demanding project, can be a good thing as it provides challenge and can help us grow. However, unrelenting pressure for a sustained period of months, or more probably years, is bad for our physical and mental health. This becomes even more acute if we are facing stress in our home life, such as financial pressures.

One of the most important models in understanding the effects of work demands is burnout theory. The social psychologists Christina Maslach and Susan Jackson developed the Maslach Burnout Inventory (MBI) in 1981, which considered burnout in three dimensions: emotional exhaustion, depersonalization, and personal accomplishment. Emotional exhaustion is considered the core of burnout. The Dutch psychologists Arnold Bakker (featured in this book) and Evangelia Demerouti developed this further in 2001 with their job demands–resources model, which shows that high job demands drain us of energy, causing emotional exhaustion.

As mentioned earlier, the Japanese have a word for sudden death—usually heart attacks or strokes—through overwork: *karoshi*. This is brought on by years of excessive work pressure, typically the sheer volume of work and little control in being able to manage it. The effects of burnout are discussed further in the later section on the physical health pillar.

The key ambition of any organization is to set the correct demands to the individual so that they can perform to their best. The role of a manager is critical as they are close enough to determine where this level should be set.

Work Control

The other aspect of the job demands–resources model comes into play in the work control element. Lack of resources—for example, time, training, support from colleagues, equipment, and inefficient IT systems—undermine our ability to cope with the demands of a job. Emotional exhaustion is inversely related to the extensiveness of resources.

One of the biggest resources that people may be lacking in an unhealthy workplace may simply be control over *how* they actually do their work. Lack of control—such as little or no say over the way they work, and not being allowed to focus on the task—exacerbates the pressure of a demanding workload. It is well known that being micromanaged is one of the main killers of motivation at work. Micromanaging is often a default behavior of line managers with a transactional style. However, healthy workplaces select and develop their line managers to produce a *situational leadership style* where leaders are able to step away from the detail.

Having flexibility in when to take a break is important particularly for cognitive tasks where breaks can help us refresh and solve problems. However, some job roles, such as production lines, are not structured to allow people to stop whenever they want. These employers need to compensate for the lack of flexibility in breaks by maximizing the opportunity for employees to give their input into how work is done in order to improve quality control and suggest improvements and innovations. Even the ability to press a button and stop the production line to address an issue can be seen as giving some control to those employees associated with this task.

The third component of Deci and Ryan's self-determination theory (1985) is important in work control. This is autonomy, by which they do not mean working independently, but in having agency and free will to make their own choices in how the work is done. When someone is motivated by autonomy, their job performance, engagement with the job and organization, and their well-being is higher than it would be if they are told what to do under a "command and control" style of management.

Financial Well-Being

After bereavement, serious illness, and relationship breakdown, one of the biggest non-work stressors that people face is financial pressure. Bringing money worries into work affects our ability to do our job. This has been demonstrated all over the world. For example, research by the Chartered Institute of Personnel and Development (CIPD) in the United Kingdom in 2017 showed that as a result of money worries, 19% of employees had lost sleep, 10% had found it hard to concentrate or make decisions, and 8% had spent working time dealing with money problems. For 6% of employees, money worries had caused health problems.

Healthy workplaces contribute to financial well-being by giving people the tools to improve their financial literacy, as well as being supportive of those who are in difficulty with access to financial counseling services and in some cases loans to stop the debt spiral.

People can often hide financial difficulties, making it more difficult to access help and support.

CONNECTION

One of our fundamental human needs is that of having positive and constructive relationships with our fellow humans. This is the connection pillar.

Connection is important as it builds empathy. As human beings, we are wired to connect with other people. A team of neuroscientists at the University of Parma in Italy discovered "mirror neurons" in the mid-1990s. These are a type of brain cell that responds both when we perform an action and when we see someone else performing the same action. These neurons help explain how and why we instinctively understand other people's thoughts and feelings and empathize with them.

Neuroscience also shows us that many of the positive behaviors associated with the connection pillar encourage production of the hormones serotonin and oxytocin. When we feel that we belong and are supported and that the organization has a sense of community, then these hormones are more likely to be produced, leading to lower stress levels and the improved ability of our bodies to repair themselves.

Connection is closely linked to the sociological concept of cohesion. Social cohesion is the strength of interpersonal bonds among group members. Healthy workplaces have higher social cohesion. Another aspect of cohesion is "task cohesion," which is a feeling of shared commitment to the team's (or organization's) objectives, and thus links to the purpose pillar discussed earlier in this chapter.

Cohesion is considered by psychologists to be one of the most important properties of small groups and has been extensively studied in diverse environments such as industry, the military, and sports teams. Research shows that group cohesion is related to outcomes such as work group performance, job satisfaction, and well-being. For example, cohesion in the military has been found to have a strong positive relationship with physical and psychological outcomes such as well-being, enjoyment, and belonging. Higher levels of cohesion are associated with lower rates of stress and post-traumatic stress disorder.

Sociologists consider that we each belong to a primary group, usually family and close friends. Primary groups tend to be long-lasting and are marked by members' concern for one another, where the goal is actually the relationship itself rather than achieving another purpose. The workgroup is typically a "secondary group," which is more transactional in nature and where the team is working toward shared goals. However, in healthy workplaces, teams can develop many of the characteristics of a primary group, which is why people can say that their team—or even their employer—"feels like a family."

Connection is, however, a very personal thing. The amount and nature of connection that we consider appropriate varies from person to person according to factors such as personality and neurodiversity, cultural background, and life stage.

Diversity and Inclusion

In order to be our best at work, we need to be able to be our authentic selves, regardless of our personal characteristics such as gender, age, ethnicity, and sexual orientation. If we constantly have to hide a facet of our personality in the workplace, this can affect our mental health. The development of LGBTQ+ groups, for example, have allowed a significant group of people not only to take pride in who they are but celebrate it.

Vernā Myers, the TED speaker, author, and vice president of Inclusion Strategy at Netflix, is often quoted on this topic by saying, "Diversity is being invited to the party; inclusion is being asked to dance." However, many have built on this, stating that empowerment is feeling comfortable to ask someone to dance ourselves, not feeling that we need to wait to be asked.

Many organizations have made great strides in becoming more diverse in terms of gender, ethnicity, and sexual orientation but have been slow to introduce cognitive diversity. If your organization needs high levels of innovation, then cognitive diversity is essential. If everybody thinks the same way, the organization probably won't be creative enough to get those breakthrough ideas.

Sometimes people run the two words of *diversity* and *inclusion* together as if they are one and the same, but that is not the case, and unfortunately inclusion has often straggled behind. Organizations need to give everybody the opportunity to contribute, speak up, and share their ideas. All too often there is simply not the space or will to let this happen. Those organizations that pursue a policy of inclusion, ensuring every voice is heard, are the ones that will win and are the ones that care about the health and well-being of their employees. It is unhealthy for anyone to feel they cannot express their views, opinions, or even be themselves because of fear of repercussions.

A diverse and inclusive environment gives people psychological safety. This concept was defined by William Kahn in 1990 as "being able to show and employ one's self without fear of negative consequences of self-image, status or career." Harvard psychologist Amy Edmondson has since applied the concept to team functioning in agile working. Google's famous Project Aristotle study of team and manager effectiveness found that psychological safety was one of five key characteristics of successful teams.

Emotional Expression

Building on the inclusion in the preceding section, emotional expression is being able to speak up and be oneself at work, and it is therefore a consequence of psychological safety. It is not good for our mental health to feel that we cannot speak up about our concerns or not be able to express ourselves. In an environment where we do not feel safe to be ourselves, we will not feel able to use all our talents. However, a culture of emotional expression drives mutual support and loyalty where emotional intelligence (EI) can become an organizational asset.

The concept of EI has gained traction since Daniel Goleman's book of the same name in 1995. Zeidner et al. (2012) found that greater EI facilitates more positive emotional states and fewer negative moods, thereby achieving a greater sense of well-being. This helps reduce stress.

Sanchez-Alvarez et al. (2015) carried out a meta-analysis of 25 studies with a combined total of 8,520 participants and found a significant relationship between high EI and subjective well-being: "In general, individuals who perceive, know and manage their emotions might deal better with emotional issues, and therefore experience greater psychological wellbeing."

Peer Support

Given that we spend a high proportion of our waking lives at work, the presence of supportive relationships with one's peers is an important factor in our mental health. We need to feel that we get on with our colleagues and can count on them for support. This is most likely to happen in a psychologically safe environment where people are more likely to share information, ask for help and feedback, suggest new ideas, and learn from mistakes.

This element has become more important as organizations have become flatter and people need to work across organizational boundaries. This is about a culture that fosters collaboration to improve the way things are done rather than internal competition, which can result in the hoarding of resources and knowledge and the creation of silos. In the knowledge economy, an emphasis on the sharing of tacit knowledge can become the basis of competitive advantage.

Manager Support

Surveys have consistently found that one of the main reasons people leave organizations is because of poor line management. Although people do quit for other reasons, such as a lack of growth opportunities, there is certainly much truth in the old adage "People join organizations but leave their bosses." Managers have a big impact on employee experience and well-being. Managers who are not clear on their expectations, are poor at giving constructive feedback, and are ineffective at communicating and implementing change will demotivate their teams and cause stress. These managers often perceive the manager-direct report relationship in transactional terms.

Unhealthy organizations often do not have good processes for selecting and developing line managers, which means that the quality of line managers can vary widely and demonstrate inconsistent behaviors. These workplaces display the phenomenon of the "accidental manager," where people are appointed to line management roles because of their technical skill: "You are a great salesperson; now become a sales manager!" In many cases the result is the exchange of a great salesperson for a poor sales manager. Of course, some will turn out to be effective managers, but this is far from guaranteed.

Healthy places to work give line managers the support to develop so that they can, for example, give constructive feedback and lead change effectively. This is a transformational leadership style.

A 2018 literature review by psychologists at the Universities of Surrey and Exeter in the United Kingdom showed a number of ways in which leadership behavior affects well-being. This relationship can be positive, such as the traits associated with transformational leadership, or can be negative, leading to burnout, exhaustion, and poor-quality sleep.

Relationships

This element takes a broad overview of the strength of relationships across the organization beyond that with one's peers and line manager, and the extent to which the organization is seen as supportive in times of crisis.

Clayton Alderfer's existence-relatedness-growth (ERG) theory from 1969 updated Abraham Maslow's hierarchy of needs (1943) by arguing that we can fulfill different needs simultaneously and it is not always based on progression once the previous need is fulfilled—for example, the starving artist example where the desire for growth surpasses the basic needs of existence such as food and water. The relatedness component concerns our requirements for social interaction and external self-esteem. This element measures the extent to which we perceive our efforts at work are appreciated, which can have an impact on our self-esteem.

Brian Lakey and Edward Orehek's relational regulation theory (2011) describes ways in which social support in interpersonal relationships affects mental health. This shows that we regulate our emotions with everyday conversations and shared activities rather than through conversations on how to cope with stress. This regulation is relational in that the people who provide support, conversation topics, and activities that help regulate emotion are specific to the individuals involved: we all do this in a way that works for us individually.

Belonging

The need to belong is one of the most basic human needs. This applies as much to work groups as it does to our other family and social groups. This element provides a high-level measure of the strength of connection in the organization and as such is a summary of the combined effects of the previous five elements of this pillar.

Firstly, it measures the extent to which people feel that they will not be let down by their colleagues. Being able to rely on one's colleagues is a critical aspect of a high-trust, high-well-being workplace. Conversely, the feeling that one will be let down by one's colleagues creates stress and inhibits building strong relationships.

Secondly, it measures the extent to which people will stay with the organization even if higher pay is available elsewhere. This intention to stay (ITS) statement in the Healthy Place to Work survey is an important outcome. An organization with a poor workplace culture will foster a transactional mindset in which people are much more likely to move for monetary reasons. A healthy place to work, on the other hand, is much more likely to be able to retain people, even if they are able to obtain slightly better remuneration elsewhere.

Social Well-being

A healthy place to work recognizes that people's lives outside work are important and that we are all members of a wider society. Our broader social networks are important for sustaining mental health. Strong personal networks boost our emotional stability and well-being. They are particularly important for supporting us and acting as a sounding board when we face problems.

An important aspect of social well-being for many people is volunteering, which helps them connect to wider society. Volunteering can take many forms, but whatever form it takes for us individually is good for mental health as it helps build aspects of our life purpose in a way that the workplace may not necessarily be able to do. Volunteering can help us develop our skills, feel good about ourselves, and build confidence.

PHYSICAL HEALTH

While the first three pillars in toto cover many aspects of mental health, the fourth pillar covers the visible and tangible aspects of health, such as whether people have a nutritious diet and exercise adequately.

This pillar mirrors the biological aspect of the biopsychosocial model of health. While we cannot change our genes, we can do things to improve our physical health—getting good sleep, being physically active, and eating a nutritious diet—that will ameliorate our genetic propensity to certain conditions. Good physical health helps build our mental resilience.

While many people will be familiar with the Latin phrase *mens sana in corpore sano* (a healthy mind in a healthy body) and the good intentions it implies, a challenge we all face is not to make poor health decisions when under stress and pressure. Extensive research from all over the world shows that job-related conditions exert a big influence on individual decisions that affect health, such as unhealthy eating, smoking, drinking, and drug abuse. For example, a study of workers in Japan showed that high levels of job-related stress were linked to overeating and obesity. Another study of over 46,000 smokers showed that they were more likely to smoke, and to smoke more, when under work stress.

Work Environment and Safety

Abraham Maslow's hierarchy of needs (1943) is one of the most famous theories used in people management. At the bottom are our physiological needs for food, water, and safety. A good work environment will meet these needs by being, above all, safe. This is particularly important in manual roles such as mining, construction, manufacturing, and agriculture, where people may be using dangerous equipment.

The Health and Safety Executive (HSE) in the United Kingdom has estimated that there are at least one million injuries caused by workplace accidents each year and that poor health and well-being is a significant contributing factor.

People need to see that health and safety legislation is complied with and that they can speak up if they see risks being taken and corners being cut. This is what is known as behavioral safety, which goes beyond rules, procedures, and legislation to driving a deep safety culture on a zero-incident basis. In healthy workplaces this is closely linked to the values and purpose of the organization.

In an office environment, people want to be able to do their best work, which means different workplaces for different types of work and different working styles such as collaboration spaces and quiet areas.

Fitness

Physical activity helps with mental health as it can lift one's mood. It is also important in controlling one's weight. Because of this, according to the World Health Organization, physical activity lowers the risk of cardiovascular disease, of type 2 diabetes, and of certain cancers. It also strengthens the body's physiology and systems' functioning. These combined effects contribute to the slowing of aging.

Some job roles involve a great deal of physical activity. Employers need to ensure that this is done in a way that does not cause injury or excessive fatigue. Conversely, other roles involve little or no physical activity: combined with other health risks associated with a sedentary lifestyle, these roles are detrimental to health. In this case employers need to encourage physical activity (taking a short walk at lunchtime, using the stairs instead of the elevator, etc.). Studies have shown that regular moderate physical activity during the working day can increase workplace productivity and lower absenteeism and staff turnover.

Energy and Rest

Sleep and rest are very important for maintaining our health. Lack of sleep can be caused by shift work, working long hours, or other stress at work or in one's personal life.

When we are under stress, the stress hormone cortisol suppresses the repair mechanisms in our bodies. When under stress for a sustained period, the reduced effectiveness of the repair mechanisms compromises our immune system. This increases our health risks—for example, heart and other cardiovascular diseases and cancer. This is why burnout is such a risk.

Sleep deprivation also leads to lower emotional resilience and greater irritability. In the short term, a single sleepless night can impair performance as much as a blood alcohol level of 0.08–0.1% (the legal limit for driving in many countries). We become less alert, are more prone to making mistakes, and find it harder to learn. A sleep-deprived workforce is one at greater risk of health and safety incidents. Tiredness contributes to many accidents, and it has been estimated that 20% of motorway accidents are due to fatigue.

Diet

Most workers will have one main meal during a typical eight-hour working day. It is important that employees have access to healthy food while at work but also have enough knowledge to be able to make healthy eating decisions during the rest of the day.

Skipping lunch because one is too busy to stop can have side effects. It can lead to low blood sugar (hypoglycemia), which can shorten attention span and slow the speed at which humans process information. This can lead to lower productivity and more workplace accidents. The World Health Organization estimated in 2003 that adequate nourishment can raise national productivity levels by 20 percent.

Undernutrition—where people don't get enough to eat, thereby missing vital nutrients—is a factor in many developing countries. For example, iron deficiency is an important factor in restricting growth and general health in poor communities in many countries. According to the WHO, iron deficiency results in extreme fatigue for 740 million adults worldwide, thus harming productivity and contributing to accidents. Physical work capacity and performance can be impaired by as much as 30 percent.

Conversely, many rich economies are suffering from an epidemic of obesity because of easy availability of processed foods with high fat and sugar content. The International Labor Organization states that in the United States, 39.2 million work days per year are lost to illness related to obesity.

Improving our diet can make a big difference. For example, the Mediterranean diet—a balanced diet rich in fish, vegetables, fruits, nuts, whole grains, legumes, and olive oil, with little red meat and moderate alcohol consumption—has been shown to support brain function as we age. It has also been associated with a lower risk of heart attack and stroke in women.

THE FOUR PILLARS AND 21 ELEMENTS

The Healthy Place to Work survey is an opportunity for an organization to gain valuable data on the health and well-being of its workforce. This data is the starting point in responding strategically to the biggest issues affecting their employees. By drilling down through geographies, locations, departments, teams, and so forth, they can focus their resources with precision and start the process of improving the state of health of their workforce.

These improvements often lead to higher productivity, efficiency, effectiveness, and innovation. In turn, organizations report lower staff turnover and lower absenteeism. Finding a workplace that really cares about its workforce is exceptional. Employees quickly realize they are lucky and then reciprocate with good work and extra effort.

When an organization focuses on the model of the four pillars and 21 elements in this chapter, they are building a resilient workforce and ensuring the continued sustainability of their business.

DR. ELS VAN DER HELM

One bad night's sleep can dramatically affect our performance. If you extrapolate that effect across a full workforce, you may understand why it is important to learn how to sleep well. According to sleep expert Dr. Els van der Helm, we are missing out on one of the biggest performance drivers in our organizations, and she has the data to prove it!

> People will rather buy a sleep tracker, new bed, or a new little gadget, instead of thinking about their behavior and what to change.

Why We Need Sleep

During deep sleep, our brains are clearing out toxins that have built up throughout our day and moves them into our lymph system. In people who suffer from chronic sleep deprivation, the process does not operate effectively.

> We see this in both IQ and EQ, whether it's our ability to plan and organize to recognize patterns in a sea of information, whether it's thinking creatively, but also on the EQ side, sleep plays a really important role in our ability to manage our own emotions, to recognize emotions in others, whether it's in their face, or in their tone of voice, and our ability to show empathy or to trust other people.

The connection between good health and good sleep is extremely high.

Quality sleep is associated with better long-term outcomes, whether it's your chance of developing dementia, cardiovascular disease, or even cancer.

Quantity versus Quality

It is not all about simply the number of hours you are asleep, but equally important is the quality of the sleep you are getting.

If you can fall asleep within 30 minutes, if you wake up during the night for a maximum of 5 minutes (10 minutes if you are over 65), if you don't wake up too early, then you are achieving quality sleep.

Quality also relates to the consistency of sleep you get each night and whether you are in sync with your bio rhythms—this is particularly important in an organizational context when not everybody can be treated the same. Some simply won't perform well at an 8 a.m. meeting because their body has not fully woken up; equally, being forced on a red eye flight on a Monday could ruin your Sunday night sleep pattern.

The Role of the Organization

Organizations have a role to play according to van der Helm. The leaders need to act as role models. They need to build awareness and knowledge among their teams about the importance of rest and recovery. They need to provide tools that allow employees personalize their work engagement in a way that works for them. This also extends to company policies around work scheduling, and finally incentives can work to reward managers who focus on the health and well-being of their team.

I think there's often this perceived tension between well-being and organization performance.
A manager that just burns through their team members has consequences versus the leader that is really boosting their well-being.

Stress and Sleep

There is a clear relationship between sleep and stress, and some leaders understand better the impact stress has on their sleep and the impact sleep has on their stress, specifically on their ability to deal with stress effectively.

There are always those people who just know how to do it—they have low stress levels, low sleep debt, and high sleep quality.

Many think quality sleep relates to how you spend the last hour before bed, but van der Helm is clear that it is a result of how you spend your whole day.

This is about what you do the entire day. If you have a crazy back-to-back day, you're just building up your stress hormones, and it's really hard to get them down in the evening and then have a good night of quality sleep. This is very much around building in recovery moments during the day.

Inspirational Leadership

Quoting research from Christopher Barnes from the University of Washington, van der Helm showed that sleep plays a key role for those wanting to be seen as inspirational.

Research showed not only that well-rested leaders are more inspiring but that their teams that are well rested are easier to inspire.

ARNOLD BAKKER

Arnold Bakker is an internationally known organizational psychologist who lectures frequently to professional groups, business audiences, and students. Together with Evangelia Demerouti, he developed the job demands–resources (JD-R) theory: one of the most-cited theories in psychology and management literatures.

> If you are a good organization and care for your people, you'll spot when they are going through a tough time and help them deal with it.

The JD-R theory provides a structured approach to view a job in terms of the demands it placed on the employee (work overload, interpersonal conflict, job insecurity, role ambiguity, etc.) and the job resources (feedback, coaching, autonomy and control, career development and learning, social supports, etc.) that may mitigate those negative effects of job demands.

> With our theory of job demands and resources, we are building on the shoulders of giants.

Personal Resources

Bakker and Demerouti's theory was broader and less role specific than the work of their predecessors, providing a more general application and flexibility. Their model evolved to include personal resources rather than just job resources.

When it comes to the lower-order factors like beliefs about your optimism, self-efficacy, self-esteem, hope, and resilience, these are malleable. Personal resources can be changed.

According to Bakker, people need to be really proactive and change things themselves in an active way, for example by using job crafting, through playful work design, by using their strengths, and in many other ways by using their voice.

Self-Undermining Behavior

In terms of risk prevention, organizations should not only monitor the level of job demands and level of fatigue but also the levels of self-undermining behaviors.

That is an early warning sign for me; if there is self-undermining behavior and people admit that they create conflicts and create confusion, then you should immediately intervene.

The Personalization of Job Design

The ability to be able to craft your job so it suits you is essential so that you can balance the job demands and resources, and this needs to be completed on an individual basis rather than at the organizational level.

Job design efforts shouldn't be the same for everyone in the same organization; they should be different for different people.

Job Crafting versus Playful Job Design

Bakker contrasts job crafting—changing work tasks, work environment, or creating new resources or support—with the new concept of playful job design. He believes employees have the autonomy to make their work more fun by using humor, fantasy, or setting mini challenges.

By approaching the same task in a playful way, you're more likely to do it because it's more entertaining, it's more meaningful, you feel that you achieve something; if you make it more fun, you have a better time while doing it.

He personally sets competitive challenges around dealing with a targeted number of emails in an hour or slipping a word that makes no sense into a conversation to see if anyone will notice!

Leaders Need to Focus on Worker Well-Being

Bakker believes that many leaders today don't fully connect the dots between the well-being of their people and the performance of their organizations. He believes they need to be measuring workforce health and well-being at least every six months.

> They're interested in money, in investments, in tomorrow's stock market. I wish that these economists and financially oriented people would know more about worker well-being, because that will bring them eventually more money, and that will attract more people to stay in the organization.

But progressive companies respond to the needs of their employees.

> If you're a good organization, you take care of your people, and when they are going through a rough time, then maybe you need to offer them more job resources, a little bit lower demands, so that they can move on to another period where things are a bit more normal.

General managers who have been trained to look at efficiency and financial output often look at performance, but they forget to monitor people's well-being.

The Next Biggest Challenge

Bakker believes the next biggest challenge for workers will be their ability to collaborate with robots.

> You could say that robots and computers and artificial intelligence can take over the dirty work. But if we do that and make everything more efficient, then humans do not have slack time to be more creative and problem solve. So that will put everything even under more strain.

INTERNATIONAL WELL BUILDING INSTITUTE

Ann Marie Aguilar
Senior Vice President; EMEA Region

"If you can design a building with gradients of thermal comfort, even between 1 and 3 degrees, people will work where they are most comfortable . . . . give people individual control over their environment."

In this book we have outlined the 25 elements that make up a healthy place to work. One of those elements relates to work environment and safety, and a related statement asks whether people believe they work in an "energizing physical environment." To get a better understanding of some of the factors that will determine whether an environment is energizing we turned to the International WELL Building institute and their Senior Vice President Ann Marie Aguilar, who outlines the 10 aspects that they assess and their component parts.

Air

Achieve high-level indoor air quality across a space's lifetime. This includes air quality management, smoke-free environment, ventilation design and particle filtration, construction pollution management, improving supply air, air quality monitoring and awareness, pollution infiltration management, combustion minimization, isolating sources of contaminated air, and microbe and mold control.

Water

Access to high-quality drinking water and water management. Performance metrics and monitoring, legionella control, enhanced quality, drinking water promotion, moisture management, and hygiene support.

Nourishment

Encourage better eating habits by creating food environments where the healthiest choice is the easiest choice. Fruits and vegetables, food advertising and education, nutritional transparency, mindful eating spaces, refined ingredients, food preparation guidelines, portion management, on-site food production, special diet accommodations, and responsible food sourcing.

Light

Benefit from daylight and lighting systems designed to increase alertness, enhance experience, and promote sleep. Appropriate light exposure, daylight simulation, visual lighting design, visual balance, circadian lighting design, electric light quality, glare control, occupant lighting control, and daylight design strategies.

Movement

Promotes active living through environmental design strategies, policies, and programs. Active buildings and communities, site planning and selection, ergonomic design, physical activity opportunities, active furnishings, physical activity promotion, circulation network, physical activity spaces and equipment, and facilities for active occupants.

Thermal Comfort

Maximize your productivity through improved HVAC (heating, ventilation, and air conditioning) system design and by meeting thermal preferences. Performance metrics, thermal zoning, individual controls, radiant thermal comfort, ongoing monitoring, and humidity control.

Sound

Improve your experience with optimal acoustical comfort parameters. Sound-reducing surfaces, minimum background sound, enhanced audio devices, sound mapping, maximum noise levels, sound barriers, reverberation time.

Materials

Reduce human exposure to hazardous building materials. Materials transparency and optimization, waste management, minimal/low hazard pesticide use, cleaning products and protocols, lead, asbestos, PCB (polychlorinated biphenyls) and mercury safety, CCA (chromated copper arsenate) and lead management, site remediation, material and COC restrictions.

Mind

Support cognitive and emotional health through design, technology, and treatment strategies. Mental health promotion, stress management, connection to nature, restorative opportunities and spaces, connection to place, tobacco cessation, mental health services and education, substance use services.

Community

Establish inclusive, integrated community through social equity, civic engagement, and accessible design. New parent support, civic engagement, diversity and inclusion, emergency resources, health and wellness promotion, accessibility and universal design, emergency preparedness, occupant surveys, health services, and benefits.

A thoughtful approach to the design of a workplace/workspace is so important on so many levels but none more so that the fact that it can drive healthy behaviors. The interaction of employees and their environment is a critically important aspect delivering sustainable performance.

While many will view the workplace or workspace on a functional level, the more insightful will invest time and energy in creating a design that delivers on multiple levels.

For more go to @makeworkhealthy podcast.

CHAPTER 14

A Healthy Conclusion

When we began writing this book, we felt what we were proposing was revolutionary. It would require a serious rethink of the relationship between work, the workplace, and the organization. It was clear that work wasn't working for many. Work was causing pain, suffering, and in some cases death. For some it was a choice between work and life, and it needed a radical redesign to stop the harmful effects.

The world was surprised that employee engagement was at rock bottom levels, not realizing there was a deep level of resentment within many workers as work was forcing them into routines that were counterproductive to their health and the health of their families. In fact, they felt like 21st-century slaves.

In our work we saw the greatest levels of resentment when there was a major mismatch between skills and talents of individuals and a misalignment to the cultures, leaders, and organizations where they worked. We had experienced many people who looked internally emotionally dead as they felt trapped in a role, workplace, and company that didn't play into their talents or align with them as people. This misalignment was making them sick.

At the same time, we could see a demographic time bomb about to explode where governments were being forced to spend an increasing percentage of gross domestic product (GDP) on health care services to meet the needs of their populations. This was exacerbated by an aging population that was living longer with complex medical needs. The pharmaceutical and health care industries were providing more and more solutions at constantly increasing costs, creating a dystopian world where soon only the wealthy would be healthy.

Something had to change to avoid this impending doom. Our request was to the second biggest force in society, business, to step forward and lead, reimagining work, workplace, and organizational performance; radically changing how work was delivered and crucially making work healthy; replicating the model represented by the Quaker companies of the 1800s and early 19th century, like Cadbury and others, taking a deep sense of care for their employees and their families, providing them with housing, education, and work that allowed them to develop, grow, and flourish.

239

This new approach would see employees fit their work around their lives and not their lives around their work. It would require an unparalleled level of flexibility from employers, allowing people to design their own work while still getting the job done. We were convinced that the key to success in the new world of work was a dedication to the health of the workforce and the systems that drove the organization to be an environment conducive to health rather than sickness. Companies would now be measuring and managing workforce health as a key determinant of success.

A DIFFERENT APPROACH

In the pages of this book, we shared the science of well-being, using empirical evidence to highlight the most important components. This included the theoretical work of giants whose shoulders we were now standing on, like Albert Bandura, Edward Deci, Richard Ryan, and many others. This was the basis for the creation of the Healthy Place to Work model showing what needed to be measured and analyzed—based on four pillars and 21 elements. Importantly every element was actionable and could be responded to effectively. This wasn't just a nice theory; this worked in practice.

We mapped the journey for those who were inspired to move the dial in their organizations; we talked about culture, systems, practices, policies, and behaviors. We showed the symbiotic relationship between the organization and the individual, a co-dependent relationship. We identified the points where individual and organizational interests collided to achieve sustainable individual and collective organizational performance. Data points reflected the perceptions of people and provided clear visual representations of the journey to be undertaken. The destination was clear but the route not always, as there was no one-size-fits-all solutions to the specific issues identified in particular organizations. Importantly it was context dependent. The responses to the presenting issues needed to be carefully constructed so that they resolved the concerns that needed to be addressed.

As data flowed in from across the globe, the correlations became clear. There were a range of elements with regard to individual employees' health status that affected their performance at work. While the organization was not responsible for those personal items, the organization needed to be concerned and show support in those areas if it was to be seen as a caring company who viewed these people as human beings. It was also within the organization's self-interest to respond if it wanted to ensure the achievement of peak performance on the job. This symbiotic relationship between the employee and organization was critical. The research data showed clear links between people's personal health and their on-the-job performance. It also showed there was a clear correlation, but not necessarily causation, between people's personal perceived health status and their view of the organization and its leadership—namely, if they had positive health status, their view of the leadership and organization was in turn positive, and this led to better performance around productivity, creativity, less conflict, more agility and adaptability, collaboration, and performance.

At this stage it was clear that progressive leaders needed to take a radically different approach to workforce health, abandoning the tactical, tickbox, superficial, event-based, programmatic, HR-led approach and replace it with a more strategic, data-driven, evidence-based, systems approach, focused on embedded cultural change, an approach that would be owned by the C-suite who would be role models and one which focused on resilience, sustainability, and organizational performance. Measuring and managing workforce/workplace health would be one of the most importance activities in the company, as it would be a predictor of future performance and be critical for shaping the risk profile of the organization going forward. This approach would require organizations to become radical in terms of how, where, and when work was delivered. They would show great flexibility and would allow individuals design their own roles to suit their lives. This would see a monumental shift in approach with power shifting to employees, who simply were not going to sacrifice themselves and their health to deliver organizational performance. But was the business world ready for this transformation?

THE PANDEMIC: HEROES TAKE A BOW AND WORKERS DELIVER AGAIN

Well, whether organizations were ready or not became a moot point because the COVID-19 pandemic happened, and the world of work changed. A virus invisible to the human eye was now the biggest force for change, and *everything* changed. Some claim that those changes would have happened anyway and COVID-19 just accelerated the process. Suddenly health became the number one priority for everyone—governments, state agencies, businesses, and everything else paled into insignificance. It was incredible to see the past limitations simply removed and overcome. Money was not an issue. Governments seemed to have unlimited resources to plow into the health care services. Businesses were only interested in how they could get solutions and less interested in the costs associated. Workers were furloughed. People who previously complained about work now complained about not having work; they missed the camaraderie of friends and co-workers, they missed getting out and about, the cut and thrust of business life, the flying and traveling that seemed a hassle a few months earlier became a missed pastime, and isolation was now the enemy.

Frontline workers had no choice but to brave through, taking on a new role in life as heroes. Those whose roles had previously been viewed as lowly with the commensurate pay scale were now elevated to the status of "essential"; those on the front line were now waging a war against an invisible enemy with few resources or protections. Many sadly lost their lives. The workplace yet again was a dangerous place to be. But selfless employees turned up in the face of fear. They were mission driven. They had passion and purpose. They were indeed our 21st-century heroes, and we should never ever forget what they did and how many laid down their lives to save us.

COVID-19 was reshaping our world. It had our attention. There was only one way to stop it. Our wonderful scientists were working in their workplaces long hours. Vaccines that previously were developed in years were now brought to market in months; what was impossible became possible and happened. The world heaved a universal sigh of relief as once more we could reenter the world from our cocoons and isolation thanks to the brilliant work from microbiologists, virologists, and scientists all over the world, whose dedication, skills, and talents provided a "get out of jail card" to the world's population.

As the poet William Butler Yeats wrote: "All changed, changed utterly: A terrible beauty is born."

The people reemerging from their homes and apartments were not the same people who left society earlier. They were changed by the experience. They had stepped off the rat race. They had time to think—always a dangerous thing! The idea of operating with unrelenting levels of stress until retirement and then dying didn't seem attractive anymore. They woke up to their lives and reassessed. Many decided enough was enough. They resigned from their jobs. The universal deal that everybody had bought was suddenly broken, and all bets were off. The debate started. It wasn't a few individuals in isolation reimagining their futures; it was a large swathe of people deciding they wanted real change. It became the Great Resignation.

Businesses and companies were forced to respond to COVID-19 with remote working. Employees had now proved that what they had previously requested (requests that were in the main rejected) could actually work, and in fact worked much better than anyone predicted or imagined. Yes, it was not the same, but wasn't that the point? People didn't want the same. For those who had caring duties, families, great relationships, long expensive commutes, they made it work. The battle for a new form of workplace was fought and won. Many women were also finding remote working making work possible, which was crucial as there was a deficit in resources and the talent that businesses were desperate to attract. People with disabilities were suddenly able to join the workforce with ease. The talent pool for organizations became global because geographic restrictions were removed. Suddenly, even the biggest companies that had demanded that people return to the workplace were backtracking, and hybrid working became the thing every white-collar worker was doing.

Employees were having conversations with their managers and agreeing on new ways of working. Job crafting became sexy. Individuals designed their roles and work engagements in ways that better suited their lives, and the businesses and organizations thrived. The impossible was suddenly possible. Work was finally starting to work for some.

A NEED FOR A MAJOR SHIFT

Throughout this book we interviewed thought leaders and exemplar companies who had created new ways of working years ago, but it took a pandemic to get others to see the light. We have enjoyed telling the success stories as an inspiration to others to come on the journey. But we need to go further, much further. We need a major paradigm shift. We need to challenge all the old ways that made employees sick and replace them with cultures, systems, practices, and processes that make work healthy.

All the issues obsessing the minds of HR directors from pandemic recovery, long COVID, attraction and retention, talent management, remote and hybrid working, wellness, mental health, diversity and inclusion, belonging, resilience, purpose, sustainability, and so forth, could all come together under one word—and that word was health. The ultimate obsession and the ultimate focus was to make work healthy and keep it healthy, in the belief that organizational performance would follow.

But this was not the whole story. Core to the model we propose is a salutogenic orientation—a significantly different orientation. It might be subtle as an idea, but the implementation impact, if delivered correctly, is life changing. We need to stop seeing health as the absence of illness and to focus on the aspects that make us healthy and resilient and our lives sustainable. The concept at its core is the development of a sense of coherence, which is composed of three parts: comprehensibility, manageability, and meaningfulness.

- Comprehensibility in cognitive terms means that we need the world around us to be ordered and consistent, not constantly chaotic; we need to understand and make sense of the madness.
- Manageability is a feeling that we have the resources at our disposal to cope with everything life throws at us. Those resources could be cultural, societal, financial, and related to our support network.

- Finally, meaningfulness is the emotional aspect. Is the challenge worthwhile? Is the purpose powerful enough to see us through with energy and determination? While all these were true for the individual, the question posed was how relevant this could be to organizational performance. It became clear that with the speed of change and the increasing need to be adaptable and agile, an organizational sense of coherence wasn't just nice to have but essential.

Leaders now needed to constantly communicate to bring clarity to those that followed. Their primary role was sense making for the organization and shaping the context in which they were operating. Secondly, they needed to ensure that the organization was providing the supports necessary for the employees to operate at the levels that were required. This meant dismantling the processes that were not working and replacing them with ones that did. Finally, those leaders had to pump the purpose throughout the organization, ensuring that every individual felt committed and connected to the cause. These leaders now viewed the organization from a salutogenic perspective; they aimed to reduce the pathogens, such as excessive demands, poor behaviors, power and politics, and low standards of safety, and increase the salutogenic aspects such as positive supportive leadership, dedicated social support, learning and development, better job design and role clarity, and increased autonomy.

In the post-pandemic world of work, these leaders and managers needed to be salutogenic managers and salutogenic leaders; their number one priority was the health and well-being of their people. They became obsessive about the numbers and spotting the times, the people, and the locations where work was not working and negatively affecting people's health. They would jump in and respond immediately to fix the process, practice, or behavior that was problematic in a systemic way rather than just for that instance. The knowledge allowed the organization to learn and adapt so it was constantly improving and continuing to be a healthy place for all employees. The leaders knew in the hybrid/remote world of work that if they wanted employees to make sacrifices to commute and leave their homes, the leaders had better create compelling, multi-functional workplaces that were designed for effective contribution, collaboration, and deep work all in the one place.

But many leaders reading this would question whether that is really necessary. To them it seems like a lot of work. They would prefer business as usual. Well, unfortunately that world of work as we knew it is gone, and it was never aligned with sustainable performance anyway.

BOARD MEMBERS' ROLES AND RESPONSIBILITIES

Throughout this book, we have been blessed with the generosity of exemplar companies that have shared their stories, insights, and practices. These should inspire every reader to understand that organizations are changing and implementing new approaches to respond to the new environment. They are living in a beta world where everything they are doing is experimental and they are learning as they move forward. We thank them deeply for sharing their insights on the approaches that have worked and for their humility in telling us about the things that have not so that our readers can accelerate their learning without making costly mistakes.

We would also like to thank the thought leaders who have operated in this world of work for many decades, thinking deeply, writing papers, conducting research, testing hypotheses, and importantly drawing conclusions; to you all we are deeply indebted. The last of those thought leader profiles is in this chapter by Jim Loehr because his thoughts are extremely relevant to leaders and those in a privileged position to have a real and dramatic impact on the lives of the people in their care and in their employment.

Before we close, let us turn our attention to the board of directors. Many will see their role as one of oversight: ensuring that the governance protocols are implemented correctly; setting strategy for the organization, supporting the CEO, and giving direction to ensure the organization is on the correct path. More and more the role of the board encompasses the concept of sustainability. Many will look closely at the UN Sustainability Goals to ensure that the organization they are part of is focused and committed to delivering and playing their part in the achievement of these goals and being seen as good corporate citizens.

Flowing from these goals came the ESG movement. This initially placed attention on ensuring that investors targeted corporations that did not solely focus on profit maximization but also had concerns around ethical considerations. ESG, related to environmental, social and governance reporting, brings a whole new level of transparency to this arena in the hope of moving the dial and making an impact for good.

Boards now need to be aware of the impact of the businesses that they are directing, both positive and negative:

- They need to have data to understand the environmental impact of their corporation and business. This is two-fold. Climate change is racing ahead, and unless we reverse the effects, the future of Mother Earth is in peril. Secondly, consumers are watching like never before. Greenwashing is being called out where it occurs, and tick-box activity in this arena is pointless and, in fact, counterproductive. The impact on a brand is significant and can be terminal.

- The S in ESG relates to social reporting and the way in which businesses treat their employees, clients, and society in general. As you can imagine, the health and safety of their employees is front and center with regard to their impact. Securing a data source that provides transparency and evidence is crucial for boards to have insight into the effect the organization is having on its people. It is also important to provide a degree of separation between the CEO's own reporting and that of independent data available to the board. In fact, we are seeing more and more boards requesting this information so that they are able to satisfy their requirements in this regard.
- The final part of ESG is the G for governance, and this includes a range of issues from taxation to anti-corruption.

The key message for board members is that pursuit of profit alone is not the extent of their responsibilities. Being good corporate citizens requires a broader set of reporting requirements, and the UN goals and specifically ESG reporting are a critical element now and into the future. But even if this wasn't a legal requirement for many (such as larger corporations), the progressive ones would be doing this anyway as there is an increasing demand from the public (and most probably many of whom will be clients) to see the brands they spend their money focusing on doing good while doing business. The two are not inconsistent; in fact, they are often integral.

A LEGACY IN THE MAKING

Jim Loehr, who is profiled in this chapter, talks extensively about impact, but he also talks about something very relevant to leaders, and that is legacy. For many, legacy is seen as taking on greater significance when you come to the end of your career, and you have most of your business achievements behind you. In fact, maybe when you "have it made" your mind turns to more esoteric types of subjects of a higher echelon to do with how you may be viewed after you have retired, left office, or died. In fact, probably the most famous story in this regard relates to Alfred Nobel, who read his obituary, which had been posted incorrectly and was far from complimentary and in fact associated him with profiteering from war. He was so affected that he would go on to leave all his fortune at the time of his eventual death eight years later to the development of the Nobel Prize, promoting those who had conferred the greatest benefit to humankind.

The key with legacy is not to wait until you are old and gray to decide how you will be remembered or how people will view your impact; it is to decide today. It doesn't matter whether you are 18 or 80; right now you can decide how you want to be remembered, and what words would you like people to use to describe you and your impact. Then you need to get busy making it happen.

Often people end up in leadership roles and are so busy and focused on either keeping the show on the road, driving growth, beating the competition, or developing the next big thing that they simply never stop to consider their impact, both actual and potential. Being a leader in an organization is important because the decisions you make have an impact not only on the lives of your employees but also on their families and society as a whole. Often, it is only when this fact is highlighted to leaders that they stop and suddenly recognize just how important their position is to so many. The leader of an organization has a significant impact on the culture of the organization, and the culture drives the values, behaviors, and norms. Leaders have the potential to change people's lives in a very positive way.

When it comes down to it, the most valuable asset we possess is our health. If a leader can positively influence the health of their people (employees), they are making a real difference, and they should start immediately.

Work and the workplace have a huge impact on the health of employees. Leaders need to redesign work and workplaces so they can make work healthy. The workplace needs a major reset, we need to challenge everything, and our lens needs to be workforce health, believing that performance will follow. We need to deconstruct and reconstruct every practice to ensure it is fit for purpose. We need to rebalance power and control, demands and resources. We need to reimagine work and the workplace. We need to stop treating employees as replaceable resources and see them for what they are: human beings.

We need to understand that the workforce that turns up for work today is different from the one that left yesterday, and leaders need to have their finger on that pulse and spot the changes daily and respond. That takes measurement and management. We need to incentivize all people managers to focus in an authentic way on the health of their people, making it their number one priority, now even more crucial in a virtual world. We need to view the workplace as a complex system of energy where the leader's role is the transformation of that energy from potential to kinetic (energy in motion). We need to treat employees like volunteers, pumping them full of passion and purpose. We need to give people a career, not just a job. We need to redesign work with our employees, building in moments of recovery throughout our day. We need to stop social pollution. We need to make work the best part of people's day. We need to do it all together because creating a healthy place to work is a team sport. We need to stop focusing on cure and start focusing on prevention.

We need to be dedicated to creating healthy workplaces with healthy cultures, systems, practices, behaviors, and policies. We need to focus in a salutogenic and holistic way on making every single employee and contractor physically, mentally, socially, emotionally, and spiritually stronger.

Together, let's make work healthy.

JIM LOEHR

A world-renowned performance psychologist, researcher, and author of 17 books, including his bestseller *The Power of Full Engagement*, Jim Loehr is the co-founder of the Johnson & Johnson Human Performance Institute, which helps train and inspire more than 250,000 business, sports, medicine, and military leaders worldwide.

> I want to be actively engaged in having the most exhilarating life possible, and making sure whatever trajectory I am on, I am watching this very carefully through this magnificent lens of reflective consciousness.

After interviewing Jim Loehr, coauthor John had to check his family tree to see if they were related. They share the same passion, the same purpose, and the same views on so many topics that related to high performance and energy.

Legacy Drives Purpose

The late Stephen R. Covey encouraged his readers and listeners to always begin with the end in mind (*7 Habits of Highly Effective People*). Well, Jim Loehr is also a fan of that philosophy because for him it is all about legacy. Often people wait until they are at an advanced stage of life to start considering their impact, but Jim believes that it is useful to do so at any time, and in fact the best time is now. Why? Because if people think deeply about the legacy they want to leave, they will become much clearer about their purpose in life. Purpose drives meaning, meaning drives passion, and passion fuels performance. As a sport and performance psychologist, Loehr has been studying this very thing for many years.

The Privilege of Leadership

Ultimately your legacy will be determined by how others view you and the impact you had on their lives. Leaders are in a very privileged position to impact the lives of so many people. More important than what you say is how you make people feel and how you treated them along the journey. A leader's character will shine through above any of their extrinsic achievements.

The Big Lie

Loehr believes that most people are sleepwalking through life, playing by other people's rules, being what other people have told them to be, believing that being successful in business, their role, their job, their wealth (society's markers of success!), and so forth, is what really matters in life; however, they are mistaken, and they need to wake up and set their own markers of success for their lives and be clear about the purpose of their life and the meaning in their time on earth.

The Energy to Live a Purposeful Life

Once people have a clear purpose in their life, they need energy to fulfill it, and Loehr is clear that to have a big life, you need big energy. Key to having big energy is constant recovery. He talks passionately about the need for microbursts of recovery during our daily lives, building them into our habits, routines, and rituals. It helps to automate health-related decisions as that saves energy. For Loehr, a successful and healthy life is not about time management but rather about energy management.

It is the energy you give to someone else (being present), not the time, that shows you care. The renewal of energy physically, mentally, emotional, and spiritually is the key to success in life.

Loehr believes many people blame their illnesses on excess stress, but his research has led him to the view that insufficient recovery is normally the problem. In fact, he sees stress as necessary for a high-performance life as it is a stimulus for growth, but the growth happens during recovery. The fitter you are (in the broadest definition of "fit"), the less time you need for recovery.

Hopefully you will be inspired to decide today what your legacy will be and convert that into a clear purpose for your life; be disciplined in living consistently with that purpose, remembering energy management and recovery is how you will achieve it.

Notes

Aguirre, D., Brown, A., and Harshak, A. (2010, October 5), "Making Change Happen, and Making It Stick: Delivering Sustainable Organizational Change," *Strategy + Business*, https://www.strategy-business.com/article/00057.

Alderfer, C.P. (1972, February 29), *Existence, Relatedness, and Growth; Human Needs in Organizational Settings* (First Edition), Free Pr.

Anderson, D.L. (2016, November 28), *Organization Development: The Process of Leading Organizational Change*, Sage Publications, Inc.

"Anemia," World Health Organization, https://www.who.int/health-topics/anaemia#tab=tab_1.

Antonovsky, A. (1979), *Health, Stress, and Coping*, Jossey-Bass Inc., San Francisco.

Antonovsky, A. (1987), *Unraveling the Mystery of Health: How People Manage Stress and Stay Well*, Jossey-Bass.

Antonovsky, A. *"The Salutogenic Model as a Theory to Guide Health Promotion,"* *Health Promotion International*, Volume 11, Issue 1, March 1996, pp. 11–18, https://doi.org/10.1093/heapro/11.1.11.

Aristotle. (2000). *Aristotle: Nicomachean Ethics* (Cambridge Texts in the History of Philosophy) (R. Crisp, Ed.), Cambridge: Cambridge University Press,. doi:10.1017/CBO9780511802058.

Bakker, A.B., and Demerouti, E. (2007, April 3), "The Job Demands-Resources Model: State of the Art," *Journal of Managerial Psychology*, 22(3), 309–328, https://doi.org/10.1108/02683940710733115.

Bandura, A. (1979), *Social Learning Theory*, Englewood Cliffs, NJ: Prentice Hall.

Bandura, A. (1986), *Social Foundations of Thought and Action: A Social Cognitive Theory*, Prentice Hall.

Bandura, A., and Adams, N.E., "Analysis of Self-Efficacy Theory of Behavioral Change," *Cogn Ther Res* 1, 287–310 (1977), https://doi.org/10.1007/BF01663995.

Bersin, J. (2021), "The Healthy Organization: Next Big Thing in Employee Wellbeing," https://joshbersin.com/2021/10/the-healthy-organization-the-next-big-thing-in-employee-wellbeing/.

Buchanan, D., Fitzgerald, L., Ketley, D., Gollop, R., Jones, J.L., Saint Lamont, S., Neath, A., and Whitby, E., (2005), "No Going Back: A Review of the Literature on Sustaining Organizational Change," *International Journal of Management Reviews*, Vol. 7, No. 3, pp. 189–205, September 2005.

Buchel B., and Davidson, R. (2011), "The Art of Piloting New Initiatives," Post-Print hal-02312029, HAL.

"Cardiovascular Diseases (CVDs)," World Health Organization, www.who.int/newsroom/fact-sheets/detail/cardiovascular-diseases-(cvds).

251

Cervera, César (8 May 2019), "La jornada de ocho horas: ¿un invento 'sindicalista' del Rey Felipe II?" [The eight-hour day: a "unionist" invention of King Philip II?]. www.abc.es (in Spanish). ABC.

"Costs to Great Britain of Workplace Injuries and New Cases of Work-Related Ill Health–2018/19," Health and Safety Executive HSE, https://www.hse.gov.uk/statistics/cost.htm.

"Council Recommendation of 22 May 2018 on Key Competences for Lifelong Learning," European The Council of the European Union, https://eur-lex.europa.eu/legal-content/EN/TXT/PDF/?uri=CELEX:32018H0604(01)&rid=7.

Conway, E., Fu, N., Monks, K., Alfes, K., and Bailey, C. (2016), "Demands or Resources? The Relationship Between HR Practices, Employee Engagement, and Emotional Exhaustion Within a Hybrid Model of Employment Relations," *Hum Resour Manage*, 55: 901–917. https://doi.org/10.1002/hrm.21691.

Covey, S. R. (1989), *The 7 Habits of Highly Effective People*, Free Press.

Csikszentmihalyi, M. (1990), *Flow: The Psychology of Optimal Experience*, Harper & Row.

Deci, E., and Ryan R. (1985), "Self Determination Theory," In P.A.M. Van Lange, A.W. Kruglanski, and E.T. Higgins (Eds.), *Handbook of Theories of Social Psychology* (pp. 416–436), Sage Publications Ltd., https://doi.org/10.4135/9781446249215.n21 (1985).

Detels, R., Gulliford, M., Karim, Q.A., and Tan, C.C. (2015, April 26). *Oxford Textbook of Global Public Health* (6th ed.), Oxford University Press.

DiFonzo, N. (2008, August 29), *The Watercooler Effect: An Indispensable Guide to Understanding and Harnessing the Power of Rumors* (1st ed.), Avery.

Di Meglio, F. (2022), "Renegotiating the Psychological Contract for the Post-COVID World," www.hrexchangenetwork.com/employee-engagement/articles/renegotiating-the-psychological-contract-for-the-post-covid-world.

Dockterman, E. (2021), "42% of Women Say They Have Consistently Felt Burned Out at Work in 2021," *Time Magazine*, https://time.com/6101751/burnout-women-in-the-workplace-2021/.

Dweck, C.S. (2016), *Mindset: The New Psychology of Success*, Scribner Publisher.

"Employee Financial Well-Being: Why It's Important," (2017), CIPD in partnership with Close Brothers, Research Report, https://www.cipd.ie/Images/financial-well-being-why-its-important-report_tcm21-17441.pdf.

Engel, George (April 8, 1977), "The Need for a New Medical Model: A Challenge for Biomedicine," *Science* 196 (4286): 129–136. Bibcode:1977Sci...196..129E. doi:10.1126/science.847460. PMID 847460.

Eurofound, (2014), "Towards Better Living and Working Conditions," Publications Office. https://data.europa.eu/doi/10.2806/66091.

"Focussing on Wellness and Prevention," Johnson & Johnson Feb 7, 2014, http://www.jnj.com/about-jnj.

Fox, M. (2022), "Here's What Gen Z and Millennials Want from Their Employers amid the Great Resignation," CNBC, www.cnbc.com/2022/05/18/what-gen-z-and-millennials-want-from-employers-amid-great-resignation.html.

Gainer, R. (2008), "History of Ergonomics and Occupational Therapy," *Work* 31(1):5–9.

Goleman, D. (1995, September 1), *Emotional Intelligence: Why It Can Matter More than IQ* (1st ed.),. Bantam.

"Good Health Is Good Business. Here's Why," McKinsey Global Institute, www.mckinsey.com/mgi/overview/in-the-news/good-health-is-good-business.

"Guide: Understand Team Effectiveness," re:Work, https://rework.withgoogle.com/print/guides/5721312655835136/.

"Healthy People 2000," CDC, Centers for Disease Control and Prevention, https://www.cdc.gov/nchs/healthy_people/hp2000.htm.

Hook, G.E. (November 1995), "Ramazzini: Father of Environmental Health?" *Environ. Health Perspect.* 103(11):982–983.

Humphries, J. (2010), *Childhood and Child Labour in the British Industrial Revolution* (Cambridge Studies in Economic History - Second Series), Cambridge: Cambridge University Press.

Kahn, W.A. (1990), "Psychological Conditions of Personal Engagement and Disengagement at Work," *The Academy of Management Journal*, 33(4):692–724, https://doi.org/10.2307/256287.

Kamesaka et al. (2016): Kamesaka, Akiko; Tamura, Teruyuki: 労働時間と過労死 不安 ("Working Hours and Karōshi Risk Assessment," in Japanese), (2016), ESRI Discussion Paper Series 325, Economic and Social Research Institute (ESRI).

Keatinge, G., "Charles Turner Thackrah: The Effects of Arts, Trades and Professions on Health and Longevity." *Br J Ind Med.* 1958 Apr;15(2):137–138. PMCID: PMC1037850.

Kudel, I., Huang, J.C., and Ganguly, R. (2018, January), "Impact of Obesity on Work Productivity in Different US Occupations," *Journal of Occupational & Amp; Environmental Medicine*, 60(1):6–11, https://doi.org/10.1097/jom.0000000000001144.

"Losing from Day One: Why Even Successful Transformations Fall Short," (2021), McKinsey & Company, https://www.mckinsey.com/capabilities/people-and-organizational-performance/our-insights/successful-transformations.

Lakey, B., and Orehek, E. (2011, July), "Relational Regulation Theory: A New Approach to Explain the Link between Perceived Social Support and Mental Health," *Psychological Review*, 118(3):482–495, https://doi.org/10.1037/a0023477.

Marques, A., Peralta, M., Martins, J., Loureiro, V., Cortés Almanzar, P., Gaspar de Matos, M. (2018), "Few European Adults Are Living a Healthy Lifestyle," *American Journal of Health Promotion*, https://research.unl.pt/ws/portalfiles/portal/11656704/Marques_Am_J_Hea_Prom_2018_1.pdf.

Mattke, S., Harry H. Liu, John P. Caloyeras, Christina Y. Huang, Kristin R. Van Busum, Dmitry Khodyakov, and Victoria Shier, "Workplace Wellness Programs Study: Final Report," Santa Monica, CA: RAND Corporation, 2013.

Maul, D. (2019), "The International Labour Organization: 100 Years of Global Social Policy," De Gruyter.

"McKinsey Global Institute,"The Future of Work after COVID-19," (2021), www .mckinsey.com/featured-insights/future-of-work/the-future-of-work-after-covid-19.

Mittelmark, M.B., Sagy, S., Eriksson, M., Bauer, G.F., Pelikan, J.M., Lindström, B., and Espnes, G.A. (2016, September 2), *The Handbook of Salutogenesis* (1st ed. 2017), Springer.

Morton, A.L., *The Life and Ideas of Robert Owen*, New York, International Publishers, 1969.

Murdaugh, C. L., Parsons, M. A., and Pender, N. J. (2018), *Health Promotion in Nursing Practice* (8th ed.), Pearson.

Myers, V.A. (2012, April 1), "Moving Diversity Forward: How to Go From Well-Meaning to Well-Doing," American Bar Association.

Nembhard, Ingrid, M., and Amy C. Edmondson, A.C., "Psychological Safety: A Foundation for Speaking Up, Collaboration, and Experimentation in Organizations,'" in Gretchen M. Spreitzer, and Kim S. Cameron (eEds), *The Oxford Handbook of Positive Organizational Scholarship, Oxford Library of Psychology* (2011; online edn., Oxford Academic, 21 Nov. 2012).

Nishitani, N., and Sakakibara, H. (2006), "Relationship of Obesity to Job Stress and Eating Behavior in Male Japanese Workers," *Int J Obes* (Lond), https://pubmed .ncbi.nlm.nih.gov/16247505/.

"Nuria Chinchilla: The Power to Change Workplaces," Case: OB-67, Stanford Graduate School of Business, https://blog.iese.edu/nuriachinchilla/files/2010/12/the_power_ to_change_workplaces.pdf.

"Nutrition," World Health Organization, https://www.who.int/health-topics/nutrition#tab= tab_1.

Orchard, C. (2015), "The Business Benefits of a Healthy Workforce," Harvard T.H. Chan School of Public Health, www.hsph.harvard.edu/ecpe/the-business-benefits-of-a-healthy-workforce/.

Organizational Health Development (OHD) Model, (Bauer and Jenny, 2012), Jenny and Bauer, 2013.

Pfeffer, J. (1999), "The Knowing-Doing Gap," Stanford Graduate School of Business, www.gsb.stanford.edu/insights/knowing-doing-gap.

Pfeffer, J., and Sutton, R., *The Knowing-Doing Gap: How Smart Companies Turn Knowledge Into Action*, Boston, Mass. Harvard Business School Press, 2000.

"Physical Activity," World Health Organization, https://www.who.int/news-room/fact-sheets/detail/physical-activity.

Priesemuth, M. (2020), "Time's Up for Toxic Workplaces," *Harvard Business Review*, https://hbr.org/2020/06/times-up-for-toxic-workplaces.

Reardon, J. (1998), "The History and Impact of Worksite Wellness," *Nurs Econ* 16(3):117–121.

Riekert, K.A., Ockene, J.K., and Pbert, L. (2013, November 8), *The Handbook of Health Behavior Change*, 4th ed., Springer Publishing Company.

Roser, M., Ortiz-Ospina, E., and Ritchie, H. (2013), "Life Expectancy," Our World in Data, https://ourworldindata.org/life-expectancy.

Rucker, M. (2016), "The Interesting History of Workplace Wellness," https://michael-rucker.com/well-being/the-history-of-workplace-wellness/.

Ryan, R.M., and Deci, E.L. (2000), "Self-Determination Theory and the Facilitation of Intrinsic Motivation, Social Development, and Well-Being," *American Psychologist*, 55(1):68–78, https://doi.org/10.1037/0003-066X.55.1.68.

Sánchez-Álvarez, N., Extremera, N., and Fernández-Berrocal, P. (2015b), "Maintaining Life Satisfaction in Adolescence: Affective Mediators of the Influence of Perceived Emotional Intelligence on Overall Life Satisfaction Judgments in a Two-Year Longitudinal Study," *Frontiers in Psychology*, 6, https://doi.org/10.3389/fpsyg.2015.01892.

Sánchez-Álvarez, N., Extremera, N., and Fernández-Berrocal, P. (2015, August 11), "The Relation between Emotional Intelligence and Subjective Well-Being: A Meta-Analytic Investigation," *The Journal of Positive Psychology*, 11(3):276–285, https://doi.org/10.1080/17439760.2015.1058968.

Seligman, M.E.P. (2006), *Learned Optimism: How to Change Your Mind and Your Life*, Vintage.

Stelter, N. (2019), "Workplace Stress–the \$300B Business Problem That's Only Getting Worse," https://business.kaiserpermanente.org/insights/mental-health-workplace/workplace-stress-business-problem-getting-worse.

Threlkeld, K. (2021), "Employee Burnout Report: COVID-19's Impact and 3 Strategies to Curb It," www.indeed.com/lead/preventing-employee-burnout-report.

US Dept of Health & Human Services, US Public Health Service, (1993), "1992 National Survey of Worksite Health Promotion Activities: Summary," *American Journal of Health Promotion*, 7(6):452–464. https://doi.org/10.4278/0890-1171-7.6.452.

Volk, S., Lowe, K.B., and Barnes, C.M. (2022, August 15), "Circadian Leadership: A Review and Integration of Chronobiology and Leadership," *Journal of Organizational Behavior*, https://doi.org/10.1002/job.2659.

World Health Organization and Burton, J., (2010), "WHO Healthy Workplace Framework and Model: Background and Supporting Literature and Practices," World Health Organization, https://apps.who.int/iris/handle/10665/113144.

World Health Organization, "The Ottawa Charter for Health Promotion," Geneva, Switzerland: WHO, 1986 Nov 21.

Zalaquett, P., R.J. Wood, Eds. (1997), *The Maslach Burnout Inventory Manual*, Scarecrow Press.

Zbrodoff, S. (2012), "Pilot Projects—Making Innovations and New Concepts Fly," Paper presented at PMI Global Congress 2012—EMEA, Marsailles, France, Newtown Square, PA: Project Management Institute.

Zeidner, M., Matthews, G., and Roberts, R. D. (2012), *What We Know about Emotional Intelligence: How It Affects Learning, Work, Relationships, and Our Mental Health (A Bradford Book)*, Bradford Books.

Assessment and Impact— Supportive Leadership and Resources Correlate to Improved Employee Health Status

This appendix presents an impact model of organizational wellness culture and resources on employee health. Eight types of organizational wellness culture developed by top managers and other resources to promote employee health are assessed, including: congruence (fit), organizational values, wellness culture, work environment and safety, work control, work demands, manager support, and peer support. Four aspects of employee health were comprehensively assessed, including the financial, social, psychological, and physical health. Data were collected from 18 companies from more than eight countries including UK, Ireland, Brazil, Denmark, Mexico, Philippines, Sweden, and the USA, which employ 12,019 employees.

CONTEXT

Trinity College Dublin (Na Fu and her team) was asked to independently analyze a data set from Healthy Place to Work International to determine the impact of organizational culture and resources on employee health. While we had seen firsthand the impact that individual leaders and the overall approach of organizations C-suite had on the general level of health of employees we wanted to see if this was replicated across the board. It was important to any organization that was considering investing time and resources to support their people that they had data to support the overall view that the investment would result in an improvement in performance.

It was our experience that leaders could not take a half-hearted approach to employee health. They need to be seen as role model driving and supporting a wellness culture through their business. If the leaders were not seen as role models, well-being initiatives were doomed to failure as the necessary changes required would not receive support and gain traction.

It is about creating systems and a structure that places recovery into everybody's daily routine. It is not about words but actions, it's not about programs but embedded changes, it's not nice to have but essential.

METHOD

In this section, we report the data collection and sample profile.

Data Collection

Between 2021 and 2022, the Healthy Place to Work worked with 18 companies from more than eight countries including UK, Ireland, Brazil, Denmark, Mexico, Philippines, Sweden, and the USA, which employ 12,019 employees.

An online survey was sent out to all employees in these organizations with the internal support from the senior management team. Reminders were sent out to encourage participation. In total, 6,049 responses were received, and the response rate was 49% (ranging from 27% to 94% at company level).

During the data screening and cleaning stage, invalid responses (e.g. selected the same response for all items) were removed (the valid response rate was 46% (ranging from 26% to 94% at company level), which is comparable to existing research focusing on employee experience and well-being (e.g. 39% in Conway et al. 2016).

Table A.1 presents the sample and response rates across organizations.

TABLE A.1   Sample and Response Rate

ID	Region	Sample size	N	Response rate
1	Europe	6367	2504	39%
2	North and South America	5386	3124	58%
3	Asia	112	98	88%
4	Global	154	92	60%
Total	**18 companies in 8+ countries**	**12,019**	**5,818**	**48%**

Sample Profile

Among the respondents shown in Table A.2, 50% were male, 46% were female, and 4% indicated other in gender. In terms of age, 14% were less than 25 years old, 35% were between 26 and 34 years old, 30% were between 35 and 44 years old, 15% were between 45 and 54 years old, and 6% were 55 years and more. For tenure, 38% had worked in their organizations less than 2 years, 34% were between 2 and 5 years, 16% were between 6 and 10 years, and 12% had more than 10 years' tenure. Majority of respondents (78%) were staff (non-management), 17% were managers/supervisors, 8% were at the middle management level, and 4% were at the executive/senior management level. Majority of respondents (78%) were full-time workers and 22% were part-time workers. Almost half of the respondents were from Ireland and UK (41%) and Mexico (46%), followed by Brazil (7%), Denmark (2%), Philippines (2%), Sweden (.3%), USA (.2%), and other (global, 1.5%).

TABLE A.2 Demographic Characteristics of the Sample

Items		Sample distribution
Gender	Male	50%
	Female	46%
	Other	4%
Age	Less than 25 years	14%
	Between 26 and 34 years	35%
	Between 35 and 44 years	30%
	Between 45 and 54 years	15%
	55 years or more	6%
Tenure	Less than 2 years	38%
	2 to 5 years	34%
	6 to 10 years	16%
	11 to 15 years	7%
	16 to 20 years	2%
	Over 20 years	3%
Job grades	Staff (non-management)	71%
	Manager/Supervisor	17%
	Middle Management	8%
	Executive/Senior Management	4%
Contract type	Full-time	78%
	Part-time	22%

(Continued)

TABLE A.2   (Continued)

Items		Sample distribution
Country	*Brazil*	7%
	Denmark	2%
	Ireland and UK	41%
	Mexico	46%
	Philippines	2%
	Sweden	.3%
	USA	.2%
	Other (global)	1.5%

KEY FINDINGS

We analyzed the impact of organizational wellness culture and resources on employee health. A series of explorative and confirmative factor analyses were conducted to establish the reliability and validity of the scales. The results are available upon request. Figure A.1 presents the HPTW impact model where the key constructs and variables are included.

In the model, four aspect of employee health were included, i.e. the financial, social, psychological, and physical health. For social and psychological health, each aspect has three dimensions (emotional expression, work relationships and inclusion for social health; learning mindset, self-efficacy in health, and self-efficacy in job and career for psychological health). For physical health, two dimensions are diet and fitness and energy and rest.

For the organizational resources, eight factors are included, i.e. congruence (fit), organizational values, wellness culture, work environment and safety, work control, manageable work demands, manager support, and peer support.

Linking Organizational Resources with Employee Financial Health

Financial health refers to employees who have relatively stable and good financial status. Healthy places to work need to provide employees compensation and rewards to enable employees to live a relatively good life.

As shown in Table A.3, all organizational resources have significantly positive impact on employee financial health when entered individually. When they were all considered, wellness culture and manageable work demands are the most significant factors to increase employee financial health.

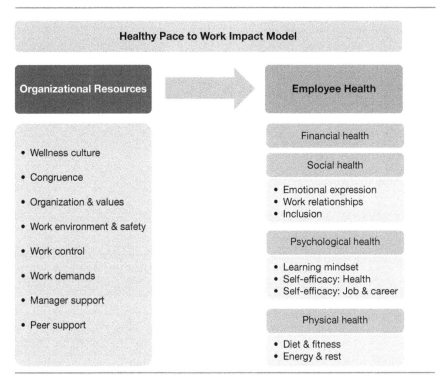

FIGURE A.1   HPTW Impact Model.

Wellness culture requires senior leaders care about the well-being of employees, and they demonstrate healthy behaviors, so employees perceive that their organizations genuinely care about their people's health.

Providing employees with manageable work demands where employees can do their work within their normal working hours also requires organizational leaders to design the jobs to have the right level of work demands for their people.

Linking Organizational Resources with Employee Social Health

Employee social health refers to employees' relationships with their family and co-workers, as well as their individual emotional expression. It is an important aspect of employee health. Organizations need to provide sufficient resources for employees to express their emotions and to develop good relationships with family members and co-workers.

TABLE A.3 Impact of Organizational Resources on Employee Financial Health

Organizational resources	Financial health	
	A	B
Wellness culture	+	+
Congruence (fit)	+	
Organizational values	+	
Work environment and safety	+	
Work control	+	
Manageable work demands	+	+
Manager support	+	
Peer support	+	

Note: Due to the high correlation between the organizational resources, separate regression models were tested for each organizational resource on financial health, shown in column A. Column B shows the results of the stepwise regression where only the most significant factors are retained. All regression analysis controlled for age, gender, tenure, job grades, and contract type (1 = full time; 0 = part time).

As shown in Table A.4, all organizational resources have significantly positive impact on employee overall social health and each aspect of it, when being entered individually. When they were all considered, different impacts were found.

Overall, wellness culture is significantly related to the employee overall social health and each aspect of it. The strong message is that senior managers and leaders need to develop a wellness culture, which will be critical for building and maintaining employee social health. They can do that via shifting the mindset toward caring about the well-being of employees and demonstrating healthy behaviors themselves, so employees perceive that their organizations genuinely care about its people's health.

Similar messages were found via the significant impact of organizational values on the employee overall social health and each aspect of it. Three items were used to measure organizational values, i.e. "People at this organization act in line with our values," "This organization clearly values high performance," and "This organization will act effectively on the results of this survey." Namely organizations need to live their values, which will help to build their employees' social health.

In addition, both manager and peer support were found to be significantly related to overall social health and each aspect of it. This is consistent with the finding on the senior leaders' role in creating wellness culture and living with

TABLE A.4   Impact of Organizational Resources on Employee Social Health

Organizational resources	Overall social health		Emotional expression		Work relation- ships		Inclusion	
	A	B	A	B	A	B	A	B
Wellness culture	+	+	+	+	+	+	+	+
Organizational values	+	+	+	+	+	+	+	+
Manager support	+	+	+	+	+	+	+	+
Peer support	+	+	+	+	+	+	+	+
Congruence (fit)	+	+	+		+	+	+	
Work environment and safety	+		+		+	+	+	
Work control	+	+	+	+	+		+	
Manageable work demands	+		+		+		+	+

Note: Due to the high correlation between the organizational resources, separate regression models were tested for each organizational resource on employee overall social health and the three aspects of social health, shown in column A. Column B shows the results of the stepwise regression where only the most significant factors are retained. All regression analysis controlled for age, gender, tenure, job grades, and contract type (1 = full time; 0 = part time).

values, which are important for employee social health. In the organizations with positive wellness culture and values, employees are more likely to experience higher levels of support from their managers and colleagues, which again is important for their health, socially.

Congruence (fit) is found to be positively associated with the overall social health, and work relationships. Work environment and safety are found to have a significant impact on work relationships. Work control is found to improve employee overall social health and individual emotional expression. Manageable work demands are positively linked with inclusion.

Linking Organizational Resources with Employee Psychological Health

Employee psychological health refers to employees' learning mindset, self-efficacy in their health, and self-efficacy in their jobs and careers. It is another important aspect of employee health. Organizations need to provide sufficient resources for employees to develop a learning mindset, as well as to improve their self-efficacy in health and their jobs and careers.

TABLE A.5   Impact of organizational Resources on Employee Psychological Health

Organizational resources	Overall psychological health		Learning mindset		Self-efficacy: Health		Self-efficacy: Job and career	
	A	B	A	B	A	B	A	B
Wellness culture	+	+	+	+	+	+	+	+
Work control	+	+	+	+	+	+	+	+
Manageable work demands	+	+	+	+	+	+	+	+
Congruence (fit)	+	+	+	+	+		+	+
Organizational values	+	+	+	+	+		+	+
Manager support	+	+	+	+	+		+	+
Work environment and safety	+	+	+		+	+	+	+
Peer support	+		+		+		+	

Note: Due to the high correlation between the organizational resources, separate regression models were tested for each organizational resource on employee overall social health and the three aspects of social health, shown in column A. Column B shows the results of the stepwise regression where only the most significant factors are retained. All regression analysis controlled for age, gender, tenure, job grades, and contract type (1 = full time; 0 = part time).

As shown in Table A.5, all organizational resources have significantly positive impact on employee overall psychological health and each aspect of it, when being entered individually. When they were all considered, different impacts were found.

Overall, wellness culture is significantly related to the employee overall psychological health and each aspect of it. The key point is that senior managers and leaders need to develop a wellness culture, which will be critical for building and maintaining employee psychological health.

In addition, both work control and manageable work demands, two elements related to job design, are positively related to the employee overall psychological health and each aspect of it. This finding requires senior managers and leaders to invest in job design to enable employees to have some autonomy (e.g. deciding when to take a break; having a say over the way they work), and to have manageable job demands (e.g. achievable deadlines and being able to do their work within their normal working hours).

Congruence (fit), organizational values, and manager support are important for the overall psychological health, learning mindset and self-efficacy in jobs and careers. Work environment and safety are important for the overall psychological health, self-efficacy in health and jobs and careers.

Linking Organizational Resources with Employee Physical Health

Employee physical health refers to employees' diet and fitness and energy and rest. It is another important aspect of employee health. Organizations need to provide sufficient resources for employees to develop physical health, which is directly influencing their productivity and performance.

As shown in Table A.6, all organizational resources have significantly positive impact on employee overall psychological health and each aspect of it, when being entered individually. When they were all considered, different impacts were found.

Overall, work environment and safety and manageable work demands wellness are significantly related to the employee overall physical health and both aspects of it. The critical finding is that senior managers and leaders need to design safe and healthy physical place (e.g. keeping employees safe at workplace, providing healthy food). Senior managers and leaders also need to invest in job design to enable employees to have manageable job demands (e.g. achievable deadlines and being able to do their work within their normal working hours).

Wellness culture, organizational values, and work control are found to be significantly related to employee overall physical health and energy and rest. Congruence (fit) is positively related to energy and rest.

Linking Employee Health with Employee and Organizational Outcomes

Regression analysis was conducted to test the impact of health on individual (general health) and organization (intention to stay and sick leave) performance. As shown in Table A.7, the four aspects of employee health are positively associated with employee intention to stay and general health and negatively associated with sick leave, which is an important indicator for organizational productivity.

TABLE A.6 Impact of Organizational Resources on Employee Physical Health

Organizational resources	Overall physical health A	B	Diet and fitness A	B	Energy and rest A	B
Work environment and safety	+	+	+	+	+	+
Manageable work demands	+	+	+	+	+	+
Wellness culture	+	+	+		+	+
Organizational values	+	+	+		+	+
Work control	+	+	+		+	+
Congruence (fit)	+		+		+	+
Manager support	+		+		+	
Peer support	+		+		+	

Note: Due to the high correlation between the organizational resources, separate regression models were tested for each organizational resource on employee overall social health and the three aspects of social health, shown in column A. Column B shows the results of the stepwise regression where only the most significant factors are retained. All regression analysis controlled for age, gender, tenure, job grades, and contract type (1 = full time; 0 = part time).

TABLE A.7 Impact of Employee Health on Employee and Organizational Outcomes

Variables	General health	Intention to stay	Sick leave
Financial health	+	+	-
Social health	+	+	-
Psychological health	+	+	-
Physical health	+	+	-

Note: Due to the high correlation between the organizational resources, separate regression models were tested for each organizational resource on employee overall social health and the three aspects of social health. All regression analysis controlled for age, gender, tenure, job grades, and contract type (1 = full time; 0 = part time).

SUMMARY

Organizational resources are critical for employee health. Based on the data surveying over 12,000 employees in 18 companies from over eight countries, strong empirical evidence has been found for the impact of organizational resources on four aspects of employee health, i.e. financial, social, psychological, and physical health, which in turn increases employee general health, intention to stay, and reduces sick leave, important toward organizational performance.

In particular, organizational wellness culture, developed by senior leaders and managers, is found to be significantly linked to all four aspects of employee health, and almost every element in these health aspects. Similar findings are revealed in relation to organizational values, another important management practice that senior leaders and managers need to pay attention to. In addition, job design, e.g. providing work autonomy and manageable job demands, is also playing an important role in promoting employee health. These findings call for business leaders to take a significant step toward changing to prioritize workforce/workplace health in the belief that it will eventually deliver performance. This change needs to start with the leaders at the top of the organization.

Acknowledgments

First and foremost, we are indebted to the many experts and organizational leaders we interviewed that generously shared with us their time, insight, and stories. We interviewed leaders at Centiro, Thames Water Company, RSCPA, Danske Bank, Deloitte, Kingston Council, Version 1, Cohesive, Takeda, ISS, Aviva, International Well Building Institute, Leek United Building Society, IIH Nordic, Concentrix, PwC, SAP, Futurice, P&G, Dubai Police, Amêndoas do Brasil, and SAS. We concluded each of these interviews inspired and resolved that creating healthy workplaces is not only possible, but there are many paths to achieving your own healthy workplace. We also interviewed a range of thought leaders that have shaped our current understanding of well-being in the workplace allowing us to present not only our own experience but offer a greater depth of understanding and experience. Included in this book are the voices of Wilmar Schaufeli, Georg Bauer, Ron Goetzel, Peter Cheese, Dave Ulrich, Jeffrey Pfeffer, Paul Litchfield, Susie Ellis, Els van der Helm, Arnold Bakker, and Jim Loehr.

While our names are on the cover, this book is the accomplishment of many people. There is a large team behind us, both at Wiley and Healthy Place to Work. Thank you to the editorial team at Wiley including Jeanenne Ray, Jozette Moses, and Michelle Hacker. This book began to take shape under the hands of Georgette Beatty, Lori Martinsek, and Vinolia Fernando. Peter Morris, TJ Byrne, Charles Fair, Doireann Gough, and Aideen Waters at Healthy Place to Work were instrumental in guiding our efforts, and we appreciate the effort of our many advisors and supporters including Michelle Ferrari and Angeles De Gyves, Jose Tolovi Jr., Maria Gruden and Eva Martin, Ian McCool, Malcolm Knox, David Cullen, Romulo Romero, Roy Cruz, and Stella Yulo. We would like to thank Na Fu from Trinity College and Professor Patrick Flood from Dublin City University. The Team at OGX including Peter Nicholson, Peter Paris, Senan Lynch, and Ailish Nicholson all played an important role in positioning, graphic development, and marketing support. Three other people deserve special thanks. Genoveva Llosa, a former editor at Wiley engaged with us early on and helped shape our initial thinking and approach to the book. Lisa Shannon, another former Wiley editor, provided invaluable feedback on our drafts. And finally and importantly, Ron Immink took our work to the next level and challenged us to be bolder in our messaging and approach; he made sure that we made consistent progress toward its completion. It proves the axiom that it really does take a village.

From John: I'd like to thank my wonderful wife Kelly, my son Dylan, daughters Amy and Hannah, and loyal dog Sammy, who patiently watched every keystroke from the bay window. To all my friends who listened to my thoughts about the process of writing a book! To all the people who shared their personal experience of working in toxic workplaces.

From Michael: I'd also like to thank my friends and colleagues who encourage me along the way including David Robrert, Heather Hackman, Annie Sinzinger, Lisa Ratner, Lisa Satawa, Drew Goldstein, my colleagues in the iCoach program that cheerleaded along the way, and my colleagues at Loeb Leadership, Dion Leadership, and the Droste Group for their encouragement and support. And thank you to my dad and brother, James Burchell and Daniel Burchell, who were always there with unconditional love and support.

About the Authors

JOHN RYAN

John Ryan is the founder and CEO of Healthy Place to Work. John established Healthy Place to Work to make a difference and improve employees' working lives by supporting organizations to focus on the health of their people as a strategic driver of organizational performance.

With over 25 years' experience consulting with organizations in a range of industries including pharmaceutical/medical devices, IT, energy, telecommunications, and professional services, John has a very hands-on approach to transformational change. A business graduate of Dublin City University, he initially followed his lifelong passion of radio and became a broadcast journalist, later transferring to a sales leadership and learning and development role in the Yellow Pages industry, which allowed him to support the development of many businesses exposing him to the challenges that entrepreneurs and CEOs were facing in their daily lives.

He has a particular passion for the public sector and working with the organizations delivering services to the public along with the not-for-profit sector. John is a former mayor of his town and county in Ireland.

John entered the human capital business initially as a transformation consultant working with a range of organizations including Allianz, EMC/Dell, Motorola, and BAE Systems later heading up the Great Place to Work Institute in the Republic of Ireland, where he led several transformation projects while achieving significant growth in revenues and brand.

John lives in Bray, Ireland. You can find out more about John at www.healthyplacetowork.com and on LinkedIn at https://www.linkedin.com/in/john-ryan-ireland/.

MICHAEL BURCHELL, EdD

Dr. Michael Burchell is an executive coach and independent consultant. Michael is an expert in human capital strategy and transformational change, and is the co-author of two previous books, *No Excuses: How You Can Turn Any Workplace into a Great One* (2013) and *The Great Workplace: How to Build It,*

How to Keep It, and Why It Matters (2011). He is a seasoned executive counselor in organizational effectiveness, including workplace culture change, employee engagement, diversity and inclusion, and human capital strategy.

Michael brings over 30 years of experience in post-secondary education, manufacturing, and workplace consulting. As an executive vice president at United Minds, group managing director for Great Place to Work®, and organization expert for McKinsey & Company, Michael has worked with leading global organizations in enhancing the employee experience through design, data, coaching, team development, and facilitation.

Michael holds degrees from the University of Southern California and Colorado State University and a doctorate degree from the University of Massachusetts Amherst in diversity and social justice eEducation, where his doctoral research focused on diversity and inclusion strategies in the L&D function.

Michael makes his home in Alexandria, Virginia. You can find out more about Michael at www.michaelburchell.com and on LinkedIn at https://www.linkedin.com/in/drmichaelburchell.

Index

Evelyn Waugh
and the
Modernist
Tradition

With a new introduction by the author

George McCartney

GW00481262

Transaction Publishers
New Brunswick (U.S.A.) and London (U.K.)

Second printing 2004

New material this edition copyright © 2004 by Transaction Publishers, New Brunswick, New Jersey. Originally published in 1987 by Indiana University Press.

Library of Congress Catalog Number: 2003060767
ISBN: 0-7658-0555-3
Printed in the United States of America

Library of Congress Cataloging-in-Publication Data

McCartney, George.
    [Confused roaring]
    Evelyn Waugh and the modernist tradition / George McCartney ; with a new introduction by the author.
        p. cm.
    Originally published: Confused roaring. Bloomington : Indiana University Press, 1987.
    Includes bibliographical references (p.) and index.
    ISBN 0-7658-0555-3 (alk. paper)
    1. Waugh, Evelyn, 1903-1966—Criticism and interpretation.   2. Modernism (Literature)—Great Britain. I. Title.

PR6045.A97Z735   2003
823' .912—dc22   2003060767

For Anne-Marie

CONTENTS

In Memory of Frank Brady
1924-1986

Formerly
Distinguished Professor of the Graduate School
And University Center of the City University of New York
And
Chairman of the Yale Boswell Editions

I remain indebted to Frank Brady for encouraging me to write this book. His support was invaluable; the loss, incurable.

INTRODUCTION TO THE TRANSACTION EDITION

Most would agree Evelyn Waugh was a satirist. His practice of the sardonic art, however, has puzzled many. His novels and essays do not conform to the traditional understanding of the genre. While they deploy satire's standard arsenal – wit, irony, ridicule, parody, caricature, and more – they conspicuously refrain from assessing behavior against traditionally accepted standards of morality and decorum. While reading a Waugh novel, we can hardly deny we're in the grip of a master satirist. Yet, when we close the book, it is not an easy matter to say what has been satirized. This may seem paradoxical, but the contradiction disappears if we alter our expectations regarding satire's purpose. A personal anecdote may help clarify this issue.

In his memoir, *Will This Do?*, Auberon Waugh reports a telling incident from his father's dining table. During the rationing mania following World War II, some British bureaucrats took notice of a recent shipment of bananas, a fruit that had been long absent from English diet at the time. Since the amount was limited, equitable distribution posed a difficulty. They decided the moral solution would be to provide every child in the realm with one banana. This meant three for the Waughs. "The great day arrived," Auberon recalls,

> when my mother came home with three bananas. All three were put on my father's plate, and before the anguished eyes of his children, he poured on cream, which was almost unprocurable, and sugar, which was heavily rationed, and ate all three. [1]

Was this an act of selfish gluttony or a lesson in the unforeseen consequences of good intentions? Ignoring this obvious and theoretically exculpatory question, Auberon instead declares he never again "treated anything [his father] had to say on faith or morals very seriously." Who could fault Auberon's decision? After all, we do not go to Waugh for preaching. We turn to him for his inexhaustible wit, his superb mastery of language, and, if we care for such things, his vision of human destiny in what seemed to him a culturally bankrupt world. You do not have to be

ix

decently fair-minded to deliver these goods; in fact, decency might have been an obstacle to Waugh's literary purposes. He certainly makes it seem an impediment in his fiction. His gallery of characters is comprised of decent but tepidly ineffectual bores, on one hand, and energetic rogues, on the other. The second group is forever besting the first in circumstances that either horrify or amuse us according to our respective sensitivities in such matters.

Putting aside sensitivity for the moment, it seems clear Waugh was after something deeper than traditional morality and religious conventions. He was taking aim at the philosophical premises on which moral codes and belief systems are founded, the assumptions generally left unexamined by all but theologians, philosophers, intellectuals, and, of course, satirists such as himself. He wanted to amuse his readers, certainly, but he also wanted to shake them from their slumbers. He was convinced the Western world they took for granted was standing on rotten pilings, infested by the misguided and irresponsible premises of contemporary intellectuals, especially those in the modernist camp. It is not surprising, then, that before all else his satire takes aim at these premises.

This, in short, is the primary contention of *Evelyn Waugh and the Modernist Tradition*. When it was first published in 1987, I had hoped it would demonstrate that Waugh's concerns continued to be ours. Re-reading it today, I can't help thinking that Waugh's preoccupations are even more pertinent than they were then or, for that matter, seventy years ago at the beginning of his career. I also wanted to make the case that his best novels were as original in style, structure, and thought as those of the modernist generation that had preceded his own and were, in fact, partially indebted to them. Although Waugh had little use for the philosophical assumptions implicit in the works of Virginia Woolf, James Joyce, and D.H. Lawrence, he clearly had gone to school to them. It seemed clear to me that he had consciously constructed an alternate modernism, one that took full account of the radical changes that were transforming so much of Western culture in the twentieth century. In a form of literary jiu-jitsu, Waugh appropriated many of the tactics of the modernist masters to refute their vision of a world liberated from traditional constraints. In novel after novel, Waugh portrayed the consequences of jettisoning the traditions that had created the society and culture of Western Europe since the collapse of the Roman Empire. While he had no illusions about preserving all that was so quickly being lost, he was convinced the core of the older order's sensibility would be retained. He believed it would become the cornerstone for whatever new edifice was being built by an increasingly technological society. While he could never be fully in sympathy with such a world, as a matter of faith he concluded it would have to be built on the Greek, Hebrew, and Christian past. Only this tradition, he reasoned, could guarantee a recognizably human future for our species.

While a note of despair frequently sounds in Waugh's writing, it is never without a chord of optimism, however muted. Some have read his 1946 novel, *Brideshead Revisited*, as a protracted dirge for the passing of the civilizing force of an aristocratic culture. But, read more closely, it turns out to be something quite different. True, its narrator, Charles Ryder, and, one can't help suspecting, its author, deplore the decline of the recusant Roman Catholic family who once flourished on the Brideshead estate. Ryder is especially appalled by the abuse their stately country seat must endure when the British army requisitions it to quarter three platoons during World War II. Nevertheless, the last scenes in the novel reveal something quite different and, ultimately, more important than a wealthy family's losses. While the courtyard and fountain outside the estate's private chapel may be littered with the sandwich wrappers and cigarette butts carelessly discarded by the bivouacking soldiers, inside these same working and middle class men dutifully pay respect to what is of infinitely greater moment than hallowed architecture. They are attending mass in the chapel where the tabernacle candle still burns in testimony to what Waugh believed to be central to European culture: the sacramental guarantee that God's Real Presence continues to work in history.

Not only the bread and wine of the mass, but also Brideshead Castle has a sacramental role to play. Although built to house an aristocratic family, it comes to provide shelter, physical and spiritual, to all classes. These scenes put to rest the canard that Waugh was an incurable snob sniveling about a lost golden age of aristocratic grandeur. Yes, he was undoubtedly guilty of fawning over his aristocratic friends, but this weakness made him all the more effective in writing about class privilege. Like F. Scott Fitzgerald, one of the few American authors he admired, his acquaintance with privilege made him one of its finest critics. More than this, his sense of history enabled him to see well beyond local customs and mores. Although thoroughly conservative, Waugh could entertain change with equanimity. In a short story "Out of Depth" (1932), he imagines a contemporary Londoner magically translated five centuries into the future. For reasons unspecified, English civilization has collapsed and the population has reverted to primitive life. As in the fourth century, Britain is once again under imperial rule. This time, however, the colonizing conquerors are African. In the story's last moments, the time-traveling protagonist is making his way through the resurgent wilderness that has overtaken London when he comes upon a "shape in chaos." It turns out to be a "log built church" in which "disheveled white men were staring ahead with vague, uncomprehending eyes to the end of the room where two candles burned. The priest turned towards them his bland, black face. 'Ite, missa est.'" This Latin closing to the mass is usually taken to mean more than simply, "Go, the mass is ended."[2] With the omission of "finita," the formula can be read to say, "Go, the mass is," suggesting the mass never ends, a reading that surely would have pleased Waugh who entered the Church because it stood for him as the only permanent "shape in chaos."

One doesn't have to be religious to recognize the power of such an allegiance to a theologically guaranteed still point. For Waugh, it provided a fixed vantage from which to put the turmoil of modern life into perspective. It is in his second novel, *Vile Bodies* (1930), that this nostalgia for permanence is first announced by Father Rothschild, an enigmatic Jesuit whose name links him to the famous Jewish family of financiers and philanthropists. Rothschild's Hebraic-Christian origins and his prodigious learning (he carries in his valise "six important new books in six languages") establish him as the embodiment of Western culture, a condition that duly deputizes him to assess contemporary events. It is his considered opinion that "our age suffers from an almost fatal hunger for permanence." [3] Seventy years on, who could doubt the justice of this analysis when so many seem so lost in the welter of a madly materialist culture driven by the twin values of wealth and power? This, in part, explains Waugh's continued popularity.

While Waugh has always been held in high regard in England, his fortunes in America have been less consistent. When I first took notice of his fiction thirty years ago, his American audience regarded him as a minor novelist with pronounced satiric tendencies. By the late 1980s, however, this judgment had begun to change. His name began to be invoked by people as ideologically divergent as John Kenneth Galbraith, William F. Buckley, Gore Vidal, and Barbara Bush. His reputation had regained the luster it enjoyed in the days when Edmund Wilson and Henry Luce found themselves in unwonted agreement on the merits of his work. His name appeared with surprising frequency as a touchstone in essays, book reviews, and even film criticism. By unspoken consent, "pure Waugh" became shorthand for describing ludicrously excessive behavior perpetrated by those in a position to know better.

What had happened? Several things I suspect. First, there were the sixties by which, of course, we mean the seventies, a time of unusual social change and cultural dislocation not unlike the 1920s and 1930s when Waugh began his writing career. The gracefully controlled anarchy of his works seems especially suited to such periods of confusion. Then there was the John Mortimer's television dramatization of *Brideshead Revisited*, Waugh's most popular novel although far from his own favorite. This was followed by Charles Sturridge's 1988 film adaptation of *A Handful of Dust*. Both dramatizations helped introduce Waugh to a wider audience than he had enjoyed previously.

Critical attention also began to grow. While most sympathetic commentators had a high regard for Waugh's work from the beginning, many had not taken its full measure. At mid-twentieth century, they had placed him somewhere above Graham Greene and Kingsley Amis, but nowhere in sight of James Joyce and Samuel Beckett. Others found his ideas ridiculously antiquated even as they marveled at his style and wit. It was generally agreed that whether you took Waugh seriously or not, he was a writer nearly everyone could enjoy. After all, how many others have the art to make their readers laugh out loud? Today these judgments have not been so much discounted as superceded. Critics and biographers have gathered momentum in their determination to establish Waugh in the first ranks of our Anglo-American literary tradition.

There are many reasons for this renewed critical and popular interest in Waugh but four seem especially prominent. First, he was always entertaining. This is why Waugh has never required the support of university required reading lists to maintain an audience. People do not read his books because they have to but, rather, because they want to. Second, Waugh is unquestionably one of the twentieth-century's master stylists. Third, his themes stand as a refreshingly acerbic rebuke to the received opinions of our time. Fourth, few writers have been as prescient.

As an entertainer, Waugh is peerless. Even in his minor pieces, he sets the standard to which others aspire. Here he is in a trifle of a short story entitled "Period Piece." The narrative concerns Lady Amelia, an elderly widow trained to refinement but inclined to vulgarity. She "had been educated in the belief that it was the height of impropriety to read a novel in the morning. Now, in the twilight of her days, when she had singularly little to occupy the two hours between her appearance downstairs at quarter past eleven, hatted and fragrant with lavender water, and the announcement of luncheon, she adhered rigidly to this principle." Once luncheon is over, however, she feels at liberty to indulge her recently acquired passion for American authors "in the school of brutal realism and gross slang." As her secretary reads to her in "delicately modulated tones . . . in a scarcely comprehensible idiom, the narratives of rape and betrayal, Lady Amelia occasionally chuckle[s] over her woolwork."[4] This juncture of delicacy and brutality is one of Waugh's signature strategies. He specialized in walking and frequently crossing the border between savagery and civilization, suggesting the demarcation had become hopelessly smudged in the modern era.

As for style, Waugh's was a supremely supple instrument capable of making whatever it touched indelibly memorable. In the opening pages of *Decline and Fall*, we are introduced to a pack of Oxford vandals with these sentences: "A shriller note could now be heard rising from Sir Alastair's rooms; any who have heard that sound will shrink at the recollection of it. It is the sound of county families baying for broken glass."[5] No less a stylist than Tom Wolfe has confessed to finding Waugh's lupine conceit irresistible. In *Bonfire of the Vanities* he borrows it to describe the 1980s frenzy on Wall Street as "the sound of well-educated young white men baying for money on the bond market."[6] In his 1946 preface to *When the Going Was Good*, a collection of his earlier travel writing, Waugh expressed his mock regret at not having stayed home to defend England from the encroaching "savagery" that he claimed to have invaded its shores. Like others of his generation – Graham Greene and Peter Fleming, to name two – he could not resist the lure of faraway places. "We turned our backs on civilization. Had we known, we might have lingered with 'Palinurus' (Cyril Connolly who refused to abandon home comforts); had we known that all that seeming-solid, patiently built, gorgeously ornamented structure of Western life was to melt overnight like an ice-castle, leaving only a puddle of mud; had we known man was even then leaving his post. Instead we set off on our various stern roads; I to the Tropics and the arctic, with the belief that barbarism was a dodo to be stalked with a pinch of salt."[7] The forty-seven-word second sentence of this eighty-five-word passage is built up with rococo intricacy as clause after clause is punctuated with the mock groans of regret in "had we known." The ice castle is especially well chosen with its suggestion of formidable skill and energy used to produce something fragile and fleeting. It cannot but become a "puddle of mud." (Not a mud puddle; that, of course, would have ruined the sentence's rhythm.) But the *coup de grace* comes with the equation of barbarism with a dodo. With an elegant reversal, Waugh establishes that far from extinct, barbarism flourishes vibrantly at home.

Then there is Waugh's notorious assault on contemporary pieties. Like his close friend Graham Greene, he harbored a congenital distrust of decency and innocence. This may explain why he wrote *The Loved One* in a manner calculated to offend the unsuspecting. The narrative concerns Dennis Barlow, an opportunistic British poet who has been sponging on his uncle's hospitality in the barbarous climes of Hollywood. He comes home one evening to what would be a thoroughly discomfiting surprise to anyone less self-absorbed.

> Never, it so happened had he seen a human corpse until that morning when, returning tired from night duty, he found his host strung to the rafters. The spectacle had been rude and momentarily unnerving; perhaps it had left a scar somewhere out of sight in his subconscious mind. But his reason accepted the event as part of the established order. Others in gentler ages had had their lives changed by such a revelation; to Dennis it was the kind of thing to be expected in the world he knew.

Although Dennis is a rotter of the first order, the narrative voice implies approval of the *sang froid* with which he greets his good uncle's demise. Note how Waugh strategically delays the revelation in this scene by injecting the otherwise pointless phrase "returning home from night duty" before springing the hard-boiled cliché of contemporary crime fiction. Gruesome as the scene is, Waugh manages to treat it with a detached, unflappable humor. After all, in the world we know, why wouldn't one string oneself from the rafters?

Last, Waugh's prescience. In ways he could not have foreseen fully, his fiction anticipated the return in the 1970s of the medieval argument between the realists and the nominalists. This was when fashionable literary critics began to embrace deconstruction theory and launched an attack on logocentric nostalgia which, they argued, naively assumed external reality corresponded to our representations of it. Jacques Derrida and his followers sought to subvert the common-sense assumption that language reports the world as it is and that we can therefore arrive at some reasonable understanding of the essential nature of things. This argument continues to embroil intellectuals today albeit with less urgency than it did, say, fifteen years ago. Still questions about language's transparency and the possibility of objective knowledge continue to bedevil us.

Waugh had detected this same dilemma in literary modernism. He was constitutionally averse to the apparent solipsism he sensed in Woolf and Joyce. It is not difficult, then, to imagine how he would have reacted to the neo-Kantian school of deconstruction and its descendants that were, until recently, regnant in academic literary studies. He would have had little patience with their contention that we are locked in a seamless web of linguistic signs and therefore cannot possibly know reality as it is in itself. Tony Last's fate in *A Handful of Dust* can be read as a proleptic parody of this position. At the novel's conclusion, Tony is punished with a peculiarly literary damnation for having turned his back on twentieth-century life and lived as though he were a nineteenth-century gentleman on his inherited estate. When modernity breaks into his Victorian dream, he hasn't the resources to combat its depredations. Instead, he tries to escape by fleeing to Brazil to pursue rumors of a lost city that has miraculously established and preserved civilized European values in the jungle. This gambit leads him with inexorable irony into the hands of Mr. Todd, an illiterate Amazonian of mixed Indian and European parentage who nurtures a sentimental taste for British literature. We last see Tony doomed to read the complete works of Charles Dickens to Mr. Todd again and again, endlessly. He finds himself permanently sealed in a wholly linguistic universe, indicting himself with the words of Dickens' dreamy simulacrum of the Victorian life to which he was once so thoroughly committed.

Waugh's position regarding objective truth can be divined in a letter he sent to George Orwell in 1949. He had just finished reading *1984* and wanted Orwell to know how much he enjoyed it. He did, however, have a reservation. "I think your metaphysics are wrong." He went on to point out that by denying the reality of the soul, the narrative's protagonist, Winston Smith, in effect surrenders in advance to the dehumanizing ethos of the narrative's ruling government.[8] It seems evident that Waugh was questioning Orwell's epistemology as well as his metaphysics for *1984* turns on a fundamental epistemological question: what we can know of reality with certainty? Coincidentally enough, Waugh was at work on *Helena*, a narrative that, in its own way, was interrogating the same issue.

Both Orwell and Waugh were committed to exposing the destructive effects of modern thought, especially when it expresses itself as a ruthless relativism ready to liquefy objective truth in the solvent of expedience. This is why the protagonists of both novels undertake desperate struggles to establish standards of objectivity with which to judge assertions of truth. Both Winston Smith and Helena seek some principle that can guarantee there is a reality independent of the mind. They both sense that without grounds for such a conviction, those in power will inevitably package truth to fit their own designs.

In *1984*, Orwell pushes the tendencies of contemporary relativistic thought to their limits and reveals the consequences of believing in nothing. To paraphrase G.K. Chesterton, he exposes the danger of losing one's faith in a knowable world outside the mind. It is not that one will believe in nothing, but rather that one is liable to believe in anything. In Orwell's totalitarian state, this is precisely what is required of the citizenry. They are expected to pass the test of indiscriminate faith. They must believe in what they know to be false. Not just pretend, but believe it unreservedly. This is an exercise in mental gymnastics Orwell famously named doublethink.

The government that can get its people to doublethink perfectly, to give full-hearted endorsement to what they know to be incontestably false, has, in effect, destroyed the grounds of intellectual and moral dissent in advance. In such a state of epistemological incoherence, the individual loses the fulcrum of objective truth. There is nothing on which to exert the lever of personal conviction against officially sanctioned lies. When Winston Smith is apprehended, he's put through sustained brainwashing designed to make his mind "perfect." Part of the process requires that he deny fundamental mathematics. When O'Brien, Winston's torturer-cum-father-confessor, proposes that two plus two equal five, he is not satisfied when Winston acquiesces to the absurdity. He demands that Winston *believe* the sum is five. "Only the disciplined mind can see reality, Winston," O'Brien explains. "You believe that reality is something objective, external, existing in its own right. . . . But I tell you, Winston, that reality is not external. Reality exists in the human mind, and nowhere else. Not in the individual mind, which can make mistakes, and in any case soon perishes; only in the mind of the Party, which is collective and immortal. Whatever the Party holds to be truth *is* truth." When Winston protests that this is nonsense, O'Brien calmly demurs. He points out reasonably that whatever happens outside the mind is unknowable and whatever happens within is fully controllable. "We make the laws of nature," he boasts. "Reality is inside the skull. . . . There is nothing that we could not do. Invisibility, levitation — anything. I could float off this floor like a soap bubble if I wished to." Without an objective standard to appeal to, Winston flails about to regain his intellectual footing. "The belief that nothing exists outside your own mind — surely there must be some way of demonstrating that it was false?" When he desperately insists that "there is something in the universe — I don't know, some spirit, some principle — that you will never overcome," O'Brien asks, "Do you believe in God?" Winston doesn't. "Then what is it, this principle that will defeat us," O'Brien demands. "I don't know," Winston replies, appealing vaguely to "the spirit of Man." The novel's bleak ending does not make this seem an effective recourse. [9]

It is typical of Orwell's integrity that he did not make things easy for himself. Elsewhere he had argued cogently that belief in absolutes, whether God or political ideology, diminishes the individual human being. Yet, in *1984*, he displayed the individual's vulnerability in a world stripped of any fixed coordinates external to the mind. In such a world, power, not impartial inquiry, must always be the final arbiter of truth. O'Brien's arguments are eerily similar to those being promoted by many intellectuals today.

Unlike Orwell, Waugh did believe in absolutes. In *Helena* he openly marshals them to defeat O'Brien's claim that reality is purely a mental affair. The narrative retells the story of St. Helena (c. 255 – 330), mother of Constantine, alleged to have found the True Cross in Jerusalem.

Helena is presented as a plainspoken woman. She is constitutionally unreceptive to intellectuals who delight in speculation for its own sake, refusing to commit themselves to any definite principles. Her tutor, Marcias, is such an intellectual. A eunuch who has become a professional Gnostic, he lectures on the mystery religions. At the end of a presentation on the significance of the fertility goddess, Astarte, Helena demands, "When and where did all this happen?" Marcias dismisses her question as childish. "These things are beyond time and space." Helena is not so easily put off. "It's all bosh," she finally concludes, turning her back on Marcias' vaporous speculations. Marcias is portrayed as an irresponsible intellectual -- a clever, talented man, obviously sophisticated and well read, but without convictions, a type that appears frequently in Waugh's novels. At bottom, he cares little for the consequences of his teachings except as they help or hinder his career. When things become at all difficult, he simply retreats into his mind, "sailing free and wide in the void he made his chilly home." He is as sterile intellectually as he is physically. [10]

As Helena recoiled from the mystery cults of her time, so Waugh rebelled against what he took to be the subtle evasions of modern thought. Either there was a truth to be found or there was none at all. Either the human mind could discern a purpose to existence or life was meaningless. For Waugh there was no middle ground.

In telling the tale of Helena's discovery of the True Cross, Waugh was testifying to his conviction that we are meant to discover our purpose in and through the ordinary world of the senses. To put it another way, he believed physical reality was sacramental. When Helena undertakes her mission, she has no interest in theological speculation, nor does she care for the subtle distinctions of Christian dogmas. Her search is not intellectually inward, but sensibly outward. Her vindication is to be achieved not by retreating from but rather by engaging with the ordinary world. She is convinced that once she finds the "solid chunk of wood"[11] on which Christ was crucified, she will have also reached a crucial intersection of time and eternity, thought and being. This plain, homely artifact will prove that the external world responds to our longing for meaning and certainty. If she is right, then our minds' representations, from the most pedestrian to the most sophisticated, even those that are misshapen or entirely mistaken, can never be wholly futile. They arise from our interaction with the meaningful reality that surrounds us. As such, our perceptions and thoughts always carry with them revelatory potential. Waugh was convinced that viewed correctly daily experience did nothing less than inform us, however imperfectly, of our purpose as created beings.

Helena's mission, then, speaks of Waugh's belief that in the beginning was the Word and the Word was made flesh, which is to say, in the argot of current literary criticism, that the original sign and its referent were one and the same. It followed for Waugh that, however uncertainly and fleetingly, all subsequent words must have the power to put us in touch with the real presence of reality's eternal being, no matter how confusing our day-to-day experiences. Truth was to be located neither in the mind nor the world but rather at their fruitful intersection. In his opinion, this homely position was enough to explode the lures of contemporary gnosticisms, including a good deal of modernist fiction.

It need hardly be said that many do not find Waugh's religious convictions congenial, including many in his own church. This makes his current return to popularity all the more intriguing. Whatever one thinks of his answers, he was raising the right questions and they continue to speak to our current anxieties. What can we know with certainty? How can we achieve a moral consensus without an appeal to absolute principles? Are we, as the neo-Kantian schools suggest, trapped in the web of our own semiology, forever uncertain about the nature of external reality? And, if so, can there be any sound reasons to refrain from scrapping traditional concepts altogether and refashioning human nature to meet the political exigencies of the day?

We might enlist the services of a recent United States president to help clarify the issue. Asked whether his assertions were true or not, William Clinton famously evaded the question. "It depends," he allowed, "on what the meaning of 'is' is." There can be little doubt this remark says more than President Clinton intended. It sounds, not unsurprisingly, very much like the kind of subtle distinction prized by one or another school of contemporary critical thought. As O'Brien demonstrated for Winston, once the notion of objective truth is surrendered, we have entered into a species of relativism that allows reality to be fashioned to the needs of the moment. Thus it becomes increasingly difficult to question the "truth" devised by powerful institutions or, for that matter, powerful individuals.

One doesn't have to subscribe to Waugh's beliefs to appreciate the importance of his literary purpose. His resistance to the philosophical implications of modernist thought is undeniably tonic to a time when so many find it so difficult to distinguish between the genuine and the bogus in human affairs.

Notes

1. Auberon Waugh, *Will This Do?* (New York: Carroll & Graf, 1998, 1991), p. 67.
2. Evelyn Waugh, "Out of Depth," *The Complete Stories of Evelyn Waugh* (Boston: Little, Brown), pp.138 – 39.
3. *Vile Bodies*, pp. 1, 183.
4. "Period Piece," *The Complete Stories of Evelyn Waugh*, p. 149.
5. *Decline and Fall*, p. 2.
6. Tom Wolfe, *The Bonfire of the Vanities* (New York: Farrar, Straus, Giroux, 1987), p.57. Wolfe cheerfully confirmed his borrowing from Waugh in correspondence with me.
7. *When the Going Was Good* (Harmondsworth: Penguin, 1946, 1968), p. 8
8. *The Letters of Evelyn Waugh* (New York: Ticknor & Fields, ed. Mark Amory, 1980), p. 302.
9. George Orwell, *1984* (New York: New American Library, 1981, 1949), pp. 205, 218-22.
10. *Helena*, pp. 121, 9.
11. Helena, p. 196.

ACKNOWLEDGMENTS

I would like to express my gratitude to the people and institutions who made it possible for me to write the book that follows. There is first my mentor, David Gordon of the Graduate School and University Center of the City University of New York, who assisted me in writing the dissertation from which this study grew. His editorial advice and patient encouragement were invaluable. Without them, I would not have been able to complete the first phase of my project.

Robert Day, Irving Howe, Alfred Kazin, and Michael Timko also read the dissertation, contributing important insights, which I hope I have been able to incorporate successfully into the book.

I owe debts of gratitude to the American Council of Learned Societies and the National Endowment for the Humanities for the financial assistance that permitted me to take fifteen months leave from my teaching duties and put the manuscript into its final shape. It was during this time that I had the pleasure of visiting the Humanities Research Center at the University of Texas in Austin. While there I was graciously assisted by Cathy Henderson and her staff in my research of the center's Evelyn Waugh holdings. Later the same year, I traveled to London, where I was able to draw upon the resources of the British Museum; I also had the honor of meeting Auberon Waugh, who was good enough to clarify a number of issues regarding his father's life and career.

I also wish to thank the people at my school, St. John's University, who assisted me. Dorothy Canner's word processing staff typed my drafts with care and dispatch. My chairman, Jack Franzetti, listened, sympathized, and gave of his time to write letters and memoranda on my behalf. And, finally, I owe a special debt of gratitude to Dean Catherine Ruggieri of St. Vincent's College on whose faculty I teach. Her unfailing support and generous vision have opened more than a few doors for me.

Portions of the first three chapters appeared in *The American Spectator* 18 (January 1985). I thank Wladyslaw Pleszczynski, the *Spectator*'s managing editor, for permitting me to reprint this material.

TEXT CITATIONS

Quotations from Waugh's works generally come from the Little, Brown edition (see Selected Bibliography). The works are identified in the text by title and the quotations are cited by page numbers in parentheses. Wherever a reference might be ambiguous, I have included a title abbreviation with the page reference as follows:

CRSD *Charles Ryder's Schooldays and Other Stories*
LO *The Loved One*
MAA *Men at Arms*

INTRODUCTION

Although Evelyn Waugh rarely missed an opportunity to flaunt his traditionalism, he was not a traditional satirist. If conventional satire seeks to
correct morals and manners, then his work clearly does not conform to the
genre. What can the moralist make of the world Paul Pennyfeather and
Margot Metroland inhabit, a world in which decent people are invariably
boring and the wicked consistently charming? When critics try to evaluate
Waugh's novels in terms of moral satire, they either give up the effort, deciding there is no coherent purpose to be discovered, or reduce the works
to a formula that inevitably fails to account for their anarchic vitality.[1] As
for Waugh himself, he flatly denied he was writing satire at all. The genre,
he argued, "flourishes in a stable society and presupposes homogeneous
moral standards. . . . It exposes polite cruelty and folly by exaggerating
them. It seeks to produce shame. All this has no place in the Century of the
Common Man where vice no longer pays lip service to virtue."[2]

Of course, this disclaimer is probably best understood as Waugh's con-
summate satiric ploy. Whether or not it was meant as such, it does reveal
his primary concern: the bankruptcy of a civilization unable or unwilling to
sustain its commitment to the metaphysical principles that had made moral
distinctions possible in the first place. If Waugh is to be considered within
the genre at all, it must first be said that his satiric objective was not moral
but metaphysical and it is on this ground that his work achieves its consistency of purpose. Lapses in conduct, however outrageous, were never his
preoccupation, though frequently his delight. He fully expected people
would behave badly with or without moral standards and had no hesitation
in admitting his own failings. Nor did he think his century any less moral
than those that had preceded it. In his view, the real issue was the general
disillusionment with the notion of absolutes, whether moral or metaphysical. After the tragic wastefulness of the Great War, "the standards of civilization" had come into question. Their legitimacy, he complained, no
longer seemed self-evident. Instead of submitting to their "rigid discipline," people were inclined to cultivate "a jolly tolerance of everything
that seemed modern."[3] For Waugh, this amounted to a profoundly dis-
piriting dereliction that could only serve to undermine the intellectual resolve necessary to maintain civilized order. "It is better to be

narrow-minded," he reasoned, "than to have no mind, to hold limi
rigid principles than none at all."[4]

Waugh's first novel loudly demonstrates the consequences of tolerating
a mindless lack of principles. It opens and closes with the "confused roaring" raised by the sons of England's ruling families "baying for broken
glass" as they carouse through Oxford's colleges destroying every symbol
of art and learning they come upon.[5] Their behavior goes conspicuously
unchecked by the university's authorities who have chosen instead to hide
in their darkened rooms. Such is the modern world, Waugh implies, where
willful energy, lacking the discipline of a self-assured moral intelligence
founded upon inarguable principles, expresses itself resentfully in random
acts of destruction.

The one constant in Waugh's fiction is his portrayal of what happens to
a society that disregards the metaphysical coordinates which had once
given it a sense of purpose. This was a condition he thought especially apparent in the contemporary enthusiasms for experimental art and technological innovation. He read both as symptoms of a general decline into an
aimless pursuit of the new. The prospect might be enticing, but it was
nonetheless futile. It only excited a boundless appetite for fashion that deserved the ridicule he was glad to heap on it.

For all his disapproval, however, Waugh's response to the modern was
marked by certain fruitful ambivalence. In his official pose he was the cur-
mudgeon who despised innovation, but the anarchic artist in him frequently delighted in its formal and thematic possibilities. He was never
quite the scourge of the new he pretended to be, though he did work on
the role.

Writing of himself in the third person in his autobiographical novel, *The
Ordeal of Gilbert Pinfold*, he announced that his "strongest tastes were
negative. He abhorred plastics, Picasso, sunbathing and jazz—everything
in fact that had happened in his own lifetime" (p. 11).[6] He went to a good
deal of effort and expense to remove himself from the world that featured
these abominations. At the age of thirty-four, this once intensely urban so-
cialite set up house in the West Country far from London where he could
ostentatiously turn his back on modernity in all its guises. When he began
to lose his hearing in later life, he was pleased to transform his affliction
into an emblem of his chosen isolation. Instead of an efficient battery-run
hearing aid, he carried about a comically oversized Victorian ear trumpet,
wielding it with blatant buffoonery as if he wanted to visually dramatize his
inability to hear what the world had to say to him. But, for all his advertised
disgust with contemporary developments, he kept remarkably informed
about them. Throughout his writing career we find him addressing modern
art, functional architecture, photography, and film—"everything in fact

that had happened in his own lifetime." As a young man he rode motorcycles, flew with a stunt pilot, produced a film in which he co-starred with
Elsa Lanchester, and commuted to Paris by plane. During the war, he volunteered for commando service, reporting later that his parachute training
was particularly exhilarating even if he did break his leg on his first jump.
For all his country-squire affectations, Waugh was very much a man of his
century.

It has too often been assumed that Waugh was a sharper-tongued Wode-
house, a more substantial Firbank, or, to borrow Sean O'Faolain's formula,
"a purely brainless genius, with a gift for satire," who created his own idiosyncratic world redolent of Edwardian nostalgia.[7] A closer reading suggests he had far more in common with modernists like Wyndham Lewis
and T.S. Eliot. Like them he was keenly interested in the peculiarities of
life in the twentieth century. True, he was never comfortable in this century. But it is hard to imagine him at home in any other. He certainly had
little love for the nineteenth. In novel after novel, he ridicules those of his
characters who try to go on living as though the Great War had never happened, as though the achievement of true happiness were only a matter of
perpetuating the attitudes and values of the previous age. He portrays
their world to be as laughably fraudulent as Llanabba Castle in *Decline and
Fall*, an ordinary enough nineteenth-century country house the front of
which has been made over to give it the appearance of venerable antiquity.
This was the work of an enterprising mill owner who could not abide his
workers' enforced idleness during the "cotton famine" caused by the
American Civil War. Believing in enlightened self-interest and having
nothing better to do with his employees, he had them build a "formidably
feudal" facade for his home enhanced by "at least a mile of machicolated
wall" and gates that are "towered and turreted and decorated with heral-
dic animals and a workable portcullis" (p. 18). Under the circumstances,
the labor was cheap and the results charmingly Gothic. It was just this sort
of blend of pragmatism and sentimentality for which the nineteenth century stood indicted in Waugh's mind. It was guilty of exploiting a cultural
past for its purely decorative value, while neglecting its moral and metaphysical implications.

When this kind of travesty of tradition provoked Waugh to satiric attack,
he often found his appropriate weapon among the artifacts peculiar to the
twentieth century he professed to despise. He was vividly instructed in this
strategy while at Oxford, if not earlier. In his travel book *Labels* (1930), he
recalls how stunt flying could unsettle secular assumptions to salutary
effect.

> During what proved to be my last term at Oxford, an ex-officer of the R.A.F.

appeared in Port Meadow with a very dissolute-looking Avro biplane, and advertised passenger flights for seven and six-pence or fifteen shillings for "stunting." On a very serene summer evening I went for a "stunt flight." It was a memorable experience. Some of the movements merely make one feel dizzy, but "looping the loop" develops in the mind clearly articulated intellectual doubts of all preconceived habits of mind about matter and movement. . . . In "looping," the aeroplane shoots steeply upwards until the sensation becomes unendurable and one knows that in another moment it will turn completely over. One looks down into an unfathomable abyss of sky, while over one's head a great umbrella of fields and houses have suddenly opened. Then one shuts one's eyes. My companion on this occasion was a large-hearted and reckless man; he was President of the Union, logical, matter-of-fact in disposition, inclined towards beer and Ye Olde Merrie Englande, with a marked suspicion and hostility towards modern invention. He had come with me in order to assure himself that it was really all nonsense about things heavier than air being able to fly. He sat behind me throughout, muttering, "Oh, my God, oh, Christ, oh, my God." On the way back he scarcely spoke, and two days later, without a word to anyone, he was received into the Roman Church. It is interesting to note that, during this aeroplane's brief visit to Oxford, three cases of conversion occurred in precisely similar circumstances. I will not say that this aeronaut was directly employed by Campion House, but certainly, when a little later, he came down in flames, the Jesuits lost a good ally, and to some people it seemed as if the Protestant God had asserted supremacy in a fine Old Testament manner.[8]

Despite the cool irony of his tone, Waugh cannot conceal the enthusiasm he takes in reporting this innovative approach to evangelizing. He clearly approves. After all, this is no world in which to be comfortable. We should be reminded of its fundamental strangeness, its endless capacity for betraying human expectations. If an improbable feat of aeronautical daring accomplished this purpose, there was every reason to commend it. The airplane became an important element in Waugh's imagination, appearing time and again in his fiction usually as an adjunct to some abrupt revelation or disaster. Often both at once. Nothing served so well to dramatize modernity's assault on conventional attitudes. In 1951, according to Christopher Sykes, Waugh commissioned a painting by Richard Eurich depicting the interior of a plane's passenger cabin. The occupants are portrayed in a way that makes it unmistakably clear the plane is about to crash. "Every possible detail contributing to horror and irony was included at Evelyn's insistence." When Sykes wondered if visitors were shocked by it, Waugh replied, "I hope so."[9]

Waugh took a perverse delight in discomfiting the complacent. This was modernism's special value to him. Like stunt flying, it turned the ordinary world upside down, giving one a glimpse of the abyss guaranteed to unsettle everything one had taken for granted. Although he seems to have become increasingly reluctant to admit it as he grew older, the young Waugh found in modern art the kind of derisive but liberating iconoclasm Ortega y Gasset had applauded for its power to clear away the conventional esthetic pieties that only served to obscure one's view of the world as it was after 1914. Waugh might not have liked what was revealed—the metaphysical emptiness, the abdication of reason, the aimless pursuit of sensation—but he preferred to look at the disease rather than hide behind a facade of nineteenth-century reasonableness pretending nothing had changed.

It was more than fashionable cleverness that led him to make a functional architect of the Bauhaus school the cranky moral center of his first novel. Otto Silenus announces a specifically modernist critique of the nineteenth-century humanism Waugh detested for its deluding sentimentality. Silenus is convinced that "all ill comes from man" and, consequently, "the problem of all art [is] the elimination of the human element from the consideration of form" (p. 159). When he is commissioned to replace an aristocrat's sixteenth-century home with "something clean and square" (p. 156), he constructs a new residence in ferro concrete and aluminum to achieve an industrial look, explaining that "the only perfect building must be the factory, because that is built to house machines, not men" (p. 159). Besides, man "is never happy except when he becomes the channel for the distribution of mechanical forces" (p. 159). Like D. H. Lawrence's futurist artist, Loerke, in *Women in Love*, Silenus gladly subordinates his art to the contemporary spirit of commercial expedience. Yet he is not a hack; he has not sold out in any usual sense. In fact, he displays a certain perverse integrity in his determination to express the ruling passion of his age honestly, regardless of its dehumanizing consequences. Whatever else it accomplished, Waugh suggests, modernism unapologetically confronted its audience with the sour truth of the twentieth century's streamlined transience in which traditions are swept away as soon as they prove inconvenient and present arrangements sustained only as long as they are profitably functional.

Late in his career, Waugh testified to his involvement with contemporary experimental art. Writing of his vocation, he stated that "the artist, however aloof he holds himself, is always and specially the creature of the Zeitgeist."[10] It was his complicated response to modernism, the Zeitgeist of his formative years, that imparted a distinctive shape and energy to his fiction. At every turn, his writing pays parodic tribute to modernist art and literature. Although he deplored many of the movement's aims, he nevertheless admired its methods, borrowing them freely whenever it suited his purpose to do so. Like Wyndham Lewis, he developed an alternate modernism. Whether it was his playful handling of Nietzschean and Bergsonian themes, his ironic reworking of Bauhaus and Futurist theories, or his borrowings from film technique, Waugh gave every evidence that he was consciously taking his place in what he called "the advance guard" despite his notoriously "antique" tastes.[11]

Waugh's ambivalent reaction to modern art and thought was part of a larger pattern. He was one of those artists who thrive on contradiction. Although he declared himself committed to the "standards of civilization," he was unmistakably intrigued by savagery.[12] He prized rationality, but could never entirely resist the lure of anarchy. This is why he was at once fascinated and repelled by modernism's assault on conventional expectations. It spoke to him of the anarchic impulse he alternately indulged and resisted in himself. Much of his work sprang from his sustained and animated argument with what he perceived to be the excesses of the avant-garde. It was through this argument that he confronted what was at best an uneasy truce and at worst a volatile standoff between his orthodox and wayward selves, transfiguring his private struggles so that they represented the characteristic tensions of his time. Accordingly, our consideration of Waugh's interest in modernism begins with this uneasy truce, expressed in his fiction as a comically disabling severance of intellect from will.

I

CONFUSED ROARING

Evelyn Waugh's first novel, *Decline and Fall,* begins with a lopsided struggle between order and energy. Paul Pennyfeather, a thoroughly civilized theology student who has spent his first twenty years living within the "preconceived bounds of order and propriety," finds himself suddenly overwhelmed by the "confused roaring" of the tumultuous Bollinger Club, an improbable gathering of unruly aristocrats whose only organizational purpose is to celebrate their annual dinner as drunkenly and destructively as they possibly can. Their revelry has become fully frenzied when Paul chances to meet them on the college quad. It is a fateful encounter that will alter radically the reasonable course of his prudently managed life. Waugh anticipates their meeting by juxtaposing two carefully constructed scenes: in one the revelers rave wantonly through the night; in the other Paul carries on in his meticulously disciplined fashion.

> A shriller note could now be heard rising from Sir Alastair's rooms; any who have heard that sound will shrink at the recollection of it; it is the sound of the English county families baying for broken glass. Soon they would all be tumbling out into the quad, crimson and roaring in their bottle-green evening coats, for the real romp of the evening. . . . It was a lovely evening. They broke up Mr. Austen's grand piano, and stamped Lord Rending's cigars into his carpet, and smashed his china, and tore up Mr. Partridge's sheets, and threw the Matisse into his water jug; Mr. Sanders had nothing to break except his windows, but they found the manuscript at which he had been working for the Newdigate Prize Poem, and had great fun with that.

As the Bollingers proceed with their ceremonies of destruction, Paul approaches the quad unawares.

> Paul Pennyfeather was reading for the Church. It was his third year of uneventful residence at Scone. He had come there after a creditable career at a small public school of ecclesiastical temper on the South Downs, where he had edited the magazine, been President of the Debating Society, and had, as his report said, "exercised a wholesome influence for good" in the House of which he was head boy. At home he lived in Onslow Square with his guardian, a prosperous solicitor who was proud of his progress and abys-

8

mally bored by his company. Both his parents had died in India at the time when he won the essay prize at his preparatory school. For two years he had lived within his allowance, aided by two valuable scholarships. He smoked three ounces of tobacco a week—John Cotton, Medium—and drank a pint and a half of beer a day, the half at luncheon and the pint at dinner, a meal he invariably ate in Hall. He had four friends, three of whom had been at school with him. None of the Bollinger Club had ever heard of Paul Penny-feather, and he, oddly enough, had not heard of them. Little suspecting the incalculable consequences that the evening was to have for him, he bicycled happily back from a meeting of the League of Nations Union. There had been a most interesting paper about plebiscites in Poland. He thought of smoking a pipe and reading another chapter of the *Forsyte Saga* before going to bed. (pp. 2–5)[1]

With the confrontation that follows, Waugh announced what was to be his major theme. All his subsequent work grows out of an irreconcilable opposition between energetic willfulness and effete reasonableness, here represented by the barbarous Bollingers and the overly civilized Paul Pennyfeather respectively.

Despite their aristocratic pedigrees, the Bollingers both in appearance and behavior are a rabble of yahoos. The language describing them has been chosen carefully to suggest their degenerate natures. They number in their ranks "epileptic royalty from their villas of exile; uncouth peers from crumbling country seats; smooth young men of uncertain tastes from embassies and legations; illiterate lairds from wet granite hovels in the Highlands; ambitious young barristers and Conservative candidates torn from the London season and the indelicate advances of debutantes." The "sonorous of name and title" are epileptic, uncouth, illiterate, uncertain, and torn; they come from crumbling homes and squalid hovels. Together they comprise the force of primitive disorder let loose once more upon an unsuspecting world.

The ruling class may have turned against civilization, but Paul Pennyfeather has not noticed their treason. Until he crosses their path, his own commitment to civilized values remains unshaken, although, like many another of Waugh's well-intentioned, well-bred young men of the middle class, he has only the dimmest notion of the principles on which these values have been built, principles that have been carelessly set aside by those in power. Reading Galsworthy's *Forsyte Saga* in measured installments, Paul is absorbed in the Edwardian dream of an ordered, benevolently progressive world achieved and maintained by prudence and industry. His carefully managed life of hard, steady work relieved by precisely measured indulgences—three ounces of tobacco a week, a pint and a half of beer each day—testifies to his nineteenth-century middle class faith that moderation is the way to a better life. Because he is a man convinced that the course of events is amenable to reason, he attends the League of Nations Union and takes serious interest in Polish plebiscites. But when he runs afoul of the Bollingers, the irrational invades his measured life, changing it "incalculably." He finds himself thrust from his predictable existence into boundless possibility. From a world established on a set of reasonable assumptions, he tumbles into a state of unmanageable turbulence. Among the Bollingers he discovers that the civilized distinctions he has always taken for granted suddenly and unaccountably lose their power to organize experience.

> Out of the night Lumsden of Strathdrummond swayed across his path like a druidical rocking stone. Paul tried to pass. Now it so happened that the tie of Paul's old school bore a marked resemblance to the pale blue and white of the Bollinger Club. The difference of a quarter of an inch in the width of the stripes was not one that Lumsden of Strathdrummond was likely to appreciate. "Here's an awful man wearing the Boller tie," said the Laird. It is not for nothing that since pre-Christian times his family has exercised chieftainship over uncharted miles of barren moorland. (p. 5)

Acting as chief over uncharted wasteland is not likely to encourage an aptitude for fine discriminations. Civilized distinctions—that quarter-inch difference in the tie's stripe—can no longer defend against the muddled barbarians. And rightly so, we are made to feel. Those who make the distinctions appear pallid when put up against the robust revelry of those drunk with the vitality of experience unmediated and therefore uncontaminated by conventional preconceptions.

Set upon by the Bollingers, Paul is promptly engulfed in their "kaleidoscope of dimly discernible faces" (p. 2). The individual committed to standards of social and esthetic order is submerged by the anonymous horde intent upon destroying form and harmony. The Bollingers are natural enemies of disciplined order, as demonstrated by their destruction of the grand piano, the Matisse, and the manuscript. The uniqueness of his identity already compromised by Lumsden's confusion about his tie, Paul then suffers the removal of his trousers and is sent scurrying across the college quad, his common humanity clearly exposed. For this "flagrantly indecent" (p. 7) behavior, he is sent down while the Bollingers are merely fined. Paul's "guilt" in this matter is compounded by his inability to meet the stiff fines the college authorities expect men of character to pay for their escapades. Once Paul's limited financial means have been ascertained, the college's Master lets it be known that his is "not the conduct we expect of a scholar. . . . That sort of young man does the College no good" (p. 7). Expelled from his scholarly retreat, Paul must confront the "real world" for the first time. There he is whirled from one outrage to the next, first becoming a marginal schoolmaster at a wildly negligent institution for demonstrably ineducable boys, then nearly marrying an aristocratic white slaver, next going to jail for unwittingly assisting her criminal schemes, and finally escaping his imprisonment by feigning death so that he can return to his theological studies at Scone College disguised as his own cousin. Paul's movements establish a circular pattern Waugh returns to in many of his novels.[2] It might be described as a decline from the decorum of a genteel life into the "confused roaring" of modern primitivism, a fall from the vantage point of orderly perception into a welter of promiscuous sensations that finally sends naive victims such as Paul scrambling to regain the protection of their earlier cloister.

The ease with which savagery supplants civilization in Waugh's twentieth century is largely due to a general abdication of authority. It seems those putatively in charge lack the will to impose the order they represent. Paul's brief encounter with the Bollingers is witnessed by Mr. Sniggs, the college's Junior Dean, and Mr. Postlethwaite, the Domestic Bursar, who prudently remain in their rooms throughout the evening's commotion with their lights off, the better to avoid any possible confrontation with the revelers. When Mr. Sniggs notices Paul approaching the host of celebrants, he mistakes him for Lord Rending and anxiously wonders whether they should do something to protect the young nobleman from injury. But Mr. Postlethwaite will have none of it.

> "No, Sniggs," said Mr. Postlethwaite, laying a hand on his impetuous colleague's arm. "No, no, no. It would be unwise. We have the prestige of the senior common room to consider. In their present state they might not prove amenable to discipline. We must at all costs avoid an *outrage*." (p. 6)

Both officials are greatly relieved when they discover the Bollingers' victim is only Paul Pennyfeather, an untitled individual of no account. In a lawless world there is little profit in defending the weak.

Having abandoned their commitment to civility, the administrators only concern themselves with their own protection and enrichment. The world has turned barbarous again, Waugh suggests, because the delegated custodians of civilized values have neither the courage nor the conviction necessary to their task. But the problem of authority goes much further than a cowardly bureaucracy. Sniggs and Postlethwaite are only the symptoms of the general failure of society to sustain a convincing rational order. The Bollingers overwhelm Paul not so much because these officials refuse to intervene on his behalf, but rather because, without any genuine conviction to support it, his dreary reasonableness cannot stand up to their drunken enthusiasm. "Paul had no particular objection to drunkenness—he had

read rather a daring paper to the Thomas More Society on the subject—
but he was consumedly shy of drunkards" (p. 5). Paul can entertain the
idea of drunkenness, but he has no stomach for the breathing, brawling
drunkard. It is precisely this disjunction between idea and experience that
fascinated Waugh. In his novels, actuality always proves too slippery and
upsetting for the intellectual categories that had once seemed to make
sense of it. Until meeting the Bollingers, Paul had been protected by the
intellectual environment of his college, an environment that seemed to respect the importance of ideas. But once actuality invades, these ideas
prove ineffectual either because they are bankrupt in themselves or because the people who officially subscribe to them do so without conviction.

Waugh's is a polarized world in which thought and desire have gone
their separate ways; with few exceptions, everyone ignores what once was
thought to be the civilizing struggle between reason and feeling. As a result, people have become either hopelessly prudent or heedlessly impulsive. Some retreat into nostalgic cloisters of intellectual order untested by
worldly events, while others plunge into the flux of immediate experience
unconcerned with tiresome metaphysical questions about meaning and
purpose. Neither group is quite human.

To explain this rift between intellect and will, Waugh introduces Otto
Silenus, the wonderfully gloomy German architect whose avant-garde design theories parody those of the 1920s Bauhaus movement. A philosopher
of sorts, Silenus carries the mock argument of the narrative on his unlikely
shoulders and in so doing introduces a wild pastiche of popular intellectu-
alizing that serves Waugh's purposes as both parody and illumination.

Silenus has discovered a difference in human nature more fundamental
than gender: "Instead of this absurd division into sexes they ought to class
people as static and dynamic. There's a real distinction there, though I
can't tell you how it comes. I think we're probably two quite different species spiritually" (pp. 283–84). Life, according to Silenus, is "like the big
wheel at Luna Park" (p. 282).

> You pay five francs and go into a room with tiers of seats all round, and in the
> centre the floor is made of a great disc of polished wood that revolves
> quickly. At first you sit down and watch the others. They are all trying to sit
> in the wheel, and they keep getting flung off, and that makes them laugh,
> and you laugh too. It's great fun. . . . The nearer you can get to the hub of
> the wheel the slower it is moving and the easier it is to stay on. There's gen-
> erally some one in the centre who stands up and sometimes does a sort of
> dance. Often he's paid by the management, though, or, at any rate, he's al-
> lowed in free. Of course at the very centre there's a point completely at rest,
> if one could only find it. I'm not sure I am not very near that point myself. Of
> course the professional men get in the way. Lots of people just enjoy scram-
> bling on and being whisked off and scrambling on again. How they all shriek

and giggle! Then there are others, like Margot, who sit as far out as they can and hold on for dear life and enjoy that. But the whole point about the wheel is that you needn't get on it at all, if you don't want to. People get hold of ideas about life, and that makes them think they've got to join in the game, even if they don't enjoy it. It doesn't suit every one. (pp. 282–83)

Silenus's parable illustrates the rupture between thinking and doing. At life's game, one is either an impotent spectator or a mindless participant. There's no middle ground.

The name Silenus is full of suggestion. The Silenus of classical myth was the mentor of Dionysus, whom he encouraged to follow the promptings of instinct and will regardless of consequence. Otto Silenus's divided world seems remarkably similar to the one announced by the mythical Silenus, especially as imagined by Friedrich Nietzsche. Consider the following passage from *The Birth of Tragedy* concerning the natural antagonism between Apollonian and Dionysian imaginations. Nietzsche's distinction parallels both Otto Silenus's division of the human species and the collision between the static Paul Pennyfeather and the dynamic Bollingers.

And now let us imagine how the ecstatic sounds of the Dionysiac rites penetrated ever more enticingly into that artificially restrained and discreet world of illusion, how this clamor expressed the whole outrageous gamut of nature—delight, grief, knowledge—even to the most piercing cry; and then let us imagine how the Apollonian artist with his thin, monotonous harp music must have sounded beside the demoniac chant of the multitude! The muses presiding over the illusory arts paled before an art which enthusiastically told the truth, and the wisdom of Silenus cried "Woe!" against the serene Olympians. The individual, with his limits and moderations, forgot himself in the Dionysiac vortex and became oblivious to the laws of Apollo. Indiscreet extravagance revealed itself as truth, and contradiction, a delight born of pain, spoke out of the bosom of nature. Wherever the Dionysiac voice was heard, the Apollonian norm seemed suspended or destroyed.[3]

Was Waugh parodying Nietzsche? There is nothing that confirms he read Nietzsche other than some general remarks he made concerning his interest in philosophy at this time in his life.[4] But the parallels seem strong enough on their own without recourse to external proofs of influence. No less seriously and certainly no less playfully than Nietzsche's treatise, Waugh's first novel explores the antagonism between Apollonian order and Dionysian energy. Paul Pennyfeather is "the individual with his limits and moderations." The "demoniac chant of the multitude" is taken up in the "confused roaring" of the Bollingers. Paul lives in a world of settled arrangements; his sense of himself and his world depends upon his unexamined assumption that reality or being is inherently stable. According to Nietzsche, this is an illusion that beguiles most civilized people. Becoming is the only fundamental reality; human thought, however, requires that it be translated into the supposed categories of Being.[5] Running with the flux of Becoming, the Bollingers overwhelm the trivial artifice of Paul's measured world. Described as "a kaleidoscope of dimly discernible faces," the Bollingers comprise an undifferentiated Dionysian force intent upon annihilating the individual. In Nietzsche's vision of the Dionysian principle in its esthetic guise, "each single instance of such annihilation will clarify for us the abiding phenomenon of Dionysiac art, which expresses the omnipotent will behind individuation, eternal life continuing beyond all appearances and in spite of destruction. The metaphysical delight in tragedy is a translation of instinctive Dionysiac wisdom into images. The hero, the highest manifestation of the will, is destroyed, and we assent, since he too is merely a phenomenon, and the eternal life of the will remains unaffected."[6] The willful Bollingers engulf Paul and obliterate his rationally constructed individuality. They strip his pants from him in a parodic ritual that sacrifices reason to the will. This is why the narrator must later interrupt his story to tell us in an ironically self-conscious aside that "the whole of this book is really an account of the mysterious disappearance of Paul Pennyfeather, so that readers must not complain if the shadow which took his name does not amply fill the important part of hero for which he was originally cast" (p. 163). In a world in which reason has lost its struggle with the will, "Paul Pennyfeather would never have made a hero, and the only interest about him arises from the unusual series of events of which his shadow was witness" (p. 164). This also explains why Paul can so readily "die" and be reborn as his own cousin. Paul's death and rebirth parody Nietzsche's doctrine of the Dionysian will with its belief in an eternal return which guarantees that everything eventually comes full circle, the undifferentiated life force endlessly reproducing the same individuals and events through an eternity of time.

Paul's allegiance to Apollo is far too faint to stand up to Dionysian turbulence when it erupts in his life. He exemplifies one of Waugh's recurring themes: decency without force. Without strong convictions, educated people like Paul may continue to observe codes of morality and manners handed down to them from previous ages but generally think it embarrassing to have to examine the theological and metaphysical principles upon which their behavior rests. Tony Last in *A Handful of Dust* provides the perfect example. A decent, devoted family man, he glories in his nineteenth-century estate of pseudo-Gothic design, fulfills all the conventional obligations of a gentlemen, attends chapel on Sundays, and generally reveres the tradition into which he was born. But he does not bother himself about the metaphysics that originally gave his way of life its purpose. When the local parson tries to console him in his grief over the death of his

son, he gets rid of the man at the earliest possible moment and then remarks, "after all the last thing one wants to talk about at a time like this is
religion" (p. 158). Religion for Tony is a cultural ornament, a museum
piece to be preserved with the same sort of care he expends on his pseudo-
Gothic house. Beyond its esthetic value, however, it has little more to offer
than a few ethical precepts founded upon an uplifting fiction. It was precisely this tendency to reduce religion to a cultural artifact that Waugh
came to abhor. When he converted to Roman Catholicism in 1930, he
wrote of modern sophisticated religious thinking that hesitated to commit
itself to any definite beliefs: "If its own mind is not made up, it can hardly
hope to withstand disorder from outside."[7] He thought it futile to use religion as a sort of picturesque inducement with which to cultivate decency
and social feeling. Stronger fortification was needed to withstand the savagery that had always besieged civilization.

Paul Pennyfeather, we are told, could "be expected to acquit himself
with decision and decorum in all the emergencies of civilized life" (p. 163).
His problem is that so very little civilized life remains and its polite emergencies seem exceedingly insignificant in the hurly-burly of modern times.
This is the truth Paul discovers when his commitment to a reasonable ethic
of moderation proves to be the flimsiest of defenses against the wild excesses of the Bollingers. This encounter parodically inverts Nietzsche's
mocking reference to Anaxagoras, the ancient philosopher who had argued that "in the beginning all things were mixed together; then reason
came and introduced order." Anaxagoras, Nietzsche observes, "with his
concept of reason, seems like the first sober philosopher in a company of
drunkards."[8] What better describes Paul among the Bollingers? Only in
this case, reason does not prevail. Instead, the Bollingers put Paul through
a regressive rite of passage that reintroduces him to the original chaotic
mixture of things, a primitive stew which reason's puny distinctions cannot
reduce to order.

Paul is awakened from his Victorian dream of an ordered, purposeful life
enshrined in a "code of ready-made honour that is the still small voice,
trained to command, of the Englishman all the world over" (p. 252). His
eyes open on a new reality. Now he is encouraged to go his way "careless
of consequence" (p. 133) and advised to "temper discretion with deceit"
(p. 24). Nineteenth-century decorum has given way to what Edmund Wilson describes as Waugh's twentieth century, a world of "perverse, unre-
generate self-will" that gives "rise to confusion and impudence."[9] Here
Paul is taken up by Margot Beste-Chetwynde (pronounced beast-
cheating), an amoral charmer who has climbed into the aristocracy by
means of a strategic marriage and then, so it is rumored, hastened her wid-
owing. She is a creature of undisguised self-assertion who supports herself

by running a chain of brothels in South America. Unaccountably, she
chooses Paul to be her next husband. Their marriage, however, is called off
at the last minute when he is arrested for having unwittingly taken part in
her white slave trade. It is then that Paul fully realizes there is "something
radically inapplicable about this whole code" of "ready-made honour" (p.
252) by which he lives. It does not fit the age of Margot. At his trial on
charges of procuring, he must decide whether to give evidence against her
or allow himself to be convicted for her crimes. Paul does the honorable
thing: he sacrifices himself. He cannot help but concede the "undeniable
cogency" of her son's remark: "You can't see Mamma in prison, can you?"
As the narrator explains, the more Paul considered this rhetorical question,
"the more he perceived it to be the statement of a natural law. He appreciated the assumption of comprehension with which Peter had delivered it.
As he studied Margot's photograph . . . he was strengthened in his belief
that there was, in fact, and should be, one law for her and another for himself" (pp. 252–53).

> He *saw* the *impossibility* of Margot in prison; the bare connection of voca-
> bles associating the ideas was obscene. . . . if the preposterous processes of
> law had condemned her, then the woman that they actually caught and
> pinned down would not have been Margot, but some quite other person of
> the same name and somewhat similar appearance. It was impossible to im-
> prison the Margot who had committed the crime. (p. 253)

If Margot could actually be "caught and pinned down," she would no
longer fulfill her role; she would become merely a mortal, subject like everyone else to the usual constraints of humankind. But Margot is not mortal; she is a goddess of Becoming, a pure Dionysian principle quite beyond
the censure of a spiritless morality. To expect her, then, to be responsible
for her deeds is to ask her to be someone other than who she is. Margot's
vital energy knows no restraint. Paul, on the other hand, for all the powers
of discrimination bequeathed him by an Oxford education, is shadowy and
effete; he has neither the conviction nor the energy to act decisively.
There is one law for those who reside in the static world of fixed principles
and another for those who live in the dynamic world of unprincipled self-
assertion. Not only is this the reason he cannot testify against her; it is also
the reason he cannot marry her. As Silenus points out, they are "two quite
different species spiritually."

This division of characters into irreconcilable extremes has been frequently taken as a symptom of Waugh's moral confusion. James F. Carens,
for instance, argues that

> the satirist seems to imply that amoralism may be justified by the very nature
> of things, that there are those such as Paul, who live within the law and are

judged by it, while there are others, such as Peter and his mother, who, by virtue of their dynamism and, perhaps, their position, are outside the "whole code of ready-made honour," inherited by Paul but "inapplicable" to them.[10]

This is true enough on moral grounds. But these are not the grounds upon which Waugh chose to work. The characters and situations in his novels—certainly his early novels—dramatize epistemological concerns anterior to moral considerations. They are frankly abstractions deployed in his analysis of the modern world. Even by the standards of satire, these characters are too flatly one-sided to be seriously considered as moral agents. This is the point, of course. Paul and Margot have been effectively removed from any known moral arena. They exist as polar remnants of a disintegrated humanity: one forever imprisoned by the bankrupt categories of a failed order, the other boundlessly self-assertive because she is untrammeled by any consideration of moral consequences. For Paul to testify against Margot would be as supererogatory as if one were to indict the will for having appetites. There is not much point in arraigning the given. For his part, Paul is prevented from exerting his temperate influence because the "code of ready-made honour" with which he has been brought up has become "radically inapplicable" in a society that has forfeited its belief in the possibility of moral absolutes. Reason can exert no force without a fixed fulcrum. The chapter in which Paul goes to jail, "Stone Walls Do Not a Prison Make," takes its title from Richard Lovelace's "To Althea from Prison," but Waugh ironically tweaks the original meaning. In Paul's case there is no need for walls; he is already imprisoned by the values of a tradition that people like Margot simply ignore. He might as well complain against his temperament as protest his prison sentence. Either grievance would be futile.

In its title, *Decline and Fall* suggests first the most famous of historical descriptions of barbarian assaults on an enfeebled civilization, Gibbon's *Decline and Fall of the Roman Empire*. But when Professor Silenus declares that Margot and Paul are of different species spiritually, his finding echoes that of his countryman Oswald Spengler. In *The Decline of the West*, a work that can be read as a continuation of Gibbon's, Spengler argued that the human race is divided into geographical groups, each manifesting a unique soul that distinguishes it from all the rest. Spengler's book appeared in an English translation in 1926, so it does not seem unreasonable to suppose Waugh had it in mind when writing *Decline and Fall* in 1928. Presumably he had at least a superficial knowledge of it some time earlier or he would not have referred to it as one of "two or three very solemn" works he packed for his 1929 trip abroad.[11] Although he recorded nothing else about it, there can be little doubt that Spengler's apocalyptic pessimism would have appealed to the young Waugh, one of whose poses required that he adopt a sardonic knowingness. Certainly Spengler's argument would have provided Waugh with another explanation of the world in which his little lost characters find themselves, and it would have had the virtue of being an explanation that coordinated neatly enough with Nietzsche's polarization of human nature.

Spengler isolates eight distinct world cultures and then outlines the habitual, one might say reflexive, perception of the world characteristic of each. Working in the tradition that passes from Kant through Nietzsche, he naturally assumes that a culture is best understood in terms of its own special epistemology. Whether in the arts or sciences, a culture's thought reflects the largely unconscious assumptions of its peculiar world view. The static-dynamic polarity so dear to Professor Silenus appears in *The Decline of the West* as the opposition that distinguishes the essential differences between the classical Greek and the Faustian European cultures. (As Spengler uses these terms, they parallel Nietzsche's contrast of the Apollonian and Dionysian.) These labels are not meant to be applied to historical periods exclusively. They serve as well to make the familiar distinction between classical and romantic sensibilities that is not limited to any particular time. Historical conditions in a given age tend to favor one of several competing sensibilities. The favored one becomes dominant and characterizes the period. This does not mean other predilections disappear; they simply become less visible because the individual finds it less advantageous to express them. Used here, Spengler's categories will refer to sensibilities rather than specific ages.

Comparing the classical sensibility with the Faustian romantic, Spengler wrote that

> the "Nature" of Classical man found its highest artistic emblem in the nude statue, and out of it logically there grew a static of bodies, a physics of the near. . . . Faustian man's Nature-idea was a dynamic of unlimited space, a physics of the distant. . . . Apollinian theory is a quiet meditation. . . . The Faustian is from the very outset a working hypothesis.

For the classical sensibility ideas are timeless Platonic forms; they are fixed coordinates which we use to make the world intelligible. We can rely on them to shape our understanding of the flow of experience. In contrast, Faustian or romantic man values ideas not as ends in themselves but rather as means with which to exert his will over his surroundings; he maintains no absolute truths, only hypotheses devised as momentary expedients. Spengler's descriptions of the Classical and Faustian sensibilities find their way into Waugh's novels in various guises, most notably in the recurring motif of the anachronistic naïf bedazzled by one of modernity's goddesses, roles first filled by Paul Pennyfeather and Margot Beste-Chetwynde. Classical epistemology is capable of supporting Paul Pennyfeather's ready-made code of honor. The romantic sensibility with its provisional categories suits Margot, whose precarious career demands infinite adaptability. The classical attitude cautions us to live within the limits of the possible; the romantic urges us to transcend all boundaries. It is this binary opposition that Waugh parodies with Silenus's static-dynamic polarity. As Nietzsche seems to have done, so Spengler also served his abiding theme.[12]

Spengler's thesis further explains why the narrator of *Decline and Fall* insists upon Paul's inability to play the heroic role for which he had originally been cast. The traditional hero finds his strength in his cultural identity. Convinced of the values with which he has been raised, he stands ready to project them into the world around him. Once he is deprived of this type of unreflective conviction, Paul can only retreat from the barbarous shock of Waugh's twentieth century. The supposed custodians of tradition no longer believe in their ability to make a difference in such a world. Like Silenus's gallery of static spectators they must content themselves with watching impotently from the sidelines.

According to Spengler's analysis, Paul is a natural victim of his age. Spengler argues that the West had developed beyond the stage of societal cohesion by the modern period and was in the twentieth century loosely held together by the fading memory of a once vital and compelling body of convictions. Using a cyclical schema applicable to the growth and decay of societies in general, he observes that in the early cultural periods of a society's development individuals, singly and collectively, feel themselves bound up with the fate of their community. The meaning of their lives flows from the shared beliefs and traditions that have served them in their common struggle for survival. But once a society succeeds and flourishes as a civilization, its defensive cohesion begins to dissolve as it takes on an aura of skeptical cosmopolitanism. The populace tends to cluster in cities in search of economic opportunity. Wealth becomes a measure of value more important than honor, tradition, or property. (In *Decline and Fall* the Junior Dean and Domestic Bursar gauge the Bollinger infractions not in terms of moral but rather financial value. As they sit idly by, their only concern is how much they will be able to fine the celebrants for their drunkenly destructive behavior. They even pray that the revelers might attack the chapel so that the maximum in punitive damages can be levied against them.) With growing affluence and security, the cities swell with self-interested *déracinés* who have little sense of common destiny with their neighbors. The resulting ethos encourages the society Waugh portrays, a society in which it is every man for himself. *Sauve qui peut* serves as the ironic refrain of his last novel, *Unconditional Surrender*. It is clearly meant

ect the final wisdom of Western decadence at mid-century, a world
it with untempered self-regard.

There are a number of ways to express Waugh's central theme, some
more complicated than others. Perhaps the best formulation is the simplest
and oldest: the perennial human failure to behave reasonably. As themes
go, there is certainly nothing new here, nor was there meant to be. The
Western tradition begins with the fundamental conflict between knowing
and doing. The gears of intellect and will are meant to mesh, but more often grind. This is the stuff of all human drama, but it seemed to Waugh that
this failure had become especially acute in the twentieth century. In earlier ages the inevitable discord between reason and impulse was explained
as a result of willful selfishness. One was capable of knowing how to act but
chose to do otherwise. This was called sin. There was general agreement
that the morality of individual acts could be assessed according to objective standards. What disturbed Waugh was that in our relativistic age morality had become disputable not only in specific cases, but also in
principle. This is why Waugh disclaimed the title of satirist in 1946, arguing that satire is not possible in an unstable society that does not subscribe
to "homogeneous moral standards." The satirist "seeks to produce shame"
and this, he contended, was clearly impossible in a world in which "vice no
longer pays lip service to virtue."[13] Another way of putting this is to say
that without conviction in a transcendent purpose to life, it becomes impossible to discriminate among ethical systems; one will seem no more
metaphysically compelling than another. At any given juncture, then, the
will is left to choose from competing rationales. For Waugh this amounted
to an abdication of reason's authority, which was bound to result in the
mindless self-assertion he thought characteristic of modern life. It was this
supposed decline of the traditional intellectual and moral order that so fascinated him, compelling his satiric response.

II

DESIRE, DOUBT, AND THE SUPERB MEAN

Polarization and counterpoint are constant features in Waugh's fiction. They were the structural analogues to the divisive tensions he sensed both within and outside himself. His first published story, "The Balance," turns on the counterpoise between sentimental narrative and comic commentary. It unfolds as though it were a silent film about young, affluent worldings, caught in the toils of romance. We "watch" the narrative at a movie house with two serving women on their night off who, for our edification, provide a noisy but very sensible assessment of the "soft" proceedings.[1] By juxtaposing party scenes in *Vile Bodies*, Waugh satirizes the generational division that afflicts his society. While the elders settle into Anchorage House, a revered family seat, for an evening during which they will reassure themselves that all is right with their world, some miles away their offspring stumble about in a tethered dirigible that floats a few feet above the ground. These Bright Young People, eager martyrs to modernity, are quite willing to suffer the nausea that inevitably results under the combined influence of drink and the uncertain footing of their swaying quarters. *Black Mischief* alternates between scenes of shiftless Londoners and feckless Africans. In *Work Suspended* and *Sword of Honour* protagonists meet their unseemly doubles from whom they belatedly discover unwelcome truths about themselves.

All these examples are permutations of Waugh's original preoccupation with the uneasy balance between rational order and willful energy. This said, it must be emphasized that he focused precisely on the dividing fulcrum, not one side or the other. Divergent critical opinion has tended to place him in one scale or the other, reductively labeling him a compulsive conservative or an unprincipled anarchist. In truth, he was a bit of both. Harold Acton put it best when he described Waugh as a "prancing faun, thinly disguised by conventional apparel. His wide-apart eyes, always ready to be startled under raised eyebrows. . . . The gentleness of his manner could not deceive me . . . so demure and yet so wild! A faun half-tamed

21

by the Middle Ages, who would hide himself for months in some suburban retreat, and then burst upon the town with capricious caperings."[2] Waugh's personality was a battle zone of contending forces. He was by turns reflective and impulsive, traditional and anarchic, reclusive and cosmopolitan. In *Decline and Fall* he projected these tensions into Paul Pennyfeather's diametrically opposed colleagues, Mr. Prendergast and Captain Grimes, who, taken together, vividly illustrate the consequences of living in a world in which reason has lost touch with impulse. Standing at allegorical extremes from one another, Prendergast personifies intellect immobilized by doubt while Grimes expresses will unhindered by reflection.

Captain Grimes is the incorrigible rascal who flouts morals and manners so cheerfully that no one would ever want him brought to account. He may be a bisexual bigamist who leaves schoolmastering in Wales for pimping in South America, but these faults cannot be held against a man who so genially admits, "I can stand most sorts of misfortune, old boy, but I can't stand repression" (p. 264). Following the dictates of his impulses wherever they lead, he repeatedly lands "in the soup" (p. 31), as he puts it. His casual treatment of complaisant women together with his excessive interest in adolescent boys has made it necessary for him to cultivate the wiles of a confidence man and the skills of a quick-change artist to merely survive as he keeps one small step ahead of the authorities. And survive he does with splendid resilience. While in the armed service, he is given the choice between a dignified suicide and a squalid court-martial for disgraceful—probably homosexual—behavior. Left alone with a revolver to do the decent thing, he gets drunk instead. Grimes is not one to be cowed by somebody else's conception of honor. Intuitively he knows the world to be a much dicier place than any code of ethics can explain. He also knows his luck. It is a fellow Harrovian who discovers him in the stupor of his double infamy. Recognizing Grimes as a public-school man, this loyal advocate of the old-boy tradition soon has him shipped to Ireland to work in the postal service for the war's duration. Later, when Grimes's erratic, not to say erotic, teaching career takes him to Paul's school, Llanabba Castle, he finds himself forced into marriage with the headmaster's daughter. To escape this odious involvement, he pretends suicide by swimming out to sea. Shortly after this adventure, he appears at Margot's to apply for a managerial position in one of her brothels. Sometime later, when Paul goes to prison, there is Grimes again. Having decided that three years is too long to serve for bigamy, however, he soon escapes under the cover of fog during a work detail. When he is not located in the countryside surrounding the prison, the guards confidently agree that he has drowned in the bogs of

Egdon Mire, a Hardyesque fate that long experience has taught them no
mortal can evade. But Paul knows better.

> Grimes, Paul at last realized, was one of the immortals. He was a life force.
> Sentenced to death in Flanders, he popped up in Wales; drowned in Wales,
> he emerged in South America; engulfed in the dark mystery of Egdon Mire,
> he would rise again somewhere at some time, shaking from his limbs the
> musty integuments of the tomb. Surely he had followed in the Bacchic train
> of distant Arcady, and played on the reeds of myth by forgotten streams, and
> taught the childish satyrs the art of love? Had he not suffered unscathed the
> fearful dooms of all the offended gods of all the histories, fire, brimstone and
> yawning earthquakes, plague and pestilence? Had he not stood, like the
> Pompeian sentry, while the Citadels of the Plain fell to ruin about his ears?
> Had he not, like some grease-caked Channel swimmer, breasted the waves
> of the Deluge? Had he not moved unseen when darkness covered the wa-
> ters? (pp. 269–70)

Grimes is another character who approaches the condition of pure Dionysian becoming—formless, protean, infinitely adaptable. That echo of
Genesis in the last sentence of this passage—"Had he not moved unseen
when darkness covered the waters?"—mockingly suggests that Grimes is
like the clay of brute matter before the form of being has imparted shape
and destiny to its unconditioned potency. Indeed, his name further supports this reading: he is the original grime of the world always ready to subvert the tidy housekeeping of civilization by letting in the primal messiness
once more. Like Margot, Grimes is one of Waugh's willful gods going his
way "careless of consequence" (p. 133), slipping society's restraining nets
with an ease as astonishing as it is comical. He is an untamable life force,
pure energy; disruptive of good manners, certainly, but quite beyond
moral censure.

Grimes's opposite is Mr. Prendergast, the agnostic parson who has given
up his ecclesiastical living and stooped to schoolmastering, a profession notoriously open to rascals such as Grimes and failures such as himself. An
abysmally incompetent teacher, Prendergast has spent the last ten years as
the butt of schoolboy pranks, most of which he fecklessly calls down upon
himself. He wears a cheap and obvious wig that naturally becomes the irresistible target of his students' cruelest jokes. As he explains to Paul, once
he put the wig on he felt he could not go back. Removing it might cause increased mischief, a risk he is unwilling to run. Prendergast does not have
the will to expose himself honestly, and without this power of will he is ineffectual in all his efforts. At their first meeting, Prendergast offers Paul
some port. Having had a glimpse of conditions at Llanabba, Paul eagerly
accepts. But they find there is only one glass in the commons room, the one

from which Prendergast is drinking. Prendergast makes a feeble attempt to locate another, but quickly gives it up. The failed clergyman possesses the wine but he cannot produce communion; there is promise but no delivery. He does not have the power to give anyone, including himself, what is needed.

On their second meeting, Prendergast tells Paul his story. "I should be a rector with my own house and bathroom . . . only I had *Doubts*" (p. 36), he confides. It was not "the ordinary sort of doubt about Cain's wife or the Old Testament miracles" that had unnerved him.

> I'd been taught how to explain all those while I was at college. No, it was something deeper than all that. I *couldn't understand why God had made the world at all.* . . . You see how fundamental that is. Once granted the first step, I can see that everything else follows—Tower of Babel, Babylonian captivity, Incarnation, Church, bishops, incense, everything—but what I couldn't see, and what I can't see now, is *why* did it all begin? I asked my bishop; he didn't know. He said that he didn't think the point really arose as far as my practical duties as a parish priest were concerned. (pp. 36–39)

Prendergast raises the fundamental issue but hasn't the will to resolve it. Instead, he foolishly jumps at the chance to return to the cloth as a prison chaplain when he discovers the post does not require him to subscribe to any particular creed at all. Of course, such agnostic felicity cannot last. Among his caged flock there is a religious lunatic unhindered by any doubts at all. His beliefs are as unswerving as they are unexamined. Convinced that the angel of the Lord has commissioned him to murder the faithless, this self-styled "lion of the Lord's elect" (p. 240) decides—with some cause—that Chaplain Prendergast is not a Christian and so murders him by sawing his head from his body with tools conveniently provided him by the prison's enlightened arts and crafts program, which stresses the criminal's need for emotional release through artistic self-expression.

Prendergast's inability to sustain a coherent religious vision is one of the many instances in which Waugh satirized the modern abdication of intellectual authority that calls forth the fanatic. Whether religious or political, these zealots are led by the inner light of untutored emotion alone. Surrounded by an ostensibly sane citizenry whose lives lack a rationally defined purpose, their peculiarly mindless dedication gives them devastating strength. Prendergast's grisly end provides Waugh with a metaphor of his central theme: twentieth century man decapitated, his intellect severed from his will. When reason neglects its reign, impulse usurps its place with predictable results.

Reported casually, Prendergast's fate seems neither all that shocking nor particularly lamentable. Instead, we are made to feel he got no more than he deserved. He is one of Waugh's well-meaning humanists, personally inoffensive but culturally lethal. Without convictions of any kind, these characters wander through the novels vaguely unnerved by the chaos that surrounds them. Their failure to sustain the tradition of which they are the immediate beneficiaries has emptied their world of purpose and left those who are more willful and less scrupulous either to drift into aimless dissipation or to channel their otherwise undirected energy into one of the many perverse ideologies that plague the day. This was Waugh's assessment of a culture that has lost confidence in itself and its ability to make sense of the world. It explains the frequent appearance of fanaticism in his fiction. In *Vile Bodies* Lady Melrose Ape, the stalwart, lightly bearded evangelist modeled on Aimee Semple McPherson, wows London with her feel-good religiosity and her troupe of nubile singing angels, while Colonel Blount rents his ancestral estate to serve as the location for an "all-talkie super-religious film" (p. 202) about the eighteenth-century religious enthusiast John Wesley. In *Black Mischief* a young Oxford-educated African emperor is convinced that he is the apostle of Progress "at [whose] stirrups run woman's suffrage, vaccination and vivisection." He confidently declares, "I am the New Age; I am the Future" (p. 22), as he builds railroads that go nowhere and equips his barefoot, spear-carrying army with a tank. Aimée Thanatogenos in *The Loved One* unreservedly devotes herself to Dr. Kenworthy's euphemistic mortuary and its denial of death. These and other true-believing lunatics like them are desperate symptoms of a society that has lost its way.

The early novels are populated by half-human characters who are either dynamically willful or statically reflective. The world of Captain Grimes and Mr. Prendergast has given up the dialectical struggle between classic restraint and romantic striving. There is, however, one remarkable exception: Imogen Quest in *Vile Bodies*. She is one who has "achieved a superb mean between those two poles of savagery Lady Circumstance and Lady Metroland" (p. 158), Lady Circumstance being all purblind allegiance to an otiose nineteenth-century ethic and Lady Metroland (Margot Beste-Chetwynde in a later incarnation) seething with insatiable modernity. Imogen, unlike almost every other young person in Waugh's novels, is happily married and content with her lot in life. "From the first she exhibited signs of a marked personality . . . her character . . . a lovely harmony of contending virtues—she was witty and tender-hearted; passionate and serene, sensual and temperate, impulsive and discreet" (p. 158). Imogen, in other words, is a whole, self-sufficient individual capable of balancing the claims of reason and impulse in her life. In fact, she is too blessedly sane to be true. She is, of course, imaginary, a joke of sorts. Her "lovely harmony" of romantic impulse and classic poise turns out to be a fiction made up by

Adam Fenwick-Symes, the novel's protagonist. As a gossip columnist for a paper appropriately named the *Daily Excess*, Adam finds himself strapped for material and so, in the dishonorable tradition of his trade, he resorts to invention. Imogen becomes his most successful creation. In fact, she positively captivates his readers, inspiring them with her benevolent normality. "And this knowledge of the intangible Quest set, moving among them in uncontrolled dignity of life, seemed to leaven and sweeten the lives of [his] readers" (p. 159). Soon Adam's readers, including his employer, Lord Monomark, are clamoring to meet Imogen. But Adam goes too far, and disaster falls. In detailing Imogen's social activities, he makes a serious mistake when he announces her plans to give a party and, for the sake of verisimilitude, includes an address in his report. "On the following day Adam found his table deep in letters of complaint from gate-crashers who had found the house in Seamore Place untenanted" (p. 159). When soon after Lord Monomark approaches him requesting an introduction, Adam has no other recourse but to improvise a hastily arranged Jamaican holiday for the Quests, their stay indefinite.

Modern England is clearly no place for civilized men and women. Imogen's "superb mean" has become the stuff of whimsical nostalgia; her balanced life is no more than an attractive fiction and even at that it cannot survive the gate-crashing barbarism of the twentieth century. Imogen's leavening power fades from the world, leaving people bereft and bewildered. Certainly what we overhear in Adam's desultory conversation with his fiancée, Nina, reflects a profoundly irresolute mind that Imogen would find intolerably alien.

> "Nina, do you ever feel that things simply can't go on much longer?"
> "What d'you mean by things—us or everything?"
> "Everything."
> "No—I wish I did."
> "I dare say you're right. . . . I'd give anything in the world for something different."
> "Different from me or different from everything?"
> "Different from everything . . . only I've got nothing. . . . what's the good of talking?"
> "Oh, Adam, my dearest . . . "
> "Yes?"
> "Nothing." (p. 273)

Neither Adam nor Nina has the strength of Imogen's "marked personality" and without it they have little chance to direct their lives purposefully. Instead, they allow themselves to be carried away by the sweep of sensational but pointless events, including an endless series of parties— "Masked parties, savage parties, Victorian parties, Greek parties, Wild

West parties . . . almost naked parties . . . parties in flats and studios and
houses and ships and hotels and night clubs, in windmills and swimming
baths," sickening boat and plane trips, grotesque evangelists, suicidal auto
races, "all that succession and repetition of massed humanity . . . those vile
bodies" (pp. 170–71). The surfeit of excitement finally reduces them to
listless passivity. In these early novels, the impoverished mind typically
founders in a vertiginous swirl of sensation. None of the characters has the
poise to manage his experience of a wildly fragmented culture.

The world divided between a fading vision of classical order and the
lively anarchy of romantic excess—this was Waugh's concern from the
hectic humor of his early satires to the elegiac ironies of the *Sword of Honour* trilogy. His treatment of the issue was all the more effective because he
resisted facile moralizing. Nor, despite what some have said, did he merely
champion past order over present disorder.[3] Even when Waugh donned
his conservative cap the better to advocate a stern application of traditional restraints to modern behavior, he always made allowance for the
healthy play of impulse. The latitude of his position can be demonstrated
by comparing what he had to say about discipline and repression with the
remarks of his friend Ronald Knox, whose thought Waugh greatly respected. There are two passages in particular that display these apparently
like-minded men reaching tellingly different conclusions. The first comes
from Knox's *God and the Atom*, a work exploring the theological and social
consequences of living in the atomic age that Waugh urgently pressed on
friends and acquaintances as necessary reading.

> I take it that we do not exceed the bounds of legitimate metaphor, if we think
> of the human personality in this way. At the core of it, there is a bundle of in-
> stincts, impulses, prejudices, phobias and what not, each of them bound, and
> each, though often in a very slight degree, straining at its bonds. They are
> held together and held in by the elastic band of Repression; some of it con-
> scious, much more of it unconscious, or half-conscious at the best. If the
> band snaps, the result is lunacy; all the hidden impulses of a man's nature re-
> gain their freedom, held in only by random, external checks. If the band
> slips, the result is that sudden brain-storm or black-out which the psychol-
> ogists have christened schizophrenia; the subject "forgets himself," is un-
> true to his normal habits of behaviour; it may be, only for a short interval.
> But in the ordinary life, the elastic band holds, and the hidden impulses re-
> main bound, only betraying themselves by casual mannerisms and fidget-
> ings, by the images that haunt us in our dreams, and so on. What must be the
> strength, when you come to think about it, of this band which holds our psy-
> chic life in position, consisting in part, but only in part, of that free will
> which we consciously exercise![4]

The second passage comes from one of Waugh's characteristic essays, a
piece of journalism Waugh was commissioned to write in 1929 concerning

the impact of the Great War on the generation coming of age in the 1920s and 1930s. He finds it unsurprising that these young people should be "undiscriminating and ineffectual." The blame can be laid especially on the mood of tolerance that followed the war.

> The only thing which could have saved these unfortunate children was the imposition by rigid discipline, as soon as it became possible, of the standards of civilization. This was still possible in 1918 when the young schoolmasters came back to their work. Unfortunately, a very great number, probably the more influential and intelligent among them, came with their own faith sadly shaken in those very standards which, avowedly, they had fought to preserve. They returned with a jolly tolerance of everything that seemed "modern." Every effort was made to encourage the children at the Public Schools to "think for themselves." When they should have been whipped and taught Greek paradigms, they were set arguing about birth control and nationalization. Their crude little opinions were treated with respect. Preachers in the school chapel week after week entrusted the future to their hands. It is hardly surprising that they were Bolshevik at eighteen and bored at twenty.
>
> The muscles which encounter the most resistance in daily routine are those which become most highly developed and adapted. It is thus that the restraint of a traditional culture tempers and directs creative impulses. Freedom produces sterility. There was nothing left for the younger generation to rebel against, except the widest conceptions of mere decency. Accordingly it was against these that it turned. The result in many cases is the perverse and aimless dissipation chronicled daily by the gossip-writer of the Press.[5]

Examined closely, these two defenses of repression turn out to be quite different. At first Waugh seems to be saying much the same thing as Knox except for the curmudgeonly pose with which he calls for whipping the young and sneers at their "crude little opinions." But Waugh's emphasis differs sharply. For Knox repression is an elastic band that holds back dangerous impulses, a sort of moral girdle. For Waugh it provides the tension necessary to channel one's energy usefully. Repression in this view is basic to culture not merely for moral reasons but also, and perhaps just as importantly, for esthetic reasons. Repressive culture in the form of discipline and standards provides the means, not to hold back impulse, but rather to strengthen and direct it. One hesitates to say it, knowing Waugh's opinion of the good doctor, but this is pure Freud. Confronted with the constraints of the civilized order, libidinous and creative energies must find cleverer ways of expressing themselves than if they were allowed free, undirected play. Without Apollonian restraint, Dionysian impulse dissipates itself in futile, aimless expression. Conversely, and this is sometimes left unremarked in discussions of Waugh, without Dionysian ebullience, Apollonian order is lifeless.

On the evidence of his essays and reviews, Waugh clearly believed that

in an ideally constituted society classic restraint and romantic energy
would temper one another. Yet he seems to have taken inordinate delight
in demonstrating their contemporary incompatibility. So much so that,
even after allowing for the distortion of satire, we must stop to ask whether
his fiction is giving us the peculiar world of his experience or his peculiar
experience of the world. Do Waugh's novels reflect, in however exaggerated a manner, the world as it is, or do they represent his special way of
seeing things? The answer must be yes to both questions. The truth is that
Waugh, like many artists, throve on contradiction. Although he promul-
gated the redemptive virtues of traditional Western culture, he was, as
Harold Acton put it, "always ready to be startled" by the spectacle of barbarism wherever it was to be found. He seems to have been quite determined to see his cherished values flouted. Certainly he spent enough time
searching round the world for what he considered examples of man's inherent disregard for civilized order. Believing barbarism "was a dodo to be
stalked with a pinch of salt," he went "to the wild lands where man had deserted his post and the jungle was creeping back to its old strongholds." It
was in "distant and barbarous places," he reported, that his literary sense
came alive, especially at "the borderlands of conflicting cultures and states
of development, where ideas, uprooted from their traditions, became
oddly changed in transplantation."[6] This is not surprising. The savagery
and civilization he discovered flourishing promiscuously together in Abyssinia, Kenya, and Brazil were sure to intrigue one so divided between the
appeals of order and anarchy within himself. This is why he found California so captivating. Here he stalked the lurid inanities of Forest Lawn cemetery. It was, in his words, "a first-class anthropological puzzle of our own
period," a cemetery that welcomed suicides but refused burial to Fatty Ar-
buckle "because, although acquitted by three juries of the crime imputed
to him by rumour, he had been found guilty, twenty years or so earlier, of
giving a rowdy party."[7] Such a travesty of civilized protocol could not fail
to quicken the imagination of one for whom outrage was a positive addiction. The payoff was his gloriously ghoulish novella, *The Loved One.*

All this is to say that Waugh's own unresolved tensions prepared him to
satirize an age that professed allegiance to a code of behavior founded
upon principles it had called into doubt. As one who must frequently have
felt himself cramped by his chosen orthodoxy, he could not have failed to
notice the lure of moral relativism. Why struggle, why suffer for a tradition
with no more valid a claim on one's loyalty than another or than none at all,
if such were imaginable? Much of Waugh's writing is about resisting the
proposition implicit in this question.

Waugh's inner division also accounts for the practical decisions he made
as a writer. His natural penchant for polarizing experience along the axes

of reason and will provided him with extraordinarily effective means for satirizing his world. As a satirist, he did not want to use ambiguous shading and textured nuance. He was attempting to create fiction that would be as hard-edged and reductive as the schematic cartoons he drew to illustrate his early novels. These drawings serve as visual analogues to his writing. In both media he employed a firm, resolute stylization that portrays disorder without succumbing to it.

When Waugh's life is aligned with his writing, it becomes unmistakably clear that the divorce between reason and impulse dramatized in his novels began in himself. It is nothing less than his signature, to be read with equal clarity in his subject matter and his style. Although he entertained a life-long preoccupation with reason and decorum, he frequently behaved with gargantuan rudeness. He made a point of announcing that his conversion to Roman Catholicism was quite without emotion, a matter of cold, rational conviction, and yet, on other occasions, he could be brutishly unreasonable.[8] Having become exasperated with the fulsome praise *Brideshead Revisited* so often attracted, he put an abrupt end to one woman's fawning. "I thought it was good myself," he snapped, "but now that I know a vulgar, common American woman like yourself admires it, I am not so sure."[9] After reducing another admirer to tears, he was asked how he could behave so badly and profess to be a Catholic. His now famous rejoinder was, "You have no idea how much nastier I would be if I was not a Catholic. Without supernatural aid I would hardly be a human being."[10] There's no getting round the contradiction: Waugh was a man who declared himself committed to the "standards of civilization," yet conducted his life with legendary incivility.[11]

This contradiction seems to have produced in Waugh what might be called a polaristic imagination that strengthened his art while leading him to take political stands from which a more practical man would have prudently shied. This is apparent in both his fiction and his life. In *Sword of Honour* his protagonist, Guy Crouchback, rejoices when he receives news of the Hitler-Stalin Warsaw pact. The agreement may seriously threaten the Allies but it simplifies the ideological issues. Now, Guy thinks, he can go into battle with the clear conscience of a principled warrior fighting the dehumanizing collectivism of "the Modern Age in arms" (p. 8). If this is meant ironically—as I think it is in a partial and complicated way—then the irony is directed not only at the fictional character but also at Waugh's younger self. Waugh had recorded the following thoughts on the Hitler-Stalin agreement in his diary, 22 August 1939: "Russia and Germany have agreed to neutrality pact so there seems no reason why war should be delayed." Later, when it became clear that British policy favored working with the Russians, he wrote:

The papers are all smugly jubilant at Russian conquests in Poland as though this were not a more terrible fate for the allies we are pledged to defend than conquest by Germany. The Italian argument, that we have forfeited our narrow position by not declaring war on Russia, seems unanswerable.[12]

Better the risk of an ideologically pure fight against near impossible odds than the contamination of a prudent but compromising alliance. Waugh never wholly abandoned this position. His was always the wish for neat divisions, clear lines of allegiance, uncompromised efforts. How could such a wish not decay into the embittered nostalgia that periodically darkened his later years?

Waugh used a similar polarizing strategy to describe Ronald Knox some thirty years after *Decline and Fall*. In his preface to Knox's *A Spiritual Aeneid* he borrowed his friend's own terms to portray his nature.

He [Knox] liked the classic division of mankind into the "drastic"—the men of action and decision who know what they want and how to get it, who have little patience with the hesitation of others, who never shrink from "making a scene"—and the "pathetic" who take what is on the table when it is offered them, who suffer neglect rather than assert their rights, who hate to inconvenience anyone.

In this sense he was eminently pathetic.[13]

By calling Knox pathetic, Waugh meant he was a man willing to suffer the world in order to understand it. The drastic man, by contrast, is so driven to dominate his surroundings that he plunges himself into the sweep of events before he has time to assess their significance. These categories do little more than make the familiar distinction between the man of action and the intellectual, but, familiar as it is, Waugh's use of it is peculiarly characteristic of him.

The drastic-pathetic polarity Waugh uses to place Knox is, of course, another version of Silenus's division of mankind into static and dynamic subspecies. Waugh's admiration for the "pathetic" Knox suggests there was an aspect of himself that was drawn to Paul Pennyfeather's static soul, a part that desired the intellectual order and steadfastness of Platonic categories only fully available to those willing to remove themselves from the world's seductions. This explains in part, but only in part, why he became a Catholic. As a seemingly timeless institution, the Church offered a retreat from modernity's "confused roaring." But Waugh was too worldly for the kind of cloister in which Knox, a priest and Oxford don, prospered. However reclusive he became in later life, he could never permanently resist the temptation to behave drastically, not to say rudely, when opportunity arose. His desire for metaphysical stability had as much to do with his apprehension of his own wayward inclinations as with the alarm he felt when confronted by what seemed the dissolution of Western culture.

As an artist Waugh used his divided nature to construct a sort of knock-about allegory that satirized the troubled relations between reason and impulse in a world that had, so to speak, lost its head. Many have assumed he was on the side of reason in this issue. Certainly Waugh's essays support this reading. His comments on literature and art reveal a man generally more intrigued by intelligent craftsmanship than with esthetic passion. Intense feeling was pointless without artistic discipline. In 1946 he flatly declared that "the artist's only service to the disintegrated society of today is to create little independent systems of order of his own."[14] But this was Waugh's official self simplifying the issue he treated rather more complexly in his fiction. It is often assumed that despite his own flagrant indulgences, Waugh was committed to an ascetic, life-denying version of Christianity that secured order at the cost of vitality. But if this were the case, we must wonder why his willful rogues are so engaging and his Paul Pennyfeathers so lackluster. Even indisputably committed Catholics such as Bridey in *Brideshead Revisited* often come off as sententious bores, admirably devout, perhaps, but unquestionably limited. Contrary to some moralistic readings, Waugh's satire does not fasten on the will and instincts as though they were the exclusive source of the world's evil. Mockery was enough for the folly of his impulsive rogues. He reserved his scorn for his law-abiding bores, the decent, reasonable characters like Paul Pennyfeather and Mr. Prendergast who conduct themselves prudently according to their inherited morality but either doubt or ignore the principles on which it was founded. This is true throughout his works and is expressed quite vividly in a surprisingly explicit passage from "Charles Ryder's Schooldays," the fragment of a novel that was to depict the youth of the character who narrates *Brideshead Revisited*. When young Charles willfully steps from the prescribed path of his public school's routine, his state of mind is described with a startling allusion.

> Today and all this term he was aware of a new voice in his inner counsels, a detached, critical Hyde who intruded his presence more and more often on the conventional, intolerant, subhuman, wholly respectable Dr. Jekyll; a voice, as it were, from a more civilized age, as from the chimney corner in mid-Victorian times there used to break sometimes the sardonic laughter of a grandmama, relic of Regency, a clear, outrageous, entirely self-assured disturber among the high and muddled thoughts of her whiskered descendants. (CRSD, p. 282)

It seems to me that the reversal in this passage expresses something of Waugh's essential vision. To see what this is, we must ask the obvious question it raises: in what sense could Jekyll be thought subhuman and Hyde civilized? This seems merely perverse until we reconsider Robert Louis Stevenson's late-Victorian parable and discover that by taking it out of the hands of the depth psychologists Waugh has conveyed the tale's real meaning in his seemingly casual allusion. Once suggested, it is obvious. Of course, Jekyll is the real monster of the story and Hyde his maddened victim. Jekyll is a monster of rationality and good intentions whose belief in man's perfectability requires that he brutally deny the Hyde in himself. As the story makes clear, Hyde is not the product of repression psychoanalytically understood. His appearance is not the result of unconscious denial. Long before Jekyll concocted his transforming potion, he had been acting quite consciously on his Hyde-nature in furtive nocturnal philandering. The purpose of his experiment is neither to repress nor subliminate his troublesome Hyde-self. Rather he wants to purge and ignore it so that he can get on with his ambitious program of scientific and social reform undistracted. Hyde, then, is the product of Jekyll's refusal to take responsibility for the flawed condition of his human nature. Undirected and unleavened by a morality that accepts sin as an inevitable, even salutary part of human experience, he splits in two. There is the noble, intellectual Jekyll, well-intentioned but ultimately irresponsible, and there is the bestial, impulsive Hyde, growing more uncontrollably powerful with each new outrage. Despite his anguished handwringing Jekyll must bear the moral if not the legal responsibility for the Hyde he has created by turning his back on his willful nature. Waugh's Jekyll is modern secular society whose professed moral relativism and progressive materialism require that it ignore a difficult truth: the energy that sometimes erupts as feral viciousness is the same that at other times springs forth as moral virtue.

Jonathan Swift had made the same point in Gulliver's fourth voyage to the Land of the Houyhnhnms, where Gulliver is so seduced by the dream of pure reason that he does everything in his power to deny his Yahoo humanity. Gulliver like Jekyll is a moral infant who desires nothing less than a shadowless life in which choice is invariably rendered uncomplicated. The point of both characters is that they reject the moral adventure implicit in being creatures endowed with free will. Each would rather forfeit his freedom than face the anguish of ambiguous moral decisions. They want blueprinted guides to behavior, foolproof and fully guaranteed. They long for a sunny world of childish irresponsibility in which their lives will be laid out, every wrinkle anticipated and smoothed in advance. Waugh directed his satire at just this sort of irresponsibility. Both in his fiction and in his journalism he attacked those of his contemporaries who relied on reasonableness and decency alone to face an increasingly uncivil world. Characters such as Paul Pennyfeather and Mr. Prendergast were muddle-headed Jekylls naive enough to behave as though good intentions alone could banish the Hyde both within and outside themselves. Waugh's argument is always that people who persist in the simpleminded belief that unaided decency will prevail in human affairs must continue to be at the mercy of the savagery they refuse to acknowledge.[15] By dividing human nature into Silenus's static and dynamic subspecies, Waugh in effect was bringing our attention to the delicate and often uneasy balance between Jekyll and Hyde, Houyhnhnm and Yahoo in us all. Put too much weight on Jekyll's side and you get Mr. Prendergast, a well-meaning but bumbling humanist who lacks the force of will to put his good intentions into effective action. Pile on with Hyde and you get Captain Grimes, the irrepressible rascal whose outrageous carelessness may seem jolly enough at first but has an unfortunate way of sliding irreversibly toward havoc.

This Jekyll and Hyde relationship between reason and will was, of course, a common theme in the late nineteenth and early twentieth centuries. We find the major novelists preoccupied by it. Their emphasis, however, differs markedly from Waugh's. Conrad, Mann, Lawrence, Woolf, and Joyce all portray European man as a victim of his overly intellectual culture. It was a disease that had enfeebled his will and left him devoid of healthy spontaneity. The generally prescribed cure called for turning off the intellect so that one could abandon oneself passionately to the flow of immediate experience. Health and wholeness could be regained by those who were able to mute the commands of convention and listen once more to their instincts.

Waugh was as aware as Mann and Joyce of the supposed enfeeblement of will that afflicted the thoughtful segment of the European population. In his own way he was no less attentive to the excesses of abstract thought than were Lawrence and Woolf. There is no doubt he agreed with Yeats that the best lacked all conviction, while the worst were filled with passionate intensity. His diagnosis of these familiar symptoms, however, was decidedly different. In his satires it is not the dominance of one faculty over the other but the failure to sustain a dialectic between them that has left contemporary society divided between mindless action and spineless reflection. Unhampered by conventional moral restraints, the doers of his fictional world go their way "careless of consequence" while the thoughtful find themselves chained by the forms of a tradition they observe but no longer believe in.

Perhaps the clearest statement of Waugh's position can be found in the work of Martin D'Arcy, the Jesuit who assisted him in his preparations for entering the Roman Catholic Church and with whose works he must have been thoroughly familiar. One of D'Arcy's principal arguments in *The Nature of Belief* (1931) may be read as Waugh's recurring thesis abstractly formulated. Taking the Thomistic view of the relation between thought and desire, D'Arcy argues that "they are both distinct and inseparable; the mind is a paralytic and the will is blind, and to meet concrete situations the two must help each other out." The will is naturally inclined toward truth, beauty, and goodness but can go astray unless reason guides it. Human nature, however, is fallible; it cannot be depended upon to behave reasonably in all situations. A man's mind is shaped by his experiences into a "pattern or complex" that "reinforces the native power of intellect." But if "the affective or desirous constituent of the complex usurp the authority of the main constituent, the mind," then "distortion comes about." According to D'Arcy, these "distinct but inseparable" faculties can only find their proper balance in subordination to God's design in which knowledge and power are not antagonistic but rather complementary. This follows the Thomistic conception of God. The essential simplicity of the divine nature does not admit any distinction between intellect and will. As a created being, then, man fulfills his nature to the degree that he approximates, at his own level, the divine unity of knowledge and deed. The solution to the perplexing conflict between thought and desire is faith in a divinity that bridges the distance between them. Only commitment to an absolute can strike a balance between the reflective intellect and the impulsive will.[16]

D'Arcy's work clearly explains what became Waugh's own view of the contemporary obstacle to living a purposeful, civilized life in the twentieth century and how Waugh proposed to overcome it. We can see him addressing himself to related theological issues in his nonfiction as early as 1930, the year of his conversion.[17] With few exceptions, however, he did not do so in his fiction until 1946 when he wrote his first avowedly "Catholic novel," *Brideshead Revisited.* In his earlier and some of his later works, he preferred to represent the crippling division between intellect and will with categories he adopted and parodied from modern philosophy and esthetics. To understand how and why this was so, it is necessary to explore the influences on his thought that preceded and, in some measure, prefaced his commitment to Catholicism.

III

AN UNGUIDED AND HALF-COMPREHENDED
STUDY OF METAPHYSICS

As an undergraduate in the early 1920s, Waugh worked on the *Oxford Broom*, a publication founded and edited by his friend Harold Acton. Its first number included an unsigned manifesto, "A Modern Credo," which asserted in its opening paragraph that

> human nature requires an absolute. The exquisite chaos of modern thought offers this one incomparable opportunity—the creation of new absolute values. Recent intellectual sap has yet to vitalize any adequate forms of existence, and an imaginative apathy is still in vogue. But what sporadic imagination has survived is inevitably God-seeking.

The credo goes on to patronize Plato as one who had supplied a useful "life-concept" for earlier ages but can no longer be taken literally. There must be a quest for a modern "life-concept," one that "can scarcely come about merely through the cerebral or sensual irritations of our usual existence. Something slightly less primordial is required and more sufficient. . . . The ultimate requisite is always idealism incarnate."[1]

Whether or not Waugh had a hand in this piece of undergraduate self-importance, it certainly reflects the longing for certitude and wholeness evident in the novels he was to begin publishing a few years later. In fact, its argument is remarkably similar to the one Father Rothschild makes in *Vile Bodies*. Rothschild, the enigmatic Jesuit who becomes the unlikely moral spokesman of Waugh's second novel, seems to epitomize Western tradition. His name and vocation suggest antecedents in Judaism, Christianity, and European liberal capitalism. This background together with his extensive connections among the rich and powerful ideally situates Rothschild to assess his society—as he does whenever he can get someone to listen. But, oblige him as they occasionally will, none of his influential contacts pay serious attention when he explains that since the

36

Great War the Western world has been plagued by a "radical instability . . . a fatal lack of permanence" (p. 183), which has left the younger generation desperately disillusioned. Rothschild knows what the older, prewar generation refuses to believe: that while many of these heirs to Western civilization want nothing more than a sense of purpose, as many more have given up all hope of ever finding one among the fragmentary remnants of their cultural tradition. Without direction, both groups pursue an endless round of casual debauchery. As Rothschild tries to make clear, a hedonism as willfully improvident as theirs indicates something more than youthful irresponsibility. The Bright Young People have succumbed to a serious case of metaphysical despair. Waugh knew their world first-hand, and, while there is little doubt he was attracted to its energetic pursuit of pleasure, he came to be disenchanted with its emptiness. By 1930 he decided to satisfy his own longing for permanence by entering what he considered a rational faith that gave life a purpose beyond the enjoyment of the moment. But, as his letters and diaries testify, he sought explanations in secular thought well before his conversion.

Having lost his faith as a young man, Waugh turned to philosophy in search of some reliable principles with which to order his life. Instead he discovered "the exquisite chaos of modern thought." Writing of his early intellectual development, he once recalled how he had been deprived of the consolations of his boyhood faith. An Oxford theologian who came to teach at his public school during the First World War had unmoored him from his world of settled certainties and cast him adrift to discover for himself how best to satisfy his metaphysical longings. "This learned and devout man," he explains, "inadvertently made me an atheist" the day he informed Waugh's class that none of the Bible's books were written by their supposed authors and then invited his students "to speculate in the manner of the fourth century, on the nature of Christ." Once this worthy had "removed the inherited axioms" of his faith, Waugh found himself quite unable "to follow him in the higher flights of logic by which he reconciled his own scepticism with his position as a clergyman." And so, one supposes, the feckless Mr. Prendergast first entered Waugh's imagination.[2]

It was during this period of schoolboy doubt that Waugh read Pope's *Essay on Man*. The notes in his edition led him to Leibnitz, after which he began what he refers to as "an unguided and half-comprehended study of metaphysics," advancing only "far enough to be thoroughly muddled about the nature of cognition. It seemed simplest to abandon the quest and assume that man was incapable of knowing anything."[3] But, of course, he did not.

Seven years later (1925), his diary records that he was reading Henri Bergson. What did he make of the philosopher of Becoming? Typical of

Waugh, his entries include nothing in the way of evaluative comment. He only notes that he was "reading a little Bergson."[4] But a few years afterward, Bergsonian concepts appear in his fiction, most notably and comically in *Vile Bodies* in which he plays with the metaphysical differences between Being and Becoming. In this episodic novel, the one chapter that might be thought pivotal concerns an automobile race. As was his manner in this period of his career, Waugh has his narrator interrupt this story and, with apparently sublime indifference to his unfolding plot, indulge in what seems a digression but turns out to be in its own bizarre way absolutely pertinent to the novel. He pauses in the midst of describing the race preparations to meditate with Olympian aplomb on the fruitful comparison to be made between passenger and race cars.

> The truth is that motor cars offer a very happy illustration of the metaphysical distinction between "being" and "becoming." Some cars, mere vehicles with no purpose above bare locomotion, mechanical drudges such as Lady Metroland's Hispano Suiza, or Mrs. Mouse's Rolls-Royce, or Lady Circumference's 1912 Daimler, or the "general reader's" Austin Seven, these have definite "being" just as much as their occupants. They are bought all screwed up and numbered and painted, and there they stay through various declensions of ownership, brightened now and then with a lick of paint or temporarily rejuvenated by the addition of some minor organ, but still maintaining their essential identity to the scrap heap.
>
> Not so the *real* cars, that become masters of men; those vital creations of metal who exist solely for their own propulsion through space, for whom their drivers, clinging precariously at the steering-wheel, are as important as his stenographer to a stockbroker. These are in perpetual flux; a vortex of combining and disintegrating units; like the confluence of traffic at some spot where many roads meet, streams of mechanism come together, mingle and separate again. (pp. 227–28)

With this comic distinction between the cars of Being and Becoming, Waugh parodies the philosophical argument as to whether essence or existence should be granted ontological primacy. Traditional metaphysics, following Plato, used the term Being to refer to that which constituted the permanent essential core of things providing their identity and intelligibility. The accidental appearances of individual existents might change from one moment to the next, but their participation in Being guaranteed that underneath the shifting surfaces of daily experience there was an abiding stability. The more existential turn of modern thought, however, led many in philosophy to argue that this traditional assumption of Being's stabilizing priority in the order of things obscured and devalued the vitality of existence. Of the leading philosophers of this century who have concerned themselves with metaphysics at all, most have focused on change rather than permanence, relativity rather than identity, time rather than eternity.

Instead of a universe of definable beings and settled purposes, thinkers such as Bergson and Alfred North Whitehead had depicted an unfinished world evolving toward an unknown but vaguely beneficent end. Ceaselessly unfolding, the open-ended Becoming of their existential reality had been liberated from the fixity and closure of Being.

This struggle between essentialist and existentialist ontologies was much on Waugh's mind when he was writing *Decline and Fall* and *Vile Bodies*. It was a time when he seems not to have fully resolved the issue for himself. It is not surprising, then, to discover that, along with references to Bergson, he was also alluding to a critic and a theorist who were both affected by the philosopher's ideas. *Vile Bodies* includes a mock footnote to explain the provenance of some absurdly avant-garde party invitations. These, it turns out, were adapted from Wyndham Lewis's short-lived but influential Vorticist journal, *Blast*, and Filippo Tommaso Marinetti's *Futurist Manifesto*. The reason for Lewis's appearance is clear enough. His 1927 treatise, *Time and Western Man*, had attacked Bergson's thought at great length from a classical essentialist perspective. If Waugh was familiar with this work, as one must suppose he was, there is no doubt it appealed to his polaristic imagination. Lewis was the perfect counterweight to Bergson. Marinetti's role is not so immediately apparent, but Waugh seems to have associated his celebration of technological speed and efficiency with Bergson's concept of Becoming. Although he only mentions Marinetti once in a footnote, Waugh's choice of race cars as the embodiment of Becoming had to be more than coincidentally similar to the Futurist's paeans to the "intoxication of great speeds" in roaring cars.[5]

I want to consider first what Waugh found useful in Lewis and Bergson and then take up the Marinetti connection.

In 1930 Waugh paid tribute to Lewis, calling him the Samuel Butler of his age. Like Butler, he was a valuable "critic of contemporary scientific-philosophical systems" and, more than this, had "the finest controversial style of any living writer."[6] So impressed was Waugh, he seems to have set himself to imitation, telling his literary agent that he was ready to write more "Wyndham Lewis stuff" for the magazine editors he was cultivating at the time, a decision that may have been both literarily and economically motivated.[7] At this point in his career, Waugh was avidly courting notoriety. What would be more to his purpose than to become as controversial as Lewis? It would no doubt bring him more and better-paid assignments and he was never unduly delicate about writing occasional pieces to suit a paying market. But, economics aside, Waugh's intellectual preoccupations were such that he could hardly have failed to respond to Lewis's ideas.

For his part, Lewis wrote approvingly, if with some of his typical condescension, of Waugh's early novels.[8] While there is little danger of mistaking Lewis's writing for Waugh's, one cannot help but notice the similarities in their thought and temperament. Both had a highly developed visual sense: Lewis was a respected painter, Waugh an accomplished illustrator. Their training in the visual arts seems likely to have contributed to their dedication to an objective narrative style. Each in his own way composed his fiction with what Lewis called "the method of the external approach . . . the wisdom of the eye."[9] This was the strategy Lewis had suggested in *Satire and Fiction* (1930), a work Waugh reviewed enthusiastically, calling special attention to Lewis's "observations about the 'Outside and Inside' method of fiction," which, he declared, "no novelist and very few intelligent novel readers can afford to neglect."[10] Waugh was responding to something more than technical advice. Lewis had emphasized the importance of writing objectively from the outside as a strategy to hold psychological investigation to a minimum. It was imperative that the novelist resist the temptation of subjective sentimentality. Few counsels could have been as agreeable to a natural satirist such as Waugh, whose purpose was to depict the superficiality of modern life. Lewis and Waugh shared other predilections. Both were politically rightward. Each lamented the bankruptcy of traditional modes of order, and fastened upon this presumed cultural failure as an opportunity to create his own idiosyncratic vision. True, their novels have little in common. Lewis's lumbering narratives gain whatever crude energy they have from his unique brand of bullying animosity. Nothing could be further from Waugh's unlabored ironies and easy poise. His work exhibits none of Lewis's gnashing irascibility. Still, they shared common ground in their opposition to the modernist fashions that were taking hold in the art and thought of their day.

Although Waugh never referred to it directly, Lewis's argument in *Time and Western Man*, published a year before *Decline and Fall*, seems to have supplied him with a good deal of satiric ammunition. In this flagrantly unfashionable treatise, Lewis defends Western philosophy's traditional enthronement of the intellect. Reason, he argues, is in imminent danger of being subverted by modern philosophical trends which characteristically worship the will. When, to demonstrate his point, he exhibits Bergson's philosophy of Becoming as a prime source of contemporary metaphysical confusion, his influence on Waugh seems all but inarguable. As we have seen, Bergsonian Becoming plays a central role in *Vile Bodies*. There are other allusions to the issues Lewis raised with regard to Bergson. In *Decline and Fall*, for instance, the enigmatic Otto Silenus imparts something of the Lewis touch to a speech that parodies Hamlet's disgust with human nature as though its major fault was its tendency to illustrate so convincingly Bergson's concept of Becoming.

What an immature, self-destructive, antiquated mischief is man! How obscure and gross his prancing and chattering on his little stage of evolution! How loathsome and beyond words boring all the thoughts and self-approval of this biological by-product! this half-formed, ill-conditioned body! this erratic, maladjusted mechanism of his soul: on one side the harmonious instincts and balanced responses of the animal, on the other the inflexible purpose of the engine, and between them man, equally alien from the *being* of Nature and the *doing* of the machine, the vile *becoming!* (p. 160)

Along with the Shakespearean cadences, Silenus seems to be echoing Lewis in one of his more misanthropic moods. He attacks the "vile becoming" in terms only slightly more vehement than those Lewis used to argue that Bergson's thought was a major threat to Western man's understanding of himself. In fact, here and elsewhere the affinities between Lewis and Waugh are such that a close examination of Lewis's criticism of Bergson can be used to excavate the unspoken assumptions on which Waugh's fiction stands.

Bergson presented Lewis and Waugh with a convenient target. His work distilled and popularized intellectual trends that traditionalists like themselves thought inimical to civilization. With his democratic assumption that all experiences—sensory and emotional as well as intellectual—were equally worthy of philosophic attention, he was sure to affront those who held to the classical notion that only a discriminating mind disciplined by the 2500-year tradition of Western thought could properly engage the rigors of metaphysical reasoning. His advocacy of intuition as a philosophical tool must have made it seem he was practicing a do-what-you-feel philosophy that located truth in the intensity of the unmediated moment rather than in the rationally demonstrable premises of classical philosophy. Today, Bergson seems rather less formidably subversive than Lewis liked to make him out, but he did call into question Western assumptions about knowledge and truth.

Bergson's thought turns on the opposition between Being and Becoming. His object was to examine the limitations of classical philosophy and find a way to overcome them. In its quest for the bedrock certainty of timeless Being, he argued, the essentialist metaphysics of the West had been chasing a will-o'-the-wisp. Reality was not to be discovered in static concepts, but in the relentless process of evolutionary growth he called Becoming. The reason this had not been understood previously was the Western tendency to trust only the analytical intellect when making metaphysical inquiries. Philosophers had come to assume that reality was only that which the intellect could objectify and communicate by means of representation in language and symbol. Other forms of knowledge—sensate and intuitive—were discounted. They were tainted by their immediate contact with the changeable and therefore unreliable world of material existence. Bergson questioned this evaluation, reminding his readers that the intellect's prized version of reality was, after all, an abstraction from immediate experience.

In Bergson's assessment, this emphasis on intellectual knowledge at the expense of other forms of apprehension exacts a serious toll. Maintained strictly, it manages to alienate us from the world of our immediate perception. Reality becomes an object out there that presents itself to our subjective awareness from across an epistemologically impassable gulf. Since the intellect traffics in representations, it is always and necessarily at one remove from concrete experience. It is as though the reasoning mind were only able to apprehend the visible shell that has just been discarded by the numinous principle within. In order to think or speak about experience at all, we enter into a collaborative fiction by which we pretend that this remnant fossilized by the intellect is the real thing so that we can attach stable, clearly identifiable qualities to it. The thing-in-itself, life itself, which is fundamentally a process of Becoming in time, always eludes our static categories. According to Bergson, this purely intellectual approach to experience cannot help but produce a sense of homelessness. By standing apart from its object of thought, the mind necessarily feels itself to be in an adversarial relation to it. There is a remedy, however. Bergson urges that we "install [ourselves] within change," that is, allow ourselves to experience the moment directly without the intervention of analytical judgment about its significance. In the moment of intuitive experience, there is no gap between the perceiving subject and perceived object; they join in direct, unreflective intuition. Only this total embrace of experience can give us that awareness of the irreducibly real that puts us into emotional and imaginative harmony with our world. This is the incommunicable, almost mystical experience of *durée* in which we unmistakably contact the numinous principle of existence: Becoming. Despite the quasi-sacramental character with which it is described, *durée* turns out to be within the bounds of ordinary experience. As Bergson emphasizes, it is commonly available in those moments of unreflective awareness when we are self-forgetfully engaged with the external world. The problem, Bergson argues, is that the Western philosophical tradition has not valued this experience properly.[11]

Bergson's thought is basically romantic and optimistic; it celebrates each coming moment as one more in "the perpetual climax of the now," to borrow the phrase of another romantic, Norman Mailer, and shares the egalitarian spirit found in Emerson and Whitman.[12] Every new moment collects and advances all previous moments. Time is democratized so that each instant fulfills itself in the universal Becoming. There are no declines, no falls from anterior ideals, only the sense of an ever-improving, gradual evolutionary development. Like Waugh's cars of Becoming, everything is in a "perpetual flux," always becoming but never being itself. It follows that there are no points of definition from which to measure improvement or deterioration. Each existent is no more nor no less than it can be in each successive moment. This, of course, is a vision guaranteed to provoke anyone who either believes in or longs for absolute standards.

Bergson's general argument in *Creative Evolution* was a prime exhibit of the romantic vision that Lewis thought so harmful. In *Time and Western Man* he argues that Bergson's philosophy is subversive to Western civilization because it threatens the privileged positions of reason and individualism in our culture.[13] It naively urges us to abandon the distinction between subject and object so that we can plunge into the temporal flow of experience. Lewis is at pains to warn us that however intense or rapturous this union of subject and object may be, it can only serve to blur our understanding of ourselves and our surroundings. To enter what Lewis calls Bergson's "time-world" requires that we surrender to the confusion of Becoming. It is a devolution into the amorphous world of primitive consciousness in which the self is so thoroughly involved in its experience that the intellect loses the leverage it needs to abstract itself from the immediate moment and thus becomes powerless to formulate the generally applicable distinctions necessary to establish civilized order.

Lewis recognizes, grudgingly it seems, that Bergson's intuitionism can be emotionally rewarding, but he is nonetheless cautionary, describing this reward as though it were a pleasurable but potentially addictive drug. Excessive use can result in passivity and loss of initiative with the fall of civilization to follow hard upon. If not a willful misreading, Lewis's version of Bergson might be considered a creative exaggeration. As no doubt he would have agreed, his argument has the tendentiousness useful for satire. He makes his point by overstating his case. Adopting something of a siege mentality, he warns that surrendering the intellect's spatial world of static forms will unavoidably undermine the fortifications of culture. The uncertainty of Becoming is a weak substitute for the stability of Being. In Bergson's philosophy, Lewis explains,

> pattern, with its temporal multiplicity, and its *chronologic* depth, is to be substituted for the *thing*, with its one time, and its *spatial* depth. A crowd of hurrying shapes, a temporal collectivity, is to be put in the place of the single object of what it hostilely indicates as the "spatializing" mind. The new dimension introduced is the variable mental dimension of time. So the notion of the transformed "object" offered us by this doctrine is plainly in the nature of a "futurist" picture, like a running dog with a hundred legs and a dozen backs and heads. In place of the characteristic static "form" of Greek

philosophy, you have a series, a group, or as Professor Whitehead says, a re-iteration. In place of a "form" you have a "formation."

In other words, Bergson replaces clear thinking with vague approximation. With this analysis of the consequences of Bergson's epistemology, Lewis seeks to prove that far from putting us in touch with reality, the philosophy of Becoming, for all its emphasis on the immediate, offers instead just another instance of the abstract posing as the concrete.

This has important consequences. Lewis reasons that an epistemology that favors ongoing formation over static form will naturally encourage a politics of passivity. Without definite starting and stopping points, it is difficult, if not impossible, to make firm judgments about one's experience. Individualism tends to get lost in the drift of mass opinion. Just as the rowdy Bollingers overwhelmed the orderly Paul Pennyfeather, so the Bergsonian "crowd of hurrying shapes" confounds "the single object" of the classical mind. Because the philosophy of Becoming deprives us of the intellectual tools with which to segment and arrange experience, we lose our purchase upon the terms of our existence. Unable to exercise the civilizing force of the intellect in balance with the will, we lapse into the amorphous world of primitive consciousness and allow our surroundings to shape us, especially the pressure of group thought. The resulting consciousness, for Lewis, is as tribal as it is modern.

> It is definitely our segregations that are to be broken up, our barriers to be broken down. The paradigmatic "objects" that are held up to us, as our mirrors or as pictures of *our* reality, are of that mixed, fluid and neutral character; so that, if we survey them long enough, and accept them as an *ultimate* —as a metaphysical, as well as scientific—truth, they will induce us, too, to liquefy and disintegrate, and to return to a more *primitive* condition.

Lewis finds Bergson's thought most disturbing in its apparent depreciation of the European philosophical tradition. For Lewis, classical metaphysics in the West was to be accounted a positive achievement of the moral will on behalf of intellectual sanity. By insisting that essence precedes and defines existence, Western thought had imposed boundaries on experience that made it manageable. It is this vision that Lewis wants to sustain. Rather than the dynamic flow of *durée*, he offers as his chosen reality the sculptural statics of Platonic forms glimpsed at just those moments when the object of perception most realizes its essence. In this epistemology, the mind is discriminating rather than passive in its pursuit of understanding. It actively seeks the essential nature of things by isolating what is humanly intelligible in them. Lewis approves of this deductive approach to knowing because he adheres to "classical science" in which an object realizes itself, working up to a climax, then it disintegrates. It is its apogee or perfection that is it, for classical science. It is the rounded thing of common sense. Eternity is, for classical science, registered in those moments, or in those things.

The purpose of Bergson's thought, according to Lewis, is to replace this essentialist epistemology of the clearly defined idea with a cloudy, quasi-mystical existentialism that claims to locate reality in the shapelessness of the passing moment. But Bergson's pursuit of truth in the flux was, Lewis argued, even more of a chase after the will-o'-the-wisp than Western philosophy's longing for Being. Worse, it threatened to undermine the stabilizing categories of the commonsense world of ordinary men that rested, however unconsciously, on the metaphysics of Being. Lewis does not make claims for the ontological reality of Platonic forms; he merely observes that life is more orderly and therefore more civilized when it is assumed that permanent principles underlie the flow of appearances. Lewis's point is that whatever reality is, Bergson's particular version of it is but one among many and to insist on its metaphysical preeminence is irresponsibly misleading. Of course, he involves himself in a difficulty here. Even as he argues for fixed principles, he confesses his own relativism. For all his emphasis on reason, Lewis was arguing for what he felt as much as what he thought. Waugh would try to resolve this contradiction through his faith in a transempirical reality.

Lewis was convinced Bergson was "more than any other single figure . . . responsible for the main intellectual characteristics of the world we live in." This included contemporary esthetic assumptions. He was particularly exercised that under Bergson's influence artists had come to assume that their appointed task was to develop strategies that would bypass the intellect. Modernist writers and artists were increasingly intent on capturing those moments of unreflective communion that put one in touch with reality unmediated by any preconceptions whatsoever. Lewis considered this at best sentimental nonsense, at worst potentially subversive of Western sanity. It could only serve to encourage the sort of decadent subjectivism he had detected in such writers as Virginia Woolf, Gertrude Stein, and James Joyce, writers who had turned away, so he thought, from the "Great Without" of the ordinary factual world to dawdle among the velleities of their pampered sensibilities. In Lewis's opinion, such suspension of rational thought was a failure to meet one's responsibility to impose human order on the world.[14]

Waugh's parody of Being and Becoming suggests he agreed with Lewis, even if he was not so militantly ferocious about it. Bergsonian philosophy, according to Lewis, is an "egalitarian science" which recognizes no "objects," that substitutes for them a cluster of "events" or of perspectives, which shade off into each other and into other objects, to infinity. Reality is where things run into each other, in that flux, not where they stand out in a discrete "concreteness."[15]

Waugh provides the appropriate image of this reality with his cars of Becoming in *Vile Bodies*. His description closely parallels Lewis's account of Becoming and even contains one of Lewis's favored words, vortex. These Bergsonian cars, "masters of men," are in a "perpetual flux; a vortex of combining and disintegrating units; like the confluence of traffic at some spot where many roads meet, streams of mechanism come together, mingle and separate again" (p. 228). As for Lewis, so for Waugh: Bergsonian Becoming is a metaphysics that threatens to dissolve the classical world view, submerging the individual in the flux of relativism. Traditional metaphysics was like the cars of Being which maintain "their identity to the scrap heap" (p. 227); it provided stability and continuity. In Waugh's vision, however, the cars of Being have been left behind. In their stead, the cars of Becoming have taken the field, "those vital creations of metal who exist solely for their own propulsion through space" (p. 227). But, vital and efficient as they are, these cars are liable to the same charge Lewis had leveled at Bergson's Becoming. They are more abstract than concrete, more romantic notion than sensible reality. They lack definition and purpose and are much too mercurial to be put to ordinary human ends. Always about to become themselves, they are never actually anything at all. This is the true Bergsonian élan vital: not to exist at any one time in any one place, but rather to be in a "perpetual flux." As the cars roar around the track, they make frequent pit stops to replace worn parts. Like the river of Heraclitus, they are never quite the same car from moment to moment. They are always in the process of becoming the car they will be in the next moment. Rather than an objective car tangibly continuing its existence in time, they present instead the abstract notion of car-ness. This is Waugh's figure of Bergsonian Becoming, then, a world of ceaseless change in which there are no befores or afters, but only a blurred now. This is the modern age in which the clear and distinct idea has surrendered to the shapeless smear of sensation. It was apparently important to both Lewis and Waugh as essentialists that they disprove Bergson's claim that intuition put one in direct contact with reality. Lewis's argument and Waugh's metaphors are meant to illustrate that, upon close analysis, Becoming is far more abstract than the intelligible forms of Being. Neither may bring us substantially closer to the ever-elusive thing-in-itself, but the cars of Being offer this advantage: they permit us to keep our heads and steer our own course, rather than be carried away by a vehicle whose only purpose is its own "propulsion through space" and for whom its driver "clinging precariously at the steering-wheel [is] as important as his stenographer to a stockbroker" (pp. 227–28).

Having examined Lewis's importance to Waugh, we can understand why Lewis is linked to Marinetti in *Vile Bodies.* If Lewis's critique of Bergson shaped Waugh's theme, then Marinetti seems to have supplied his image. Waugh's paean to the racing car closely resembles the kind of celebration of the new technological age found in the modern art manifestos of the early twentieth century, particularly Marinetti's Futurist proclamations. It seems safe to assume that Waugh intended the race episode to satirize not only Bergson's *Creative Evolution* but also the Futurist's worship of speed, mechanism, and inhuman efficiency, or what Lewis scornfully called the cult of "automobilism." Waugh's explicit mention of the *Futurist Manifesto* suggests that the cars of Becoming were a deliberate parody of Marinetti's penchant for saluting the automobile as the instrument which would liberate Europeans from their sentimental attachment to a dead cultural past. As Marinetti wrote:

> The intoxication of great speeds in cars is nothing but the joy of feeling oneself fused with the only *divinity.* Sportsmen are the first catechumens of this religion. Forthcoming destruction of houses and cities to make way for great meeting places for cars and planes.[16]

> We say that the world's magnificence has been enriched by a new beauty; the beauty of speed. A racing car whose hood is adorned with great pipes, like serpents of explosive breath—a roaring car that seems to ride on grapeshot—is more beautiful than the *Victory of Samothrace.*[17]

These passages seem a likely source for Waugh's mock tribute to "the real cars." As if to underscore the connection, the most formidable contestant in the race is named Marino, who is known as "a real artist" (p. 238) for his brutally competitive driving. His name, his reckless driving, and his designation as an artist all point to Marinetti as Waugh's model.

A figure such as Marinetti could not have failed to ignite Waugh's imagination. His wild disregard for the cultural past perfectly incarnated Waugh's worst fears about the age of the Common Man, as he liked to call the twentieth century.[18] But other than as a bogeyman, Marinetti must have struck Waugh as being no more than his time deserved. At least he spoke the truth others were too squeamish to admit. Who could deny the perverse justice in Marinetti's call for an unsentimental, dehumanized art that would deal honestly with the mechanism and speed that had helped to create a world of headlong change? Although Marinetti's practical objectives could have hardly been less congenial to Waugh, his esthetic provided the means with which the artist in Waugh could accurately portray the consequences that follow from an uncritical indulgence of the Bergsonian sensibility. In a racing car one could embrace Bergson's *durée* at its most intense; the heady acceleration of the twentieth century provides immediate kinetic gratification to those willing to abandon themselves to its participatory excitement. As handled by Waugh, Marinetti's Futurism and Bergson's Becoming are closely allied. They both turn their attention to the immediate sensate moment, neglecting questions about before and after, motives and consequences.

Futurist and abstract artists make appearances throughout Waugh's work. They are usually in the background, like the geometric abstractionist in "The Balance" and the Belgian Futurist in *Brideshead Revisited*, but their presence points to Waugh's continuing preoccupation with the significance of modern art. Futurism was particularly useful to him. It offered opportunities for portraying the inhuman consequences of Bergsonian existentialism. He seems to have found in Marinetti's "automobilism" a particularly apt figure for depicting the diminishment of the individual in this century. *Vile Bodies* creates a world in which people have become as replaceable as the standardized parts of their cars. The anonymous race-car drivers are especially expendable. These are the

> Speed Kings of all nationalities, unimposing men mostly with small moustaches and apprehensive eyes; they were reading the forecasts in the morning papers and eating what might (and in some cases did) prove to be their last meal on earth. (p. 223)

The Speed Kings have come to win the prize trophy, "a silver gilt figure of odious design, symbolizing Fame embracing Speed" (p. 230). In the modern world the prize goes to those who can best keep pace with Becoming; those who lag behind among the timeless categories of Being are not in the race at all. This, of course, is another version of Silenus's Big Wheel metaphor with which he separated the dynamic from the static as though they were distinct species. But here the dynamic participants enjoy no advantage over the static spectators. The cars of Becoming master those who drive them. These "unimposing men" lose their individuality to the race; as Paul Pennyfeather had faded into the background of "dimly discernible faces" when he fell from his spectator's position into the "confused roaring" of the Bollinger dinner, so these drivers become indistinguishable from one another as they hide behind their identical "small moustaches and apprehensive eyes." One of the characters exclaims, in a rare moment of insight, "How people are *disappearing*" (p. 266). Paul Pennyfeather had been the mysteriously disappearing hero of *Decline and Fall*. In *Vile Bodies* his disappearing act has become the general condition of society. Individuality is one of the casualties of the dehumanizing speed of a technological society.

Like the cars of Becoming, Waugh's characters lead foreshortened lives. They have little sense of continuity and purpose. Stripped of both their cultural and personal past, they are swept along in a "perpetual flux, a vortex of combining and disintegrating units." Impermanence is the one given in their existence. Waugh signals this by making disguise a prominent feature of his novels. In *Decline and Fall* a butler may be a gangster, a tavern keeper, or Arnold Bennett. In *Vile Bodies* a Jesuit, a rascal, and an aristocrat all affect false beards while titled gentlemen scurry from one party to the next working as gossip columnists. Colonel Blount writes Adam, his prospective son-in-law, a thousand-pound check, signing it Charlie Chaplin. Many improbable complications later, Adam returns to Blount's home disguised as the man his former fiancée has married instead of him. His imposture goes undetected. While one set of characters passes through a seemingly endless succession of disguises, another set responds to the resulting confusion by lapsing into the forgetfulness of cheerful senility. Lottie Crump in *Vile Bodies* is among the earliest of this type. Based on Rosa Lewis, the famous London hotelier, she has solved the problem of memory and identity in her busy world by reducing everyone she meets to namelessness: "You all know Lord Thingummy, don't you?" "There's Mr. What-d'you-call-him." "Your Honour Judge What's-your-name, how about a drink for the gentlemen?" (pp. 43–45) Her policy seems quite logical. Anonymity becomes the most salient characteristic of a world in which people and events so readily shift and slide from under their identifying labels. Like the race cars, no one is quite the same person from moment to moment. Continuity, identity, tradition have all disappeared in the blur of unordered experience.

Speaking on behalf of the Futurists, Marinetti jubilantly proclaimed that they had created "the new aesthetic of speed." "We," he went on, "have almost abolished the concept of space and notably diminished the concept of time. We are thus preparing for the ubiquity of multiplied man."[19] Waugh no doubt agreed with this assessment of the modern sensibility, although he hardly shared Marinetti's enthusiasm for it. To his mind, aimless speed and undiscriminating democracy were the specific symptoms of a general failure of the essentialist tradition to hold its ground against the growing existentialist mood, especially as it was expressed in Bergson's concept of Becoming. His esthetic problem was to find a way to register this mood without succumbing to it. He wanted nothing to do with the expressive fallacy implicit in stream-of-consciousness narration, nor was he attracted to the studied turmoil of literary surrealism. Instead, he devised a fiction of controlled chaos. To do this, he drew upon his knowledge of avant-garde art and, turning its assumptions to his own purposes, shaped an esthetic which might be thought of as an alternate modernism.

IV

A PURE AESTHETE

Interviewing Waugh in 1960, a television journalist rashly assumed he must have turned against the attitudes of "the aesthetic set" with whom he associated at Oxford. Waugh quickly corrected him. "I'm still a pure aesthete," he declared.[1] His nonfiction bears him out. From his first book, a study of Dante Gabriel Rossetti, through his journalism and travel writing, artistic values were his constant preoccupation—so much so that esthetics came to shape his social and political views. He assessed the world in terms of its art and, more often than not, charged it with the same incoherence he professed to find in experimental painting and functional architecture.

Like Wyndham Lewis, Waugh enjoyed posing as a scourge of the avant-garde, a man who stood for the "superb mean" of classicism, honoring the values of restraint and decorum in the arts. But, as in Lewis's case, a good deal of countervailing evidence indicates that Waugh was not immune to the tradition-breaking provocations of modern art, which is not surprising in one so divided between the orthodox and the wayward. This conflict seems to have been an important source of his fiction's characteristic energy. He may have been known as the bête noire of modernist art, but that never prevented him from pilfering its innovations when they served his purpose.

Waugh frequently addressed esthetic issues in general and modern art in particular, but his observations were usually made as glancing asides that interrupted the flow of his travel books, reviews, and occasional essays, the work he did quickly to gain income and notoriety. Of his few sustained arguments, only a handful deal with literature. The others develop his ideas on art and architecture. When taken together, however, his arguments and obiter dicta on both art and literature provide a revealing look at his working esthetic; it is one that seems to have prospered on contradiction. I want to consider both sides of this conflict in order to see what it meant for his work.

The familiar Waugh of unreservedly traditional values was never shy about making his orthodox esthetic preferences know. We meet an extreme version of him in his unfinished novel, *Work Suspended*. This is the narrator's father, an accomplished painter who prides himself on being totally out of step with the avant-garde: "Only Philistines like my work and, by God, I like only Philistines." As far as he is concerned, the public is much better served with opportunities to view his copies of the old masters than to make themselves "dizzy" by "goggling at genuine Picassos."[2]

This was a character with whom Waugh could identify. In his articles and reviews he frequently took similar pleasure in ridiculing what he considered the excesses of modern art. In 1938 he satirized twentieth-century architecture as the excrescence of "the post-War Corbusier plague" during which "horrible little architects crept about [Europe]—curly-headed, horn-spectacled, volubly explaining their 'machines for living.' Villas like sewage farms, mansions like half-submerged Channel steamers, offices like vast bee-hives and cucumber farms sprang up round their feet, furnished with electric fires that blistered the ankles, windows that blinded the eyes."[3]

In 1956 he alluded to Paul Klee's work as "the acme of futility" and did not hesitate to attack those who had been championing such experiments since the turn of the century. These were the fashionable critics who liked to argue that, given sufficient time to develop "new eyes," the public would one day come to appreciate such artists. To explode this "humbug," Waugh derisively pointed out that "in the last fifty years we have seen the drawings of savages, infants and idiots enjoying fashionable favour. The [artistic] revolutionaries have grown old and died. No new eyes have grown in new heads."[4]

This was Waugh's official line, put out for public consumption. With it he was able to stage-manage his chosen role as a Tory debunker of sham fashions. But, as it was meant to do, this official front obscures his highly developed taste for esthetic experiment.

Although Waugh often affected a sneering attitude toward the representative works of twentieth-century art, he just as frequently found himself fascinated by their esthetic innovations. In a very early essay, dated 1917, he stoutly defended cubism against "deliberate misunderstanding of a prejudiced public."[5] In later years he would come to think James Joyce a madman, but in 1930 he was commending his development of narrative technique as a model for young novelists.[6] As late as 1948, he was willing to testify to his conviction that "the artist, however aloof he holds himself, is always and specially the creature of the Zeitgeist; however formally antique his tastes, he is in spite of himself in the advance guard."[7] Waugh may have enjoyed playing the unreconstructed Philistine singing the praises of eighteenth-century architecture, Victorian furniture, and artistic verisimilitude, but a close appraisal of his essays and reviews tells a somewhat more complicated story. His fiction also belies his pose. The abstract, schematic composition of his early work has much more in common with the deliberate distortions of contemporary narrative experiments than it does with the traditional novel.

Waugh may have deplored the metaphysics of modern art but he was quick enough to recognize its esthetic usefulness. A telling example of the ambivalent response it evoked from him appears in his ironic appreciation of Antonio Gaudi i Cornet's buildings, which he chanced upon while passing through Barcelona in 1929. In Gaudi's works, he declares, "is apotheosised all the writhing, bubbling, convoluting, convulsing soul of the Art Nouveau," and he relishes its having broken "through all preconceived bounds of order and propriety, and coursed wantonly over the town, spattering its riches on all sides like mud." Then he goes on to explain in detail.

> But, indeed, in one's first brush with Gaudi's genius it is not so much propriety that is outraged as one's sense of probability. My interest in him began on the morning of my second and, unfortunately, my last day in Barcelona. I was walking alone and without any clear intention in my mind, down one of the boulevards when I saw what, at first, I took to be part of [an] advertising campaign. . . . On closer inspection I realized that it was a permanent building, which to my surprise turned out to be the offices of the Turkish Consulate. Trees were planted in front of it along the pavement, hiding the lower stories. It was the roof which chiefly attracted my attention since it was coloured peacock-blue and built in undulations, like a rough sea petrified; the chimneys, too, were of highly coloured glazed earthenware, and they were twisted and bent in all directions like very gnarled fruit-trees. The front of the building, down to the level of the second row of windows was made of [a] mosaic of broken china . . . , but thoughtfully planned so that the colours merged in delicate gradations from violet and blue to peacock-green and gold. The eaves overhung in irregular, amorphous waves, in places attenuated into stalactites of coloured porcelain; the effect was that of a clumsily iced cake. I cannot describe it more accurately than that because, dazzled and blinded by what I subsequently saw, my impression of this first experience, though deep, is somewhat indistinct.

Having caught his first glimpse of Gaudi's work, he tells us that he rushed off to see as many more examples as he possibly could before he had to leave Barcelona. Of some buildings on the grounds of a recreational park he writes that as he looked at them he

> could not help being struck by the kinship they bore to the settings of many of the later U.F.A. films. The dream scene in *Secrets of the Soul*, the Oriental passages in *Waxworks* particularly, seem to me to show just the same inarticulate fantasy.

He remarks of a church

> that Gaudi has employed two very distinct decorative methods in his sculp-

ture, the one so evanescent and amorphous, the other so minute and intricate, that in each case one finds a difficulty in realising that one is confronted
by cut stone, supposing instinctively that the first is some imperfectly
moulded clay and the second ivory or mahogany. . . . [Gaudi] is a great example, it seems to me, of what art-for-art's sake can become when it is
wholly untempered by considerations of tradition or good taste. Picabia in
Paris is another example; but I think it would be more exciting to collect
Gaudis.[8]

It is not surprising that Waugh should have wanted to collect Gaudis, as
unlikely as such a project would have been. Few experiences are so vividly
gratifying as those in which we find our suspicions confirmed by events
quite external to ourselves. In Gaudi's "two very distinct decorative methods," Waugh seems to have fastened onto an architectural equivalent of his
polarized world. This was just the kind of dichotomy that provoked his
imagination. It does not seem too much to say that Gaudi's buildings expressed for Waugh the disequilibrium fundamental to his vision in which
the extremes of impulse and reason are allowed to run wild. Their "amorphous," "evanescent" yearning echoes his portrayal of desire untempered
by thought. Their "minute and intricate" details suggest the impotent
workings of an intellect unable to achieve an overall formal integration
of the parts at its disposal. Above all, the aura of impermanence captivates him. As Waugh describes it, Gaudi seems to have celebrated in stone
moments of a purely subjective intensity unfettered by the constraints of
traditional convention. Despite his proclaimed classicism, Waugh finds
himself enthralled by these buildings and their willful disregard for the
forms and proportions appropriate to their materials. His comparisons are
telling: they are like "inarticulate fantasies"; rather than solid, habitable
buildings, they look like a "rough sea petrified," an "amorphous wave,"
and a "clumsily iced cake." Although these are institutional structures
meant for the centuries, they appear to be as ephemeral as the gimcrack
settings of a cheaply produced film. Nothing could better indicate how
contemporary assumptions about the nature and value of existence had
turned the artist away from his proper object. For traditionalists like
Waugh art was the one enterprise in which men had the opportunity to
transcend the accidents of time. Yet here was an artist of considerable talent who seemed to have ignored the essential, enduring forms of things in
order to pursue instead whatever stray, accidental impression had taken
his fancy.

Gaudi's buildings must have seemed to Waugh the architectural expression of the Bergsonian flux, which he was to parody a year later in *Vile
Bodies*. They literally concretized the élan vital. Their whimsical structures flouted any known architectural decorum, declaring each shape good

and just as important as every other, provided only that it be feelingly expressed. In Waugh's eyes this could only be viewed as a deliberately ahistorical art that celebrated the rapturous moment. Looking neither before nor after, it focused entirely on the climactic now of Bergsonian experience. Instead of memorializing the perdurable forms found in classical architecture, these buildings hallowed the perishable moment by taking their shapes from transitional intervals—waves about to break, cakes about to melt. For Waugh such works were at once deliciously grotesque and lamentably appropriate, exemplifying, as they did, the instability he thought endemic to the contemporary scene.

Gaudi seems to have engaged both the conservative and anarchist in Waugh. Accordingly, his response is an ironic amalgam of censure and delight. His classically trained mind might disapprove of architecture untempered by tradition and good taste, but his esthetic instinct responded to Gaudi's idiosyncratic energy. Standards may have been neglected, but, intentionally or not, Gaudi's amazing rule-breaking inventiveness did justice to a thoroughly indecorous age. With whatever mixture of irony, Waugh admired Gaudi's genius even as he deplored the vision it served. It is precisely this divided sensibility that he brought to his fiction.

Waugh returned to some of these issues inspired by Gaudi in 1956 when he wrote an essay explaining photography's harmful influence on painting, but he did so straightforwardly without the luxury of ironic appreciation. There is no ambivalence in "The Death of Painting," just a closely reasoned esthetic argument in which he comes closer than usual to making his case against modern art. The argument is especially revealing of Waugh's predispositions because of its implied philosophical grounds. It clearly relies on metaphysical assumptions similar to those that Lewis had enlisted in his dispute with Bergson. Speaking in his official voice, Waugh attributes the decline of representational art to the camera, which had done a "mortal injury to painters" that was "both technical and moral." By seeming to take over the province of pictorial verisimilitude, it had encouraged the artist to pursue either of two unsatisfactory alternatives.

One response was to allow photography to become "the ideological justification for sloth." The artist could forfeit representation to the camera altogether and abandon the traditional discipline of his craft. Why struggle to reproduce the standard "art-school clichés" of form and perspective when the camera can do as well without the effort? Instead of laboriously developing a technique, the artist can slothfully rely upon inspiration to imbue his nonrepresentational work with artistic merit. Slothfully, Waugh insists, because "verisimilitude was what took the time and trouble." In effect, the abstract painter was evading his responsibility to re-present the world and thereby invest it with his own interpretive order.

If the artist was not interested in abstraction, there was the other alternative. He could let the camera discover his subject for him. Since the snapshot had made it possible to arrest and analyze movement at any instant, including those instants that ordinarily elude the unaided eye, the painter could attempt to recreate the novel images so revealed. Although portrayal of this sort of representational truth might be as technically challenging in its way as the discipline of conventional verisimilitude, it begot paintings preoccupied with the transient ungainliness of the inessential moment, a result Waugh thought no less misguided than the abstractionist's product. "The 'slice of life,'" Waugh remarks, "became the principle of many compositions at the end of the nineteenth century" when "for a decade or more painting and photography were very close." The artist could now paint what had never been observable before: postures, grimaces, movement in stop-action, all manner of strained, off-balance subjects, animate or inanimate, that could never have been posed in a studio. All this and more the camera had made available.

> The simplest example is that of the galloping horse. Draughtsmen had achieved their own "truth" about the disposal of its legs. The camera revealed a new truth that was not only far less graceful but also far less in accordance with human experience. Similarly with the human figure. In posing a model a painter was at great pains to place her. His sense of composition, her sense of comfort, the feasibility of maintaining and resuming the pose, were important. . . . Then came the camera shutter to make permanent the most ungainly postures.

What was wrong with this ungainly truth of the camera? Didn't it provide the artist with novel attitudes? Waugh does not spell it out, but he seems to have in mind the same objections Lewis raised with regard to Futurist paintings that attempted to portray "temporal multiplicity" by spatially assembling stop-action moments of bodies in motion. Such art focused on the instantaneous fragment of time snatched from a rhythm that had yet to achieve its formal balance. Seemingly deprived of a unifying artistic force, these fragments spoke of life as though it were aimlessly indeterminate.[9]

Like Lewis, Waugh was convinced that the epistemological assumptions of twentieth-century art had deflected it from its proper course. Instead of the classic struggle to fit the mutable subject matter of this world to the perception of the timeless and essential, modern art either escaped into abstraction or occupied itself with the temporary and accidental. Rather than serving the human need for an abiding sense of continuity and permanence amidst daily uncertainty, it either turned its back on immediate experience or seized upon those aspects of it that exemplified its transient, perishable nature.

This, more or less, is Waugh's official line regarding modernist art. His jeremiads against it alternated between the sarcastic and the portentous and there is no doubt he meant his readers to take them seriously. But this did not prevent the subversive artist in him from appreciating the technical accomplishments of his unorthodox contemporaries.

Perhaps what is most important about Waugh's esthetic analyses is that they reveal at least as much about himself as they do about the art he discusses. His inclination is to polarize his subject matter into binary oppositions that ultimately derive from his initial cleavage of thought and desire. Here the polarity is expressed as form and formlessness, but it clearly parallels his other oppositions: order and energy, the pathetic and the drastic, Being and Becoming. As with everything else he confronted, he seizes upon what he takes to be the essential contradiction in the art he examines. In Gaudi's work he isolates the seemingly irreconcilable tension between the "evanescent and amorphous" on one side and the "minute and intricate" on the other. When he considers modern art in general, he divides it into two camps. There are those who lazily withdraw from life into abstraction and those who rush headlong to embrace the passing moment regardless of all proprieties. One response is fastidiously sterile, the other excessively mimetic.

This tendency to polarize his experience was so much a part of him that it became the basic structural unit of his work. Almost anything that came within his experience was liable to turn up in his fiction as part of a binary opposition, but modern art seems to have been a preferred candidate for this treatment. Perhaps this was so because, as the *Oxford Broom's* "Modern Credo" had suggested, the artistic imagination had a responsibility to resolve the conflict between "the cerebral [and] sensual irritations," between idea and experience, "the ultimate requisite [being] idealism incarnate."[10] To Waugh's mind the modern imagination had failed conspicuously in this enterprise and deserved to be reminded of its delinquency. At the same time its failure was instructive. The twentieth-century artist might not achieve the classic balance between mind and reality that had been his calling's traditional mission, but this shortcoming accurately portrayed the general failure of the modern temperament to sustain an incarnate ideal.

Waugh's first travel book, *Labels,* and his second novel, *Vile Bodies,* published in 1929 and 1930 respectively, offer a particularly vivid example of how he used the polarity he perceived in contemporary art to shape his fiction. To trace this process is to look into his mind and method. It begins in February 1929 in Paris, where he attended an art exhibit in the Rue Bonaparte entitled *Panorama de l'art contemporain.*[11] When he came to record his impressions a year later, two paintings that had been hung side by side remained particularly vivid in his memory. "It was very French," he wrote in *Labels:*

> [Francis] Picabia and [Max] Ernst hung cheek by jowl; these two abstract pictures, the one so defiant and chaotic, probing with such fierce intensity into every crevice and convolution of negation, the other so delicately poised, so impossibly tidy, discarding so austerely every accident, however agreeable, that could tempt disorder, seemed between them to typify the continual conflict of modern society.[12]

Although Waugh mentions many other works on display, it was these two paintings that particularly intrigued him. Clearly he seems to have discovered in their juxtaposition a perfect illustration of his central theme, as a closer examination of their contrast will bear out.

Waugh does not identify the paintings by title and the only extant review of the exhibition does not itemize individual canvases; still it is possible to deduce the style and character of the works he encountered. In the preceding decade Picabia and Ernst had developed styles unmistakably their own. We can be reasonably confident of the type of painting with which each would have been represented in a fashionable art show of 1929. Picabia had become known for his blend of Cubist abstraction and Futurist drollery; Ernst, for his seething surrealism. While we can only guess, Waugh probably neglected to name the paintings because he was more interested in the contradiction they suggested than in the individual merits of either. This would explain what seems to be an obvious discrepancy in the passage just quoted. Although Waugh mentions Picabia first, the sequence of his impressions does not follow this lead. His description of Ernst's "fierce intensity" comes before his assessment of Picabia's "delicately poised" order. Waugh may have arranged his comments negligently, but they are too much to the point to have been carelessly composed. Few sentences could have caught so simply the essential difference between these two painters. The sureness of his response suggests how fully their works engaged his imagination. And how could it have been otherwise? Put side by side as they were, they visually portrayed the antagonistic extremes with which he was always preoccupied. The "continual conflict" they suggested to his mind was, of course, as much a reflection of his divided self as it was a portrayal of the contradictions of modern society. They exemplified once again the incompatibility of rational order and willful energy to which he was always preternaturally alert. Each seems to have contributed to Waugh's portrait of an age in which mind often seems to be in retreat from refractory experience.

Picabia's paintings from this period resemble diagrammatic drawings of machines to which, perversely enough, he assigned human titles such as

The Infant Carburetor, Universal Prostitution, and *The Daughter Born without a Mother.*[13] Resembling the bright color-coded illustrations one might see in an issue of *Popular Mechanics,* these canvases display sanitized mechanisms which have never been sullied with oil or grease, as if to suggest the triumph of the technical over the biological. With whatever mixture of irony, Picabia's vision reveals a self-contained technological world sealed off from dirt and decay, a Futurist celebration in which speed and geometric shape liberate man from the messy unreliability of organic nature. Picabia seems to have taken ironic pleasure in announcing the new age of triumphant mechanism. In his *Daughter Born without a Mother* one machine brings another into existence out of its own internal workings as if to parody the twentieth century's claim to be self-created, self-sufficient, and therefore radically discontinuous with the centuries preceding it. Questions about origin and purpose have been put to rest. Picabia's purely technocratic vision renders such thinking merely quaint. In the world he portrays, efficiency is all. The metaphysician's why has been exchanged for the pragmatist's how.

Ernst's surrealism, on the other hand, presents a world entirely alien to Picabia's. Between 1925 and 1928 he created a series of hallucinatory wildernesses in such paintings as *Forest, The Grey Forest, The Great Forest,* and *Forest, Sun and Birds.*[14] These canvases are crowded with fierce vegetation. Through dense shadows, we glimpse writhing shapes that seem familiar enough at first but, upon closer examination, elude our attempts to identify them. The wild organic vitality of these paintings defeats the mind's inclination to name and categorize. It is a world that evades definition at every turn because it is blankly indifferent to civilized modes of order.

The juxtaposition of these two painters could not have been better suited to Waugh's satiric imagination. They portrayed for him the alternative types of dehumanization that result when men lose confidence in the ability of reason to discover some essential order underlying the chaos of experience. In Waugh's formulation, Picabia stands for an Apollonian retreat from the disorder of immediate experience into a kind of idealized geometric poise, while Ernst represents a mindless abandonment to the Dionysian ecstasy of pure unordered sensation. Given their emblematic importance for Waugh, it is not surprising to see him echo their paintings in *Vile Bodies,* which was published the year following his trip to Paris. Near the end of this novel, he places two contrasting scenes which, like the Picabia and Ernst canvases, are "hung cheek by jowl" without benefit of explanatory or transitional signals of any kind. Their debt to the paintings seems unmistakable. In the first, Nina Blount is physically sickened by the strange perspectives of her first airplane ride; in the second, Agatha Runcible drifts into hallucination as she lies in her hospital bed dying from injuries she has sustained in an automobile accident.

> Nina looked down and saw inclined at an odd angle a horizon of straggling red suburb; arterial roads dotted with little cars; factories, some of them working, others empty and decaying; a disused canal; some distant hills sown with bungalows; wireless masts and overhead power cables; men and women were indiscernible except as tiny spots; they were marrying and shopping and making money and having children. The scene lurched and tilted again as the aeroplane struck a current of air.
>
> "I think I'm going to be sick," said Nina.
>
> "Poor little girl," said Ginger. "That's what the paper bags are for."
>
> There was rarely more than a quarter of a mile of the black road to be seen at one time. It unrolled like a length of cinema film. At the edges was confusion; a fog spinning past; *"Faster, faster,"* they shouted above the roar of the engine. The road rose suddenly and the white car soared up the sharp ascent without slackening of speed. At the summit of the hill there was a corner. Two cars had crept up, one on each side, and were closing in. "Faster," cried Miss Runcible. "Faster."
>
> "Quietly, dear, quietly. You're disturbing everyone. You must lie quiet or you'll never get well. Everything's quite all right. There's nothing to worry about. Nothing at all."
>
> They were trying to make her lie down. How could one drive properly lying down?
>
> Another frightful corner. The car leant over on two wheels, tugging outwards; it was drawn across the road until it was within a few inches of the bank. One ought to brake down at the corners, but one couldn't see them coming lying flat on one's back like this. The back wheels wouldn't hold the road at this speed. Skidding all over the place.
>
> *"Faster. Faster."*
>
> The stab of a hypodermic needle.
>
> "There's nothing to worry about, dear . . . *nothing at all . . . nothing.*"
> (The emphasis is Waugh's.) (pp. 284–85)

The descriptions of these two scenes are remarkably analogous to Waugh's impressions of the Picabia and Ernst paintings. Nina's countryside is as "impossibly tidy" as the geometries of a Picabia canvas; Agatha's hallucination has as much "fierce intensity" as any of Ernst's chaotic scenes.

In addition to the internal textual evidence that links these fictional scenes with Waugh's comments on Picabia and Ernst, two nonliterary considerations support this reading. First, there is their closeness in time: the comments in *Labels* must have been composed between 1929 and 1930, the same period in which Waugh was working on *Vile Bodies*. Second, this same travel book includes what must have been his source for Nina's distressing aerial vision. A few pages before he makes his comments on Picabia and Ernst, he describes the flight that brought him to Paris for the exhibition. It was unpleasantly memorable.

> I was sick into the little brown bag provided for me. One does not feel nearly as ill being air-sick as sea-sick; it is very much more sudden and decisive, but I was acutely embarrassed about my bag. . . . if we had been over the channel it would have been different, but I could not bring myself to throw it out of the window over the countryside. In the end I put it down the little lavatory. As this opened directly into the void the effect was precisely the same, but my conscience was easier in the matter.
> The view was fascinating for the first few minutes we were in the air and after that very dull indeed. It was fun to see houses and motor cars looking so small and neat; everything had the air of having been made very recently, it was all so clean and bright. But after a very short time one tires of this aspect of scenery. I think it is significant that a tower or a high hill are all the eminence one needs for observing natural beauties. All one gains from this effortless ascent is a large scale map. Nature, on an elusive principle, seems usually to provide its own view-points where they are most desirable.[15]

Waugh's flight to Paris seems unquestionably the personal experience on which he drew for his description of Nina's plane ride in *Vile Bodies*. Granted this, it would be reasonable to expect that he incorporated some of his other travel experiences into his fiction. So it is not surprising that his comments on Picabia and Ernst a few pages later can be applied with equal justice to Nina's sickening prospect and Agatha's fatal hallucination.

In the first scene, Nina is presented with a picture of the twentieth century done in the Futurist mode. The unnatural perspective of flight has distorted the conventional countryside scene so that it reveals its distressingly modern condition. This is a world in which standard expectations have been turned thoroughly inside out. Even the usual distinction between the organic and inorganic can no longer be taken for granted. From Nina's plane people seem to be no more than the nearly indiscernible dots one might find on a statistician's graph. The inorganic structures, however, are invested with a vitality that dominates the scene: roads have become "arterial," bungalows are "sown," factories are "decaying." Compared with them, the faceless human beings have faded into their functions, "marrying and shopping and making money and having children" with mechanical regularity. The peculiar arrangement of this last clause reinforces Waugh's point. We would expect to hear that these people are marrying and raising families, earning and spending. By shuffling these activities and adding an extra coordinate conjunction so that first "marrying" and "shopping" are linked and then "making money" and "having children," Waugh suggests syntactically that there are no value distinctions among these activities. In the twentieth century people are reduced to the measurable functions of an economist's report which refuses to distinguish between love and material consumption. In the foreground of Nina's vision, "wireless masts and overhead power cables" form the technological grid under which the century takes its shape. This is a world in which things, especially mechanical things, are more alive than people. Like the geometric poise of a Picabia painting, the scene is "impossibly tidy" and thoroughly dehumanized.

If, in fact, Waugh deliberately connected modern abstract painting with the view of the earth to be had from a plane, then he was doing no more than providing an early demonstration of the point he would make eighteen years later when he asserted that no matter what the artist's personal preferences are he is always in the advance guard.[16] Indeed, Waugh seems to have been ahead of the official avant-garde in this instance. It was not until five years after he wrote of Nina's upsetting flight that Gertrude Stein had occasion to make the same association. Her first experience in a plane led her to record impressions strikingly similar to Waugh's.

> When I looked at the earth I saw all the lines of cubism made at a time when not any painter had ever gone up in an airplane. I saw there on the earth the mingling lines of Picasso, coming and going, developing and destroying themselves, I saw the simple solutions of Braque, I saw the wandering lines of Masson, yes I saw and once more I knew that a creator is contemporary . . . he is contemporary and as the twentieth century is a century which sees the earth as no one has ever seen it, the earth has a splendor that it never has had, and as everything destroys itself in the twentieth century and nothing continues, so then the twentieth century has a splendor which is its own and Picasso is of this century, he has that strange quality of an earth that one has never seen and of things destroyed as they have never been destroyed.[17]

As Waugh seems to have done implicitly, Stein explicitly associated her aerial view of the countryside with the vision of abstract painters. It would be interesting to know if Waugh ever read this passage. One thing seems certain: if he did, he would have agreed with Stein that modernism was aspiring to the discontinuity of a radically present-tense existence, but he would have deplored her congratulatory tone. He had little sympathy for Stein, judging her work to be "outside the world-order in which words have a precise and ascertainable meaning and sentences a logical structure." As for the modernist painters she admired, he thought the "message" of such artists "one of chaos and despair which is not the message of art."[18] Yet, as was evident in his response to Gaudi and other figures such as Gropius, Waugh was hardly insensitive to contemporary experimental art, however much he complained of its improprieties. Here, too, the modernism he officially deplored seems to have become a source of unofficial inspiration. Nina's view of the "impossibly tidy" countryside is quite at one with Stein's vision of a strange "earth that one has never seen" in which "nothing continues." The only difference is that the abstract "splendor" of this new world does not lead Nina to applaud but to vomit, as it also did her creator.

Turning from Nina's distress, Waugh's narrative abruptly enters Agatha Runcible's death-bed nightmare. There is no preparation, no warning. The reader is simply plunged into the chaos of Agatha's hallucination in which her consciousness has been reduced to the rush of black road over which her imagined race car speeds at an uncontrollable velocity. Having come to grief in what the narrator describes as one of the cars of Becoming, Agatha's world has become a blur, not unlike an Ernst painting, filled with shapes without recognizable forms, experience without defining categories. Her hallucination is a surreal parody of Becoming, or, to be more precise, of Wyndham Lewis's account of Becoming. There is no perspective, no past, no future, only the confused sensation of each new moment as she rushes into it. The experience is unquestionably vibrant, "probing," as Waugh had said of Ernst's work, "into every crevice and convolution of negation." It is also fatal. When Agatha's nurse repeatedly assures her "there's nothing to worry about . . . *nothing at all . . . nothing,*" she is correct in a way she does not intend. Nothingness is indeed worrisome. The suggestion is that Becoming leads to nihilism. Pursued to its limits, it literally leaves one with nothing. For Agatha, votary and victim of Becoming, the perspectives of place and destiny evaporate like the "fog spinning past" her. The flux of unordered sensation first knocks her on her back and then overwhelms whatever ability she once might have had for steering her car. As she speeds toward the final nothingness of death, she has no chance to make sense of her experience. There is only the exhilarating but mindless imperative to go *"faster, faster."*

These two scenes mark the course through which Waugh's fiction runs. Their juxtaposition constitutes a principle at once structural and thematic. At one extreme, static, inhuman order; at the other, the unmanageable flux.

Binary oppositions such as this appear throughout his work, forming units of isotonic tension upon which his satire is constructed. The pressure they exert against one another creates the energy characteristic of his narratives. Recurring in large and small ways, some of these polarities are so strikingly obvious that they halt the story, while others linger inconspicuously just beneath the narrative surface. Either way, polarity is always near to hand. It is Waugh's signature, an idiosyncratic expression of personality anterior to any particular writing. His stories are as hostage to his binary imagination as the abstract canvas is to the modern artist's preferred shapes. Waugh announced as much with his early story "The Balance," in which an art studio figures prominently. At one point the narrator stops to observe a "promising pupil" who constructs his life-class figure drawings on geometric principles. While the model takes her break, he continues "calculating the area of a rectangle" that he has abstracted from the shape of her body. Implicit in this scene is the balance of the story's title, a balance poised uneasily at the intersection of biology and artifice. The narrative concludes with its protagonist deciding against suicide and choosing instead to pursue his craft as he reflects that art is one with "the appetite to live—to preserve in the shape of things the personality whose dissolution you foresee inevitably."[19] Waugh approaches his subject matter in much the same way, extracting design from confusion with an almost geometric stylization. But to do satiric justice to the confusion, his designs do not resolve contradictory tensions but rather intensify them. By incorporating the extremes of Picabia and Ernst, he can both satirize and defeat them.

A number of Waugh's binary oppositions have been discussed already and there will be occasion to consider others in chapters to come, but it might be useful to pause here and sample a few more in order to suggest something of their frequency and variety.

Some of these oppositions are little more than throwaway lines. In *A Handful of Dust*, Mrs. Beaver, an interior decorator ever alert to business opportunities, assesses the effects of a fire with a ghoulish inversion of the expected sentiments. It "never properly reached the bedrooms, I am afraid," she laments, but then takes heart. "Still they are bound to need doing up, everything black with smoke and drenched in water and luckily they had that old-fashioned sort of extinguisher that ruins *everything*. One really cannot complain" (p. 3). Elsewhere in the novel, we are told that Tony and Brenda Last hold themselves to a diet "although they were both in good health and of unexceptional figure. . . . It gave interest to their meals and saved them from the two uncivilized extremes of which solitary diners are in danger—absorbing gluttony or an irregular regimen of scrambled eggs and raw beef sandwiches. Under their present system they denied themselves the combination of protein and starch at the same meal. . . . Most normal dishes seemed to be compact of both so that it was fun for Tony and Brenda to choose the menu" (p. 27). The word *normal* in this passage gives the game away. Even as they take precautions against uncivilized extremes, Tony and Brenda have slipped into a world of abnormal division.

In *Scoop*, William Boot, the most reluctant of foreign correspondents, sends his news-starved editor a cable from the African republic of Ishmaelia advising him on local conditions. It concludes, "LOVELY SPRING WEATHER BUBONIC PLAGUE RAGING" (p. 208). In another scene, the elegant Julia Stitch is discovered at the Duchess of Stayle's ball "in the Duke's dressing room, sitting on a bed, eating foie gras with an ivory shoehorn" (p. 101). In *The Loved One*, the sculpture of the colossally vulgar cemetery, Whispering Glades, includes pieces exhibiting grotesque misalliances of material to subject, such as "a toddler clutch[ing] to its stony bosom a marble Mickey Mouse" (p. 80). These comic disjunctions put the reader through verbal pratfalls. Set up to expect one thing, we trip over its opposite. Some are fun, others cleverly underwrite a theme. The bathetically sentimental statue of a toddler, for instance, has a bosom as stony as that belonging to the unctuously solicitous mortician-entrepreneur, Dr. Kenworthy.

These passing instances supply the background against which Waugh. builds larger binary structures. In *Scoop* the oppositions dovetail into one another. Mr. Salter, Foreign Editor for the *Beast*, one of London's leading newspapers, recalls how he had been taken from the "ordered discrimination" of the humor page and "thrown into the ruthless, cut-throat, rough-and-tumble of the *Beast* Woman's Page. From there, crushed and bedraggled, he had been tossed into the editorial chair of the Imperial and Foreign News." His reminiscences are prompted by his present painful assignment. Under direct orders from Lord Copper, the *Beast's* owner, he must convince the retiring William Boot to leave his cloistered country home and hurl himself into the intrigue of an African civil war. *The Loved One* reveals the two faces of Dr. Kenworthy's Whispering Glades with a sudden contrast between its public and professional appearances as the narrator moves from the reception desk to the embalming laboratory.

> The pickled oak, the chintz, the spongey carpet and the Georgian staircase all ended sharply on the second floor. Above that lay a quarter where no layman penetrated. It was approached by elevator, an open functional cage eight feet square. On this top floor everything was tile and porcelain, linoleum and chromium. Here were the embalming rooms. (p. 65)

Below, the fake warmth of pseudo-traditional architecture and decoration, aged wood and soft carpeting; above, the chrome-cold intelligence that has contrived this travesty of funeral customs to profit from the public's exorbitant fear of death.

All of these juxtapositions echo Waugh's original polarity between the cloistered idea and boisterous experience, between what should be and what is. Confronted by modern reality, the intellect retires to its Picabia world of perfect, unsullied patterns, leaving the will to wander blindly through the Ernst forest.

V

SMASHING AND CRASHING
WAUGH ON THE MODERNIST ESTHETIC

If Waugh, in his official guise, was convinced that art and architecture had deserted the cause of sanity and civilization, he was no more sanguine about modernist literature. Sometimes his reactions were flat and specific. Proust was "mentally defective," "plain barmy"; he had "no plan" and the structure of his work was "raving."[1] Virginia Woolf's novels, he recorded in his diary, were no good.[2] Joyce could be detected going mad sentence by sentence in *Ulysses*.[3]

Generalizing from these specific instances, he decided that "the failure of modern novelists since and including James Joyce, is one of presumption and exorbitance. . . . They try to represent the whole human mind and soul and yet omit its determining character—that of being God's creature with a defined purpose."[4] No matter how technically accomplished, art that did not acknowledge, at least by implication, a purposeful reality beyond the sphere of human affairs was incomplete and incoherent. More particularly, the modernist author too often adopted an exorbitantly "subjective attitude to his material."[5] As Waugh implied in his portrayal of the madly self-obsessed worldlings who inhabit his novels, extreme subjectivity was a deranged willfulness that cut one off from the larger picture. It encouraged people to take themselves too seriously on psychological grounds but not seriously enough with respect to their place in mankind's common destiny. When Waugh, who always chose his words fastidiously, called the subjective tendency in modernism exorbitant, he meant just that. As far as he was concerned, it went beyond the bounds of reason.

Waugh neither argues nor illustrates his charge that the modern novel has become excessively subjective. As suggested earlier, his literary criticism generally consists of fragmentary observations. This is why his more carefully reasoned analyses of the visual arts are particularly useful. His remarks on Gaudi's architecture, for instance, serve very nicely to reveal what must have lain behind his criticism of contemporary experimental novels. It will be useful to recall them in relation to Virginia Woolf's explicit program for modernist narrative, especially since her work affronted Waugh's literary taste. In 1919, Woolf had urged novelists to leave behind the constraints of traditional narrative conventions and focus on subjective experience.

> Examine for a moment an ordinary mind on an ordinary day. The mind receives a myriad of impressions—trivial, fantastic, evanescent, or engraved with the sharpness of steel. From all sides they come, an incessant shower of innumerable atoms. . . . Life is not a series of gig-lamps symmetrically arranged; life is a luminous halo, a semi-transparent envelope surrounding us from the beginning of consciousness to the end. Is it not the task of the novelist to convey this varying, this unknown and uncircumscribed spirit, whatever aberration or complexity it may display, with as little mixture of the alien and external as possible? We are not pleading merely for courage and sincerity; we are suggesting that the proper stuff of fiction is a little other than custom would have us believe it.[6]

Woolf's commitment to the varying "uncircumscribed spirit" distinctly resembles the motive force Waugh discovered in Gaudi's shapeless architecture, which appeared to be guided by the whims of spontaneous emotion rather than the discipline of classic archetypes. Woolf's insistence that the artist find his subject in his daily impressions, whether "trivial, fantastic, evanescent, or engraved with the sharpness of steel," seems to anticipate Waugh's description of Gaudi's "two very distinct decorative methods . . . the one so evanescent and amorphous, the other so minute and intricate."[7] While it may be impossible to prove that Waugh was consciously paralleling Gaudi's sensibility with Woolf's, there is evidence that he had taken professional notice of her esthetic in the years just preceding his discovery of Gaudi on his trip to Barcelona in 1929. Certainly his description of "the romantic outlook" in his 1928 book on Dante Gabriel Rossetti recalls Woolf's celebration of life's "luminous halo."

> The romantic outlook sees life as a series of glowing and unrelated systems, in which the component parts are explicable and true only in terms of themselves; in which the stars are just as big and as near as they look, and "*rien n'est vrai que le pittoresque.*" It is this insistence on the picturesque that divides, though rather uncertainly, the mystical from the romantic habit of mind.[8]

Whether or not Waugh was thinking about Woolf when writing about Rossetti and Gaudi, he would have recognized the "romantic habit of mind" in all three. A work such as *To the Lighthouse* would certainly have struck him as being as much a product of the impulsive self and as little tempered "by considerations of tradition or good taste" as one of Gaudi's buildings.[9] As modernists, Gaudi and Woolf shared an epistemology that sanctioned an ahistorical preoccupation with the momentary sensations of purely private experience. Their metaphysics logically led to a misconceived esthetic focused on the "uncircumscribed spirit" of subjective truth. Although Waugh's argument with modernism was less the polemic he sometimes suggested and more a struggle with an opponent some of whose tactics he could not help but admire, he was nevertheless adamantly opposed to what he took to be its goal of setting up the self as the final arbiter of whatever fragment of truth could be discovered in a world emptied of theological transcendence. In his judgment, this permitted every kind of vulgar excess in the name of personal fulfillment, including Gaudi's happenstance architecture and Woolf's uncircumscribed spirit. Instead of external standards established by tradition, modernism, at least the modernism advocated by Woolf, relied on the spontaneous judgment of the self to shape artistic expression, or so it seemed to Waugh. There was no more fallible guide in his estimate.

Of course, there are modernisms and modernisms. What Waugh found objectionable was the quasi-mystical phase of the modernist development that offered itself as a replacement for lost faith. Irving Howe has described this as a fusion of ideology and sensibility that

> strips man of his systems of belief and his ideal claims, and then proposes the one uniquely modern style of salvation: a salvation by, of, and for the self. In modernist culture, the object perceived seems always on the verge of being swallowed up by the perceiving agent, and the act of perception in danger of being exalted to the substance of reality. *I see, therefore I am.* Subjectivity becomes the typical condition of the modernist outlook. In its early stages, when it does not trouble to disguise its filial dependence on the romantic poets, modernism declares itself as an inflation of the self, a transcendental and orgiastic aggrandizement of matter and event in behalf of personality.[10]

Allied with Bergsonian metaphysics, this brand of modernism offered a particularly seductive view that experience was explicable without recourse to a transcendental religious principle. Given his temperament, Waugh was sure to think this dangerous enough to require his combative attention.

Waugh's narrative strategies seem frequently constructed with this modernist esthetic in mind, as if for satiric purposes he were devising a variant and, at times, parodic version of it. Again Woolf provides a convenient contrast. She and Waugh began in essential agreement: the nineteenth-century novel had died. There was no point to rewriting it now that contemporary experience belied its assumptions about the ultimate reasonableness of the world. Having arrived at this conclusion, they go their separate ways. Woolf moves inward on her characters, attempting to render their whole minds. Waugh stays outside, rarely giving us more than a glimpse of motivation.

Woolf was reacting against her predecessors' subordination of character to social and economic issues, and their related assumption that character was a function of material conditions which could be evoked by painfully elaborate exercises in verisimilitude. In her essay "Mr. Bennett and Mrs. Brown" (1924), she imagines Arnold Bennett's handling of a hypothetical Mrs. Brown, glimpsed in the corner of a train carriage. After quoting a long passage from one of Bennett's novels filled with minute description of a middle-class home with its frayed furniture, grimy windows, and prospect of a neighbor's garden, she concludes:

> Mr. Bennett . . . is trying to hypnotize us into the belief that, because he has made a house, there must be a person living there. With all his powers of observation, which are marvelous, with all his sympathy and humanity, which are great, Mr. Bennett has never once looked at Mrs. Brown in her corner. There she sits in the corner of the carriage—that carriage which is travelling, not from Richmond to Waterloo, but from one age of English literature to the next, for Mrs. Brown is eternal, Mrs. Brown is human nature, Mrs. Brown changes only on the surface, it is the novelists who get in and out— there she sits and not one of the Edwardian writers had so much as looked at her. . . . They have developed a technique of novel-writing which suits their purpose; they have made tools and established conventions which do their business. But those tools are not our tools, and that business is not our business.[11]

"For moderns," as Woolf wrote elsewhere, "the point of interest lies very likely in the dark places of psychology."[12] Their subject was to be the self, precisely at those moments when, whether by accident or design, it eludes the conventions of its society. In this undertaking, environment was interesting only as the occasion of the self's emotionally charged sensations, for "the task of the novelist (was) to convey this varying, this unknown and uncircumscribed spirit . . . with as little mixture of the alien and external as possible." To do this, Woolf proposed to discard the novel's conventional methods of representation. Like other modernists, she thought the commonly agreed-upon categories used to explain the world and human life in it were founded upon the unwarranted assumption that the mind had access to objective truth. The commonsense reality of public opinion, however, was better understood to be the product of society's consensual delusion that phenomena could be impartially assessed and made to yield an accurate report of things as they are in themselves. For Woolf, the world was unavoidably colored by subjective longing. There were no clear boundaries separating fact from opinion, certainty from desire. Like Bergson, she refused to satisfy the intellect's thirst for objective definitions. Instead she offered a romantic epistemology that sought reality in the fleeting impressions and intuitions experienced in those moments of unreflective communion that occur before the perceiving subject has the opportunity to distinguish itself from its perceived object. Uncontaminated by culturally acquired intellectual habits, these moments were largely inaccessible to discursive reason. They yielded the kind of unconditioned experience romantics like Wordsworth celebrated for its power to remove the blinders of routine that ordinarily limit our daily awareness of the world around us. But Woolf's romanticized experience differed from Wordsworth's in one important respect. Wordsworth had postulated, however vaguely, a unifying intelligence that imparted to these moments some ultimate purpose. Woolf accepted the epistemology but rejected the teleology. For her there was nothing that bound these experiences together, nothing that made any final sense of them other than the honesty of the artist at the moment of creation. This was what lay behind her ironic contention that human nature had changed in 1910.[13] On the eve of the Great War men were beginning to realize that they were living outside the conventional structures that had been provided in earlier eras by tradition and religion.

Now that artists had been deprived of the usual sources of order, she argued that they had no choice but to explore the self apart from society. The subject matter of art was to be the immediate data of consciousness, that amorphous, endlessly fascinating interpenetration of sensation and sensibility. Novelists must give up the conventions of realism that demanded detailed observation of the social world. Instead, they would depict the genuine self in its moment-by-moment awareness—fertile, chaotic, infinitely suggestive. The self, Woolf's Mrs. Brown, must be rescued from the worn-out furniture of realism.

> At whatever cost of life, limb and damage to valuable property Mrs. Brown must be rescued, expressed, and set in her high relations to the world . . . so the smashing and crashing began. Thus it is what we hear all round us, in poems and novels and biographies, even in newspaper articles and essays, the sound of breaking and falling, crashing and destruction.[14]

This "smashing and crashing" can be heard everywhere in Waugh's fiction, but his aims are quite different from Woolf's. Waugh applied a modernist technique without a modernist ideology. The conservative in him rejected the notion that subjective truth and "the dark places of psychology" were art's special province, but the artist in him welcomed experiment. As a novelist he set himself the task of developing narrative innovations that would reflect the confusion of his age. But he was deter-

mined to do this without succumbing to the self-indulgent vagaries which
he considered the fundamental modernist mistake. He found his solution,
eccentrically enough, in the works of Ronald Firbank.

In his 1929 essay praising Firbank as the novelist's novelist, Waugh announced what must have seemed, supposing anyone noticed, a contradictory appraisal of the twentieth-century novel. On the one hand, he saluted
modern narrative innovations, such as authorial neutrality, temporal dislocation, associational psychology, and the suspension of the ordinary laws of
logic; on the other, he rejected the modernist preoccupation with subjectivity. The true innovator, he claimed, was Firbank because, while experimental, his fiction remained objective.

Waugh found in Firbank's novels a way to avoid both the restrictive conventions of realism and the psychoanalytic excesses of modernism. His el-
liptically evanescent narratives provided an avant-garde strategy that
never lapsed into self-absorbed solemnity. Firbank "emphasized the fact
which his contemporaries were neglecting," Waugh wrote approvingly,
"that the novel should be directed for entertainment." Unlike other novelists whose attempts to deal with the contemporary world had "forced
[them] into a subjective attitude to [their] material, Firbank remained objective." He did so with a wit that Waugh described as "structural." Unin-
timidated by the realist tradition of the novel, Firbank was content to be
elegantly artificial. This was extremely important for the young Waugh
who was as determined as any of his contemporaries to escape the earnest
humanism of the nineteenth-century novel. Although Waugh did not fault
the Edwardian novelists as Woolf had done for their lack of psychological
insight, he did object to their naive narrative logic that assumed the world
was reasonable and human behavior intelligible.

> Nineteenth-century novelists achieved a balance of subject and form only by
> complete submission to the idea of the succession of events in an arbitrarily
> limited period of time. Just as in painting until the last generation the aes-
> thetically significant activity of the artist had always to be occasioned by
> anecdote and representation, so the novelist was fettered by the chain of
> cause and effect. Almost all the important novels of this century have been
> experiments in making an art form out of this raw material of narration.[15]

This sounds like a passage from a modernist manifesto—and it is, in its own
way. Waugh may not have set out to rival Proust and Joyce but he did experiment with narrative form and Firbank provided a useful point of departure.

Firbank's novels are constructed with a series of counterpointed scenes
that flash on and off with disconcerting speed. The mainstays of the traditional narrative—descriptive detail, logical transitions, plausible charac-

terization, orderly chronology—have all but disappeared. His plots do not progress in a linear fashion; rather, they strike a sequence of poses, each expressing its own fey attitude. Although the scenes change rapidly, his narrative seems static. The reader is presented with a series of tenuously connected tableaux reminiscent of a frieze; but, unlike conventional friezes in which the carved relief figures have been arranged to tell a story, Firbank's figures are juxtaposed in mute irony, leaving the reader to fill in the narrative connections. At the beginning of his career, Waugh was obviously impressed by this technique. Particularly pleased with Firbank's disregard for the usual marks of plausibility, Waugh continues in this essay:

> His later novels are almost wholly devoid of any attributions of cause to effect; there is the barest minimum of direct description; his compositions are built up, intricately and with a balanced alternation of the wildest extravagance and the most austere economy, with conversational *nuances*. They may be compared to cinema films in which the relation of caption and photograph is directly reversed; occasionally a brief, visual image flashes out to illumine and explain the flickering succession of spoken words. . . . In this way Firbank achieved a new art form primarily as a vehicle for bringing coherence to his own elusive humor. But in doing this he solved the problem which most vexes the novelist of the present time.[16]

What is the problem that "most vexes the novelist of the present time"? Waugh never quite says, but we can infer that it is the same one Virginia Woolf confronted when she wrote that contemporary writers had lost the sense of certainty that is "the condition which makes it possible to write." However rebellious or experimental earlier artists had been, they generally believed their world was intelligible, at least in theory. But with the decline of belief, twentieth-century artists could no longer feel certain that the world they were representing had any validity beyond their own immediate perceptions. It followed, paradoxically enough, that for all their esthetic groundbreaking, contemporary artists were not as free as, say, Walter Scott or Jane Austen, who were supported in their enterprise by the conviction that the world they inhabited and wrote about made sense not only personally but also publicly and even cosmically. As Woolf herself put it, "to believe that your impressions hold good for others is to be released from the cramp and confinement of personality."[17]

Waugh wanted a method that would allow him to reflect the contemporary lack of certainty without cramping him in the toils of personality. Firbank was his answer. The flickering counterpoint of briefly sketched scenes edited cinematically and held together by a narrative tone best described as dandyish mockery: this was Firbank's lesson and Waugh applied it enthusiastically, pursuing what he referred to as his "absorbing task, the attempt to reduce to order the anarchic raw materials of life."[18] Of course, he could have learned these techniques elsewhere, but Firbank's absurd subject matter, weightless characters, and elliptical wit—in sum, his gossamer inconsequence—were congenial to Waugh's satiric temperament. Here were the materials and methods with which he could construct his vision of man in the contemporary world, stripped of "his systems of belief and ideal claims." Waugh had learned to explode traditional literary conventions with great enthusiasm. Plot and character are laughed away with a surreal salute. Narratives splinter into as many as six or seven unrelated scenes within a few pages. Characters are drawn with paper-thin inconsequence, introduced with no more ado than that allotted Adam Fenwick-Symes in *Vile Bodies,* of whose appearance we learn nothing more than that "he looked exactly as young men like him do look" (p. 7). Verisimilitude dissolves completely when Waugh's narrators interrupt themselves to comment on the unreality of these figures.

That established notions of character in particular should be cast aside in Waugh's fiction stresses how his assumptions differ from those of both Bennett and Woolf. Bennett saw character as the product and instrument of large socioeconomic forces; Woolf saw it as the evanescent succession of momentary feelings and responses. Waugh, however, was convinced that men take their identity from the physical and spiritual structures they inhabit. He used architecture to make his point in *Brideshead Revisited.* This novel's narrator, Charles Ryder, whom Waugh elsewhere identified as his own spokesman in cultural matters, tells us that he "regarded men as something much less than the buildings they made and inhabited, as mere lodgers and short-term sub-lessees of small importance in the long, fruitful life of their homes."[19] As a corollary to this vision of architectural continuity, a man's sense of himself may be said to derive from the culture that preceded him and that, in normal times, he can expect to succeed him. By foregrounding scenes of architectural destruction in his novels, Waugh is able to suggest just how abnormally insignificant and transient he believed life had become in the twentieth century.

The "smashing and crashing" Woolf had urged as necessary to liberate Mrs. Brown resounds in Waugh's fiction as though he had taken Woolf's advice and applied it quite literally. As a result, ancestral homes fall right and left throughout his pages. *Decline and Fall* sets the pattern for Waugh's architectural motif when Margot Beste-Chetwynde replaces her sixteenth-century home with a "surprising creation in ferro concrete and aluminum" that has been designed to eliminate "the human element from the consideration of form" (p. 59). In novel after novel, ancestral homes are razed to make way for functional structures, usually apartment buildings comprised of one-room flats suited for an unsettled generation of self-obsessed transients. This is Waugh's image of a rootless modernity in which people are too preoccupied with themselves to consider anything more than the satisfactions of the present moment. The collapse of traditional structures does not lead, as Woolf had promised, to self-discovery; rather, it reveals the shallow inconsequence of characters who are left to lead absurdly pointless lives amidst the wreckage. Some, like Tony Last in *A Handful of Dust*, temporarily stave off these bleak consequences by repairing to fake replicas of an earlier and presumably healthier age. Others are quite content to exist in the bare functional buildings of modern architecture, blandly and uncritically acquiescing in the metaphysical despair Waugh read in such structures.

Charles Ryder in *Brideshead Revisited* seems particularly close to Waugh on this point. Ryder is an artist who makes his living by painting ancestral homes just before they are torn down, and his career becomes an elegiac mission to record the remains of a dying civilization lest it disappear without a trace. Waugh seems to have thought his fiction would perform a similar function. In 1946 he remarked portentously that he foresaw "in the dark age opening that the scribes [might] play the part of the monks after the first barbarian victories." The monks "were not satirists," he reminds us, but chroniclers of civilization's decline.[20] That would be his role also: a sardonic scribe recording the negligence with which the West was letting itself slip into ruin.

But Waugh did much more than record. Armed with Firbank's structural wit, he set out to create an alternative vision to that of Woolf and other modernist novelists who were pleased to pursue and indulge the self "at whatever cost to life . . . and valuable property." Waugh took modernist assumptions to what he reasoned were their logical conclusions. Consequently, in his satires Mrs. Brown, left unsupported by the common cultural props of personality, dissolves and fades like Paul Pennyfeather into "the kaleidoscope of dimly discerned faces" that constitutes the featureless society of the twentieth century.

VI

BECOMING CHARACTERS
THE SHAMELESS BLONDE AND THE
MYSTERIOUSLY DISAPPEARING SELF

The protagonist of *Vile Bodies* is as inconsequential as any to be found in Firbank. He is introduced as he is about to cross the Channel from France to England.

> A young man came on board carrying his bag. There was nothing particularly remarkable about his appearance. He looked exactly as young men like him do look; he was carrying his own bag, which was disagreeably heavy, because he had no money left in francs and very little left in anything else. He had been two months in Paris writing a book and was coming home because, in the course of his correspondence, he had got engaged to be married. His name was Adam Fenwick-Symes. (p. 7)

Although he is still in his twenties and painfully inexperienced, the book Adam has been writing is his autobiography. Upon his arrival, the English Customs Officers promptly confiscate his manuscript along with another confessional work he is carrying in his luggage, Dante's *Purgatorio*. Both, it seems, are examples of indecent literature. "I knows dirt when I sees it or I shouldn't be where I am today" (p. 25), as one of the officers puts it. After minimal protest, Adam gives up his appeal to reason and soon finds himself in London penniless and quite without prospects. He does nothing further to regain his manuscript and we never learn anything about its contents.

Stripped of his personal past and his cultural tradition—his autobiography and his copy of Dante—he drifts lost in the present moment without plans for the future. He appears without distinguishing marks, a passive victim thoroughly acquiescent to the whims of an arbitrary society. He is one of Waugh's interchangeable people. Bereft of an abiding identity, he shuttles haphazardly from one role to another—would-be author, gossip columnist, vacuum salesman, impromptu pimp, and, finally, a soldier lost in the uncharted landscape of "the biggest battlefield in the history of the world" (p. 314). All the while he remains as featureless as his original description implies. Not only are we left in the dark concerning his physical appearance, we never learn what he thinks and feels. He comes no closer to expressing genuine emotion about his predicament than to vaguely register his discontent with "things" in general: "I'd give anything in the world for something different" (p. 273). His complaints never become more specific. He does not seem to have the resolve to know what he wants. Whatever he was before, once Adam returns to England he is transformed into a creature of Becoming, living haphazardly from moment to moment.

As a character Adam cannot be classified. It would be tempting to think of him as a Candidean innocent but he does not fit the mold. He is quite capable of worldly and even low calculation. He is not above fabricating news to fill his gossip column in the *Daily Excess* and seems to have no compunction about "selling" his fiancée to a competing suitor in order to pay an overdue hotel bill.

There is something essentially undecipherable about him. Because he is deprived of a cultural context and a recognizable psychological interior, we can neither place him nor readily discern his satiric function. He is one of the novel's several unsolved mysteries. Others include a political conspiracy of unspecified intent and the unaccountable world war with which the novel abruptly closes. Like Adam these elements are put before us without apology or explanation.

Waugh deprived his early works of background exposition wherever he could do so without rendering them wholly unintelligible. One's first reading of these novels is something like trying to follow a detective story constructed by an author who has willfully neglected to include some of his plot's important clues and motives. Initially, there does not seem to be any definite solution to the mystery that is so cheerfully flaunted. Someone or something is missing but we are never told who or why. There are criminal forces abroad but no one has any definite charges to press. Shadowy characters flicker about in the middle distance. They find themselves implicated in acts of random cruelty. Mindless violence is liable to break in on them at any moment. And all this proceeds unremarked. Wandering dazed, without the resources to protest their plight, submitting to almost any outrage that happens to come their way, Waugh's characters leave us stranded. Instead of a clearly defined norm from which to gauge lapses in manners and morals, we encounter a disturbing emptiness. Something has been left out. Indeed, Waugh's novels are distinguished as much by what they omit as by what they include. Psychological exposition is especially conspicuous by its absence.

Waugh's fiction seems at first remarkably deficient when it comes to creating the illusion of depth. His characters are stubbornly superficial; they resist all attempts to sound their psychological interiors. Their actions seem to spring into the world without the ground of inward motivation. However appalling the accidents and treacheries that routinely beset them, they rarely express their feelings. In *Vile Bodies* a young couple repeatedly make and break their engagement through the course of their frequent telephone conversations, never raising their voices or forgetting to add a polite good-bye before hanging up. Though they are the novel's central characters, we never learn what they feel about their fluctuating romance. A child in *Decline and Fall* is accidentally shot in the foot, contracts gangrene, and finally dies. His slow decline is reported casually in a series of brief asides over the space of a hundred pages. The only lament is his mother's annoyance that people will think her refusal to attend a wedding a manifestation of her grief rather than the snub it's meant to be. In the same novel the protagonist Paul Pennyfeather discovers that his guardian has used the occasion of his undeserved dismissal from Scone College as a pretext to cheat him of his inheritance. When he diffidently inquires about his rights, he receives no comfort. "Have I no right to any money at all?" he asks. "'None whatsoever, my dear boy,' said his guardian quite cheerfully." So much for Paul's rights. He never raises the issue again and we never learn how he feels about being cheated. The narrator merely observes that "Paul's guardian's daughter had two new evening frocks [that spring], and, thus glorified, became engaged to a well conducted young man in the Office of Works" (p. 12). Not only are we left wondering what Paul Pennyfeather feels about his greedy uncle, we are also kept from all but his most routine responses to the rest of "the unusual series of events of which his shadow was witness" (p. 164).

One critic refers to Waugh's refusal to display his characters' interior development as the "blank silence" that thwarts the reader's understanding at every turn.[1] There is some justice in this charge. Waugh's characters rarely give voice to their feelings. They seem to have little to say about the moral and emotional implications of their experiences however urgent, painful, or startling. In *Black Mischief* Basil Seal inadvertently partakes of a cannibal feast in which the primary ingredient is comprised of his lover's remains. Atrocious as this episode is, neither Basil nor the narrator comments on it, unless one takes as moral commentary Basil's response, on returning to London, to inquiries about his future plans: "No plans; I think I've had enough of barbarism for a bit" (p. 305). And that is all. The same silence characterizes Brenda Last's adulterous affair with John Beaver in *A Handful of Dust*. Other than her vague boredom with married life, we never discover Brenda's motives for taking up with someone who she herself admits is a hopeless dullard.

As mentioned earlier, Waugh at the beginning of his career found Wyndham Lewis's fictional theories useful, especially his ideas about characterization. Lewis was committed to an esthetic of surfaces that were to be rendered by "the external approach" with "the wisdom of the eye." This was a strategy designed to hold direct psychological investigation to a minimum and put sentimental subjectivism under proscription. Character was to be discovered not in Virginia Woolf's "dark places of psychology," but rather in the glare of boldly drawn appearances.[2] Waugh seems to have taken Lewis's prescription and added a dash of Firbank's mockery for good measure. Whether farcical or poignant, Waugh's characters are presented to us deadpan. Their narrative existence is almost wholly external. Character and event are portrayed with the flat, evenhandedness of a craftsman apparently more interested in the style of his prose than the minds of his subjects. The deliberate, ironic counterpoint between Waugh's elegant prose and his inarticulate characters suggests the utter hopelessness of things: complaints would be quite beside the point. There are no remedies. There is nothing to be done but gracefully report the futility of human existence in the twentieth century. Such were Waugh's appetites and inclinations; his satiric vision required that he create a world of shallow little characters who have no consequence because they have blandly resigned themselves to live in a treacherous world without hope of recourse to any effective moral order. These figures have been made to race through a series of mishaps laughably referred to as their lives. In a pointless world there are no depths to be registered. Since purpose is unknowable, there are only appearances to be recorded. Deprived of tradition and order, Waugh's characters have been living in a state of alarm for so long that they have become morally and emotionally numb. There is no outrage they cannot pass over in blank silence.

In the early and some of the later novels, Waugh deprived himself of the conventional narrative techniques used to construct characters. There is little if any interior monologue or omniscient eavesdropping. Instead we listen to a dandyish narrator as he calmly reports the most ludicrous and outrageous behavior in a tone of mocking detachment. This is the narrative voice that can tell us there is "tradition behind the Bollinger" and illustrate the point by recalling that "at the last dinner, three years ago, a fox had been brought in in a cage and stoned to death with champagne bottles." His only comment on this marvelously efficient, if devolutionary, version of the upper order's penchant for riding to hounds is to remark, "What an evening that had been!" (p. 1). By excluding the interior dimension, Waugh developed a tone of bitter mockery that shut out conventional sentiment. Of course, satire typically requires a diminishment or distortion of its characters' psychology in order to prevent the reader from empathizing with its targets. But Waugh's novels exclude the interior dimension so relentlessly that they must be considered a special case. Even in those that moved away from farce toward realism, Waugh continued to use his external approach. There are, however, exceptions. The later works, notably *Work Suspended* and *Brideshead Revisited,* are novels in a much more traditional manner. And there is one quite revealing partial exception in one of the earlier novels, *A Handful of Dust.*

In an interesting way it is this early exception to his general rule of the external approach that best allows us to see what Waugh is doing. Tony Last in *A Handful of Dust,* unlike the characters who surround him, comes equipped with a cultural background and an interior psychology. As a character he is constructed according to the conventions of a traditional novel while the others are presented as surfaces without interiors. This difference in characterization makes Waugh's point about the quality of twentieth-century life. It is a contrast worth examining in some detail.

Tony's initial appearance signals his anomalous condition in Waugh's fictional world. "All over England people were waking up, queasy and despondent. Tony lay for ten minutes very happily planning the renovation of his ceiling." He is not yet queasy with the sickness of Waugh's version of the modern wasteland; he has yet to recognize fear in a handful of dust and still thinks of himself as an individual with purpose, one constructively involved with maintaining a viable tradition of which his ancestral estate, Hetton Abbey, is one of the more important emblems. He believes that he can live apart from his time as though he were a self-assured Christian gentleman of the Victorian period. Accordingly, Tony is still capable of an interior life worth reporting because he insists upon thinking of himself as part of a continuous heritage that extends from the past into the future. He naturally assumes responsibility for its maintenance and renovation. At the novel's opening he has not yet suffered Adam Fenwick-Syme's fate; his personal and cultural traditions have not yet been taken from him by the Customs Officers of modern England. His ancestral home, however spurious its Gothic pretension, is the outward sign of his inward allegiance to the historical sense and it is this sense of his place in history, flawed though it is, that provides him with personal depth.

In contrast, Tony's friends and family have lost this perspective. If they think of it at all, history is a subject filled with curious events and artifacts to be studied and classified rather than a tradition to be understood and lived. Tony's brother-in-law Reggie illustrates this perfectly. When he advises Tony to accept the inevitability of change, he does so with an example taken from his experience as an archaeologist. "Why, ten years ago I couldn't be interested in anything later than the Sumerian age and I assure you that now I find even the Christian era full of significance" (p. 203). Already dead and fossilized, the Western tradition has become a matter of archaeological interest which some may find fascinating but few think relevant to the present. It is this attitude, Waugh suggests, that has permitted the sordid capitulation to efficiency in twentieth-century life typified by the drably functional housing projects spreading throughout London like a seductive disease. Unlike Tony, people generally seem eager to abandon their tradition-laden homes for the chromium-plated apartments featured in these projects. These are the anonymous, streamlined dwellings that serve as Waugh's metaphor of the rootlessness of modern urban life among the affluent. Reggie urges Tony to give up his ancestral house as he has done. "It was a nasty wrench at the time of course, old association and everything like that, but I can tell you this, that when the sale was finally through I felt a different man, free to go where I liked. . . . Big houses are a thing of the past in England I'm afraid." Tony disagrees: "I don't happen to want to go anywhere else except Hetton" (p. 206). In the conflict between Tony's guileless nostalgia and his brother-in-law's ruthless practicality, the novel dramatizes the clash between the sentiment of tradition and the deracinated transience of the twentieth century.

Tony clings to his tradition, but this involves a serious problem. His idea of tradition is as childishly sentimental as his inability to remove his boyhood toys from his bedroom. It is because he does not really understand what he is paying allegiance to that he is unable to defend it when it is attacked by the representatives of modernity, one of whom is his wife.

As the novel opens, we discover that Brenda Last has been thoroughly infected with the twentieth century's peculiar disease. Her sequestered life at Hetton Abbey has not protected her against the virulence of the wasteland. The symptoms can be read in her restless boredom and mindless superficiality. Like Tony, Brenda makes her first appearance as she awakens, but the world she rises to is quite different from his.

> Brenda lay on the dais. She had insisted on a modern bed. Her tray was beside her and the quilt was littered with envelopes, letters and the daily papers. Her head was propped against a very small pillow; clean of makeup, her face was almost colourless, rose-pearl, scarcely deeper in tone than her arms and neck.
> "Well?" said Tony.
> "Kiss."
> He sat by the tray at the head of the bed; she leant forward to him (a nereid emerging from fathomless depths of clear water). She turned her lips away and rubbed against his cheek like a cat. It was a way she had. (pp. 16–17)

Brenda's insistence upon a modern bed sounds ominous within the context of Tony's ancestral home, his cherished Victorian replica of Gothic architecture. Then the litter of letters and papers abandoned across the quilt speaks of a less purposeful awakening than her husband's.

But it is Brenda's colorless face that most gives her away even while it, paradoxically enough, obscures her personality from us. Her nereid face appears to emerge from fathomless depths of clear water. At first this description of Brenda's approach to Tony is troubling. It does not seem to make visual sense. However clear water may be, it will not remain translucent indefinitely. Light can penetrate only so far and certainly does not reach to fathomless depths. At some point even the clearest water turns opaque to the searching eye. How, then, can those depths from which Brenda rises be clear and fathomless at once? Is this an invitation to look into her depths for ourselves? Or is it a signal that there is nothing to be found there? As we examine the passage more closely, we find the fathomless/clear opposition signals how thoroughly its terms are at odds with one another. To reinforce the apparent contradiction between vision and obscurity, the text joins images of shallowness and depth in puzzling tandem. Although Brenda appears to emerge from some fathomless ocean floor, her colorless face is "scarcely deeper in tone than her arms and neck." Waugh makes her a provocatively opaque figure. As a woman who leaves her husband for her lover the day after her son's funeral and then demands that he sell his cherished estate in order to support her new liaison, she behaves with such apparently willful malice that we come to expect the narrative at one point or another to divulge the deeply rooted motives that must account for it. Is Brenda emotionally unstable? Has she been irremediably wronged by Tony at some point prior to the time of the novel? Or is she simply without conscience? We are given no explanations. There is nothing to indicate what Brenda may be feeling beyond a vague boredom with Tony's world. Nor does she ever express any serious doubt or guilt about her behavior. In keeping with her initial appearance, Brenda remains an opaque nereid throughout the novel. She is at once fathomless and shallow, inexplicable and transparent. We are teased with suggestion of depths but each time we try to plumb them we find there is nothing behind her appearances. Brenda is a creature of surfaces that should have an interior explanation and we are puzzled as much as Tony when none is revealed to us.

Without psychological explanation Brenda's willfulness seems inexcusably monstrous. Yet so little information is given, we cannot be sure of our judgment. We know her acts but we never know her. This kind of character development might not be so troublesome in a novel like *Vile Bodies* or *The Loved One* in which Waugh's satire approaches farce. But *A Handful of Dust* is in a different key altogether. Brenda's betrayal of her husband and the pain it causes him are portrayed realistically and quite movingly. Yet when we look for Brenda's motives and thoughts, Waugh serves us with his usual blank silence.

But silence, even blank silence, can have its own eloquence. With regard to Brenda, it speaks quite persuasively. Brenda's lack of resonance suggests that something is missing in her makeup. An earlier age might have called it soul. Whatever is missing, it has left her less than human. Tony's inability to see what lies at the bottom of his wife's fathomless clarity is indicative of what happens when the traditional moral categories come face to face with the dull, unresponsive void of twentieth-century life.

Read this way, Waugh's decision not to dramatize the interior dimension helps to advance an aspect of his theme. He was convinced that this century's failure to sustain credible moral absolutes had diminished the possibilities for personal independence. Rather than making up their own minds according to their understanding of a few immutable principles, people were encouraged to drift along at the whim of the Zeitgeist, hapless automatons incapable of loyalty or commitment to anything other than contemporary fashion. Brenda's liaison is a case in point. The narrator makes it emphatically clear that her affair does not spring from love or even lust. Rather she seems motivated by an externally imposed need to keep up with her fashionable set. It is what her friends are doing—taking maisonettes and arranging assignations, divorcing and remarrying. A creature of her changing times, she simply does not want to be left behind. "The danger that faces so many people today," Waugh wrote in 1932, is "to have no considered opinions on any subject, to put up with what is wasteful and harmful with the excuse that there is 'good in everything,' which in most cases means an inability to distinguish between good and bad." In his opinion, it was clearly "better to be narrow-minded than to have no mind, to hold limited and rigid principles than none at all."[3] Submitting to the fashionable relativism that had permeated moral and philosophical discussion since the beginning of the century was the same as having no mind of one's own. Waugh would have agreed with Wyndham Lewis's argument that only settled principles could provide a fulcrum on which one could leverage the force of individuality. In this line of thought, relativism had the same consequences as Bergson's metaphysic. If the relativist is true to his vision, he must let go of all philosophical positions. Positions imply stability, which the relativist has forsworn. Instead he must allow himself to be swept along in the ceaseless flux of Becoming, never able to gain the footing necessary to stand up and assert his own identity. He is perforce a creature of time and fashion.

While this argument, in one form or another, appealed to Waugh, he was not one to let matters lie so simply disposed. He was ready to concede that relativists did not, like Brenda Last, necessarily lapse into faceless conformity with prevailing fashions. Some clearly had the character necessary to exert their individuality without the support of a communal ethos. But to do so required an endless effort of will which, in Waugh's portrayal, incurred an exorbitant human cost. Mrs. Rattery in *A Handful of Dust* supplies the example here. She is one of Waugh's supremely modern types, a line of characters he originated with Otto Silenus and Margot Metroland, née Beste-Chetwynde, in *Decline and Fall*. As a thoroughly modern creature casually negligent of the artifacts of tradition and without a recognizable emotional interior, she seems at first to be the very embodiment of all that Waugh despises in the contemporary world. Yet she is the novel's only character, other than Tony himself, who is capable of loyalty and her loyalty is completely disinterested at that.

Understanding Mrs. Rattery and the type she represents is crucial for appreciating Waugh's fiction. As distant as she is from the conservative Waugh, her cool, unaffected modernity is very much of a piece with the dandyish, avant-garde pose Waugh liked to adopt as an artist. Ruthlessly unsentimental, she has the Silenus touch that Waugh found a useful antidote to the insipid pieties of humanism.

At the invitation of Tony's friend, Jock Grant-Menzies, Mrs. Rattery visits the Last estate on the eve of the fox hunt in which Tony's son will be accidentally killed.

Jock's blonde was called Mrs. Rattery. Tony had conceived an idea of her from what he overheard of Polly's gossip and from various fragments of information let fall by Jock. She was a little over thirty. Somewhere in the Cottesmore country there lived a long-legged, slightly discredited Major Rattery, to whom she had once been married. She was American by origin, now totally denationalized, rich without property or possessions, except those that would pack in five vast trunks. Jock had had his eye on her last summer at Biarritz and had fallen in with her again in London where she played big bridge, very ably, for six or seven hours a day and changed her hotel, on an average, once every three weeks. Periodically she was liable to bouts of morphine; then she gave up her bridge and remained for several days at a time alone in her hotel suite, refreshed at intervals with glasses of cold milk.

She arrived by air on Monday afternoon. It was the first time that a guest had come in this fashion and the household was appreciably excited. Under Jock's direction the boiler man and one of the gardeners pegged out a dust sheet in the park to mark a landing for her and lit a bonfire of damp leaves to show the direction of the wind. The five trunks arrived in the ordinary way by train, with an elderly, irreproachable maid. She brought her own sheets with her in one of the trunks; they were neither silk nor coloured, without lace or ornament of any kind, except small, plain monograms.

Tony, Jock and John went out to watch her land. She climbed out of the cockpit, stretched, unbuttoned the flaps of her leather helmet, and came to meet them. "Forty-two minutes," she said, "not at all bad with the wind against me."

She was tall and erect, almost austere in helmet and overalls; not at all as Tony had imagined her. Vaguely, at the back of his mind he had secreted the slightly absurd expectation of a chorus girl, in silk shorts and brassière, popping out of an immense beribboned Easter Egg with a cry of "Whooppee, boys." Mrs. Rattery's greetings were deft and impersonal. (pp. 131–32)

Mrs. Rattery is the complete twentieth-century woman, a type that fascinated Waugh. She is without background, "totally denationalized, rich, without property or possessions." The insistence on her uprootedness is reinforced by what is left out of her presentation. But for the barest circumstantial details, we never learn what has driven her to achieve her remarkable presence in the world. She is simply there, changing her "hotel on an average, once every three weeks," periodically "liable to bouts of morphine." Rootless and bored, she is the ultimate twentieth-century transient. In her ceaseless search for sensation, she willfully dictates the rhythm of her life with the use of drugs. Like Margot Metroland in *Decline and Fall*, Julia Stitch in *Scoop*, and Virginia Crouchback in the *Sword of Honour* trilogy, Mrs. Rattery is one of Waugh's goddesses of modernity; her spirit presides over *A Handful of Dust* in much the same way these other goddesses preside over their respective narratives. Like one of George Orwell's streamlined people, she has dispatched the nostalgic accessories of the past and abandoned the needless bother of an interior life as if it were so much excess baggage. Asked her opinion of the ancestral Last estate, she replies that she never notices houses one way or the other. Houses, ancestral houses at least, establish a link from one generation to the next but Mrs. Rattery simply does not value the continuity they represent. She is supremely indifferent to the conventional concerns people have for their past and future. Tony is surprised to learn she has two sons; she offhandedly explains she does not see them often but she knows "they're at school somewhere" (p. 158). Mrs. Rattery's existence is radically present tense. With no background and no interior, she is ideally suited to modern life.

Mrs. Rattery is all cool efficiency, capable of meeting the contemporary world on its own terms. Because Tony Last lives in another world, he cannot understand her. As always happens in Waugh, the traditional categories no longer fit present experience. Before she arrives, Tony conceives of Mrs. Rattery as a "Shameless Blonde," popping out of an immense Easter Egg. In fact she is so far from being a frivolous chorus girl that she seems "almost austere." Her bed sheets gauge the distance between her world and Tony's. They are neither silk nor colored as Tony seems to have expected. Instead they are functional, without ornament except for the "small plain monograms" that mark them with her practical, straightforward, and very contemporary personality. The sexual import of the sheets is quite clear. Tony, living in his sentimental Victorian dream, thinks of unmarried sexual activity as colorfully wicked, silkenly decadent. Mrs. Rattery lives under a different dispensation altogether. Sex, like any other transaction, is to be managed efficiently and practically. She comes equipped with nothing but essentials. We are made to feel that despite her mysterious presence there is nothing hidden about Mrs. Rattery, no depths to be explored. She recalls Brenda's fathomless transparency; like Brenda, Mrs. Rattery seems at first a contradictory mixture of the apparently hidden and the shamelessly revealed. Even the fact that we never learn her first name promotes this sense of a mystery that has nothing to hide. She is as functional in a peremptory sort of way as the no-nonsense formality of her surname from which the frivolous adornment of a given name has been removed. She is in fact neither more nor less than the succession of her appearances.

Tony's "Shameless Blonde" epithet is correct in a way he did not intend. Mrs. Rattery is shameless in that everything about her is completely externalized. She has no reserve, no doubt, no apology. There is no inward self, no private interior distance between what she thinks and what she does. She is indivisibly at one with her visible behavior. In other words, she is not really human but rather an exotic mixture of machine efficiency and animal vitality. In *Decline and Fall* Professor Silenus, exasperated by all that is slovenly human, pays tribute to the perfectly inhuman extremes that Mrs. Rattery seems to bring together: "On one side the harmonious instincts and balanced responses of the animal, on the other the inflexible purpose of the engine, and between them man, equally alien from the *being* of Nature and the *doing* of the machine" (p. 160). As the novel's goddess of modernity, Mrs. Rattery cannot be touched by the usual human emotions.

She arrives at Hetton by plane; like the goddess she is meant to be, she descends from the sky bringing with her the twentieth-century restlessness that will permanently disturb Tony's Victorian dream. She lives the life Brenda dimly aspires to. While staying at Hetton, she discovers Brenda has arranged for an interior decorator to modernize the morning room. Having decided the Victorian molding and dado are depressingly antiquated, Brenda has ordered that the walls be covered with functional chromium plating. Mrs. Rattery cannot resist putting on her overalls and helping the workmen, she is that committed to smoothing away the inconveniences of traditional attachments.

Tony's whimsical dream cannot stand up to Mrs. Rattery's energetic reality. It seems grimly appropriate that her visit should coincide with the death of Tony's son, John Andrew. This misfortune signals the breakup of his nineteenth-century idyll, prompting, as it does, Brenda's departure and her subsequent attempt to have Hetton sold.

There is, however, an important complication concerning Mrs. Rattery. She is not simply an occasion for Waugh to revile the present and lament the loss of a more civilized past. Although Mrs. Rattery is made to represent the modern world's gratuitous destruction of traditional values, she is also the only character in the novel whose personal behavior is wholly admirable. After John Andrew's fatal accident, she stays on at Hetton to manage the affairs that Tony is too upset to handle. She keeps unwanted sympathizers away and provides Tony with the distraction of card games, the only solace that works for him in the absence of faith. Mrs. Rattery's aid is unsolicited and disinterested. She has nothing to gain. Having seen Tony through his ordeal, she flies away before he or anyone else can thank her, never to be seen again.

Mrs. Rattery's presence in the novel puts in question the object of Waugh's satire. Is he attacking modern transience measured against traditional stability? If so, why does he portray Mrs. Rattery, the transient *déracinée*, sympathetically as a worldly wise woman with a disinterested concern for others that she puts into action by coming to their aid so effectively? If Tony Last represents traditional values, the simple moral virtues of a good nineteenth-century gentleman, why is he shown to be so childishly helpless at moments of crisis and so culpably innocent with regard to his wayward wife? We may pity Tony but we are hardly invited to sympathize with him or with what he thinks he stands for. Mrs. Rattery, on the other hand, commands our respect. Here, as elsewhere, Waugh leaves us on our own. In the absence of either psychological explanation or moral evaluation within his narrative, this work, like his other early productions, does not lend itself to a simple explication.

Mrs. Rattery is one of those characters who reveal Waugh's ambivalence about his roles as artist and conservative. There seems to be little doubt that he invested more in Mrs. Rattery than was required of her narrative function. Like Otto Silenus in *Decline and Fall*, she incarnates the modern spirit without apology and Waugh has respected her integrity in doing so. If there is no transcendent principle that makes sense of existence, then her approach to life is indeed commendable. She accepts the nihilism implicit in the world of Becoming, the "perpetual flux" as Waugh had portrayed it in *Vile Bodies*. She is content to live each moment for all it is worth without sentimental nostalgia, making what sense she can of her limited time. We can see this in her addiction to cards, her one unflagging enthusiasm. They serve to relieve the general sense of life's pointlessness by supplying her with moments of order. She kindly urges Tony to take up their existential consolation as he sits numb and inarticulate with grief for his dead son. The modern world has nothing more to offer, Waugh suggests. Traditional rituals no longer make sense of life's accidents. As mentioned earlier, Tony is merely embarassed by his minister's futile attempt to console him. Religion, after all, is "the last thing one wants to talk about at a time like this" (p. 158).

But as well as making its thematic point within the novel, Mrs. Rattery's card playing echoes Waugh's esthetic practice. As cited earlier, he believed that "the artist's only service to the disintegrated society of today is to create little independent systems of order of his own,"[4] a statement analogous to this description:

> Mrs. Rattery sat intent over her game, moving little groups of cards adroitly backward and forwards about the table like shuttles across a loom; under her fingers order grew out of chaos; she established sequence and precedence; the symbols before her became coherent, interrelated . . . then [she] drew them towards her into a heap, haphazard once more and without meaning. (pp. 150–51)

In a "disintegrated society" lacking a commonly held belief structure, Mrs. Rattery creates her own "little independent systems of order," however ephemeral they may be, enjoying her game's fleeting consolations even as she resigns herself to its ultimate futility. This is an instance of her practical, managerial approach to life. Do what you can; accept the inevitable. She responds to the apparent absence of meaning with the kind of resilience Waugh looked for in an artist. As we have seen, Waugh believed that, whatever their private convictions, artists required a special sympathy for their times if they hoped to produce significant results. Like it or not, they were in the avant-garde.[5] If in the twentieth century this meant putting on an inhuman mask, it could only be said that in a soulless age the artist cannot afford conventional human sentiment. One thinks of Waugh's disengaged narrative voice calmly, even delightedly organizing spectacles of outrage that leave his characters hopelessly stricken and befuddled.

Without a trace of nostalgia, Mrs. Rattery is entirely at home in a world emptied of transcendental explanations. When she attempts to assuage Tony's anguish, she prescribes the stoical remedy of one who has jettisoned all illusions: "Stop thinking about things" (p. 152). Here and elsewhere, her determined superficiality appears unimpeachable because it proceeds from her accurate assessment of contemporary life. She accepts things as they are. Clearly Waugh found her response to present conditions more realistic than Tony's, which is founded upon a sentimental humanism that Waugh thought quite spineless since it assumed that one could retain a sense of purpose without the vulgar bother of grappling with metaphysical questions. Commenting on *A Handful of Dust*, he claimed that it "contained all I had to say about humanism" and, indeed, one cannot read this novel without becoming painfully aware that men like Tony Last—obviously decent, well-intentioned, given to inward reflection—often cannot stand up to the casual amorality of an age that largely ignores any claims on its ethical sensibility that extend further than the practical concerns of the here and now.[6] Although Waugh despised the world Mrs. Rattery represents, we cannot help but feel that he nevertheless admired her ability to prosper under the conditions of twentieth-century life. If she achieves nothing else, she at least develops a style that banishes sentimentality and false nostalgia. She does not pretend that nothing has changed since the nineteenth century. Under different guises, Waugh returned to Mrs. Rattery again and again, obviously fascinated if somewhat appalled by the apparent ease with which the various incarnations of her species could accommodate themselves to the moral vacuity of contemporary life.

Mrs. Rattery serves Waugh's satire well. She gives the lie to those who would use tradition to evade the difficulties of the present by enshrining themselves in some charming fantasy of a harmonious past. He takes a certain pleasure in exploding the delusions of his static characters who expect to achieve peace and stability without exertion. Until Mrs. Rattery's appearance in his life, Tony Last exemplifies this line in all its guileless simplicity.

Tony reveres the past but his traditionalism is more a childish dream than a commitment to cultural continuity. He lives in an ancestral home the rooms of which have been named after the figures of Arthurian legend. It is a boy's idea of the perfect house filled with the emblems of the heroic past. But for all his veneration of this tradition, Tony seems to be willfully unaware of some of its darker themes. Although his wife's room is named Guinevere, he is too dim to read the obvious signals of her infidelity until it is much too late to do anything about it. When she leaves him, he finds himself evicted from his Tennysonian reverie. His reaction is to dash off recklessly on a private pursuit for his personal version of the holy grail. This takes the shape of a mythical city, the supposed achievement of some extraordinary civilization hidden away in the jungles of Brazil. He imagines it will replace decadent London and restore the values he had thought present in his life before his wife's betrayal. Again Tony shows himself culpably ignorant of the tradition he claims to respect. Tennyson's Arthur had warned his knights against impractical expeditions after the shadowy grail, which, after all, might have no earthly existence. It was more important to tend to the immediate problems of the realm's daily affairs, however less glamorous they might be compared with such a quest. Like so many of Arthur's knights, Tony chooses to embark on the dreamy quest for an impossible ideal rather than keep up the pedestrian struggle to support civilized values at home. He may value his tradition, but he does not trouble himself to understand it. Like Waugh's other naïfs, he has not thought through its implications and is therefore incapable of applying its lessons to the contemporary scene.

Tony's decision illustrates one of Waugh's recurrent themes: the suicidal negligence of those whose vested interest it should be to preserve Western civilization. It was obvious to Waugh that what men called civilization was a fragile fortress recently carved from the wilderness and that the maintenance of its protective walls demanded unwavering vigilance against the savagery outside to say nothing of the savagery inside. Tony's behavior is one more instance of the widespread dereliction of civilized people throughout England and Europe. Now that "man had deserted his post," as Waugh put it elsewhere, "the jungle was creeping back to its old strongholds." Soon the "seeming-solid, patiently built, gorgeously ornamented structure of Western life was to melt overnight like an ice-castle, leaving only a puddle of mud."[7]

In one way or another almost all of Waugh's novels deal with desertion or eviction from Western life. The painfully unassuming protagonist of *Scott-King's Modern Europe*, however, is no deserter, so when he finds himself facing eviction, he suddenly discovers the resources necessary to resist. Having just returned from a tour of a modern totalitarian state to the school at which he has been teaching classics for twenty-one years, he has had a glimpse of what such eviction would mean and is not about to submit quietly when his headmaster informs him that his program may have to be phased from the curriculum.

> "What are we to do? Parents are not interested in producing the 'complete man' any more. They want to qualify their boys for jobs in the modern world. You can hardly blame them, can you?"
> "Oh yes," said Scott-King. "I can and do." (p. 88)

Considerate of his usually obedient employee, the headmaster offers Scott-King the opportunity to begin teaching other courses, such as economic history, against the day when there may be "no more classical boys at all," but he dismisses this kindness as if it were an unworthy temptation.

> "I will stay as I am here as long as any boy wants to read the classics. I think it would be very wicked indeed to do anything to fit a boy for the modern world."
> "It's a short-sighted view, Scott-King."
> "There, head master, with all respect, I differ from you profoundly. I think it the most long-sighted view it is possible to take." (p. 89)

The year before writing of Scott-King's commitment to this cultural holding action, Waugh sardonically described his own mission in similar terms. As remarked earlier, he saw himself as a contemporary "scribe," who, like the monks of the Dark Ages, would preserve Europe's ideals during its decline into a period of ignorance and disorder. One of these ideals was the "complete man."

In his function as scribe, Waugh was determined to remind his readers of what they were in danger of abandoning. To do this, he arranged to contrast the shriveled expectations of his wanton deserters and reluctant evacuees with the earlier ideal of the "complete man" that achieved its supreme expression in the Odyssean hero. In the Renaissance revival of classical education, this model of confident leadership was especially prized. He was a hero whose settled vision of the world was founded upon unquestioned ethical principles. The certainty of his vision enabled him to pursue his destiny with sure determination. Odysseus and Aeneas might stray from the path of obligation occasionally but they were always aware of their deviations and eventually corrected their courses. In fact, their lapses and recoveries were portrayed as just so many further instances of their heroism. It was the apparent neglect of this heroic ideal in his own society that exercised Waugh to satiric mockery. This is nowhere so evident as in his attacks on the age's unwillingness to commit itself to definite principles. It's hard to be heroic when you no longer know what you stand for.

In Waugh's view of the matter, philosophical relativism had so infected the twentieth-century mind that life for many had become an aimless journey filled with travail and tedium relieved only by moments of intense experience. Whatever spiritual dissatisfaction this may have caused, it was not without its economic usefulness for the capitalist state ready to supply the anodyne of periodic sensation delivered in doses of ever-changing products and amusements. Accordingly, Waugh's world often seems a ceaseless pursuit of excitement in plane rides, automobile races, chromium-plated flats, ridiculous movies, and an endless series of parties that are as expensive as they are foolishly elaborate. There is little room for the Odyssean hero determined to stand by his convictions in an economic system that relies for its prosperity on a ceaselss round of purchase and disposal of insubstantial goods and entertainments. His sort of constancy might retard profits. This is why those who prosper in Waugh's fictional world are precisely those who are most flagrantly inconstant. These are the characters who have surrendered themselves happily to the world of Becoming in which each moment constitutes a total break with the last. Like Lord Copper, the bullying press baron of *Scoop*, or Sir James Macrae, the stupendously forgetful film producer of "Excursion in Reality," they live completely in the present moment, unable to recall today what they said and did yesterday. The degree of their worldly triumph is in direct proportion to the ease with which they can shed earlier commitments. Far from a liability, their forgetfulness is a positive asset.

While Copper's and Sir James's forgetfulness may be farcical, Rex Mottram's in *Brideshead Revisited* is nothing less than strategic. Mottram's is a selective amnesia. In order to enter a politically advantageous marriage, he agrees to convert to Catholicism. His previous marriage and current affair do not deter him from his goal nor does he think himself at all insincere. He is genuinely amazed that his fiancée's family should take exception to his suit upon discovering his former and current ties. Rex's opportunism is a practical consequence of the metaphysics of Becoming. In a relativistic world there is simply no point in subscribing to anything more lasting than the stratagem of the day. Through his narrator, Charles Ryder, Waugh makes it clear that he detests Mottram's type, but he is honest enough to portray this careerist as a competent man of the world. On Waugh's grounds, Mottram may be a metaphysical imbecile, but he is, nevertheless, a skilled politician who knows all the right people and understands how his society works. Regardless of law and regulation, he gets things done. He may have to resort to a shrewdly cultivated contact, a strategically chosen lover, or a smoothly delivered bribe, but, after all, his experience in modern London has taught him that success comes to those who make it a point never to respect absolute standards any further than they can serve immediate ends. By ordinary measurements Rex appears to be an accomplished man of the world, but his achievement has come at a cost. Committed only to his self-advancement, he fails to meet the requirements of Scott-King's "complete man." He is the result of an education designed to fit him for life in the modern world, and so he is something less than he seems. As the Jesuit who undertakes to assist him through his nominal conversion puts it, "The trouble with modern education is you never know how ignorant people are. With anyone over fifty you can be fairly confident what's been taught and what's been left out. But these young people have such an intelligent, knowledgeable surface, and then the crust suddenly breaks and you look down into depths of confusion you didn't know existed" (p. 193). Mottram's disillusioned wife puts it far more forcefully.

> He simply wasn't all there. He wasn't a complete human being at all. He was a tiny bit of one, unnaturally developed; something in a bottle, an organ kept alive in a laboratory. I thought he was a primitive savage, but he was something absolutely modern and up-to-date that only this ghastly age could produce. A tiny bit of a man pretending he was the whole. (p. 200)

It is precisely Rex Mottram's lack of wholeness that enables him to be infinitely adaptable to the ends of contemporary politics and commerce. In contrast, the classically trained find themselves ill-equipped to meet the demands of the modern world. As Paul Pennyfeather and Tony Last belatedly discover, gentlemanly attributes provide little defense against the unprincipled barbarism of the twentieth century.

The concept of the complete man hovers like a mocking reproach in the background of Waugh's fiction. It was against this classical standard that he measured the world. Parody was his chosen gauge.

Classical parody is an essential ingredient in many of Waugh's works. *Decline and Fall* sets the pattern by mimicking the epic journey. Once we think of the novel this way, its episodic anarchy begins to make sense. Paul Pennyfeather's adventures are not the rambling, haphazard hijinks they at first appear to be. Instead, they have been specially contrived to mark him as an inversion of the classical hero. Waugh signals his intention when he has his narrator interrupt the story line, such as it is, with a peremptory flourish to address the reader directly in a manner at once avant-grade and dandyish. He cooly reports that the character we have been reading about for more than 160 pages is only a

> shadow that has flitted about this narrative under the name of Paul Penny-feather. . . . In fact, the whole of this book is really an account of the mysterious disappearance of Paul Pennyfeather, so that readers must not complain if the shadow which took his name does not amply fill the important part of hero for which he was originally cast. (pp. 162–63)

If Paul is at all representative of the results of contemporary education then it is clear that, for the twentieth century, classical values have become little more than shadowy memories of a more civilized age.

Pursuing theological studies at Oxford, Paul thought he was on his way to becoming Scott-King's complete man, but once he is expelled and forced to enter the twentieth century outside his college's walls, he quickly becomes a two-dimensional figure of ridicule. Then, for a brief interval, the narrator allows him to materialize "into the solid figure of an intelligent, well-educated, well-conducted young man . . . . who had been developing in the placid years which preceded this story" (pp. 162–63).

As quickly as he has solidified, however, Paul disappears again because, as the narrator airily observes, he "would never have made a hero, and the only interest about him arises from the unusual series of events of which his shadow was witness" (p. 164). Here, as elsewhere in Waugh, the classical tradition is mocked. Whereas the epic hero descends into the underworld to meet the shades of the dead who impart to him the knowledge he needs to prevail in his mission, it is as a shade himself that Paul descends into the underworld of the twentieth century where he meets figures who are vibrantly, if grotesquely, alive. Rather than instilling competence, these encounters only serve to weaken further Paul's already enfeebled will.

Paul's classical Oxford education might have prepared him to deal with "all the emergencies of civilized life," but it has not equipped him for a hero's role in the barbarous conditions of the contemporary world. In a novel comprised of running gags, one of the more persistent and revealing is Paul's squeamish reluctance to play Aeneas or Dante to the fools, rogues, and madmen he meets on his mock-epic journey through the bizarre climate of the century. As in the conventional epic, each new character feels compelled to recite his life story to Paul upon their first meeting. "I expect you wonder how it is that I come to be here?" (p. 63) "I don't know why I'm telling you all this; nobody else knows. I somehow feel you'll understand" (p. 36). They will make their confession whether Paul wants to hear it or not. At first Paul politely resigns himself to his undesired role. Soon he tries to resist.

> "No," said Paul firmly, "nothing of the kind. I don't in the least want to know anything about you; d'you hear?"
> "I'll tell you," said Philbrick; "it was like this—"
> "I don't want to hear your loathsome confessions; can't you understand?"
> (p. 63)

But they don't understand; they continue to confide in him in spite of his protests. As the epic traveler, however unwilling, Paul has no choice but to listen. But listening is not learning. Paul is all too easily overwhelmed by the rogues and shameless opportunists whom he meets outside the precincts of his classical retreat. Hired to teach in a criminally negligent school in Wales, he readily complies with the headmaster's advice that "schoolmasters must temper discretion with deceit" (p. 24). Taken up by Margot Beste-Chetwynde, a Circe of modernity who collects men as one might stamps, he becomes her willing tool. When she sends him abroad to assist some young women in her employ with their travel arrangements, she neglects to explain that her business is comprised of a chain of South American brothels and the girls he is to help are in the profession. Naive and inexperienced, Paul so hopelessly lacks the resources of the wily Odysseus that he is taken in completely by this Siren. When he goes to prison, accepting the punishment that should be hers, we see that this is one Circe who need not worry about meeting her match in a masterful Odysseus.

In the novel's conclusion, Margot arranges for Paul to be smuggled out of prison and returned to his studies at Scone College. To protect him, she has arranged matters so that the authorities will be convinced Paul Pennyfeather has died and the person who has taken his place at Scone is his cousin. This parody of death and resurrection allows Paul to resume his theological studies grimly determined to avoid any further contact with the contemporary world. And so the novel turns back upon itself, an in-

verted epic journey that leaves Paul where he began.[8] Odysseus also came
full circle, but when he returned to his home in disguise, he did so only to
reveal himself and take charge of his kingdom once more. Paul, however,
returns in order to hide himself and avoid contact with the issues of contemporary life. We last see him reading about ancient heresies and de-
lighting in the punishment meted out to those who strayed from the fold.

> There was a bishop in Bithynia, Paul learned, who had denied the Divinity
> of Christ, the immortality of the soul, the existence of good, the legality of
> marriage, and the validity of the Sacrament of Extreme Unction. How right
> they had been to condemn him! . . . So the ascetic Ebionites used to turn to-
> wards Jerusalem when they prayed. Paul made a note of it. Quite right to
> suppress them. Then he turned out the light and went into his bedroom to
> sleep. (pp. 288, 293)

Whereas Odysseus had been determined to impose his values on the world
around him, Paul has forsaken the struggle to shape experience according
to either the classical or Christian vision. Instead he is reduced to taking
what consolation he can in the spectacle of other ages in which ideas were
taken seriously indeed. Having done so, he can shut his eyes and sleep
through his own.

As many another twentieth-century artist, Waugh frequently took the
measure of contemporary man by comparing him unflatteringly with the
traditional hero. Along with Paul, the protagonists of *Vile Bodies, A Handful of Dust, Scott-King's Modern Europe,* and *Sword of Honour* all suffer the
fate of T. S. Eliot's Prufrock. Each has heard "the voices dying with a dying
fall beneath the music from a farther room" and been powerless to renew
his song. They constitute an antithesis to the classical hero whose place in
the world was established by his carefully memorialized ancestry, his personal reputation, and his determination to achieve his destiny. As we have
seen, Adam Fenwick-Symes allows himself to be stripped of his personal
and cultural past when England's Customs Office confiscates his autobiography and copy of Dante. Tony Last's Arthurian quest proves as futile as it
is misguided. Scott-King manages to put up a holding action against modern encroachments on his classical program for developing the complete
man, but the prospects are not encouraging. Even in the more hopeful, at
least personally hopeful, *Sword of Honour* trilogy which features a protagonist who does not fade into insubstantial shadowiness, heroism seems
only fleetingly attainable and then only with gravely mixed results. When
he decides to become something of a gentleman warrior at the outbreak of
the Second World War, Guy Crouchback looks to the medieval crusader,
Sir Roger of Waybroke, as his model. He envisions himself battling a
league of new barbarians who have signaled unmistakably their animus to

Western civilization with the Hitler-Stalin nonaggression treaty of 1939. "The enemy was at last in plain view, huge and hateful, all disguise cast off. It was the Modern Age in Arms. Whatever the outcome there was a place for him in that battle" (MAA, pp. 7–8). Only after some painfully humiliating lessons administered by the political realities of war does Guy belatedly realize that matters are not nearly so clear-cut. His commitment to the values of the Christian Knight will not enable him to achieve the unqualified success he had hoped for when first volunteering for military service. Like Paul Pennyfeather and Tony Last before him, he discovers that the virtues of courage, honor, and fidelity are thought to be childishly naive by those who have accommodated themselves to the workings of the modern world. But worse than this, he must learn that pursuing his ideal of Christian militancy has led him seriously astray. Acting courageously and with the best intentions, he unwittingly becomes instrumental in destroying those he seeks to save. When he attempts to help a group of Jewish refugees escape their Yugoslavian captors, his efforts only succeed in removing them to another form of imprisonment and, worse, lead to the execution of the two leaders he had befriended. It seems that revering the civilized values of the past can be as delusive as the unquestioning acceptance of the progressive ideology of the present.

Waugh's decent characters are people who have misconstrued the significance of their cultural heritage. They have been encouraged to entertain a childishly idealized portrait of Western civilization that leaves them feeling completely disaffected from the present age. In some instances, their respect for the past, however intense, has about it the curator's instinct to fix objects and events, each in its proper display case. Conservators of antique charm, they cherish their cultural past but neglect what was for Waugh its essential ingredient: the faith that he was convinced had made this civilization vital and productive. Tony Last in *A Handful of Dust* wouldn't dream of missing church on Sunday. It is a weekly routine that helps him maintain his sense of familial and national history. But, sitting in his family's ancestral pew week after week, he does not hear much less believe anything his pastor has to deliver from the pulpit. His religious observance is no more than a trifling ornament to his role as country squire. It has nothing to offer him at times of crisis such as his son's death. But Tony's lack of faith does not merely deprive him of consolation, it leaves him without the strength of conviction to stand by his chosen way of life when it comes under assault by modernity.

Mr. Samgrass in *Brideshead Revisited* provides a more extreme instance of Waugh's criticism of traditionalists who have lost sight of the faith he thought tradition's only justification. *Brideshead's* narrator, Charles Ryder, describes Samgrass as an encyclopedically informed scholar whose

knowledge of history and culture is indisputably exhaustive, buts finds his
learning nonetheless spurious.

> Mr. Samgrass was a genealogist and a legitimist; he loved dispossessed roy-
> alty and knew the exact validity of the rival claims of the pretenders to many
> thrones; he was not a man of religious habit, but he knew more than most
> Catholics about their Church; he had friends in the Vatican and could talk at
> length of policy and appointments, saying which contemporary ecclesiastics
> were in good favour, which in bad, what recent theological hypothesis was
> suspect, and how this or that Jesuit or Dominican had skated on thin ice or
> sailed near the wind in his Lenten discourses; he had everything except the
> Faith, and later liked to attend benediction in the chapel at Brideshead and
> see the ladies of the family with their necks arched in devotion under their
> black lace mantillas; he loved forgotten scandals in high life and was an ex-
> pert on putative parentage; he *claimed* to love the past, but I always felt that
> he thought all the splendid company, living or dead, with whom he associ-
> ated, slightly absurd; it was Mr. Samgrass who was real, the rest were an in-
> substantial pageant. He was the Victorian tourist, solid and patronizing, for
> whose amusement these foreign things were paraded. (p. 110)

For Mr. Samgrass all of Western civilization is a glorious waxworks museum, a source of constant amusement for which he feels no responsibility.
The other characters treat him with the contempt that they do, one suspects, because they intuitively recognize his fundamental insincerity. He
becomes Sammy, the slightly repulsive little man who makes his way in the
world by toadying to the whims of his aristocratic patrons. For all his eru-
dition, he is no more than a soulless flunky, at best an object of scorn, at
worst an interfering nuisance.

If the complete man provides a positive model, Mr. Samgrass provides a
negative one. To the degree a character, even an essentially decent one,
subscribes to Mr. Samgrass's sterile knowingness, he falls just that much
further from grace, as an example also taken from *Brideshead Revisited* will
illustrate. When Charles Ryder tries to jolly Julia Flyte out of the spiritual
crisis she suffers because of her adulterous affair with him, he insensitively
resorts to an unfortunate irony, describing Julia's distress as though she
were acting a part in a play. She asks whether the play is a comedy and he
replies, "Drama. Tragedy. Farce. What you will. This is the reconciliation
scene. . . . Estrangement and misunderstanding in Act Two." Not amused,
Julia angrily retorts, "Oh, don't talk in that damned bounderish way. Why
must you see everything secondhand? Why must this be a play? Why must
my conscience be a Pre-Raphaelite picture?" (p. 291).

Indeed, Charles does see everything secondhand as in a play. Without
belief in any absolutes, the only order he can construct for himself is that
supplied by a taxonomy of the past. Present experience must always be a

belated rendition of the forms established by a cultural canon which has no essential validity beyond a genteel compact among civilized people that it should serve to arrange their lives with a sense of decorum. But grounded as it is on nothing more than a sort of gentlemen's agreement without the support of a transcendental authority, this order cannot hold. Charles Ryder's profitable painting career bears witness to its doomed fragility. As mentioned earlier, he achieves his greatest commercial success painting portraits of the great English country homes, each redolent of centuries of tradition, just before they are to be torn down and replaced by some purely functional modern structure. Like Mr. Samgrass, he knows and delights in the achievements of the past but is powerless to preserve them as anything more than occasions for "an insubstantial pageant" of pretty memories.

For Waugh, Scott-King's "complete man" was not just a matter of classical education, but a state of being achieved through theological commitment. Without belief in some absolute principle, he argued, men are not fulfilled. He made his conviction explicit in 1946, writing about his purpose as a novelist. In subsequent novels he planned to pursue two goals: "a preoccupation with style and the attempt to represent man more fully, which to me, means only one thing, man in his relation to God." "I believe that you can only leave God out by making your characters pure abstractions."[9] When Waugh wrote this, he had just published *Brideshead Revisited* in which, for the first time, he had introduced the question of God and attempted to represent people more fully than he had ever before. The results were mixed as he himself would come to think. He would try these themes again in *Helena, The Ordeal of Gilbert Pinfold* and *Sword of Honour*, but in his other fiction, excepting his unfinished *Work Suspended*, he avoided treating religious issues directly and, accordingly, drew his characters as abstractions. In *Work Suspended* his protagonist, John Plant, a successful detective novelist with no metaphysical or theological pretensions, describes just this approach to characterization.

> The algebra of fiction must reduce its problems to symbols if they are to be soluble at all. I am shy of a book commended to me on the grounds that the "characters are alive." There is no place in literature for a live man, solid and active. At best the author may maintain a kind a Dickensian menagerie, where his characters live behind bars, in darkness, to be liberated twice nightly for a brief gambol under the arc lamps; in they come to the whip crack, dazzled, deafened, and doped, tumble through their tricks and scamper out again, to the cages behind which the real business of life, eating and mating, is carried on out of sight of the audience. "Are the lions really alive?" "Yes, lovey." "Will they eat us up?" "No, lovey, the man won't let them"— that is all the reviewers mean as a rule when they talk of "life." The alterna-

tive, classical expedient is to take the whole man and reduce him to a manageable abstraction. Set up your picture plain, fix your point vision, make your figure twenty foot high or the size of a thumb-nail, he will be life-size on your canvas; hang your picture in the darkest corner, your heaven will still be its one source of light. Beyond these limits lie only the real trouser buttons and the *crêpe* hair with which the futurists used to adorn their painting.[10]

Waugh wrote this in a novel in which he was himself about to attempt a portrayal of "the whole human mind and soul" by including "its determining character—that of being God's creature with a defined purpose."[11] But until this work his practice had been to use the "classical expedient," reducing the whole man to "a manageable abstraction." This is why Firbank was so useful to Waugh. Firbank's weightlessly insubstantial characters, often little more than waggish voices hung on wonderfully implausible names like Miss Miami Mouth and Dr. Cuncliffe Babcock, were perfectly suited to Waugh's intention, which was to satirize the aimless shallowness of people living without "defined purpose."

Of course, Waugh's "algebra of fiction" did not stop with characterization. He endeavored to organize entire novels with an abstractionist's delight in mathematical poise, using stylized recurrences and juxtapositions to create his own "little independent systems of order." To do so he drew on a variety of contemporary art forms. As we have seen, he frequently put the conventions of modern architecture and avant-garde painting to satiric ends. But it was film, the uniquely twentieth-century art, that became his most abiding inspiration. Admittedly, this seems at first an unlikely proposition. Waugh frequently mocked the movie industry and seems to have given little effort to his brief tenure as a scriptwriter.[12] There is, however, abundant evidence that he entertained a lifelong fascination for the esthetic potential of film despite his continuing disappointment with most of its commerical productions. From his earliest stories he consciously constructed his narratives according to cinematic principles. Both in theory and practice, film had just what he needed to shape his antic vision of our century.

It is to this interest and strategy we now turn.

VII

FILM

THE GLARING LENS OF SATIRE

Although Waugh had little respect for the film industry and its products, he frequently expressed himself in terms of cinematic strategy. In 1921, responding to a friend whose story he had read in manuscript, he advised him to

> try and bring home thoughts by actions and incidents. Don't make everything said. This is the inestimable value of the Cinema to novelists (don't scoff at this as a cheap epigram it is really very true.) Make things happen. . . . Don't bring characters on simply to draw their characters and make them talk. Fit them into a design. . . . It [the story] is a damn good idea. Don't spoil it out of slackness or perversity. . . . Have a murder in every chapter if you like but do do something. GO TO THE CINEMA and risk the headache.[1]

Thirty-five years later, when a struggling writer asked him for some professional advice on how to proceed with a biography that was giving him trouble, Waugh suggested he think of his material cinematically.

> Could you not conceive of Maria Pasqua's life as a film? I don't mean—Heaven forbid—that it should be filmed, or that you should attempt to give it any of the character of a Hollywood script. I mean in the *mechanics* of the *imagination*. Instead of seeing it as an historical document, imagine yourself watching a film—each incident as precise and authentic as in the present version, but with the *continuity* (in the technical cinematographical sense) and selective dramatic emphasis and scenery of a film. And then write as though describing the experience. (The emphasis is Waugh's)[2]

This advice may or may not have helped his correspondents, but it certainly aids our understanding of Waugh and the mechanics of his imagination. As a satirist who frequently played the role of farceur in order to mock the decline of Western culture, he necessarily ran the risk of allowing his fiction to lapse into the shapeless slapstick his esthetic temperament abhorred. But there was to be nothing carelessly slack or perverse in his

work. Even at its most knockabout, his fiction always exhibits the craftsman's attention to design. He learned a good deal of his craftsmanship from
cinema, which supplied him with the mechanics to build underlying patterns into his narratives, no matter how helter-skelter their surfaces might
seem to the casual reader.

At least as early as his days writing undergraduate film criticism, Waugh
liked to draw upon the cinematographer's art for his illustrations. It was,
for instance, the filmmaker's mobile camera that became a key element in
his self-portrait. In his one avowedly autobiographical novel, *The Ordeal of
Gilbert Pinfold*, published in 1957, he described himself as a "combination
of eccentric don and testy colonel" (p. 13), a role he devised to keep the
unwelcome at bay. Writing about himself in the third person, he added
that "he offered the world a front of pomposity mitigated by indiscretion,
that was as hard, bright, and antiquated as a cuirass" (p. 13). From behind
this character armour

> he looked at the world *sub specie aeternitatis* and he found it flat as a map; ex-
> cept when, rather often, personal annoyance intruded. Then he would come
> tumbling from his exalted point of observation. Shocked by a bad bottle of
> wine, an impertinent stranger, or a fault in syntax, his mind like a cinema
> camera trucked furiously forward to confront the offending object close-up
> with glaring lens. (p. 12)

The contrasting similes used to illustrate mind and character in this passage are more revealing than their casual deployment would suggest. To
describe his mind, Waugh uses a cinema camera that alternates between
coolly detached long-shots of a remote world and extremely vivid close-
ups of its various outrages. As Pinfold-Waugh's camera-mind darts about
the twentieth century, however, his sensibility remains encased in its
cuirass of tradition. These images may be incongruous, but they are not
careless. The juxtaposition of cuirass and camera aptly expresses his contradictory nature, gauging as it does the tension between his public pose
and private sensibility. On one hand he is the hardened old-guard reactionary encased by views so unalterably settled that he has "never voted in a
parliamentary election, maintaining an idiosyncratic toryism which was
quite unrepresented in the political parties of his time" (p. 6); on the other,
he is the ever-alert satirist enthusiastically, if furiously, rushing out to seize
the provocation of the moment with whatever techniques his age has provided him.

Waugh the reactionary may have sought safe seclusion behind the
armament of tradition, but Waugh the artist liked nothing better than to
zoom in for close-ups of the world's scandals. As he put it himself, his tastes

might have been "formally antique" but he was nonetheless esthetically in the "advance guard."

The cuirass/camera juxtaposition is another instance of the split between the static and dynamic we have already detected in Waugh. The camera seems to have been an especially appropriate figure for him. Other than its contrast with the cuirass, the film medium, or at least its theoretical potential, touched something essential in his ambivalent nature. This is perhaps due to film's special balance of the passive and the active. As an instrument, the camera both records and shapes events; it is simultaneously detached and engaged, incorporating the worst traits of the retiring Paul Pennyfeather and the interfering Basil Seal. In part, this may explain Waugh's lifelong involvement with its possibilities. Film was an ideal tool for a satirist who was both repelled and fascinated by his subject matter.

No one familiar with the sequence of Waugh's work can be surprised by his choice of a cinematic analogy to describe the workings of his own mind. Film always played a prominent part in his life and writing. Some thirty-odd years before *The Ordeal of Gilbert Pinfold* the twenty-one-year-old Waugh helped produce and acted in an amateur film entitled *The Scarlet Woman*. Distinguished by Elsa Lanchester's screen debut, this work had a bizarre plot that included the Pope's attempt to blackmail first the Prince of Wales and then the rest of the royal family into the Roman Church.[3] Two years later he published his first piece of fiction after leaving Oxford, a short story entitled "The Balance." This experimental narrative is arranged, awkwardly at times, to resemble a silent film in progress complete with scene directions and block-lettered captions. There are even italicized remarks made by a viewing audience that is supposed to be "attending" the story with the reader.[4] His first novel, *Decline and Fall*, has for its strange spokesman Silenus, the architect who has gained his unlikely eminence in the world by designing film sets. *Vile Bodies* includes a parody of filmmaking that is as central as anything else in its relentlessly eccentric narrative, which is itself edited much like an elliptical avant-garde film devoted to individual scenes while sublimely negligent of coherent plot development. In "Excursion in Reality," a short story from 1934, and *The Loved One* from 1949 he drew upon his experience as a would-be writer-consultant for the film industry.[5]

Since the metaphorical suggestiveness and organizational strategies of film suffuse Waugh's work, it is not surprising to learn that he was convinced this medium had the potential to become "the one vital art of the century."[6] True, he did not expect it to realize this potential, given the economic constraints of producing and marketing films for a mass audience. He knew artistic considerations would be invariably the first discounted on a balance sheet tallied to accord with the priorities of a commercial film budget. Still, he insisted that film had "taught a new habit of narrative" to novelists. This might be "the only contribution the cinema [was] destined to make to the arts," but for Waugh, one surmises, this was enough to justify serious attention to its craft.[7] His early adoption of Ronald Firbank as a model, for instance, had much to do with the cinematic techniques he detected in Firbank's novels. Firbank, according to Waugh, had abandoned the linear plot in favor of a contrapuntal structure similar to montage. As we have seen, Waugh compared the effect of this practice with that of silent films "in which the relation of caption and photograph is directly reversed; occasionally a brief, visual image flashes out to illumine and explain the flickering succession of spoken words."[8] In his own novels Waugh borrowed Firbank's method in order to construct a narrative equivalent of a film edited in staccato montage. Disparate scenes, unexpectedly spliced together, rush by at a reckless pace contributing to his theme of headlong irresponsibility.

His friend Graham Greene was another filmic novelist whose craft Waugh admired. Reviewing one of his novels in 1948, he praised Greene for approaching his material as would a film director arranging his narrative so as to do away with the need for "an observer through whom the events are recorded and emotions transmitted."

> It is as though out of an infinite length of film, sequences had been cut which, assembled, comprise an experience which is the reader's alone, without any correspondence to the experience of the protagonists. The writer has become director and producer.[9]

Whether or not this fairly describes Greene's practice, it certainly explains Waugh's.

But Waugh's interest in film was more than purely technical. His attraction was at least as theoretical as it was practical. The medium's peculiar perceptual qualities seemed to express just those unquestioned assumptions of his age that he most wanted to satirize. Of course, when we come to discuss his cinematic borrowings, we will find that matters are not so neatly separable. Theory and technique, as we would expect, blend in the finished work. So before going on to review Waugh's application of cinematic strategies, it will be useful to pause for a moment and set forth in a general way how film affected his thinking and practice.

Film was the perfect analogue for Waugh's vision of a world that had forfeited the consoling stability of Being for the impassioned tumult of Becoming. He had counseled other writers to imagine themselves watching a film when attempting to organize their subject matter. He followed his own advice, but with this difference: he used cinematic strategies to organize his vision of disorder. The resulting portrait displays a world that has lost its head and with it any sense of purpose larger than personal aggrandizement. As Wyndham Lewis, Arnold Hauser, Marshall McLuhan, and other theorists have argued, film's esthetic experience is one that dissolves the conventional perspectives of time and space, presenting in their stead a dreamlike amalgam of disparate sensations held together by an associational rather than strictly sequential logic. It is a medium that can link the most unlikely images, deploy multiple perspectives as easily as changing a camera angle, and celebrate motion with an immediacy unavailable to any other art form.[10] As such, it was ideal for insulting the classical, literate mind conditioned to expect continuity and logical progression in works of art, and Waugh delighted in using it this way.

If film's formal characteristics suited Waugh's satiric ends, so did its manner of presentation. A typical film audience rarely has the opportunity or inclination to achieve that state of detached contemplation which had been the ideal of classical art. Film encourages a sensuous immersion in the flow of its images. Its appeal is primarily emotional, even visceral, and only secondarily intellectual. This is true both because of its extraordinary formal features and the way they are experienced. Unlike other arts, film traps its audience during its unreeling and leaves scant opportunity for critical reflection. The viewer in his theater seat cannot review a difficult passage at will. He cannot indulge his intellectual curiosity to reconsider individual scenes from new perspectives. At least not until he attends another screening. This temporal aspect of film most resembles music. But even music permits the kind of reviewing necessary to intellectual analysis when it is translated into a score or, in our age, recorded so that the listener can repeat passages as he wishes. Of all arts, film has proven most resistant to critical analysis because it has been generally experienced in theaters which do not permit the viewer any control over its presentation. With literature and art one can return to the works under consideration to sift and weigh impressions, correcting and amplifying them as renewed experience indicates. Until the recent introduction of inexpensive home viewing equipment, this was a luxury few of the general film audience enjoyed. Furthermore, unlike drama scripts, only a tiny percentage of screenplays are published for general consumption. As a result, viewers have not had a permanent document to refer to and have been hard pressed to formulate fully developed responses to films, let alone interpretations adequately tested by reexamination of the primary evidence. Of course this is changing now that it has become an easy matter to view a film privately with the means to control the speed and direction of its images. When Waugh was writing, however, film watching was done passively in a theater and as such it provided him with an apt metaphor of the traditionally formed mind confronted by experience over which it was powerless to exert an interpretive order. He only had to exaggerate film's formal characteristics, constructing his narratives as though he were a director sublimely indifferent to the excesses of his mobile camera and montage editing.

On the evidence of his fiction, this was film's basic appeal for Waugh. It allowed him to achieve his goals as satirist and esthete simultaneously. If the nature of cinema's structure and reception helped him evoke a society out of control, it also provided him with the means to stand aside from the confusion he portrayed and manage it. The distinction here is between experiencing film and making it. His typical early novel might be a whirligig of futility, but it is, nevertheless, assembled with the purposeful deliberation of a director standing apart from the complex operation of filmmaking so that he can make the decisions necessary to bring together its many components. The results may be a cacaphonous farce, but the reader is rarely in doubt that there is a cool, detached intelligence orchestrating the noise. This is nowhere more evident than in the discrepancy between the apparent shapelessness of Waugh's frenetic novels and the superbly mannered voice that narrates them. Waugh was drawn to the paradoxical nature of filmmaking because it was a medium that perfectly expressed the headlong nature of contemporary life, but did so only at the bidding of a serene, calculating intelligence. (Was Waugh parodying himself in *Decline and Fall* in the character of the sublimely disinterested Otto Silenus, architect and film-set designer, sitting at the still center of life's spinning wheel?) Although there is every reason to believe Waugh's art sprang as much from his emotions and intuitions as from his intellect, he seems to have been pleased to think of himself as a purely intellectual craftsman building an esthetic structure that at once expressed and contained his satiric energy.[11] His obvious enthusiasm for conceiving of himself as an unemotional, disinterested craftsman shows up in his praise of those writers like Firbank and Greene whose relation to their works is that of "director and producer." By adopting this directorial role, the novelist can deal with extremity and absurdity without seeming to be affected by them. This is, of course, another version of the split between reason and passion that marks every aspect of Waugh's work. Here it is expressed structurally.

The esthetically committed but intellectually disinterested artist is one of the recurring phenomena of our century. In "The Film Age" chapter of his *Social History of Art* Arnold Hauser argues that the twentieth-century artist sets out with "the intention . . . to write, paint and compose from the intellect, not from the emotions" as though any given artistic project were an intricate problem demanding reasoned solutions rather than subjective convictions. Hauser goes on to say that the writer has found one of these solutions in cinema. Specifically, the novelist has learned from the film editor the device of montage which so successfully represents

> the new concept of time, whose basic element is simultaneity and whose nature consists in the spatialization of the temporal element, . . . expressed in no other genre so impressively as in this youngest art, which dates from the same period as Bergson's philosophy.

Paradoxically enough, however, the intellectual artist employs cinematic logic to render the confusion and randomness of twentieth-century experience.

> The Bergsonian concept of time undergoes a new interpretation, an intensification and a deflection. The accent is now on the simultaneity of the contents of consciousness, the immanence of the past in the present, the constant flowing together of the different periods of time, the amorphous fluidity of inner experience, the boundlessness of the stream of time by which the soul is borne along, the relativity of space and time. . . . In this new conception of time almost all the strands . . . of modern art converge: the abandonment of plot, the elimination of the hero, the relinquishing of psychology, . . . and, above all, the montage technique and the intermingling of temporal and spatial forms of the film.[12]

This seems to explain film's structural value for Waugh. Here was a medium that was at once poised yet perfectly suited to represent the teeming mindlessness of contemporary society. It provided him with a method that allowed for the stillness of artistic control even as it portrayed hopeless confusion. It is no wonder that he adapted cinematic form to do justice to his vision of a divided world.

Hauser relates the technical appeal of film to the philosophical influence exerted by Henri Bergson in the opening decades of this century. There is little question of the general validity of this connection and, I think, it is one that applies specifically to Waugh. This can be detected in the manner with which both philosopher and novelist turned to cinematic analogies to express themselves.

In scenes meant to suggest the breakdown of psychic and social order, Waugh frequently employed cinematic strategies which, as often as not, were explicitly labeled as such. But film was more than a technical resource. As adapted by Waugh, it also implied an epistemology that seems to derive from his knowledge of Bergson's work. Bergson had found it useful to speak analogically of the intellect as though its processes were parallel to those of a cinematograph. This is a figure that appears in Waugh's writing repeatedly. As we have seen, in *The Ordeal of Gilbert Pinfold* he explicitly describes the workings of his own mind with a cinematic metaphor. When we recall that Waugh's first two novels contain central episodes devoted to parodying Bergson's concept of Becoming, the line of influence seems unquestionable.

In *Creative Evolution* Bergson illustrates the intellect's estrangement from reality by comparing its operation to that of cinematography. "The cinematographical instinct of our thought," he states, prevents us from fully understanding "universal becoming," the essential reality. The filmic metaphor suits his argument. Bergson wants to demonstrate that the analytical mode of thinking characteristic of Western man depends upon an artificial separation between subject and object. Film offers the perfect model. Bergson argues that we have been trained to assume that we can only come into possession of real knowledge by intellectually standing apart from the object of our interest in order to bring it into focus much as a camera must be positioned at the proper distance from what it is to film. Instead of intuiting reality from the inside, the intellect looks on, as does Pinfold's camera-eye, from the outside. By doing so, it puts itself outside its natural place in the universal becoming. Adopting the fiction of an external vantage point, it can manage Becoming by dividing it conceptually into a series of "snapshots taken at intervals of its flowing," as Bergson puts it. Like a cinema camera, the abstracting intellect reduces experience to a sequence of static representations or frames. This is why Western thinkers had never accounted for change in a convincing way. Examined by the intellect alone, change always seems an illusion. No matter how diligently it tries to account for Becoming, the intellect cannot reconstitute it. Bergson explains this in terms of "the contrivance of the cinematograph."

> Instead of attaching ourselves to the inner becoming of things, we place ourselves outside them in order to recompose their becoming artifically. . . . Whether we would think becoming or express it, or even perceive it, we hardly do anything else than set going a kind of cinematograph inside us. . . . The application of the cinematographical method . . . leads to a perpetual recommencement, during which the mind, never able to satisfy itself and never finding where to rest, persuades itself, no doubt, that it imitates by its instability the very movement of the real. But though, by straining itself to the point of giddiness, it may end by giving itself the illusion of mobility, its operation has not advanced it a step, since it remains as far as ever from its goal. In order to advance with the moving reality, you must replace yourself within it. Install yourself within change, and you will grasp at once both change itself and the successive states in which it might at any instant be immobilized. But with these successive states, perceived from without as real and no longer as potential immobilities, you will never reconsititute movement.

Reality becomes an abstraction when we, the perceiving subjects, are

→ liberation by lack of bondy

differentiated from the perceived object, inevitably prompting a sense of alienation from the world outside ourselves. Bergson recommends intuitive knowing as an antidote. Only this approach to experience produces the lively awareness of the irreducibly real necessary to foster the emotional and imaginative harmony with the world for which we long.[13]

So runs Bergson's argument. Many early twentieth-century novelists found its logic and its use of cinematic analogy pertinent to their own concerns. On the evidence of his fictional conceits, so did Waugh.

When in *The Ordeal of Gilbert Pinfold* Waugh described the workings of his own mind with a cinematic metaphor that recalled Bergson's, he was doing no more than following a personal tradition he had established many years before. Time and again, he adapted, consciously or not, Bergson's cinematographical intellect to his own very unbergsonian purposes. How else explain that in novel after novel we discover a traditionally formed, literate mind desperately "straining itself to the point of giddiness" in an attempt to assemble and interpret its cinematic experience of the world? It is as though Waugh had been literally working out the implication of Bergson's metaphor of the cinematographical intellect confronted by the unmanageable flow of Becoming. We have considered one example of this already in *Vile Bodies*, the scene in which Agatha Runcible, suffering hallucinations and strapped to her hospital bed, imagines herself trying to steer a car racing at impossible speeds over a course that offers severely limited visibility. From Agatha's prone position "there was rarely more than a quarter of a mile of the black road to be seen at one time. It unrolled like a length of cinema film. At the edges was confusion; a fog spinning past" (p. 284). This hallucinatory passage I take to be Waugh's parody of Bergson, an image of the cinematographical intellect helpless before the helter-skelter rush of Becoming. With or without explicit reference to film, it recurs throughout Waugh's fiction. Before examining its implications, I want to quote two other versions of it. Like the first, they also acknowledge their debt to film. Considered together, all three strongly argue that Waugh had quite deliberately appropriated Bergson's cinematographical intellect and bent it to his own ends.

The second example occurs in the cinematically structured story, "The Balance" (1925), when Adam Doure is shown recovering from a drunken suicide attempt. It is particularly pertinent for the way in which it distinguishes between his initial befuddlement and his dawning awareness of his surroundings. His mental confusion manifests itself as a two-dimensional cinematic experience he must endure passively until he can regain his sense of order. Once he does, the world returns in all its purposeful, three-dimensional solidity.

He still wore the clothes in which he had slept. But in his intellectual dishev-
elment he had little concern for his appearance. All about him the shadows
were beginning to dissipate and give place to clearer images. He had break-
fasted in a world of phantoms, in a great room full of uncomprehending eyes,
protruding grotesquely from monstrous heads that lolled over steaming por-
ridge; marionette waiters had pirouetted about him with uncouth gestures.
All around him a macabre dance of shadows had reeled and flickered, and in
and out of it Adam had picked his way, conscious only of one insistent need,
percolating through to him from the world outside, of immediate escape
from the scene upon which the bodiless harlequinade was played, into a
third dimension beyond it. And at length, as he walked by the river, the
shapes of the design began to advance and recede, and the pattern about him
and the shadows of the night before became planes and masses and arranged
themselves into a perspective, and like the child in the nursery Adam began
feeling his bruises.[14]

The third scene comes from the 1937 novel, *Scoop*, and recalls Agatha
Runcible's death-bed hallucinations. Lord Copper, the autocratic publisher of London's leading newspaper, the *Beast*, finds himself about to address a banquet with a speech grossly inappropriate to the ostensible guest
of honor. Written to dignify a man in his twenties, the address must now
serve for a rather disreputable looking codger of questionable sanity who
has been unaccountably installed on the dais. Seeing "the words 'young in
years' looming up at him, [Lord Copper] swerve[s]." As he glances "grimly
through the pages ahead of him," the speech takes on the high-speed characteristics of Agatha Runcible's filmic hallucination.

> For some time now his newspapers had been advocating a new form of driv-
> ing test, by which the applicant for a license sat in a stationary car while a
> cinema film unfolded before his eyes a nightmare drive down a road full of
> obstacles. Lord Copper had personally inspected a device of the kind and it
> was thus that his speech now appeared to him. (pp. 317–18)

Waugh returns to the cinematic imagery of these three scenes again and
again. Obviously, it was a comparison that resonated with special significance for him as closer examination reveals. In each a helpless character
finds himself plunged into an inexorable flow of experience that flickers,
reels, and "unroll[s] like a length of cinema film" over and around him. In
each an unmanageable rush of sensation overwhelms a mind powerless to
resist. In Waugh, reason is always about to be submerged by experience;
his characters find themselves pushed into a two-dimensional filmlike
world in which the usual distinctions between background and foreground, essential and incidental, evaporate like the "fog spinning past" the
helpless Agatha Runcible. There is no chance to direct one's life toward a
purposeful end; there is only the all-consuming now of immediate sensa-

tion. Daily experience resembles a badly composed film in which everything has a flattened, foreshortened quality. Peripheral details shove themselves into the foreground, short-circuiting depth perception. The resulting scene visually portrays a world deprived of the classical perspective that had once enabled people to steer their lives along a course of rational and moral distinctions. Now, like Agatha, they find themselves flat on their backs, unsupported by a coherent ethos. Abandoned to a brutally foreshortened perspective, they are nevertheless expected to steer for themselves as best they can.

Although Waugh's characters seem only dimly aware of it, the possibility of fitting contemporary experience into an intelligible pattern has long since passed. Forswearing absolutes, the twentieth century has allowed the objective world to slip through its fingers. What it calls reality is so fluidly elusive that nothing so feeble as an idea can restrain its mercurial course. With neither an objective, stable reality nor an epistemology that allows one to behold it from a civilized distance, the individual, like Paul Pennyfeather, disappears, merging with the "kaleidoscope of dimly discernible faces" of the undifferentiated masses.

Bergson's image of the cinematographical intellect turns up in Waugh's fiction with a vengeance. It becomes his metaphor of the civilized mind's loss of conviction in its ability to impose order on what is otherwise a senseless onslaught of daily experience. Typically, his characters must suffer one of two possible fates. There are the thoughtless, who, having embraced Bergsonian Becoming, are left to swim with the flux of a relativistic world in which the value of existence is gauged by the intensity of the moment rather than its proximity to an ideal. These are the characters who have lost any sense of commitment to a design that might transcend their immediate experience. Then there are the reflective types, who must stand on the bank and watch the flailing swimmers breast the stream as well as its shifting currents will allow. Without faith in the ordering power of ideas, they have no counsel or aid to offer their floundering opposites. They can do little more than watch experience unreel like "an infinite length of film" full of spectacle but devoid of purpose.

VIII

THE SATIRIST OF
THE FILM WORLD

Film unquestionably provided Waugh with some of his most characteristic strategies and metaphors. In this chapter I will examine the most prominent of them. For the sake of clarity and convenience, I have arranged them under five headings: incoherence and the subversive detail, the narrator as director, discontinuity, leveling, and primitivism. I do not mean to suggest that this list is immutable. Its divisions are not sealed off from one another. A strategy or metaphor examined under one heading may at times serve as well to exemplify another. My only purpose in making these admittedly artificial distinctions is to organize what I have to say about Waugh's application of film to his fiction.

Incoherence and the Subversive Detail

In his analysis of Graham Greene's narrative technique, Waugh noted that "the affinity to the film is everywhere apparent" and then illustrated his point with Greene's use of "significant detail," the writer's equivalent of film's close-up images. With a cinematic metaphor, he compares the narrator to a "camera's eye which moves from the hotel balcony to the street below, picks out the policeman, follows him to his office, moves about the room from the handcuffs on the wall to the broken rosary in the drawer, recording significant detail. It is the modern way of telling a story."[1]

Waugh does not elaborate further, but one must suppose he was thinking not only of film but the course of the modern novel since Flaubert. The modernity of this technique resides in its seeming absolution of authorial responsibility. The reader is left to discover meaning for himself. With respect to the novel before him, he finds himself in much the same position he is in when confronting a universe deprived of the intervention of a divine intelligence. He must pick his way among the details and come to his own conclusions. Of course, this is modern fiction's fiction. As Waugh points out, the writer is stage-managing the details from behind the scenes all along, imbuing them with significance that will lead the alert reader to the "correct" conclusion. An experimental work comprised of a plotless gathering of apparently random observations will turn out on closer examination to cohere around an authorial attitude. Even in the case of a writer who sets out to prove that life has no purpose the resulting work will necessarily bear the impress of his artistic purpose. This may be no more than his negative demonstration, but it will nevertheless provide his work with a coherence he professes to find absent in the world around him.

As Martin Price reminds us, novelistic details are often "pulled between the demands of structure and the consistent texture of a plausible fictional world." He goes on to observe that "their nature is not unlike those of our own lives that are jointly to be explained by outward circumstance and inward motive."[2] In *Fiction and the Camera Eye* Alan Spiegel analyzes this use of detail in cinematic terms reminiscent of Waugh's discussion of significant detail. Using what at first appears to be the neutrality of a camera eye, the modern writer, according to Spiegel, presents the narrative equivalent of a film close-up. He chooses a seemingly unimportant detail from the story's realistic background and then makes it contribute to the story's "undercurrent of interior resonance beneath the narrative surface." As Spiegel sees it, this is a strategy that attempts "to resolve the dramatic incompatibility between an object's adventitious appearance as part of a chaotic and senseless material flux and its meaningful depths."[3] In other words, a writer will avail himself of the metaphoric and symbolic possibilities inherent in his setting's realistic details in order to reinforce his theme and unify his work. To take an obvious example, the snowfall that concludes James Joyce's *The Dead*, covering and joining both the natural and man-made environment, is at once real snow and an image of common mortality.

Although Waugh complained that many modern novelists were presumptuous and exorbitant in their attempts to "represent the whole human mind and soul" without reference to any ultimate design, he could admire the technical dexterity with which a Joyce deployed his "significant details" so as to invest his work with artistic if not theological unity.[4] Waugh adapted this strategy for his own works, but he did so with an important difference. He gave it an ironic twist so that it served to mock rather than affirm the longing for coherence among people who had forsaken, knowingly or not, their belief in a providential order.

Waugh, of course, made no secret of his belief that existence was purposeful. Yet he frequently arranged his details so that they signified the opposite, as if to give his readers a sardonic glimpse of a world without any meaning. This is so true of some of the early novels that there are those who have assumed the fiction is as disorderly and slapdash as the world it portrays. What Waugh called the "significant detail" in other works turned subversive in his own. In effect, he played against his reader's expectations. The modern novel has trained us to look for signals of coherence in the details an author selects for prominent display. Waugh's satiric strategy was to give close-up treatment to details that disrupt this expectation. In effect, he provides an ironically negative demonstration of Price's and Spiegel's case. The "undercurrent" of his details speaks of an incoherent world. In the early novels, it is disorder itself that paradoxically serves as the organizing principle around which character and incident revolve. His significant details typically contribute to the "chaotic and senseless material flux." Within the story they are generally placed so as to subvert any pretension to purposeful order that may be entertained by an unusually thoughtful character. These are the details that Waugh treats in merciless close-up. They are almost always of a kind with the bad bottle of wine, the impertinent stranger, and the syntactical lapse that shocked Gilbert Pinfold's mind into reacting like a cinema camera. As such, they impinge on two levels of the reader's awareness. Viewed from without, these details form part of the overall construction. But viewed from within, the same details belie the fiction of civility with which people hide from themselves those indecorous questions about life's purpose. They organize the story with their metaphorical suggestiveness, as Waugh argued Greene's significant details did, but they have been meticulously orchestrated to signify metaphysical confusion rather than coherence. Of course, this is not surprising in satire. As Alvin Kernan has demonstrated, this is a genre that often makes its point by accumulating a riot of particulars that defeat the mind's longing for order. Certainly Waugh provides enough examples to confirm Kernan's thesis. One thinks of the bewildering catalogue of parties in *Vile Bodies*.

> . . . Masked parties, savage parties, Victorian parties, Greek parties, Wild West parties, Russian parties, Circus parties, parties where one had to dress as somebody else, almost naked parties in St. John's Wood, parties in flats and studios and houses and ships and hotels and night clubs, in windmills and swimming baths, tea parties at school where one ate muffins and meringues and tinned crab, parties at Oxford where one drank brown sherry and smoked Turkish cigarettes, dull dances in London and comic dances in Scotland and disgusting dances in Paris—all that succession and repetition of massed humanity. . . . Those vile bodies. . . . (pp. 170–71)

What is the purpose of itemizing this endless proliferation but to extinguish rational assessment?

Then there is the overheard political conversation of *Brideshead Revisited*. The year is 1936 and people are talking about the problems of Edward VIII and the hostilities that will lead to World War II.

> "Of course, he can marry her and make her queen tomorrow."
>
> "We had our chance in October. Why didn't we send the Italian Fleet to the bottom of the Mare Nostrum? Why didn't we blow Spezia to blazes? Why didn't we land on Pantelleria?"
>
> "Franco's simply a German agent. They tried to put him in to prepare air bases to bomb France. That bluff has been called, anyway."
>
> "It would make the monarchy stronger than it's been since Tudor times. The people are with him."
>
> "The press are with him."
>
> "I'm with him."
>
> "Who cares about divorce now except a few old maids who aren't married, anyway?"
>
> "If he has a showdown with the old gang, they'll just disappear like, like . . . "
>
> "Why didn't we close the Canal? Why didn't we bomb Rome?"
>
> "It wouldn't have been necessary. One firm note . . . "
>
> "One firm speech."
>
> "One showdown."
>
> "Anyway, Franco will soon be skipping back to Morocco. Chap I saw today just come from Barcelona . . . "
>
> ". . . Chap just come from Fort Belvedere . . . "
>
> ". . . Chap just come from Palazzo Venezia . . . "
>
> "All we want is a showdown."
>
> "A showdown with Baldwin."
>
> "A showdown with Hitler."
>
> "A showdown with the Old Gang."
>
> ". . . That I should live to see my country, the land of Clive and Nelson . . . "
>
> ". . . *My* country of Hawkins and Drake."
>
> ". . . *My* country of Palmerston . . . "
>
> "Would you very much mind not doing that?" said Grizel to the columnist, who had been attempting in a maudlin manner to twist her wrist. "I don't happen to enjoy it." (pp. 275–76)

The self-delusion and pointlessness of such talk speaks for itself. As different as they are, the catalogue of parties and the snippets of conversation are alike in that neither receives the benefit of narrative mediation. In both passages detail and dialogue are heaped on the reader without the usual filtering mechanisms of earlier fiction. There is no context to speak of, the principle of arrangement is obscure, and the narrator's voice is either ironic or enigmatic. The effect is to create a sense of aimless futility. But Waugh did not rely exclusively on these relatively simple means to portray the incoherence of his world. Another strategy he liked to use re-

quired that he first contrive a scene redolent of cultivated taste and imbued with the stability of long tradition. Having done so, he would then
subvert it. To do this he would select an apparently incidental detail from
the background and treat it with cinematic logic, as a scene from *Vile
Bodies* illustrates quite clearly. Lord Metroland has just returned home
from a conversation with the mysterious Jesuit, Father Rothschild, and the
current prime minister, Walter Outrage. Rothschild has tried to make Metroland aware of the "radical instability" that besets the modern world.

> By ill-fortune he [Metroland] arrived on the doorstep to find Peter Past-
> master fumbling with the lock, and they entered together. Lord Metroland
> noticed a tall hat on the table by the door. "Young Trumpington's, I sup-
> pose," he thought. His stepson did not once look at him, but made straight
> for the stairs, walking unsteadily, his hat on the back of his head, his um-
> brella still in his hand.
>   "Good night, Peter," said Lord Metroland.
>   "Oh, go to hell," said his stepson thickly, then turning on the stairs, he
> added, "I'm going abroad tomorrow for a few weeks. Will you tell my
> mother?"
>   "Have a good time," said Lord Metroland. "You'll find it just as cold every-
> where, I'm afraid. Would you care to take the yacht? No one's using it."
>   "Oh, go to hell."
>   Lord Metroland went into the study to finish his cigar. It would be awk-
> ward if he met young Trumpington on the stairs. He sat down in a very com-
> fortable chair. . . . A radical instability, Rothschild had said, radical
> instability. . . . He looked round his study and saw shelves of books—the
> *Dictionary of National Biography,* the *Encyclopaedia Britannica* in an early
> and very bulky edition, *Who's Who,* Debrett, Burke, Whitaker, several vol-
> umes of Hansard, some Blue Books and Atlases—a safe in the corner painted
> green with a brass handle, his writing-table, his secretary's table, some very
> comfortable chairs and some very businesslike chairs, a tray with decanters
> and a plate of sandwiches, his evening mail laid out on the table . . . radical
> instability, indeed. How like poor old Outrage to let himself be taken in by
> that charlatan of a Jesuit.
>   He heard the front door open and shut behind Alastair Trumpington.
>   Then he rose and went quietly upstairs, leaving his cigar smouldering in
> the ash-tray, filling the study with fragrant smoke. (pp. 186–87)

After dramatizing the general breakdown of authority with this particular
comic instance of a drunken youth's hostility for his fawningly solicitous
stepfather, the scene progresses by means of visual close-ups selected from
its background. Convinced the world is cold everywhere and having been
advised by his stepson to go to hell, Metroland is in no mood to meet young
Trumpington, owner of the tall hat, who is visiting his wife upstairs. Instead, he follows his stepson's advice and does go to hell, an unacknowl-
edged hell of his own devising in which he can lapse into a complacency

that resembles nothing so much as despair. Pathetically stubborn in his need to believe all is right with his world, Metroland retreats to his study where he reassures himself that there is an ordered continuity to his existence by selectively reviewing his bookshelves. There he finds the *Dictionary of National Biography*, *Who's Who*, the *Encyclopaedia Britannica*, official publications of parliamentary proceedings, listings of the peerage and socially prominent, and maps of the world. Although there must be many other titles and objects in this room, we never hear of them. Metroland's eyes fall unfailingly on just what he wants to see: the works that establish one's place in the world by recording order and precedence and providing rational categories with which to organize experience. In his study Metroland can convince himself that he is at the center of a coherent, eminently manageable world, but young Trumpington's hat in the outer hall and the smoldering cigar left behind in the ashtray tell a very different story. Waugh deploys his "significant details" in a manner that invites a filmic reading of this scene. In doing so, he subverts Metroland's pretension to an ordered existence. Trumpington's potently tall hat has cowed Metroland into retreat. He would rather surround himself with the comforting illusion of order than confront his wife's infidelity. When Trumpington departs, leaving the field clear once again, Metroland approaches his wife disarmed, his masculine cigar left behind to burn itself out impotently among the bankrupt mementos of a once orderly society. Waugh's narrator operates as would a skillful film director marshaling the background of the scene to serve his intention. All the forces of order and tradition are no match for that incidental hat and cigar. The center cannot hold against the merely peripheral.

This suspension of the expected relationship between the central and peripheral is also apparent in *A Handful of Dust* in a scene that is less obviously cinematic but is conceived in much the same way. This is the scene in which Tony Last struggles to maintain the appearances of gentlemanly behavior in the absence of the principles upon which such behavior presumably rests. In order to expedite the divorce his wife desires, he must escort a prostitute to a seaside resort where detectives retained for the purpose will obligingly take evidence of his "infidelity." This episode shatters what remains of Tony's sense of the proprieties not only because his overprotected sensibility is offended by having to play this charade of intimacy, but also because he is forced to realize that his hired woman has more genuine concern for her child than his wife ever displayed for theirs. Knowing Tony's intentions are directed at the appearance of vice and not the deed, the woman avails herself of this opportunity to bring her daughter to a resort. She does so over the detectives' disapproval that it "sets a nasty, respectable note bringing a kid into it" (p. 185). (Of course, in

Waugh's inverted world, the respectable naturally provokes dismay.) In contrast, before their son's death, Tony's wife had spent a good deal of effort to keep the boy at a distance so that he would pose no unseemly obstacle to her adulterous adventures.

It is during this mockery of vice at the resort that Tony realizes how far he has fallen from his dream of a principled life. Bred to a world in which virtue and propriety were unfailingly honored if not always practiced, he finds himself adrift in a society that no longer subscribes to the categories of traditional morality. Nevertheless, as he prepares to take his guest to dinner, he recalls the duties of a host.

> Tony . . . reminded himself that phantasmagoric, and even gruesome as the situation might seem to him, he was nevertheless a host, so that he knocked at the communicating door and passed with a calm manner into his guest's room; for a month now he had lived in a world suddenly bereft of order; it was as though the whole reasonable and decent constitution of things, the sum of all he had experienced or learned to expect, were an inconspicuous, inconsiderable object mislaid somewhere on the dressing table; no outrageous circumstance in which he found himself, no new mad thing brought to his notice could add a jot to the all-encompassing chaos that shrieked about his ears. (p. 189)

While not explicitly cinematic, this scene turns on an extended simile that has much in common with the strategies of the more obviously filmic passages. Like them, it plays with the distinction between the central and the peripheral. Here Tony's reasonable world, all he has been trained to expect, has become nothing more than an "inconsiderable object," a cuff link perhaps, carelessly mislaid on a littered dressing table. Everything that had been central in his life has been submerged in a chaotic clutter of detail. Having misplaced the organizing power of his central vision, Tony can do no more than passively observe the random details that now haphazardly clamor for his attention. Here again we encounter a disruption of the expected relation between the essential and incidental. It is as though Tony were watching a film that failed to distinguish between foreground and background. With neither spatial nor rational distinctions, every sensation is as important and as unimportant as every other. The resulting experience resembles a nightmare in which Tony becomes a passive center encompassed by shrieking chaos.

In Waugh's fiction the traditional mind shaped by a culture of literacy finds its linear view of the world knocked askew by events that resemble a poorly edited film in which detail, proportion, and sequence defy its rational expectations. Paul Pennyfeather was able to handle the idea of drunkenness but completely unprepared to face the drunkard. Even the far more formidable Gilbert Pinfold cannot manage his experience of the modern world. His relationship with reality is a matter of momentary confrontations. He prefers to view the world *sub specie aeternitatis* from a sequestered distance. It is only the more provocative of personal annoyances that bring him "tumbling from his exalted point of observation" (p. 12) and even then there is every evidence that he is no match for these disturbances of his cultivated poise. After all, he does not stride forth to meet them. Instead, they set him tumbling. He has little chance of winning the battle on their terrain. His mind may be like "a cinema camera truck[ing] furiously forward to confront the offending object close-up with glaring lens," but his eyes are those of "a drill sergeant inspecting an awkward squad, bulging with wrath that was half-facetious, and half-simulated incredulity" (p. 12). This is hardly the portrait of one genuinely in command. With his half-facetious, half-simulated parody of a drill sergeant, Pinfold can hardly expect to quell the subversive details of a disorderly world. Having confronted them, the best he can hope to do is escape them once more by retreating to his "exalted point of observation."

There are other characters who, when faced with the cinematic disorder of contemporary experience, are quite sure they can manage it without fuss. Their confidence, however, almost always proves unfounded. In *Scoop* we find Julia Stitch doing her best but even her masterful hand cannot sustain its grip for long. When she first appears, she is

> still in bed although it was past eleven o'clock. Her normally mobile face was encased in clay, rigid and menacing as an Aztec mask. But she was not resting. Her secretary, Miss Holloway, sat at her side with account books, bills and correspondence. With one hand Mrs. Stitch was signing cheques; with the other she held the telephone to which, at the moment, she was dictating details of the costumes for a charity ballet. An elegant young man at the top of a stepladder was painting ruined castles on the ceiling. Josephine, the eight-year-old Stitch prodigy, sat on the foot of the bed construing her day's passage of Virgil. Mrs. Stitch's maid, Brittling, was reading her the clues of the morning crossword. She has been hard at it since half-past seven. (p. 5)

With its welter of disparate detail and action, few passages better illustrate Kernan's turbulent scene of satire. The reader is kept off balance by its hodgepodge of opposites (rigidity and mobility, art and business, work and play) and its odd juxtapositions of the high and low (translating Virgil and filling in a crossword puzzle) as well as the refined and decayed (the "elegant young man . . . painting ruined castles on the ceiling") Above all, there is the indecorous tendency of these elements to spill over into one another's precinct so that they cease to be clearly distinguishable. When Julia's friend, the novelist John Boot, enters her room a few lines later, she congratulates him on his latest book. But her admiration becomes entangled with her praise for the painter who has just executed, so to speak, a headless abbot on her ceiling.

> "I absolutely loved *Waste of Time*. We read it aloud at Blakewell. The headless abbot is grand."
> "Headless abbot?"
> "Not in Wasters. On Arthur's ceiling. I put it in the Prime Minister's bedroom." (pp. 6–7)

This headless inability to maintain distinctions serves as both the spring for the novel's primary action and a wry comment on the writer as illusionist.

The comic muddle of this scene prefigures the farce to follow. Julia so mismanages events that the reclusive William Boot will be mistaken for the worldly John Boot and get packed off as a correspondent to cover an African civil war, an assignment for which he has absolutely no qualifications and even less inclination. But beyond its foreshadowing function, the confusion in this scene calls attention to the fragile nature of art in an age uncertain of itself.

When John Boot misunderstands Julia, the lapse has more to do with literary than conversational conventions. After all, the speech he cannot follow would be perfectly clear in a real conversation. Just consider Julia's puzzling words once again: "I absolutely loved *Waste of Time*. We read it aloud at Blakewell. The headless abbot is grand." In an actual conversation a listener would have little difficulty distinguishing the references of these three sentences. Routine aural and visual clues—a pause, a change in tone or volume, a glance, a turning head—any one or several would unmistakably separate the last sentence from the first two so that the listener would have no doubt it applied to the painting rather than the book. It is only when the sentences are strung together on the page without aid of graphic or narrative signals that confusion arises. From what we know of Waugh's interests and methods, I think it likely that this is in part a joke at the expense of an art that has become overly self-conscious and scrupulous about its conventions. Especially at question is what the novelist must do to achieve mimesis in a world that no longer seems knowable. What meaning can language achieve when the objects of its reference have become suppositional at best? A reading of the passage that raises these questions accords with Waugh's conviction that modern art had been deprived of its representational credibility because of its pernicious and, to his mind, unwarranted assumption that there is no abiding pattern to be discovered beneath the play of experience. It is on this question that all else stands or falls. Existence either has a purposeful order or not. If not, then no degree of managerial skill, whether in life or art, will ever be sufficient to make sense of things in any essential way.

By dismissing the possibility of a metaphysical order, the artist subverts his own order-making ability. Reasoning analogically, it works something like this: if the external world has been divested of its conventional intelligibility, if its details and events can no longer be read as material and temporal signs of transcendent purpose, then the honest artist also must abandon the conventional signals that had once constituted his interpretive contract with his audience. Julia's words are strung together without benefit of paragraphing or other written devices that would signal a change in reference. The novelist's craft has been divested of the tools with which it might refer intelligibly to the external world. The confusion that follows is the only accurate mimesis of a society that has lost its conviction in the metaphysics that had once been the basis for its conventional belief in its collective destiny. Such mimesis is also Waugh's parody of the state of the arts in the twentieth century.

Julia Stitch is just one in a series of characters who play variations on Waugh's recurring portrayal of the would-be managerial mind defeated by intractable confusion. These are the characters who behave as though they were still able to impose order on the world disintegrating about them. Otto Silenus in *Decline and Fall* begins the series. His fondest wish is to find the still center of modern life's spinning wheel. Residing there would be accomplishment enough for him. But he is perpetually vexed by "the problem of all art." He cannot entirely eliminate the unpredictable "human element from the consideration of form" (p. 159). In *Vile Bodies* it is the ubiquitous, all-knowing Father Rothschild whose "happy knack" it is "to remember everything that could possibly be learned about everyone who could possibly be of any importance." But, for all his knowingness, Rothschild is remarkably ineffectual. Though he urges the soundest of counsel on those in power, they neither understand nor believe him. His Cassandra role is signaled at his first appearance. Looking down from the rail of a channel steamer, he resembles one of "the gargoyles of Notre Dame" while "high above his head swung Mrs. Melrose Ape's travel-worn Packard car, bearing the dust of three continents, against the darkening sky" (p. 2). The juxtaposition of Rothschild's gargoyle resemblance with Mrs. Melrose Ape's Packard visually prefigures the intellect's hopeless struggle with the will. Father Rothschild may be supported by the finely articulated tradition of his Judeo-Christian heritage, but he is no match for Mrs. Ape, the evangelist of enthusiasm and feel-good piety whose own beliefs are ambiguously compromised by her eagerness to turn a dollar. She is a weird mixture of primitive emotionalism and modern technology, singing her famous hymn, "There ain't no flies on the Lamb of God," as she tours the world in her Packard. But, weird as it is, this alliance of the primitive and modern overshadows Rothschild as does the hoisted Packard, harbinger of a darkening sky that will obscure whatever light of reason he might have to offer. *A Handful of Dust* also has its still center in the austerely aloof Mrs. Rattery. But even her superb competence cannot establish an abiding sense of purpose. Under her card-playing fingers "order [grows] out of chaos," but only for brief intervals between shufflings. Her game of patience provides little more than a pale memory of a more substantial order.

All of these figures blandly assume they can direct their circumstances from their privileged positions at the centers of their respective worlds. But, in truth, they are all equally subject to the same unruly currents that overwhelm characters like Paul Pennyfeather and Tony Last.

The Narrator as Director

Whether it is Otto Silenus at the hub of his spinning wheel, Julia Stitch behind her "rigid and menacing" cosmetic mask, or Gilbert Pinfold girded with his bright cuirass of pomposity, Waugh typically includes a scene in which he has placed one character at the center of his narrative turbulence as a still consciousness trying to impose order on a senseless whirl of detail. It might be a string of peremptory commands or a darting camera eye, but each exhibits a self-assured directorial style. The joke is that their style, however confident, never succeeds in imposing any but the most ephemeral meaning on their unsettling circumstances. Julia sends the wrong man to Africa and drives her sports car with so little control that she inadvertently runs it into an underground public lavatory. Pinfold tries to maintain his "exalted point of observation" behind his elaborate character armor, but guilt-driven hallucinations eventually penetrate his fortifications and take over his mind. The world is always too much for Waugh's characters. They can retreat to seemingly safe vantage points, but, until the later novels, they are invariably impotent when confronted by the clamoring din of daily life.

For all their incompetence, however, these would-be directors serve as a gloss on Waugh's narrative strategy. Julia Stitch in her bed resembles Waugh's typically unflustered narrators at the center of hectic and apparently aimless scenes; and, like Pinfold, Waugh's narrators cannot resist the spectacle of outrage to which they pay the tribute of closeup attention. But unlike Julia and Pinfold, Waugh's narrators seem content to forgo the discovery of any coherent pattern in the events they report with such sublime detachment. They know a hopeless case when they see one.

These narrators, at least in the early satires, remain above the uncontrollable fray. They do so by adopting a disinterested directorial stance with regard to the spectacle they report, never leaving the vantage point of their detachment to empathize with their subjects. It is not that they are indifferent. Far from it. They speak enthusiastically, frankly relishing the wanton vulgarity, stupidity, and criminality of their stories. But theirs is a voice that has forsworn sympathy. They typically remain unmoved by their characters' tribulations. Nor do they invite the reader to become involved. Their object is entertainment, and everything is brought off lightly by virtue of a showman's instinct. They know how to pace and stylize even the grisliest episode to bring out its humor, however lunatic.

Waugh had commended Ronald Firbank for emphasizing "the fact which his contemporaries were neglecting that the novel should be directed for entertainment."[5] Waugh's use of the word "directed" in this passage is revealing, especially in light of the praise he subsequently paid Graham Greene for developing a narrative method in which "the writer has become director and producer."[6] The idea of the writer as director calmly orchestrating action at a distance must have had a strong appeal for Waugh. What better model could he have had for the cool, intellectual detachment needed to face an unpleasant reality without being overcome by it? At will a director and his editor can quicken or retard events, cut them into instantaneous fragments, or protract them indefinitely. They can shuffle incidents into any order or apparent disorder they choose and all the while remain disinterested craftsmen intent upon reducing "to order the anarchic raw materials of life."[7] It was an approach that provided for the kind of rational management of events that Waugh desired so much and yet, paradoxically, allowed him to emphasize just how thoroughly the world of experience was beyond the intellect's control and understanding.

Waugh projected himself as director of his fictions in a number of ways. We have already considered his use of close-up and shortly will examine his approximation of cinematic montage. But it was his invention of the directorial narrator that imparted to his satires their most distinctive feature: their sustained distance between tone and incident. This distinction between voice and event parallels his fascination for the contrast between the paintings of Picabia and Ernst which had spoken to him of "the continual conflict of modern society." Waugh created a narrative voice that has all the "delicately poised," "impossibly tidy" virtues he saw in Picabia and then used it to calmly report the "defiant and chaotic" outrage of an Ernst canvas.[8] The result can be illustrated with the following representative passage taken from *Scoop* which deals with the reception accorded Europeans by a small African nation.

Various courageous Europeans, in the seventies of the last century, came to

Ishmaelia, or near it, furnished with suitable equipment of cuckoo clocks, phonographs, opera hats, draft-treaties and flags of the nations which they had been obliged to leave. They came as missionaries, ambassadors, tradesmen, prospectors, natural scientists. None returned. They were eaten, every one of them; some raw, others stewed and seasoned—according to local usage and the calendar (for the better sort of Ishmaelites have been Christian for many centuries and will not publicly eat human flesh, uncooked, in Lent, without special and costly dispensation from their bishop). Punitive expeditions suffered more harm than they inflicted and in the nineties humane counsels prevailed. The European powers independently decided that they did not want that profitless piece of territory; that the one thing less desirable than seeing a neighbor established there, was the trouble of taking it themselves. Accordingly, by general consent, it was ruled off the maps and its immunity guaranteed. (pp. 105–6)

This exquisitely misanthropic excerpt pays homage to Swift's "A Modest Proposal" and proceeds in much the same way. Its satire lurks in the interval between its tone and its subject, between the poised narrator and the hideous events he reports. With unruffled reasonableness, the narrator calmly reviews the finely graded limits within which Christian cannibalism is permissible—the Ishmaelites "will not publicly eat human flesh, uncooked, in Lent, without special and costly dispensation from their bisop." The effect is outlandishly funny just because of the Ishmaelites' attempts to introduce restraints into their cannibalistic practices. And here is the focus of Waugh's satire: the absurd disjunction between man's pretension to order and his actual behavior. Waugh's characters, whether savage or civilized, are always observing polite forms as they indulge in the most atrocious excesses. He manages this type of scene with his seemingly detached narrator, who assembles the props and background as though he were only responsible for moving the show along quickly and efficiently. We are made to feel that any pause to evaluate the behavior being reported would be as pointless as it would be tactless.

"Incident in Azania" uses the same discrepancy between narrative tone and subject matter to mock the British tradition of never letting emotion interfere with good form. Set in an African nation modeled on Abyssinia of the 1930s, its subplot concerns terrorist attacks on European and American settlers. When natives bent on extortion kidnap a missionary and send his "right ear loosely done up in newspaper and string" (CRSD, p. 103) to the consulate, the British colonists display a capacity for restraint no less impressive than does the narrator. After some initial concern, "the life of the town began to resume its normal aspect—administration, athletics, gossip; the American missionary's second ear arrived and attracted little notice, except from Mr. Youkoumian [a local merchant], who produced an ear trumpet which he attempted to sell to the mission headquarters" (p. 106).

Nothing more is heard of the unfortunate missionary until the story's close when we learn in an aside that his "now memberless trunk . . . [had] been found at the gates of the Baptist compound" (p. 115). Faced with this news, the British commanding officer is quick to respond. "It's one of the problems we shall have to tackle; a case for action; I am going to make a report of the entire matter"(p. 115). It would be difficult to imagine a scene in which voice and subject were more wildly at odds with one another.

Using directorial distance, Waugh was able to create narrators who remain untouched by the squalor and turmoil they portray. The narrative voice that speaks to us in a typical Waugh novel is at once ironic and fastidious. It is the voice of one who finds it amusing to watch others flail about in a hopeless muddle but takes care never to get too close lest he risk falling in himself. Empathy is one temptation he can resist. He knows sentiment would compromise his style and he is too much the dandy to allow that. Brian Wicker makes this point very nicely in his *Story Shaped World.*

> Waugh's contribution to the literature of dandyism consists in his development, not of the dandyish character, but of the dandyish narrator. It comes out in the special tone of the early novels, and particularly in the narrator's studied neutrality towards actions and attitudes which by ordinary decent standards, cry out to be judged. This refusal to judge, coming as it does from a recognition that the only standards available from the bourgeois world, by which to make a judgement, are themselves irredeemably corrupt, gives the early novels their scandalous and outrageous, but also their valuably invigorating character.[9]

By looking on his scene with a probing but detached camera eye, this "dandyish narrator" can delight in its outrage and excess and yet keep his distance even as he records it. He may be fascinated, but he is not involved. There is never anything remotely censorious or approving in his voice. His amused disinterestedness suspends all judgment. With his unvarying tone of sophisticated tolerance, he never expresses an emotion stronger than mild wonderment. When Margot Beste-Chetwynde in *Decline and Fall* razes her sixteenth-century home, Waugh's narrator brightly announces the "surprising creation of ferro concrete and aluminum" (p. 159) with which she replaces it. Under his imperturbable gaze, the Bright Young People in *Vile Bodies* become a "litter of pigs . . . popping all together out of someone's electric brougham" and "squealing up the steps" (p. 125). He is pleased to report in *A Handful of Dust* that an African nation's birth control campaign is so misconstrued by its proposed beneficiaries that they are convinced the strange devices supplied them by their forward-looking government will confer an eagerly anticipated increase in their already abundant fertility. In his account of an acquisitive interior decorator prowling for new business, he finds nothing untoward in her complaint that a house fire "never properly reached the bedrooms" (p. 3). This is a narrator whose voice is unfailingly calm and reasonable regardless of its subject. He speaks as one who has passed through despair. Conditions may be quite hopeless, but, looked at from the right angle, nothing is so serious that it cannot be turned to laughter. Clearly, matters have gotten thoroughly out of hand, but there is some consolation to be had in the spectacle of a world slipping so clownishly to its perdition.

Supremely detached, thoroughly shockproof, Waugh's dandyish narrator is perfectly suited to report on people grown so accustomed to the absence of honor that they have quite forgotten it was once thought essential to human life. There is no warning, no chiding in this voice, just frank amusement. What better way to imply that there is nothing unusual about the grotesque buffoonery of those who have sacrificed their souls to modernity? This, apparently, is a fate so common there is no point in ringing any alarms. Consider, for example, Simon Balcairn's suicide in *Vile Bodies*. Lord Balcairn, a young aristocrat of an ancient and richly decorated family, desperately wants to further his career as a gossip columnist on the *Daily Excess*, but when an influential society hostess bars him from her parties in perpetuity, he realizes his quest is doomed. There is nothing left to do but file one last column, an incontestably libelous attack on the smart set that has so callously driven him from its glittering precincts. His effort to sully this group's reputation will prove futile, however. Nothing can do more to diminish their integrity than their own shameless behavior. But this is the only redress the redoubtable Balcairn can think of. As though acknowledging that it will afford meager solace, he does not bother to wait for publication, but proceeds immediately to make an expedient exit by sticking his head in his oven.

> Then he turned on the gas. It came surprisingly with a loud roar; the wind of it stirred his hair and the remaining particles of his beard. At first he held his breath. Then he thought that was silly and gave a sniff. The sniff made him cough, and coughing made him breathe, and breathing made him feel very ill; but soon he fell into a coma and presently died.
>
> So the last Earl of Balcairn went, as they say, to his fathers (who had fallen in many lands and for many causes, as the eccentricities of British Foreign Policy and their own wandering natures had directed them; at Acre and Agincourt and Killiecrankie, in Egypt and America. One had been picked white by fishes as the tides rolled him among the tree-tops of a submarine forest; some had grown black and unfit for consideration under tropical suns; while many of them lay in marble tombs of extravagant design). (p. 146)

Even by the standards of satire, the distance between the narrator's tone and what happens in this scene is quite remarkable. After unemotionally reviewing Balcairn's respiratory progression from sniffing to coughing to breathing to feeling very ill, the narrator concludes with the purest mockery: "but soon he fell into a coma and died." That "but" condescendingly absolves Balcairn of his unseemly sniffing and coughing as if to say that at least in dying he has displayed a vestigial sign of the good breeding that had led his ancestors to their more glorious if equally futile ends.

Of course, Waugh provided himself the luxury of such cold indifference to individual fate by never letting his readers feel his early novels were about real people in any but the most superficially schematic manner. Dehumanizing detachment from his characters has always been the satirists's privilege. Waugh simply availed himself of the tradition. But few satirists have been so relentlessly committed to populating their works with two-dimensionally abstract figures. Under Pinfold's camera-gaze, the world is indeed "flat as a map."

The use of the directorial narrator imparted to Waugh's fiction an abstract artificiality that appealed to him both esthetically and practically. Esthetically it enabled him to suggest that experience had exceeded the ·bounds of plausible representation and so no longer seemed "real." Practically, it enabled him to take a welter of pointless activity and reduce it to a manageable circus of charlatans, clowns, and fools.

Discontinuity

If Waugh approached his fiction as a director, he did so as one with a strong predilection for radical montage. This is evident throughout his work both structurally and metaphorically. His scenes are commonly spliced together with associational rather that linear logic, and direct references to cinematic editing frequently appear among his favorite tropes of modern life. In both ways, he used film to project his sense of the fragmentary, discontinuous nature of twentieth-century experience.

Black Mischief supplies an obvious example of film editing's possibilities. Early in the narrative we are presented with a foreshortening of the process by which political crises flare into public view for a moment only to be as quickly extinguished by collective indifference. By means of some adroit scene-hopping, Waugh has captured the fabricated frenzy of the daily press and its predictable effect on a busy public. The London newspapers, in their competitive struggle to attract an ever greater number of readers, jump from one alarming event to the next with unrelieved urgency and thereby only succeed in desensitizing their readers to real human suffering. The occasion of their latest exercise in futile hysteria is the plight of Azania, an African nation torn by a civil war promoted by outside interests.

It seems a number of European nations have determined that their economic positions will be improved considerably once Seth, the Oxford-educated heir to the throne, begins his reign. Accordingly, they have encouraged this young progressive to follow the way of European enlightenment and hasten the end of his father's tenure.

> Two days later news of the battle of Ukaka was published in Europe. It made very little impression on the million or so Londoners who glanced down the columns of their papers that evening.
> "Any news in the paper tonight, dear?"
> "No, dear, nothing of interest."
>
> "Azania? That's part of Africa, ain't it?"
> "Ask Lil, she was at school last."
> "Lil, where's Azania?"
> "I don't know, father." . . .
>
> "Only niggers."
>
> "It came in a crossword quite lately. *Independent native principality.* You would have it it was Turkey."
> "Azania? It sounds like a Cunarder to me."
> "But, my dear, surely you remember that *madly* attractive blackamoor at Balliol."
>
> "Run up and see if you can find the atlas, deary . . . Yes where it always is, behind the stand in father's study."
>
> "Things look quieter in East Africa. That Azanian business cleared up at last."
>
> "Care to see the evening paper? There's nothing in it."
>
> In Fleet Street, in the offices of the daily papers: "Randall, there might be a story in the Azanian cable. The new bloke was at Oxford. See what there is to it."
> Mr. Randall typed: *His Majesty B.A. . . . ex-undergrad among the cannibals . . . scholar emperor's desperate bid for throne . . . barbaric splendor . . . conquering hordes . . . ivory . . . elephants . . . east meets west . . .*
>
> "Sanders. Kill that Azanian story in the London edition."
>
> "Anything in the paper this morning?"
> "No, dear, nothing of interest." (pp. 86–87)

Not only an example of cinematic editing, this passage also seems to be a parody of a film convention popular in the thirties that visualized the passage of time or the development of issues as a sequence of newspaper headlines each of which flies into focus on the screen for a moment and then disappears to make way for the next. Here, however, we do not see the headlines themselves but rather surmise what they must be as they are refracted in the conversation of a number of anonymous readers and journal-ists. This, Waugh implies, is the history of human concer/ journalistic age—a heap of undeveloped impressions based on a whı.. mill of poorly reported, disconnected news stories.

Beyond its structural implications for modern narrative, film also has served as a potent metaphor of this century's metaphysical disorientation and its anxiety about purposeful continuity. Many writers have used film is this way. In *Justine* one of Lawrence Durrell's characters wonders, "Are people continuously themselves or simply over and over again so fast that they give the illusion of continuous features—the temporal flicker of the old silent film?" Aldous Huxley had already answered this question in *Eyeless in Gaza* by having his protagonist flip through a series of old photographs of himself, his family and friends as though they were so many still frames from a film of his life. Instead of continuity, these pictures comprise a series of moments tenuously held together by the fiction of personal identity.

Waugh also turned to film when he wanted to express his sense of the modern world's discontinuity and unreality. Without conviction in any ultimate purpose to existence, the self and its experience become fragmented, arbitrary. As in Bergson's parody of Becoming, life unreels as a series of discrete sensations placed side by side like individual frames in a film, their continuity cranked up mechanically from the outside. There is little sense of inner growth toward a natural fruition when life becomes a series of random episodes. Under these conditions success goes to those comfortable with living in the moment without regard to the past or future. These are the economically prosperous characters such as Colonel Blount and Lottie Crump in *Vile Bodies,* Lord Copper in *Scoop,* Sir James Macrae in "Excursion in Reality," and Rex Mottram in *Brideshead Revisited.* They all succeed where others fail because they have come to terms with the world as it is. Their secret is that they forget what they are doing from one moment to the next. They prosper because they live within the instantaneous amnesia of the truly functional. They move with the flow of pure Becoming, never looking beyond the climactic now of the present moment. This serves them well, especially in business. After all, to meet the mercantile demands of the moment, one cannot always afford the cost of prior allegiances. This is the lesson Simon Lent, the protagonist of "Excursion in Reality," learns rather painfully.

Simon's celebrity as a fashionable young novelist has brought him the attention of a movie mogul looking for marketable writers. Soon Simon finds himself assigned to work on a screenplay with a continuity editor named Miss Grits. He is surprised but not displeased to discover it is Miss Grits's policy to enter into a sexual liaison with whomever she happens to be working at the moment. So he accepts her offer to become his full-time production associate and part-time lover. By mixing pleasure with business, Miss Grits meets her human needs without any undue sacrifice of the time and energy her career demands of her. It is a matter of indifference who her lovers are. They come and go, as Simon discovers to his dismay. Only her commitment to her career as a continuity editor endures. The studio no sooner relieves him of his duties as a screenwriter than Miss Grits excuses him from his more intimate labors. Obviously, Miss Grits's profession serves as an ironic comment on a personal life that seems cinematically edited, comprised as it is of discontinuous episodes spliced together to achieve an illusion of continuity. In fact, the one thing missing from her life. is any sense of a sustained purpose beyond what she contributes to the production of entertainments that are as ephemeral as they are vulgar.

The Loved One makes a similar point by contrasting two Englishmen who have gone to Hollywood to make their fortunes. One fails, the other succeeds. Their respective fates derive from their very different personalities, especially as manifested in their opposed views of past and present. Sir Francis Hinsley, the failure, is given to reminiscences that "strayed back a quarter of a century and more to foggy London streets lately set free for all eternity from fear of the Zeppelin; to Harold Monroe reading aloud at the Poetry Bookshop; Blunden's latest in the London Mercury; . . . tea with Gosse in Hanover Terrace" (p. 10). In contrast Sir Ambrose Abercrombie, an indisputable success among the English colony in Hollywood, "had a more adventurous past but he lived existentially. He thought of himself as he was at that moment, brooded fondly on each several excellence and rejoiced" (p. 10). Sir Ambrose proudly and fatuously announces that

> I've always had two principles throughout all my life in motion-pictures: never do before the camera what you would not do at home and never do at home what you would not do before the camera. (p. 9)

Ambrose succeeds where Francis fails because he has been able to discard all sense of individual continuity and historical perspective in order to become a functioning part of the unwinding film of the present moment.

Perhaps it is the ordeal of Hinsley and his actress protégée in The Loved One that best displays Waugh's satire of what it means to live without an abiding sense of personal and cultural tradition. It seems no accident that filmmaking serves as the context in which he chose to make his point. Juanita del Pablo is a Hollywood film actress known for her protean capacity to be put through one identity change after another in order to adapt her image to the fluctuations of public taste. Upon first arriving in Hollywood, she had been turned over to Sir Francis, who equipped her with an appropriate biography.

I named her. *I* made her an anti-Facist refugee. *I* said she hated men because of her treatment by Franco's Moors. That was a new angle then. It caught on. And she was really quite good in her way, you know—with a truly horrifying natural scowl. Her legs were never *photogénique* but we kept her in long skirts and used an understudy for the lower half in scenes of violence. I was proud of her and she was good for another ten years' work at least. (p. 8)

But now that the studios have decided to make only "healthy films this year to please the Catholic League of Decency," Juanita's image has become a liability.

So poor Juanita has to start at the beginning again as an Irish colleen. They've bleached her hair and dyed it vermillion. . . . She's working ten hours a day learning the brogue and to make it harder for the poor girl they've pulled all her teeth out. She never had to smile before and her own set was good enough for a snarl. Now she'll have to laugh roguishly all the time. That means dentures. (pp. 8–9)

What identity, what integrity can one have in a land where laughing rogu-ishly all the time means dentures? This is classic Waugh: the sour juxtapo-sition of false exuberance with the dreary subterfuge that supports it.

But the dreariness has gotten to Sir Francis Hinsley. Profoundly disen-chanted with the Hollywood ethos and what it has done to him, he can no longer execute his assignments with enthusiasm and dispatch. He procras-tinates until finally

Juanita's agent was pressing the metaphysical point; did his client exist? Could you legally bind her to annihilate herself? Could you come to any agreement with her before she had acquired the ordinary marks of identity? (p. 25)

Juanita's case is not unique; the metaphysical point is always pressed in Waugh. This was his way of satirizing the ready compliance with which people connive at their own dehumanization. In a society that only values power and wealth, it is not difficult to rationalize the commodification of human beings. The combined forces of Juanita's studio, her agent, and her own ambition have turned her into a product that can be parceled and re-designed to meet market demands. Her career crisis does indeed raise philosophical questions. Is it possible to preserve a coherent sense of iden-tity when one's ethical vision extends no further than the material opportu-nity of the moment? Is personal integrity possible without a general belief in the unique destiny of one's culture? For Francis Hinsley the answer is no. Unable to keep pace with the studio's mindless policy of ceaseless transformation, he finds that he himself has ceased to exist in its corporate eyes. Returning to work one day he discovers his name and belongings have been unceremoniously stripped from his office. There has been no warning, no formal discharge; he is simply treated as a nonperson, which—pressing the metaphysical point—is what he has become by accommodating himself, however reluctantly, to an enterprise that is, to use Waugh's assessment of Hollywood's film industry in the 1940s, "empty-headed and without any purpose at all."[10] Without commitment beyond the opportunity of the moment there can be no sustenance for the civilized self. And so Hinsley hangs himself.

Leveling

Waugh associated film with what he considered the leveling or egalitarian tendencies of the twentieth century. This was for two closely allied reasons, one esthetic, the other economic. The esthetic factor has been discussed already. This is film's natural penchant for sensationalism. By virtue of its formal characteristics, film is a medium that readily encourages an unreflective, emotional response to itself. This is its special appeal and one that perfectly suits the economics of filmmaking. It is precisely the kind of basic, visceral experience film creates so easily that draws the largest possible audience, and it is this mass audience that typical filmmakers have in mind when devising their entertainments. After all, with immense production costs to meet, it is hardly likely that they would be unswervingly dedicated to producing works of art for the discriminating few.

Like Virginia Woolf and James Joyce, Waugh was drawn to the esthetic possibilities of film form. At the same time, he was quite aware that its production expenses would rarely allow film to achieve its full potential. He shared Woolf's opinion that filmmakers, despite their seemingly limitless technical resources, had only succeeded in producing crude, primitive entertainments.[11] In a 1947 essay, "Why Hollywood Is a Term of Disparagement," Waugh made this jaundiced observation concerning the economic obstacles set in the way of film's ever achieving artistic distinction:

> A film costs about $2,000,000. It must please 20,000,000 people. The film industry has accepted the great fallacy of the century of the Common Man . . . that a thing can have no value for anyone which is not valued by all. The economics of this desperate situation illustrate the steps by which the Common Man is consolidating his victory.[12]

Waugh's disparagement of the Common Man should be addressed before saying anything else about this passage. Although perfectly capable of indulging elitist attitudes, Waugh did not intend this pejorative reference to the century of the Common Man as an occasion to flaunt his snobbery. In another context he had given this term a specific application that had little to do with class distinctions ordinarily understood. The Common Man, he had argued, does not exist. He is an abstraction coined by "economists and politicians and advertisers and other professional bores of our period."[13] Common Man becomes Waugh's rubric for all those forces that militate against the individual and his ability to think for himself. The point is not that Hollywood has subversive intentions with regard to the classical world view of the cultivated gentleman, but rather that, like the rest of the technologically organized world, it is dominated by the economics of large numbers. Commercial filmmakers turn out a dehumanized product because they direct their energy to serve the most inhuman of all abstractions—the statistically average consumer. Waugh's own experiences in Hollywood convinced him that film producers had no purpose other than profit. It followed logically that "anyone interested in ideas is inevitably shocked by Hollywood according to his prejudices."[14]

But Waugh did not have to travel to California to reach this conclusion. He used filmmaking as a metaphor of contemporary society's leveling tendencies seventeen years before his trip to Hollywood. In *Vile Bodies*, Colonel Blount rents his house and estate to The Wonderfilm Company of Great Britain at reduced rates so that he can play a small role in the "all-talkie super-religious film" (p. 202) of John Wesley's life. Putting himself under the authority of the film's director-producer, Colonel Blount manages to reduce himself to playing the part of a yokel on his own ancestral estate. Begging the director for a larger part among the film's rustic characters, he presents a particularly ludicrous spectacle. Here is a man of some distinction who has sacrificed the dignity of his social position in order to become part of the film world he thinks so glamorous. Yet, having done so, he cannot erase his longing for individual recognition. Assigned a role among the faceless crowd, he nevertheless wants special treatment. It's no surprise that he takes to signing his checks "Charlie Chaplin," the screen's epitome of the little man as a star.

Waugh's most sustained treatment of filmmaking as the *locus classicus* of the leveling process of the twentieth century is his 1934 short story, "Excursion in Reality," in which Simon Lent suddenly finds himself hired by phone call to write a film script for Sir James Macrae, the elusive and sleepless producer. Whisked away at any hour of day or night by chauffeur-driven cars to attend production and writing conferences that rarely materialize, Simon belatedly discovers that Macrae has employed him to work on a production of a film version of *Hamlet*. Simon's "name naturally suggested itself," Macrae remarks, because "many of the most high-class critics have commended Mr. Lent's dialogue" (CRSD, p. 153).

When Simon points out that in the case of *Hamlet* "there's quite a lot of dialogue there already," Macrae patiently explains that "it's angle that counts in the film world" and he intends to produce *Hamlet* "from an entirely new angle" (CRSD, p. 152).

> There have been plenty of productions of Shakespeare in modern dress. We are going to produce him in modern speech. How can you expect the public to enjoy Shakespeare when they can't make head or tail of the dialogue. D'you know I began reading a copy the other day and blessed if *I* could understand it. At once I said, "What the public wants is Shakespeare with all his beauty of thought and character translated into the language of everyday life." (CRSD, pp. 152–53)

Macrae is right, of course. Film is the natural medium for such a project. Of all the arts, it makes the fewest demands on its audience. The exaggerated realism of its representation endows it with a visceral immediacy that can easily narrow its focus to the foreshortened perspective of the intensely emotional moment. From a commerical point of view, there is good reason to use common, transparent language. Elevated or poetic language would only call attention to itself and thereby disrupt the audience's unreflective enjoyment of the pleasant oneiric state film can so readily produce. While such disruption might make for a more challenging esthetic experience, it would not be nearly so inviting, nor would the resulting loss of patronage make it nearly so profitable. Economic interest dictates that film's language be that of the Common Man, as simple as possible. Soon Simon takes up the enterprise's egalitarian, collectivizing spirit himself. It will be art for the masses whatever the expense to the individual. When his girl friend complains that he has changed, Simon cheerfully agrees.

> "Yes!" said Simon, with great complacency. "Yes, I think I have. You see, for the first time in my life I have come into contact with Real Life. I'm going to give up writing novels. It was a mug's game anyway. The written word is dead—first the papyrus, then the printed book, now the film. The artist must no longer work alone. He is part of the age in which he lives; he must share—only of course, my dear Sylvia, in very different proportions—the weekly wage of the proletarian. Vital art implies a corresponding set of social relationships. Co-operation . . . co-ordination . . . the hive endeavour of the community directed to a single end . . . "
>
> Simon continued in this strain at some length, eating meantime a luncheon of Dickensian dimensions. (CRSD, p. 156)

Typically, this scene concludes with yet another example of Waugh's delight in ironic contradictions. Here the Dickensian luncheon mocks Simon's pretense to advanced socioeconomic theory. It is a touch that speaks for itself without need of any critical elucidation other than to point out once again that Waugh works as would a film director, juxtaposing conflicting elements to good effect.

In his haste to become successfully modern, Simon is quite ready to sacrifice individuality. He has no qualms about leveling his artistic expression to a packageable commodity that will sell to the public. He can go along with it all, or so he thinks. But then he discovers that "the hive endeavour of the community" is not without its competitive friction. As he turns in one "treatment" of the play after another, Macrae's board of experts—"production, direction, casting, continuity, cutting and costing managers, bright eyes, eager to attract the great man's attention with some apt intrusion"—insist that the original story elements require additions and substitutions to ensure mass-audience appeal.

> "Well," Sir James would say, "I think we can O.K. that. Any suggestions, gentlemen?"
> There would be a pause, until one by one the experts began to deliver their contributions . . . "I've been thinking, sir, that it won't do to have the scene laid in Denmark. The public won't stand for travel stuff. How about setting it in Scotland—then we could have some kilts and clan gathering scenes?"
> "Yes, that's a very sensible suggestion. Make a note of that, Lent . . . "
> "I was thinking we'd better drop this character of the Queen. She'd much better be dead before the action starts. She hangs up the action. The public won't stand for him abusing his mother."
> "Yes, make a note of that, Lent."
> "How would it be, sir, to make the ghost the Queen instead of the King . . . "
> "Yes, make a note of that, Lent."
> "Don't you think, sir, it would be better if Ophelia were Horatio's sister. More poignant, if you see what I mean."
> "Yes, make a note that . . . "
> "I think we are losing sight of the essence of the story in the last sequence. After all, it is first and foremost a ghost story, isn't it? . . . "
> And so from simple beginnings the story spread majestically. (CRSD, pp. 159–60)

Of course, the play becomes unrecognizable. Pieces from *Macbeth* are worked in, and it is renamed *The White Lady of Dunsinane*, but Macrae's board remains unsatisfied. Finally, Macrae calls a halt to the original project altogether: "No, it won't do. We must scrap the whole thing. We've got much too far from the original story. I can't think why you need introduce Julius Caesar and King Arthur at all" (CRSD, p. 161). Reminded that he had ordered these additions himself, Sir James is undeterred. His feeling now is that "what the public wants is Shakespeare, the whole Shakespeare and nothing but Shakespeare" (CRSD, p. 161). And so he makes plans to film *Hamlet* in the original. Macrae is another in Waugh's gallery of eminent characters who succeed precisely because they have the happy faculty of forgetting what they have said or done from one moment to the next. Their instantaneous amnesia meshes perfectly with the fragmentary, ahistorical reality film represents so well.

The ludicrous mixture of historical periods in Simon's film script suggests the general absence of perspective in the twentieth-century filmlike world. As the story's title, "Excursion in Reality," suggests, this is contemporary reality: a ceaseless shifting of points of view that results in the breakdown of all traditional distinctions. There is no authoritative perspective from which to pull the past and present into a continuous pattern. As Macrae says, it is only "angle that counts in the film world" and one angle is as valid as another, the only question being which will make more money. As Arnold Hauser and Alan Spiegel point out, film is ideally suited to a relativistic epistemology. It is capable of suggesting the fluid, shifting perspectives of a world without any fixed principles beyond profit, the great leveler of all other value distinctions.[15]

Primitivism

The next chapter treats at length Waugh's fascination with primitivism and his belief that modern technocracy unwittingly promotes reversion to a barbarous sensibility that is so caught up with the claims of the here and now as to be incapable of civilized thought and historical perspective. At this point, I merely want to indicate that one of the ways Waugh associated the barbarous with the modern was to link film with primitivism. Whenever the twentieth century's technological art form appears in his novels, the jungle is likely to be nearby. In "The Balance" Adam Doure's contemplation of suicide is accompanied by a film montage that represents his state of mind: "fragmentary scenes interspersed among hundreds of feet of confusion" which include the recurring images of "a native village in Africa on the edge of the jungle" and a naked man dragging himself into this jungle to die alone.[16] In "Excursion in Reality" Simon Lent is brought by high-speed car to a film producer's house that is located on an estate as "black and deep as a jungle in the darkness" (CRSD, pp. 145–46). *The Loved One* opens with this description:

> All day the heat had been barely supportable but at evening a breeze arose in the West, blowing from the heart of the setting sun and from the ocean, which lay unseen, unheard behind the scrubby foothills. It shook the rusty fringes of palm-leaf and swelled the dry sounds of summer, the frog-

voices, the grating cicadas, and the ever present pulse of music from the neighboring native huts.

In that kindly light the stained and blistered paint of the bungalow and the plot of weeds between the veranda and the dry water-hole lost their extreme shabbiness, and the two Englishmen, each in his rocking-chair, each with his whisky and soda and his outdated magazine, the counterparts of numberless fellowcountrymen exiled in the barbarous regions of the world, shared in the brief illusory rehabilitation. (pp. 3–4)

The neighboring huts in these "barbarous regions" comprise the British colony of actors and screen writers who have settled in Hollywood's aggressively modern ambiance.

Why did Waugh associate film with primitivism? To answer this, we must remember that he began his career at a time when film was still new enough to shock the literate mind's sense of decorum. Waugh was not alone. Virginia Woolf and Wyndham Lewis, among others, made the same association.[17] Many artists and theorists have found film both a fascinating and disturbing medium because of the way its mode of representation subverts the assumptions of the classically formed mind. With its ability to faithfully recreate the visible world even as it suspends the logical coordinates of time and space, it offers a paradoxical esthetic that frustrates civilized expectations. Although intensely realistic, it floats on the shifting currents of dream consciousness. Under its gaze the most ordinary objects and events can loom into enormous significance while the essential elements of life get lost in its vibrant spectacle. It is no surprise that surrealists such as Luis Bunuel and Jean Cocteau experimented with film. This is a medium that lends itself to the surrealist project of bypassing the polite conventions which ordinarily serve as a comforting filter between consciousness and reality, sifting, whenever possible, the disquieting elements from daily experience. Despite the pedestrian uses to which it has been put by commercial producers, film has formal properties that seem almost capable of putting us in touch with experience unmediated by the standard preconceptions that have been instilled in us by our society.

I think it may have been this aspect of film that especially attracted Waugh. It was not that he wanted to join the surrealists in celebrating a victory over acculturation. Far from it. Instead he used what he learned from film to defamiliarize the world and thereby portray what life would be like without the ordering assumptions that give it shape and direction. For Waugh, it was precisely our shared cultural preconceptions that save us from regressing to a state of primitive consciousness, which he conceived as being lost in the moment's sensation without recourse to the detachment and perspective necessary for civilized life.

IX

CHROMIUM PLATING AND NATURAL SHEEPSKIN
THE NEW BARBARIANS

In *A Handful of Dust* it is Mrs. Beaver's devotion to the very latest in home remodeling that introduces what is to be both the novel's theme and its principle of organization. A ruthlessly efficient landlord, she is dedicated to converting traditional homes into warrens of one-room flats-to-let decorated in her chosen style, which favors chromium-plated walls and natural sheepskin rugs. This unsettling juxtaposition of the modern and primitive visually expresses the narrative's major preoccupation: the return of the barbarian in contemporary guise.

Mrs. Beaver is a promoter of the profitably modern for whom a home is a functional convenience no more personally significant than a hotel room. She is convinced that what modern people really want in living quarters is nothing more than a place "to dress and telephone" and describes herself as one who is simply meeting "a long felt need" (pp. 52–53). When Brenda Last brings this apostle of rootless transience to Hetton Abbey, her husband Tony's ancestral estate, she feels no compunction about criticizing her host's residence. Shown the morning room, she declares it "appalling" and sets about planning its renovation in spite of the difficulties posed by its Gothic structure.

> I know exactly what Brenda wants. . . . I don't think it will be impossible. I must think about it. . . . The structure does rather limit one . . . you know I think the only thing to do would be disregard it altogether and find some treatment so definite that it *carried* the room if you see what I mean . . . supposing we covered the walls with white chromium plating and had natural sheepskin carpet . . . I wonder if that would be running you in for more than you meant to spend. (p. 106)

Part of the joke in this passage is Mrs. Beaver's pause to consider how best to resolve the problem of structure. In fact, chromium plating and natural sheepskin comprise her uniform prescription for all interiors regardless of

136

architectural style. And all England seems to be taking her medicine. Everywhere one looks in Waugh's fiction traditional buildings are being razed or renovated to make way for functional flats suited to the "base love," as Tony Last puts it, of a restless generation who have not the least inclination to consider the tradition and historical development architectural style implies. The space of their lives has contracted to whatever can take place in an austerely functional bed-sitting-room. Like the decorative dado and molding of an earlier age, their personal and family loyalties are treated as the remnants of a nostalgic but inconvenient interior design better covered and put out of sight with the impersonal smoothness of a chromium-plated life-style. Marinetti would have approved of this unsentimental, streamlined renovation and its purely functional ethos. Tony Last, however, finds it insupportable. He flees England in hopes of discovering a civilized city as yet untouched by Mrs. Beaver's special brand of technological barbarism. But, as he stumbles through uncharted Brazilian jungles, he comes to realize the futility of his quest in an hallucinatory insight: "I will tell you what I have learned in the forest, where time is different. There is no City. Mrs. Beaver has covered it with chromium plating and converted it into flats" (p. 288). Chromium-plated rooms carpeted with natural sheepskin—this unlikely juxtaposition is central to the vision of *A Handful of Dust* and all of Waugh's fiction. It serves as an emblematic condensation in which his technique and theme are fused.

We have already seen how Waugh linked film with primitivism so that wherever filmmaking enters his narrative we can expect some reference will be made to the jungle. But beyond this simple coupling, he also brought savagery and civilization together with cinematic montage, frequently employing the film editor's rapid crosscutting technique. In one paragraph a character is stranded in a Brazilian jungle, his Indian guides having left him to hunt wild pigs; in the next, an M.P. argues before parliament for a new pork import policy. Waugh used this type of juxtapositional contrast quite flexibly. Here it snaps shut as though insignificant the gap between savagery and civilization. At other times, juxtaposition yields to a counterpointing technique that moves with a slower, subtler rhythm. Two examples will serve to illustrate what I mean, one from *Black Mischief*, the other from *A Handful of Dust*.

In *Black Mischief*, the small, impoverished African nation of Azania must suffer many ignominies, but none are so trying as its new leader's attempts to bring it forcibly into the twentieth century. Dazzled by the enlightenment he received at Oxford, Seth, disputed heir to the throne, returns to his homeland boldly determined to modernize his backward people. His persistent struggle to transform Azania into Europe provides the novel with its running gag. Predictably, his efforts only result in a zanier version of contemporary European lunacies. A born reformer, he wants to make Esperanto compulsory and holds a Soviet-inspired "pageant of contraception" (p. 132) in which his uncomprehending people carry banners "emblazoned in letters of appliqued silk with the motto: WOMEN OF TOMORROW DEMAND AN EMPTY CRADLE" (p. 189). Fearing his tank-equipped but barefoot soldiers will fail to win respect among the international community, he commands boots be issued and worn under penalty of hanging. Not nearly as worried about world opinion, his undernourished troops gratefully make a supper of them. But it is Waugh's charateristic use of counterpoint that makes his case most forcefully.

The absurdity of Seth's modernizing schemes is nowhere more apparent than in the implied parallel drawn between two households—one Azanian, the other English—with which the novel is framed. In the progress of the story, the narrator pauses briefly to observe an Azanian family living in a broken-down car that has been abandoned in the middle of what is supposed to be one of the country's primary thoroughfares. Evidently knowing an opportunity when they see it, these people have taken over the car and ingeniously "set up house in the back, enclosing the space between the wheels with an intricate structure of rags, tin, mud and grass" (p. 122). The accommodations may be limited, but they are happy to share them with their two goats. These people have nothing to do with the plot action and nothing more is said of them until in the closing pages we learn that for all Seth's efforts to make Azania conform to his vision of the European twentieth century, these resourceful and imperturbable homesteaders continue to block the road with their deteriorating car-house. Unable to budge them, the regime that has taken over since the collapse of Seth's utopian misrule has devised a more realistic solution. It plans to build a new road that will go around them. The situation presents a perfect image of the futility of grafting so-called progressive ideas onto a culture unprepared for such change. But there is more to it than this. True to the pun in their nation's name, the Azanian squatters turn out to be a slightly zanier version of another household in London. Before the novel's agent provacateur, Basil Seal, leaves England for Africa, he visits his friends Sonia and Alastair Trumpington, only to find them crapulous and still in bed at dinner time. Like their Azanian counterparts, they also share their quarters with lower life forms, although they do so with noticeably less equanimity.

[Basil] drove to Montagu Square and was shown up to their room. They lay in a vast, low bed, with a backgammon board between them. Each had a separate telephone, on the tables at the side, and by the telephone a goblet of "black velvet." A bull terrier and chow flirted on their feet. There were other people in the room: one playing the gramophone, one reading, one trying Sonia's face things at the dressing-table. Sonia said, "It's such a waste not going out after dark. We have to stay in all day because of duns."

Alastair said, "We can't have dinner with these infernal dogs all over the place."

Sonia: "You're a cheerful chap to be in bed with, aren't you?" and to the dog, "Was oo called infernal woggie by owid man? Oh God, he's made a mess again." (pp. 102–3)

Basil remarks "how dirty the bed is," and Sonia replies, "I know. It's Alastair's dog. Anyway, you're a nice one to talk about dirt" (p. 103). Then, having their dinner delivered, they proceed to dine together on the bed accompanied by the dogs and the mess. Many months later when Basil returns from his African adventures, the Trumpingtons are still lounging about their apartment hung over from yet another night-before. Vaguely aware that there has been a revolution in Azania and an economic crisis in England, they protest they do not want to hear any more about either. "Keep a stopper on the far-flung stuff" (p. 305), Alastair advises. The Trumpingtons and their dogs are as squalidly immovable, as impervious to external influence as the Azanian family in their abandoned car. Living amidst their own filth and litter, both families are happily oblivious to political and economic events around them. They represent the intransigent slovenliness of human physical life stripped of all ideological pretensions. As usual in Waugh the difference between primitive and civilized is made to seem negligible.

There are many instances in which Waugh used juxtaposition and counterpoint to subvert the distinction between savagery and civilization, but the most ingenious is in *A Handful of Dust.* An even more extreme example of attenuated counterpoint, it is prepared for early in the text but does not find its completion until the narrative is nearly over. Soon after the novel begins, we meet Brenda Last, the bored and restless young woman who will leave her husband for her lover just days after her son's death in a riding accident. She appears at her dressing table holding an interview with her son's governess while she makes up her face. At one point the narrator observes that "Brenda spat in the eye black" (p. 24). While the act of spitting in one's mascara may not be unusual in itself, as a narrative detail singled out for close attention in the behavior of a woman of Brenda's type, the act is at least mildly startling, especially so since she does it in the governess's presence. Why does the narrator select this detail rather than, say, Brenda's application of perfume, powder, or rouge? Of course, this is another instance of what Waugh called the "significant detail." Once we have read the novel through, it becomes clear that Brenda's spitting appears where and when it does as one element in a network of signals to the reader. Considered in light of her subsequent behavior, her spitting fits together with her initial appearance in bed, her "quilt . . . littered with envelopes, letters and the daily papers" (p. 16). Despite her refined personal appearance, Brenda is a woman who litters, spits, and seduces shamelessly in plain view of others. There is about her an essential vulgarity that allows her to become a careless, utterly self-centered seductress calmly betraying her husband to take up with a man who possesses no other interest for her than his availability at the moment she desires some excitement outside her marriage.

Having selected this spitting incident for brief but special attention, the narrator moves on with the story. But then, some 150 pages later, the spitting episode finds its primitive parallel and, in so doing, expands to its full meaning. At the end of the novel, Tony Last, driven from England by what he considers the unspeakably barbarous demands of Brenda's divorce suit, searches for an ideal city in Brazil. During his travels he learns about "Cassiri . . . the local drink make of fermented cassava." Tony's guide explains that "it is made in an interesting way. The women chew the root up and spit it into a hollow tree-trunk" (p. 240). This reference to Indian women spitting both echoes and mocks the earlier scene with Brenda. Whereas the civilized woman had used her saliva merely as an aid to her vanity, the Indian women put theirs to practical use. This is one possible reading of the counterpoint. Another might suggest that Brenda's made-up appearance, like the Indian women's cassiri, is an intoxicant vulgarly contrived to befuddle good judgment. Taken either or both ways, these two scenes form one strand in an elaborate network of juxtapositions, correspondences, and parallels with which the novel collapses the distinctions between the civilized and the savage in much the same way Joseph Conrad had done in *Heart of Darkness* by arranging his images of Brussels and the Congo so that they mirrored one another in their common rapacity and corruption. As in Conrad, so in Waugh, such comparisons belie Europe's pretense to civilization.

In Waugh's historical novel, *Helena*, Constantius, father of Constantine the Great, rhapsodizes about the Roman Wall that separates order from anarchy.

> I'm not a sentimental man, but I love the wall. Think of it, mile upon mile, from snow to desert, a single great girdle round the civilized world; inside, peace, decency, the law, the altars of the gods, industry, the arts, order; outside, wild beasts and savages, forest and swamp, bloody mumbo-jumbo, men like wolf-packs; and along the wall the armed might of the Empire, sleepless, holding the line. Doesn't it make you see what The City means?[1]

Taking his cue from this passage, Alvin Kernan has argued that Waugh's fiction portrays a world constantly under siege. The wilderness always threatens to invade the defensive walls of civilization and reassert its priority.[2] One can go a step further and say that Waugh took perverse enjoyment in making this wall his preferred vantage point. As we have seen, it was what he described as the "borderlands of conflicting cultures" that provided him with his keenest satiric inspiration. With its relentless juxtaposition of the modern and primitive, Waugh's fiction constantly calls us back to the fragile partition that separates the savage from the civilized not only in the world at large but also within ourselves. Whether his novels are dealing with the arrogant lunacy of applying European political categories to mercenary squabbles in Africa or the futility of trying to order impulse in a world devoid of moral consensus, they regularly return to this borderland experience. It is here that he can most effectively indict the civilized West for its negligence in allowing the barbarians to overrun the city once more.

Gathering his travel writing for republication in 1946, Waugh quotes Charles Ryder, the protagonist of *Brideshead Revisited*, as his spokesman. Like his creation, Waugh decided as a young man to explore the wilderness, leaving the sedate territories of Western Europe for a later day.

> "Europe could wait. There would be time for Europe," I thought; "all too soon the days would come when I needed a man at my side to put up my easel and carry my paints; when I could not venture more than an hour's journey from a good hotel; when I needed soft breezes and mellow sunshine all day long; then I would take my old eyes to Germany and Italy. Now, while I had the strength, I would go to the wild lands where man had deserted his post and the jungle was creeping back to its old strongholds." Thus "Charles Ryder"; thus myself. These were the years when Mr. Peter Fleming went to the Gobi Desert; Mr. Graham Greene to the Liberian hinterland; Robert Byron—vital today, as of old, in our memories; all his exuberant zest in the opportunities of our time now, alas! tragically and untimely quenched—to the ruins of Persia. We turned our backs on civilization. Had we known, we might have lingered with "Palinurus" [Cyril Connolly's pseudonym]; had we known that all that seeming-solid, patiently built, gorgeously ornamented structure of Western life was to melt overnight like an ice-castle, leaving only a puddle of mud; had we known man was even then leaving his post. Instead, we set off on our various stern roads; I to the Tropics and the Arctic, with the belief that barbarism was a dodo to be stalked with a pinch of salt.[3]

This jaundiced and, perhaps, half-facetious vision of civilization's collapse finds increasingly bitter expression in Waugh's diaries where he writes in 1962:

> *Abjuring the Realm.* To make an interior act of renunciation and to become

a stranger in the world; to watch one's fellow countrymen, as one used to watch foreigners, curious of their habits, patient of their absurdities, indifferent to their animosities—that is the secret of happiness in this century of the common man.[4]

The way to deal with the contemporary decline into barbarism is to remain imperturbably aloof, amused but detached like the unflappable narrative director of the early novels, who creatively reassembles the materials of the primitive and modern in subversively entertaining montages. But in 1963 he is less sanguine.

It was fun thirty-five years ago to travel far and in great discomfort to meet people whose entire conception of life and manner of expression were alien. Now one has only to leave one's gates.[5]

While there may be some irony in the first of these three passages, there is little evidence of it in two diary entries. In any event, taken together they seem to express his embitterment with a world that had divested itself of the marks of civilization. Yet this is odd. Despite the cheerless poignancy of these late entries, the evidence of his early fiction, much of it quite cheerful indeed, suggests Waugh was as convinced at twenty-five as he was at sixty that his society had forfeited its claims to civility. A crude, alien sensibility had elbowed its way onto the scene. What else do Captain Grimes, the Speed Kings, Lord Copper, Mrs. Rattery, and Rex Mottram, to name just a few, represent if not various hues in the spectrum of barbarity coloring the age? The only thing new about his later remarks is that Waugh had lost his youthful resilience. His subject had not changed, but in his sixties he was no longer as ready to be amused by its outrageous spectacle.

He always dwelled upon the juncture at which civilizing reason confronts barbarous impulse, a conflict as much internal as external. As Jeffrey Heath puts it, Waugh "never ceased to regard himself as a battleground between savagery and civilization."[6] If in his last years he sometimes thought the struggle unavailing, this did not detract from the point of his works, which was that men were to find their purpose in the dialectic of will and reason. His fear was that, between his age's complacency and its self-doubt, reason would surrender the field to the vagaries of the will. Paul Johnson has written of the conservative mind's apprehension when it confronts the intellectual history of the century, which often reads as though it were a chronicle of reason's retreat into self-absorbed systems of thought unconnected in any way with real events. He cites as his evidence modern philosophy's preoccupation with the technical problems of linguistics and semiotics to exclusion of anything remotely like metaphysical speculation.[7] As we have seen, Waugh detected similar danger signals. There are many is his writing: Paul Pennyfeather savoring the chastisement meted out to the heretics of the early church while just outside his window contemporary heretics work their destruction unchecked; the abstract artist's refusal to engage the world, preferring instead the "impossibly tidy" constructs of his own self-enclosed intellectual systems; extremely detached spectators such as Mr. Samgrass in *Brideshead Revisited*, who looks upon the world with the eye of an irresponsible solipsist seeing nothing but an "insubstantial pageant" arranged for his private amusement.

One way or another, the civilized mind in Waugh is always being seduced from its proper task, which is to grapple with the "savage at home." The temptation is to retreat from a bad world as, indeed, Waugh often did, isolating himself at his reclusive country home near Taunton. But, as he demonstrated in the autobiographical *Ordeal of Gilbert Pinfold*, as a strategy this was finally unavailing. The world is always with us; ignore it and, like Pinfold's demon-haunted hallucinations, it comes back at you all the more grotesquely.

When Waugh refers to the "savage at home," he does not have in mind an Anthony Burgess nightmare of hooligan hordes rampaging through London streets. His new barbarians are far more dangerous. Some have frankly dedicated themselves to razing the structures of Western tradition wherever they still stand. But almost worse are those who sentimentalize this tradition, whether motivated by uninformed nostalgia or simple greed. The architectural frauds that populate the novels serve as monuments to this decadent sentimentality. Tony Last's Hetton Abbey, for example, turns out to be a nineteenth-century counterfeit of the Gothic style and, as such, marks him as culturally shallow, however personally decent. It is ironically fitting that his estate should be turned into a commercial operation when his cousins take it over upon his presumed demise. Their decision to breed and sell silver foxes for hunting mocks the tradition Tony had blindly revered. Both Tony and his cousins exploit nostalgic images of the past. Tony's use of these memories is no less a travesty for being sentimental rather than mercenary. It is Dr. Kenworthy, the enterprising mortician in *The Loved One*, who takes this trend to its logical and grotesque extreme.

Waugh's fascination for the borderlands of savagery and civilization found its peculiarly appropriate climax in *The Loved One*. Opening with the conceit that California in the 1940s is one of "the barbarous regions of the world" (p. 4), the narrative quickly proceeds to demonstrate the justice of this claim. Like an inexperienced pioneer, the protagonist, Dennis Barlow, is both alarmed and curious when he encounters the outrageous banality of Whispering Glades. This is Waugh's version of Hollywood's prestigious burial grounds, Forest Lawn, where the dead go not to their rest but, according to the institution's prescribed euphemism, their slumber. Dennis finds the place exerts a strange influence that arrests his imagination.

> Whispering Glades held him in thrall. In a zone of insecurity in the mind where none but the artist dare trespass, the tribes were mustering. Dennis, the frontier-man, could read the signs. . . . The graves were barely visible, marked only by little bronze plaques, many of them as green as the surrounding turf. Water played everywhere from a buried network of pipes, making a glittering rain-belt waist-high, out of which rose a host of bronze and Carrara statuary, allegorical, infantile or erotic. Here a bearded magician sought the future in the obscure depths of what seemed to be a plaster football. There a toddler clutched to its stony bosom a marble Mickey Mouse. A turn in the path disclosed Andromeda, naked and fettered in ribbons, gazing down her polished arm at a marble butterfly which had settled there. And all the while his literary sense was alert, like a hunting hound. There was something in Whispering Glades that was necessary to him, that only he could find. (pp. 79–81)

This necessary something has to do with Whispering Glades being the ultimate meeting place of the barbarous and the modern. Here American enterprise and technology have managed to trash all of Western culture by trivializing it. Here people who obviously know little if anything about Shakespeare quote *Hamlet* as though its hero had written a play on the wisdom of calmly resigning oneself to death's inevitability. The Lake Isle of Innisfree is reproduced as an exotic improvement on lover's lane. "It's named after a very fancy poem" (p. 82), Dennis is informed by one of the many helpful attendants. It even includes the sound of humming bees thoughtfully provided by recording. No one need fear being stung at Whispering Glades. The groundskeepers have scientifically eliminated all insect life. To complete the improved, sanitized pastoral setting there is a family burial plot with a plaque designed to immortalize an enterpreneurial fruiterer famous for having bred the stoneless peach. Nothing disturbs this idyllic scene. There are none of the grim reminders of human travail so prominent in other less enlightened cemeteries. With his superbly developed marketing instincts, Dr. Kenworthy could do no less than take the wise precaution of banning all crosses and wreaths from his premises. In this wonderland of the stingless bee, stoneless peach, and crossless grave, the troubling contradictions of life have been replaced by uniformly pleasant sensations. The difficulties inherent in sustaining civilization, the tragic limitations of human life, the appalling mystery of death, all of this and more has been ignored, simply wished away in the guided-tour rhetoric of the cemetery that refers to death as a passage into "the greatest success story of all time" (p. 78). Not without reason is Dr. Kenworthy known as the Dreamer.

Dennis, the "frontier-man," can read the signs: the barbarians are already within the walls toying with the artifacts of a tradition alien to their sensibility and impenetrable to their untutored understanding. In their hands, the art and thought of the West have been reduced to decorative culture, adornments for a moment's pleasurable distraction from the real business of life. Whispering Glades is the culmination of this tendency. It offers the image of total deracination. Far worse than ignoring the cultural past, the technological barbarians have converted it into a Disneyland theme park.

Dr. Kenworthy is intent upon reproducing the art and architecture of high culture with none of its inconveniences. He scours Europe, "that treasure house of Art," for items "worthy of Whispering Glades" (p. 78). When he comes to the Church of St. Peter-without-the-walls, he is taken with its venerable Norman style but finds it "dark" and "full of conventional and depressing memorials" (pp. 78–79). Seizing the opportunity suggested by an apt misunderstanding of its name, he builds a replica literally without walls, putting glass in their stead. It is "a building-again of what those old craftsmen sought to do with their rude implements of by-gone ages. Time has worked its mischief on the beautiful original" (p. 78). But in Whispering Glades the replica is to be seen "as the first builders dreamed of it long ago . . . full of God's sunshine and fresh air, birdsong and flowers" (pp. 78–79). Dr. Kenworthy's enterprise is barbarously innocent of any sense of history or culture. Art is art as far as he is concerned. He assembles his replicas purely for decorative effect without regard to period, purpose, or influence. Art is simply what one produces to add that patina of dignity and solemnity so necessary to convince potential customers of one's earnest reliability. His vision subverts the linear sense of progressive time characteristic of the West. History does not matter. Even the past can be collapsed into the eternal now of immediate experience. Wandering among his updated and improved monuments of previous ages, twentieth-century man becomes something like an alien set down on a planet he finds interesting but quite unintelligible. His imagination lacks the necessary referential coordinates necessary to put his experience into a coherent perspective.

Because he is an artist, Dennis Barlow recognizes in a "moment of vision for which a lifetime is often too short" (p. 164) the basic alignment of the modern and primitive in this century. It is this recognition that he carries with him when he leaves Los Angeles. It is "a great, shapeless chunk of experience, the artist's load" that he bears "home to his ancient and comfortless shore, to work on it hard and long, for God knew how long" (pp.

163–64). The importance of this vision for Waugh cannot be overestimated. It is a variant of his central thesis. The emergence of the primitive sensibility in a supposedly civilized context is another version of the will escaping the bounds of reason.

Waugh wrote a good deal about what he took to be the primitive sensibility. He was obviously intrigued by the topic and frequently drew upon his travel experiences to assist him in portraying the uncivilized point of view. But it must be said that he made no pretense to being an anthropologist. His depiction of the primitive mind has much more to do with his own preoccupations than it does with his highly unsystematic observations of Africans and South Americans. That is to say, he constructed a primitive mind according to what he imagined it would be like to live with neither a meaningful tradition nor the Western conception of time. That other cultures might have their own traditions and temporal schemes was not relevant to him. Waugh was entirely unembarrassed by what the sociologists might call his ethnocentricity.[8] Western life was not one culture among many. It was the "seeming-solid, patiently built, gorgeously ornamented structure" of the only civilization worth talking about. It follows then that his portraits of other cultures only have meaning with reference to his own. He was not trying to capture the savage mind but rather to dramatize what it would be like to live beyond the walls of Western culture. This said, I want to consider Waugh's concept of the primitive sensibility which he thought was overtaking the West in our century.

In *Work Suspended* Waugh's autobiographical character, John Plant, distinguishes between the savage and the civilized mind and the respective worlds they create for themselves as he reflects on their very different experiences of mourning.

> For the civilized man there are none of those swift transitions of joy and pain which possess the savage; words form slowly like pus about his hurts; there are no clean wounds for him; first a numbness, then a long festering, then a scar ever ready to re-open. Not until they have assumed the livery of the defence can his emotions pass through the lines; sometimes they come massed in a wooden horse, sometimes as single spies, but there is always a Fifth Column among the garrison to receive them. Sabotage behind the lines, a blind raised and lowered at a lighted window, a wire cut, a bolt loosened, a file disordered—that is how the civilized man is undone.[9]

This passage turns on an axis comprised of spontaneous emotion in one direction and thoughtful deliberation in the other. Waugh's point is not that one is inherently superior to the other but rather that a person is more or less civilized according to how closely he or she manages to reside at their juncture. He conceives of the savage mind as one that lives possessed by the moment, thoughtlessly carried away with every passion. The civilized, in contrast, fortifies itself against emotional excess by deliberately filtering its feelings through a repertoire of linguistic and symbolic conventions. It is not that emotions should be inadmissible, but rather, in accord with British good breeding, that they should not be allowed unmonitored admittance. In Waugh's military metaphor, they must take on the appearance of rational discourse before being able to penetrate the defensive lines of the self. They must be given a recognizable and communicable form before they have a chance to overpower reason as, no doubt, they should when their provocation is sufficiently extreme. The savage's feelings may be intense, but they are also fleeting because they lack the formal articulation, "the livery of defense," which would allow a certain interval of detachment necessary for intellectual appreciation. Without an intellectual component, feelings cannot be connected meaningfully with the past and future. The savage may suffer no scars, but neither does he endure with a sense of history. Thus Waugh conceived of the primitive mind, which from all indications he thought of as living in an external now of Bergsonian Becoming. Possessed by the moment and self-absorbed, the primitive in Waugh's view is totally involved in his immediate sensations to the exclusion of any larger perspective that might give direction to his life. In *A Handful of Dust* Tony asks his Indian guides when they will finish the boats they are building. The answer is always "just now" regardless of how many more days the work requires. They live, Waugh implies, as they speak, in the present tense.

If this were anthropology, it would be at the very least seriously flawed. But Waugh's primitivism is purely mythical. It is meant to be used as a gauge of European behavior. As we have seen already, many of Waugh's supposedly civilized characters are just as limited. Several examples come to mind: Captain Grimes, whose only principle is to live in the moment unchecked by social conventions; Colonel Blount, whose life comes to resemble a series of film frames each entirely self-contained as he drifts forgetfully from one moment to the next; the corporate excutives like Sir James Macrae and Lord Copper, whose success depends upon their easy ability to forget today what they had decided yesterday; Mrs. Rattery, whose vagueness about her past and the location of her sons seems more a matter of pathological negligence than cool sophistication; and, more explicitly, Ambrose Abercrombie, who "live[s] existentially" never thinking of himself as anything but what "he was at that moment" (LO, p. 10).

As reflected in Waugh's writing, primitivism is not a matter of a particular time or place. It exists wherever and whenever mind allows itself to acquiesce in the "confused roaring" of immediate sensation and surrenders the resources of literacy and reason that enable it to transcend the sensate moment. He was not anthropologically concerned with the primitive in Africa or Brazil; he was, however, philosophically preoccupied with what he took to be the growth of primitivism at home. Primitivism meant abandoning the classical perspective based on a metaphysic of fixed essences in favor of engaging the fluid experience of Becoming. Waugh thought this alternative epistemology dangerously decadent.

This response seems to have been something more than the reactionary paranoia of an anxious conservative. The first decades of the twentieth century did in fact hear some sophisticated arguments favoring what Waugh considered a program for cultural regression. The metaphysical speculations of Bergson and other vitalist philosophers appealed to those looking for an animistic relation to the world to satisfy their longing for a sense of the mystical wholeness that had gone out of their lives along with their traditional faith. Others, more cold-blooded, searched for some purely secular substitute for theological certitude. John Maynard Keynes offers a revealing glimpse of what was nothing short of a search for a new ethic that would provide all the comforting security of the old orthodoxy with none of its inconvenient strictures. Writing in 1938, Keynes recalled how he and his friends among the Bloomsbury set came under the influence of G.E. Moore's *Principia Ethica*, which, as they understood it, taught that

> nothing mattered except states of mind, our own and other people's of course, but chiefly our own. These states of mind were not associated with action or achievement or with consequences. They consisted in timeless, passionate states of contemplation and communion, largely unattached to "before" and "after." Their value depended, in accordance with the principle of organic unity, on the state of affairs as a whole which could not be usefully analysed into parts. For example, the value of the state of mind of being in love did not depend merely on the nature of one's own emotions; but also on the worth of their object and on the reciprocity and nature of the object's emotions; but it did not depend, if I remember rightly, or did not depend much, on what happened, or how one felt about it, a year later. . . . How did we know what states of mind were good? This was a matter of direct inspection, of direct unanalysable intuition about which it was useless and impossible to argue.

With ironic humor Keynes goes on to say that he and the others conveniently disregarded the chapters of Moore's work that discussed practical morality. Although these Bloomsburians were surely unlike Waugh's rascal, Captain Grimes, in every other respect, they shared with him the desire to go their own way "careless of consequence."

> We were living in the specious present, nor had begun to play the game of

consequences. . . . We entirely repudiated a personal liability on us to obey general rules. We claimed the right to judge every individual case on its merits, and the wisdom, experience and self-control to do so successfully. This was a very important part of our faith, violently and aggressively held, and for the outer world it was our most obvious and dangerous characteristic. We repudiated entirely customary morals, conventions and traditional wisdom. We were, that is to say, in the strict sense of the term, immoralists. . . . In short, we repudiated all versions of the doctrine of original sin, of there being insane and irrational springs of wickedness in most men. We were not aware that civilization was a thin and precarious crust erected by the personality and the will of a very few, and only maintained by rules and conventions skillfully put across and guilefully preserved. We had no respect for traditional wisdom or the restraints of custom. We lacked reverence, as [D.H.] Lawrence observed—and as Ludwig [Wittgenstein] also used to say—for everything and everyone. It did not occur to us to respect the extraordinary accomplishment of our predecessors in the ordering of life (as it now seems to me to have been) or the elaborate framework which they had devised to protect this order.[10]

In contrast to Keynes and his friends, Waugh seems always to have been keenly aware of civilization's precarious state. One suspects this alertness had quite a lot to do with his own reckless enjoyment of the passionate moment to which the Bloomsburians theoretically aspired. Certainly Waugh was no stranger to impulsive behavior, as anyone who has read his biography and diaries knows. Whether it was carousing with friends or insulting celebrated acquaintances, Waugh was not one to exercise undue self-restraint. While an Oxford undergraduate, he sought to squelch charges of homosexuality leveled against his club by assuring those appointed to investigate it that on sight of an attractive woman in the street his colleagues unfailingly had a "complete orgasm."[11] Presumably exaggerated, this claim nevertheless testifies to Waugh's readiness to celebrate the passion of the moment, especially when such behavior served to put puritans to rout. On assignment in Yugoslavia during the Second World War, a man in his forties with a wife and children at home, he nevertheless, to Randolph Churchill's angry dismay, defiantly disdained shelter and walked about in the open while bombing raids were in progress.[12] There is no question that Waugh had a lively taste for living in the moment. If we did not have these anecdotes as evidence, there would be his unaffected fondness for those of his characters who regularly abandon themselves to impulse. Whatever his neurotic problems, Waugh was wise enough to understand *la nostalgie pour la boue*, the periodic need to throw off the trammels of civilized decorum. What he objected to was the modern disposition to justify impulsive behavior on grounds of principle.

There is, after all, little to choose between devotion to "states of mind" in "the specious present" and Captain Grimes going his way "careless of consequence." Delightful as such spontaneity may be when embraced as a fundamental principle of conduct, it can be expected to further the work of civilization just about as far as Grimes does, which is to say not at all. Exclusive preoccupation with private satisfaction leaves little room to develop a sense of responsibility to others; nor does it encourage a serious regard for historical continuity.

Waugh addressed this defection from civilized responsibility when he read *The Unquiet Grave,* a collection of *pensées* and aphorisms much in the Bloomsbury mode by his friend Cyril Connolly writing pseudonymously as Palinurus. Waugh registered his disapproval in the margins of his personal copy. At one point Connolly pays tribute to the intense moment as the means by which we can experience the nonrational oneness beyond intellectual distinctions: "Underneath the rational and voluntary world is the involuntary, impulsive, integrated world, the world of relation in which everything is one; where sympathy and antipathy are engrossed in their selective tug-of-war." Next to this passage, Waugh has inscribed in his firm, precise hand, "Not understood by Waugh or Palinurus." Elsewhere Connolly's mystical meliorism prompts Waugh to echo Keynes's judgment concerning those who are willfully optimistic about human self-improvement. "Ignorance of the doctrine of the Fall of Man" is Waugh's diagnosis and then, not at all like Keynes, he prescribes a dose of orthodoxy: "Almost all Cyril's problems are fully and simply explained in the catechism."[13] For Waugh neither "passionate states of contemplation" nor "the world of relation in which everything is one" offered any permanent solution to man's state. To be human was to be fallen, that is, self-conscious, self-absorbed, and irremediably alienated from the natural world. Despite the modern religion of self-fulfillment, there was for him no remedy, no return to prelapsarian wholeness.

Brenda Last in *A Handful of Dust* is one of Waugh's clearest examples of the consequences of trying to live in what Keynes called "the specious present" as if one could return to a state of innocence in which one's behavior had no untoward consequences. While hardly a Bloomsbury intellectual, she is portrayed as one who has inherited the self-absorbed attitude described by Keynes, and we are made to feel that she is savagely determined to let nothing get in the way of her desire for intense experience, not even the death of her son. Like the primitive in John Plant's description, she allows herself to be possessed by the whim of the moment.

A bit bored with her marriage, she acquires a lover in much the same way she might choose a new dress, not for its distinctive design but its ready serviceableness. Having done so, she then cajoles her culpably innocent husband into letting her rent one of Mrs. Beaver's chromium-plated bed-sitting rooms in the city on the pretext of needing a place to stay while taking a course in economics. The flat enables her to conduct her liaison with relative ease and it soon becomes the center of her life. During one of her extended visits to London, her son, John Andrew, suffers his fatal riding accident. Brenda takes this occasion to break with Tony. She correctly anticipates that without offspring their marriage is pointless and it is this pointlessness that Brenda chooses eagerly, decisively. Pointlessness suits Brenda; it justifies her behavior. In a world without purpose, pursuit of the intense moment, the vivid "state of mind," is not merely permissible, it is almost a moral obligation owed to the only authority that can possibly count: the self and its immediate desires.

When Brenda first makes veiled reference to her intended departure, Tony tries to replenish her hope in the future by naively suggesting that though their loss is tragic they can look forward to children yet to come: "We're both young. Of course we can never forget John. He'll always be our eldest son but . . . " (p. 169). Brenda, however, will not hear of a future of any kind especially one with more children: "Don't go on, Tony, please don't go on" (p. 170). She will have nothing to do with going on. To go on means to live responsibly, sustaining the continuity of past, present, and future. But Brenda has elected to live in the shameless now of her immediate feelings unburdened by the dreary weight of befores and afters. It is her emotions that count, nothing else. With its anonymous, cool efficiency, her one-room flat houses the careless transience of the life to which she aspires. She is so obsessed with "the specious present" of her emotional life that she cannot even respond to her son's death. When Tony's friend, Jock, first tells her of John Andrew's accident, she confuses her son's given name with her lover's, John Beaver. After Jock explains further, she realizes her mistake.

> She frowned, not at once taking in what he was saying. "John . . . John Andrew . . . I . . . Oh thank God . . . " Then she burst into tears.
> She wept helplessly, turning round in the chair and pressing her forehead against its gilt back. (p. 162)

Typical of Waugh, he closes this scene with a visual detail that carries its weight on two counts. First, the gilded chair-back echoes Brenda's feeble attempt to cover up the enormity of her unspeakable gratitude, founded, as it is, upon the emotional betrayal of her son. Second, it indicates the superficial nature of the life she has chosen to lead in which personal loyalties need be no deeper than convenience dictates. She need not mourn John Andrew unduly. He belonged to Tony's world; he was the offspring who was to carry the family tradition from the past into the future. Wanting none of this, Brenda leaves Tony the evening following their son's funeral to attend a party with her lover. She cannot wait to declare her newly intensified feeling for him although to do so means she must figuratively step on her son's grave. "Until Wednesday, when I thought something had happened to you, I had no idea that I loved you" (p. 171). Wednesday was the day Brenda was told of her son's death. Pursuing the illusory satisfactions of a cheap story-book romance, she casually discards both her past and her future and expects Tony to do likewise. In their divorce negotiations, she does not think it untoward to demand that Tony sell his ancestral estate so that he can support her new life with Beaver. The shabbiness of her dereliction is captured in the exchange that follows her perfervid declaration of love to Beaver. By way of reply, he can think of nothing better than, "Well, you've said it often enough" (p. 171). But this does not deter Brenda. "'I'm going to make you understand,' said Brenda. 'You clod'" (p. 171). They are both little better than clods; they have slipped into the amorphous mud of their emotional whims where they are content to abandon the moral burdens of a civilized consciousness and drift aimlessly in the immediacy of the passing moment.

Worst of all, they haven't even the excuse of a grand passion, theirs being the most remarkably tepid of affairs. If neither infatuation nor lust motivates them, what does? Beaver's interest is at least comprehensible, if more than a little tawdry. He wants Brenda's money. What Brenda wants we are left to guess. She easily admits Beaver has little to offer. He is neither attractive nor charming and is decidedly without either financial or social assets. Her only motivation seems to be a need to keep up with her enlightened friends, all of whom are determined to be as modern as possible, which means, among so much else, an open flouting of sexual conventions. Beaver has nothing to recommend him but his availability. Because no one else wants him, he is there when she needs someone with whom to prove herself liberated from traditional restraints. The irony, of course, is that in seeking to escape one orthodoxy, she has only succeeded in succumbing to another. She has bought the modern prescription of self-indulgence, which in Waugh's view is in its way no less compulsory than Tony's Victorian code of manners.

In its closing, A Handful of Dust uses a more explicit juxtaposition of the savage and civilized to portray the twentieth century's abdication of historical responsibility. This abdication results in the expulsion of the novel's characters from what Keynes referred to as "the game of consequences" into a form of primitive timelessness in which the mind surrenders itself to the oblivion of the present moment. Lost and delirious, Tony wanders through the Brazilian jungle tormented by hallucinatory visions in which England and the wilderness fuse indistinguishably. A vision of Brenda appears wearing a soiled cotton gown, the typical dress of the local Indian women, and reminds him that he must attend the regular Wednesday County Council meeting at Hetton. When Tony objects that it is not Wednesday, Brenda assures him repeatedly that "time is different in Brazil" (p. 279). It is revealing that Tony's objection has to do with time. England and the jungle have become so identified in his mind that he does not even consider the obstacle of distance. Further, he has not yet grasped that the re-emergence of a primitive sensibility has undermined the conventional Western sense of ordered time and replaced it with an all-consuming now that makes schedules irrelevant. Mr. Todd will help him understand.

Tony's fate is to be evicted from time. When we last see him, he has just awakened from two days of drugged sleep to discover his watch has been stolen and he has missed a party of Englishmen who have been beating the Amazon jungles to locate him. It seems his host and captor, a backwater village tyrant named Mr. Todd, knowing in advance of the search party's approach, has prevented his rescue by giving him a powerful sleeping potion under the guise of a ceremonial Indian drink. He has taken his prisoner's watch and handed it over to the searchers as proof that Tony had come to his village and subsequently died. There is even the burial site of a previous captive to add color to his story. So the search party returns to England with the watch and the false report, and Mr. Todd keeps his Englishman whom he has appointed to read and re-read to him the complete works of Dickens. With his official death accomplished, Tony wakes to the realization that he is trapped in one of the barbarous borderlands of the twentieth century where the past and present, primitive and modern confront one another in a timeless stalemate. On one side there is the murderous illiterate who indulges a sentimental attachment to Dickens ("There are passages . . . I can never hear without the temptation to weep" [p. 302], Mr. Todd informs Tony); on the other, a young woman who insulates herself from her maternal feelings and responsibilities with the impenetrable armor of a chromium-plated life-style.

With Tony's fate established, the scene shifts abruptly to Hetton Abbey in England where we learn

> everything was early that year for it had been a mild winter. High overhead among its gargoyles and crockets the clock chimed for the hour and solemnly struck fourteen. It was half past eight. The clock had been irregular lately. (p. 303)

The irregular clock at Hetton is of a piece with Tony's missing watch and the hallucinatory refrain that had assaulted him in the wilderness, "time is different in Brazil." Time is different everywhere. Tony and what he represents have been expelled from historical time just as decisively as the would-be modern characters who have deliberately chosen to turn their backs on history. He and Hetton Abbey exist only as badly weathered arti-facts of an earlier age that had believed in its mission, its consequence, and its destiny. As noted earlier, Tony's brother-in-law, an amateur archaeolo-gist, had settled the matter when he remarked that he once "couldn't be in-terested in anything later than the Sumerian age" but now finds "even the Christian era full of significance" (p. 203). From the modernist point of view, which Waugh implicitly satirizes, Western Europe is just one more culture; its fate is no more important than that of any other. It does not have a unique destiny but rather moves through the expected cyclical pat-tern of rise and fall. Like any other culture that has completed its cycle, Western civilization offers the archaeologist an interesting dig but tells him little more about man than that his aspirations are finally futile.

And so Tony is deprived of his illusion that he has ever exerted temporal consequence. He discovers he had been living in a dream of historical des-tiny. There is no history for him any longer. His life will not form a link in the continuous development of a purposeful future; he will have neither heirs nor an estate to bequeath to the future. Doomed to the Sisyphean task of reading the entire works of Dickens over and over again to his Bra-zilian captor, Tony exemplifies all those decent, well-meaning people who avoid taking a real stand vis-à-vis the modern world. Tony had affected the forms of the Victorian gentleman without troubling himself to examine the assumptions upon which these forms were based. When Mr. Todd asks him if he believes in God, Tony replies, "I suppose so. I've never really thought about it much" (p. 291). Indeed, while at Hetton he attended church reg-ularly but only as a matter of form. The point here is not so much whether he believed or not, but rather that he did not come to terms with the issue of belief that underpinned the code of ethics to which he subscribed.

Having attempted to escape the present moment by retreating to a com-forting illusion of what nineteenth-century life was supposed to be, Tony finds himself lifted out of history. His grimly appropriate fate is to be trapped in a repetitive cycle of Dickensian grotesquery that mocks the make-believe world he had tried to establish for himself at Hetton Abbey.

X

THE WISDOM OF THE EYE

Waugh generally associated barbarism with noise and civilization with vision. This was a natural corollary of his dialectic of Dionysus and Apollo, the gods of music and light respectively. So it is not surprising to discover that much of his organizational strategy springs from an inherent tension between ear and eye. Examples are virtually everywhere in the novels, but it is *A Handful of Dust* that offers the most telling. In its closing episode one of the younger inheritors of Tony Last's estate has carelessly left her two-stroke motorcycle in front of the entrance to Hetton Abbey. This detail seems innocent enough until we recall the circumstances of the accident in which Tony's son, John Andrew, met his death. It was the explosive report of a motorcycle's backfire that set the tragic event in motion. Far from innocent, the image of the motorcycle is placed where it is as an emblem of everything that has gone wrong with the world in which Tony finds himself. As a closer examination of John Andrew's accident will demonstrate, it is the explosive noise of the motorcycle that fatally signals a culture's passing.

Tony's world comes to an end the day his son joins the neighbors in a traditional fox hunt. Having learned to handle his new pony with a fair degree of competence, John Andrew is to be allowed to ride with the adults for the first part of the day's course. Among the members of the hunting party there is a Miss Ripon who, at her father's insistence, has mounted an unruly horse she does not feel confident of controlling. Her father wants to sell the horse and thinks the fox hunt a good opportunity to display the animal. But, as the villagers observe, it is "a beast of a horse to ride" and "Miss Ripon had no business out on *any* horse" (p. 139). When another member of the party decides to come out on her two-stroke motorcycle, the stage is set for disaster. As several of the riders proceed along the road, they encounter a country bus. Miss Ripon's horse begins to shy but she keeps it under control until the motor bike, running in neutral gear to let her pass, suddenly backfires with a sharp detonation. The sound thoroughly panics Miss Ripon's horse. In its scramble to get away from the motorized vehicles, the frantic animal knocks John from his own mount and kicks him in the head. The boy dies instantly. In the aftermath everyone agrees that "it was nobody's fault; it just happened" (p. 145). Repeated four times in as many pages, these words soon sound hollow, as though spoken by those in desperate search of an absolving formula. The hectic defensiveness with which everyone uses the same expression cannot but arouse the reader's suspicion. In one way, of course, the ritual-like utterance is just the simple truth: indeed, no one intended John Andrew's death. In another, however, we are made to feel that those who have resorted to this formula have entered into an unwitting complicity with forces they are either unable or unwilling to recognize.

What are these forces? They are implied by the circumstances of the accident itself which, in effect, becomes their lethal intersection. John Andrew, the heir who was to carry on the tradition Tony valued so highly, is cut down by what has so often proved a perilous fusion: commercial interest (Mr. Ripon's insistence that his horse be displayed as a salable commodity regardless of the danger it poses) and modern technology (the motorcycle and the bus). The combined forces of the twentieth century abruptly and irrevocably deprive Tony of his Victorian idyll. Mechanized speed and the manipulation of goods purely for profit—neither is conducive to a code of gentlemanly values. Tony, the last gentleman as his surname suggests, fails to realize that he lives in a society that not only tolerates but encourages an ethos of immediate gratification, which in practical terms translates as economic ruthlessness exacerbated by a carelessly managed technology.

The novel's conclusion is unmistakable on this point. With Tony thought dead in Brazil, his ancestral estate has been taken over by the formerly impoverished branch of the Last family, who have turned matters to account by scientifically breeding silver foxes in wire cages in preparation for market. So much for fox hunting, so much for tradition. Waugh had already used this conceit to satirize the decay of tradition in *Decline and Fall*. A caged fox plays an integral role in one of the more bumptious excesses of the Bollinger Club. "There is tradition behind the Bollinger; it numbers reigning kings among its past members. At the last dinner, three years ago, a fox had been brought in a cage and stoned to death with champagne bottles" (p. 1). The twentieth century expresses itself with backfiring motorcycles and caged foxes, explosive technology and exploitative commerce. These are the forces that destroy ancestral houses in order to make room for blocks of characterless one and two-room flats. The results are at once absolutely modern and perfectly primitive. In *Brideshead Revisited* Charles Ryder is informed that Anchorage House will be taken down to be replaced by a building with "shops underneath and two-roomed flats above." Having just returned from his expedition in the Brazilian wilderness, he sees the demolition of traditional architecture in favor of contemporary efficiency housing as "just another jungle moving in" (p. 232).

In order to emphasize its dual nature as a talisman of careless savagery and reckless modernity, Waugh anticipates the closing image of the motorcycle in *A Handful of Dust* with another one that is set in the jungles of Brazil. At one point in his fevered wanderings through the wilderness, Tony comes to believe he is in the midst of a group of bicyclists wheeling around him. This scene recalls all those others in which a befuddled consciousness finds itself in the midst of swirling confusion. There seems to be only one component missing to complete its reprise of the format: noise. At this point in his life, Tony is too well acquainted with modernity not to notice its absence. He has become used to associating meaningless din with the breakdown of the social and moral order; earlier in London, he had perceived the sense of futility closing in on him as an "all-encompassing chaos that shrieked about his ears" (p. 189). Conditioned as he is, he cannot resist advising the imaginary cyclists to get motor bikes because, as he explains, they are "much faster and noisier" (p. 287).

For Waugh's purposes the motorcycle was an especially apt metaphor because it combined the acoustic primitivism of *Decline and Fall's* "confused roaring" with the technological speed of Silenus's pointlessly spinning wheel. As with the race cars in *Vile Bodies*, its barbarously vulgar noise is unredeemed by any sense of civilized gain. The would-be motorcyclists of Tony's hallucination wheel about him, describing as they do an image of circular futility. This is what it is like to live without historical vision lost in the delirium of immediate experience. Instead of the poised perspective of a linear tradition unfolding from an intelligible past into a purposeful future, contemporary life has devolved into a repetitive and meaningless circuit of feverish sensations, a circuit that carries a message no more articulate than a roaring engine.

Clearly, Waugh thought that this immersion in the present moment at the expense of the historical imagination was regressive. It could only foster an increasingly primitive imagination. His characters are routinely enveloped by hubbub and tumult. This is why such a cacophony of "confused roaring" stalks his pages. As we have seen, *Decline and Fall* opens and closes with the "confused roaring" of "English county families baying for broken glass" (p. 2). The whining racing cars of *Vile Bodies* drown all possibility of intelligible speech. As if to enforce the disastrous nature of this failure to communicate rationally, the novel's final sentence closes the acoustic circuit common to the world of Waugh's satire with the image of a mechanized war loudly waged with pointless savagery: "And presently, like a circling typhoon, the sounds of battle began to return" (p. 321). The climax of *Black Mischief* occurs against the background of an African feast filled with tribal sounds: "round and round circled the dancers . . . tireless hands drumming out the rhythm; glistening backs heaving and shivering in the shadows" (p. 302). It is at this moment, immersed in the aboriginal pulse beat, that Basil Seal discovers he has inadvertently taken part in a cannibal feast in which the remains of his lover were a primary ingredient. When the eponymous hero of *The Ordeal of Gilbert Pinfold* succumbs to paranoid delusions, they manifest themselves as the encircling voices of unseen conspirators whose plots he believes he is overhearing by chance. The hallucinations that hound him to and over the precipice of madness are exclusively aural. Their lack of any visual dimension is precisely why he finds it so difficult to quell them. Guy Crouchback in the *Sword of Honour* trilogy finds the loud popular music played on the wireless by the enlisted men as an unwarranted assault on his peace of mind. But it is Tony Last's entrapment at the close of *A Handful of Dust* that best expresses the hostility between ear and eye that recurs throughout Waugh's work.

When Waugh imagined his most ghastly nightmare, it turned out to be one in which the eye is held hostage, literally hostage to the ear. In *A Handful of Dust* a civilized man finds himself trapped in a tribal setting precisely because he is literate and can read Dickens to his barbarous captor. Tony Last's fate was for Waugh a model of what he feared was happening to the contemporary world in which the fine discriminations of a literate, visual culture seemed to be in the process of being submerged by the featureless sensate life of a semiliterate, even illiterate, aural culture filled with the confused roaring of a technologically dependent people heedless of their origins in the generations that had preceded them.

Waugh's treatment of auditory space was more than a fictional conceit. His portrayal of noise as a personal and cultural affront speaks of a man who fundamentally distrusted the world of the ear. His disdain for the sense of hearing was so exaggerated that in his diaries he wrote of deafness as a blessing.

> The Church, in our last agony, anoints the organs of sense, sealing the ears against the assaults of sound. But nature, in God's Providence, does this long before. One has heard all the world has to say, and wants no more of it.[1]

Of all the senses hearing is most disconcerting to those like Waugh who are determined to keep the world at a distance. One can avert the eyes from what one does not want to see. To a limited degree, touch, taste, and smell can be kept from undesired contact. But the ear can neither be closed nor averted. It is the most passive of the senses. Least able to exert control over its circumstances, it is entirely vulnerable to its aural surrounding. Whatever defensive measures one puts up, the world can always penetrate the self's fortress through the unguarded portals of the ears. Unless, of course, one suffers a loss of hearing.

This is why Waugh did not merely celebrate his deafness, but also used it as a weapon. Claud Cockburn records a particularly apt anecdote in this regard. It concerns Waugh's mischievous use of the outsized ear trumpet he affected in his later years and is worth repeating at length.

> His ostentatious, self-dramatizing rejection of reality required, in middle life, an equally ostentatious symbol. He found it in the form of an enormous ear trumpet. He must, I suppose, have had it specially custom-built. For although in shape and general design it resembled the ear trumpets depicted in Victorian cartoons . . . it seemed larger than any ear trumpet anyone had ever used before. . . . The function of the ear trumpet was not simply to assist hearing. On the contrary, it was to emphasize and portray, in an unmistakable physical manner, the laborious difficulty its owner had in understanding any communication the modern world might be seeking to make to him.
>
> It was both an advertisement of his personal attitude, a form of rebuke, and a weapon. I once saw it thus used, inflicting terrible wounds. . . .
>
> He had come to London to attend some very high-toned literary lunch or dinner. The guest of honor and principal speaker was some pompous statesman, a member, I think, of the Cabinet, with unjustified pretensions as a scholar and writer. It was understood that he was going to use this feast as the vehicle or sounding board for a major pronouncement on the future of civilization or something of that kind. . . .
>
> The chairman spoke briefly, and the trumpet seemed to be devouring his words. Then the guest of honor rose to speak, with all the confidence of a man who had won much acclaim for wit, wisdom, and polished oratory. The receiving end of the trumpet was trained upon him. He had been speaking for perhaps a minute when Evelyn was seen to be unscrewing the thing from his head. He removed it from his ear, placed its great bulk on the tablecloth in front of him, and sat gazing intently at his plate. The guest of honor could have dealt easily with some rude heckler. But the gesture with the trumpet utterly dismayed and discomfited him. He stared at the contraption with incredulity. He paused and slightly stammered. Probably for the first time in decades of public speaking, he lost the thread of his discourse. His pronouncement to the nation rambled almost incoherently. The reporters present stopped taking notes. He sat down after speaking for less than half the time allotted to him. As he did so, Evelyn picked up the trumpet and began adjusting it once more to the listening position.[2]

And so, after a fashion, Waugh was able to triumph over the confused roaring in his later years.

Even as a young man he had little use for the world of the ear. Both Harold Acton and Christopher Sykes make this a special point of their respective accounts of him. Each recalls that for all his absorption in the esthetics of the eye, Waugh had no parallel appreciation of music. For Acton this was the only source of serious difference he had with Waugh. "There is only one rift in our lute," he wrote in 1948; Waugh "has no ear for music and can barely tell one tune from another."[3]

The tension between ear and eye was fundamental to Waugh's sense of a world divided between savagery and civilization. In his fiction, savagery always manifests itself aurally. It is typically represented as a juncture of noise and illiteracy. Civilization, on the other hand, makes itself known visually. This is especially true of all those tranquilly described scenes in which his more fortunate characters have an opportunity to contemplate the architecture of ancestral homes, if only, like Charles Ryder, in the brief interval before their razing. With this sustained argument between hearing and seeing, Waugh's novels frequently seem to be early demonstrations of the differences between aural and visual cultures that Marshall McLuhan would be diagnosing more than a quarter of a century later. In fact, in both his life and his works Waugh seems fit to be a textbook case for the media theorist, and one is surprised to discover that he is not a featured exhibit in McLuhan's work. Here was an artist who unmistakably stood at the borderland between traditional Western civilization and what McLuhan described as the technological re-tribalization of modern man. He could not have been better situated to illustrate McLuhan's theories. After all, what else is Tony Last's fate but an anticipatory parody of McLuhan's central thesis that the primitive culture of the ear has returned to dislodge the dominance of the literate culture of the eye?

I want to pursue this connection further for what it reveals of Waugh's characteristic asumptions. Before I do, however, I should say that I am not making a case for McLuhan's theories. McLuhan has been widely criticized for being overly reductive and there seems to be justice in the charge.[4] He often makes extraordinarily inflated claims for the explanatory power of ideas that seem more provocative metaphors than closely reasoned, fully supported arguments. In fact, McLuhan himself liked to hedge his bets by calling his more ingenious speculations "probes" as if to suggest their tentative nature and perhaps to allow himself some room to maneuver should they fall flat under the prodding of critical examination. However this may be, when his ideas are applied to Waugh, they make a surprising fit. To see this, it will be useful to outline McLuhan's major themes and consider how Waugh anticipated them.

In *The Gutenberg Galaxy* and *Understanding Media*, McLuhan distinguished between literate and preliterate man by examining the differences in their characteristic modes of perceiving the world and themselves. His findings led him to construct a theory of media-induced epistemologies. These, he claimed, had the power to shape minds and through them the world at large. According to McLuhan's argument, the literate man tends to be visual, individualistic, and detached, while the preliterate is aural, communal, and involved. The reasons for these differences stem from their respective means of disseminating information. Literate man in his typographical environment is above all a visual creature. He takes in the information he needs to live through his eyes, reading silently and alone. This naturally encourages the development of self-sufficient individualism. The manner in which print presents itself also plays a part in creating the characteristic Western sense of the world. As McLuhan's phrase has it, the medium is the message. The printed page with its linear arrangement of a typographically uniform phonetic alphabet exerts subliminal influences of far-reaching consequences. The phonetic alphabet alone, McLuhan contends, is largely responsible for cultivating the attitudes necessary to develop the advanced technology for which the West is at once famous and infamous. Because the phonetic alphabet is an easily manipulated code founded upon a system of signs arbitrarily attached to their referents, it has encouraged a habit of mind by which symbols are used not only to represent the external world, but also to direct it.

To demonstrate his point, McLuhan compares Western with other cultures and finds that historically the push for technological innovation has been nowhere so insistent as it has been in the West. Until this century, it did not exist with anything like a similar intensity in cultures whose literacy originated in ideographical, hieroglyphic, or pictographic writing. It was not that other peoples were without the knowledge and materials. In some instances, such as the Chinese, it could be argued that they were far more sophisticated than Occidentals. They did not have the Western way of looking at the world, however, a habit of mind first nurtured by the phonetic alphabet and later intensified by movable type. In cultures using pictographic writing, signs originate as visual approximations of their referents. The symbol is shaped to fit what it represents. Accordingly, the culture produced by this form of literacy moves people to adapt themselves, as they do their signs, to the natural world about them. Western civilization, on the other hand, has grown up with a phonetic alphabet in which individual characters do not represent anything other than a neutral sound that bears no necessary relation to anything outside itself. Unlike pictographic writing, phonetic characters were never married to particular external referents. They were always ready to be combined, disassembled, and recombined into signs whose reference to the external world is generally a function of collective usage over time. Once this maneuverability was enhanced by the advent of movable type, the resulting pattern of the printed page became the organizing grid through which the West viewed the world. The linear uniformity of mechanical typography with which Europeans began to devise written models of the world in the Renaissance led them to think of their external environment in linear terms. Space became a continuously extended field in which every effect could be understood to follow logically from an antecedent cause. The world opened as a series of perspectives that could be controlled as one could control the printed page. The characteristics of Western man's information media, McLuhan argues, have imbued him with a view of the world that is essentially technological. Under the regime of phonetic literacy and movable type, he has been disposed to think that the material objects of his environment can be as readily taken apart and reassembled as the manipulable code with which he signifies them. The world presents itself to him as an object decidedly external to himself to be perceived, evaluated, and altered under his detached, directorial eye. Bergson had traced the cause of the split between subject and object to the intellect's natural tendency to abstract from immediate experience. McLuhan argues the phonetic alphabet was a critical factor. Whatever the cause, both emphasize that this fissure between self and world stimulates a strong sense of individuality that expresses itself as the will to master material existence. But such a pronounced sense of self carries with it a liability. Stretched too far, the distance between subject and object produces feelings of alienation and impotence. This is especially true when the world frustrates typographically conditioned expectations and stubbornly resists human designs. If it is this latter experience on which Waugh's fiction dwells, this is because the world he portrays has lost its metaphysical confidence that there is any necessary congruence between mind and matter. Gilbert Pinfold looks upon the world *sub specie aeternitatis,* but cannot really manage it. Other characters assume their ideas will make sense of reality only to find reality does not share their assumption. The more sensitive retreat to unworldly sanctuaries. The thicker-skinned by virtue of their invincible ignorance stay in the game but are no more successful at imposing order on a world grown refractory in the absence of any transcendental authority.

In contrast to the literate sensibility, McLuhan's preliterate lives in a world of the ear. Under wilderness conditions in which danger is more likely to be heard before it is seen, hearing will often be more important than seeing. Consequently, a primitive's aural sensitivity will be far more acute than that of people living in a domesticated environment. He does not perceive his surroundings as a civilized person does. Space does not open into a series of indefinitely extensible perspectives ready to be arranged to his liking. Instead it is alive, vibrant, constantly surrounding and absorbing him with a ceaseless pulse of aural messages. He approaches it more in the hope of placating than mastering it. Neither able to interrupt nor direct his aural world, the preliterate experiences his surroundings and himself as a field of interpenetration. Nor does he make the sharp distinction between subject and object common to literate, visual cultures. Because he must listen to his tribal community not only to learn his tradition, but also for the information he needs to survive, he tends to have a less highly developed sense of individuality. He finds his identity in the tribal group. Further, McLuhan argues, the preliterate is not prepared to develop the technological habit of mind. With neither a phonetic nor pictographic system of writing, his symbols have limiting abstracting ability; they are not sharply distinquished from the concrete particulars they are meant to represent. He is conditioned to adapt himself to the natural world by various homoeopathic and totemic strategies. Relying on his ear for his identity and safety, preliterate man is necessarily submerged in his tribal community and immediate experience to a degree that severely limits his capacity for the Western style detachment and analytical reasoning that comprise the foundation of technology.

McLuhan makes this comparison of aural and visual cultures in order to clarify what he takes to be a basic change in contemporary consciousness. His point is that in superseding the mechanical technology of the industrial world, twentieth-century electronic technology has reorganized our sensorium. It has brought into existence an all-encompassing information environment that resembles more closely the preliterate's predominantly aural apprehension of reality than it does the literate's visual experience of it. The proliferation of information sources—many of them transmitted aurally—encircles contemporary man in an elaborate web that interconnects him with everyone else in what McLuhan calls the global village. McLuhan does not purport to evaluate this situation; he claims merely to describe it and tries to interpret what it means for man's sense of himself.[5]

The validity of McLuhan's speculations is not at question here. What is important is that the shift in cultural sensibility he describes is the same one Waugh portrayed in his fiction long before either *The Gutenberg Galaxy* or *Understanding Media*. Unlike McLuhan, however, Waugh did evaluate the change. His fiction portrays what McLuhan would later describe as the return to the auditory space of primitive consciousness. As we have seen, Waugh dramatized this as a way of apprehending the world that encouraged a kind of surrender to immediate experience. The consequence of such surrender could only lead to a sense of futility. Without the detachment necessary to rise above the sensate moment, one is deprived of the leverage necessary to put experience into any kind of manageable perspective. Or so Waugh thought. This is why so many of his novels rework the standard Candide plot. His naïfs are forever being evicted from a sequestered life into the roa·ing confusion of the present moment. From *Decline and Fall* onward, he portrayed the age's problem in terms of a fall from a tranquil perspective into the blare of disordered sensation. The possibility of a purposeful vision depends upon having the will to detach, to abstract oneself from the immediate moment. This cannot be accomplished in the world of the ear where the borders between the self and its surroundings are indistinct. It is only in the world of the eye that the individual can maintain the distance between subject and object necessary to a focused perspective.

It was Waugh's visual predisposition that led to his appreciation of what Wyndham Lewis called the Great Without, "the method of external approach . . . the wisdom of the eye, rather than that of the ear."[6] Like Lewis, he was unwilling to surrender metaphysical clarity. He assumed the self to be a rational spectator of a world that answers to the dimensions of human understanding, however much it may exceed them. Waugh's fierce determination to believe that existence made sense was his way of confronting the fear his fiction dramatized obsessively, the fear that the contemporary world had abandoned the achievement of the traditional essentialist epistemology in favor of the confused roaring of acoustic primitivism in which the individual dissolves into the communal mass. His work is one long report of what he seems to have thought was a collective lapse into an amorphous state of diminished consciousness.

Waugh is often called a reactionary and, indeed, he was, but not merely in the pejorative political sense. He was in reaction against the trend established by his immediate modernist predecessors, such writers as Proust, Woolf, and Joyce, and continued by many of his contemporaries. This was the strain of modernism that sought a new species of redemptive experience to be achieved by closing the distance between subject and object. These modernists were attempting to recreate—if only momentarily within the boundaries of their art—the prelapsarian harmony between self and world that Bergson had celebrated as the way to restore metaphysical health to a culture grown spiritually sterile. For Waugh, however, the world was irretrievably fallen. There is no redemptive sustenance to be drawn from a rapprochement of subject and object. In fact, his blessed moments, when they occur, are almost always characterized by silent detachment. Paul Pennyfeather's experience is typical. He finds the four weeks of solitary confinement he spends at Blackstone Gaol "among the happiest of his life" (p. 229). Then there are all the recluses who achieve what little peace of mind they can by living apart from others. Theirs is a negative, limiting sort of achievement that generally proves to be a remedy worse than the disease it would cure. There are, however, other more positive examples of isolation's rewards. Three instances are especially telling in this regard. The first comes from "The Balance," the second from *The Ordeal of Gilbert Pinfold*, and the third from *Unconditional Surrender* (published in America as *The End of the Battle*), the final volume of his Second World War trilogy, *Sword of Honour*.

Adam Doure, the protagonist of the 1926 story "The Balance," recalls an incident from his seventh year in which he climbed to the top of some precariously balanced nursery furniture only to have it collapse beneath him, precipitating a startling and painful fall to the floor. Looking back on it, he finds it to have been the first time he fully recognized himself to be distinct from the world about him. The experience has remained with him as his first intimation of the rewards of detachment.

> Adam had been too well brought up to remember very much of his life in the days before he went to his private school, but this incident survived in his memory with a clearness, which increased as he became farther removed from it, as the first occasion on which he became conscious of ill as a subjective entity. His life up till this time had been so much bounded with warnings of danger that it seemed for a moment inconceivable that he could so easily have broken through into the realm of positive bodily harm. Indeed, so incompatible did it seem with all previous experience that it was some appreciable time before he could convince himself of the continuity of this existence; but for the wealth of Hebraic and mediaeval imagery with which the idea of life outside the body had become symbolized, he could in that moment easily have believed in his own bodily extinction and the unreality of all the sensible objects about him. Later he learned to regard these periods between his fall and the dismayed advent of help from below, as the first promptings towards [the] struggle for detachment.[7]

The next two passages describe a very different sort of fall. Both are based on a single incident from Waugh's life which, despite its painful conclusion, also served to reveal the rewards of detachment. During his mottled career as an offiicer in the Second World War, he briefly undertook some parachute training. Although he seriously injured his knee on his first and last jump, he found the experience thoroughly exhilarating. "For one who values privacy there is no keener pleasure than the feeling of isolation as you float down, but it is all too short-lived, the ground is very hard and the doctors decided—as I could have told them—that I was too old to hope for many such pleasures."[8] It is this episode that turns up prominently in *The Ordeal of Gilbert Pinfold*, published in 1957.

> Once during the war [Pinfold] had gone on a parachute course which had ended ignominiously with his breaking a leg in his first drop, but he treasured as the most serene and exalted experience of his life the moment of liberation when he regained consciousness after the shock of the slipstream. A quarter of a minute before he had crouched over the open manhole in the floor of the machine, in dusk and deafening noise, trussed in harness,

crowded by apprehensive fellow-tyros. Then the despatching officer had
signalled; down he had plunged into a moment of night, to come to himself
in a silent, sunlit heaven, gently supported by what had seemed irksome
bonds, absolutely isolated. There were other parachutes all round him holding other swaying bodies; there was an instructor on the ground bawling advice through a loudspeaker; but Mr. Pinfold felt himself free of all human
communication, the sole inhabitant of a private, delicious universe. The rapture was brief. Almost at once he knew he was not floating but falling; the
field leaped up at him; a few seconds later he was lying on grass, entangled
in cords, being shouted at, breathless, bruised, with a sharp pain in the shin.
But in that moment of solitude prosaic, earthbound Mr. Pinfold had been
one with hashish-eaters and Corybantes and Californian gurus, high on the
back-stairs of mysticism. (pp. 208–9)

In 1961, the material that had gone into the making of Gilbert Pinfold's experience reappears in *The End of the Battle* when Guy Crouchback makes
his first and last parachute jump:

The harness was more uncomfortable than it had seemed on the ground.
They sat bowed and cramped, in twilight, noise, and the smell of petrol. At
length the despatching officer and his sergeant opened the man-hole. "Coming into the target area," he warned. "First pair ready." . . .
Guy jumped. For a second, as the rush of air hit him, he lost consciousness.
Then he came to himself, his senses purged of the noise and smell and throb
of the machine. The hazy November sun enveloped him in golden light. His
solitude was absolute.
He experienced rapture, something as near as his earthbound soul could
reach to a foretaste of paradise, *locum refrigerii, lucis et pacis.* The aeroplane
seemed as far distant as will, at the moment of death, the spinning earth. As
though he had cast the constraining bonds of flesh and muscle and nerve, he
found himself floating free; the harness that had so irked him in the narrow,
dusky, resounding carriage now almost imperceptibly supported him. He
was a free spirit in an element as fresh as on the day of its creation.
All too soon the moment of ecstasy ceased. (pp. 129–30)

Allowing for their obvious circumstantial differences, there is a pattern
common to these passages. In each a character suffers a fall that thoroughly
unsettles his conventional habit of mind so that he is forced to recognize
his estrangement from the world of his ordinary perception. Curiously,
this sharpened awareness of his fundamental alienation does not instill the
metaphysical unease that, say, a Jean-Paul Sartre might have derived from
it. Instead Waugh's protagonists savor these experiences as moments that
foretell some future transfiguration which will render their present confusion and suffering intelligible. Between his fall and the realization of his injury, Adam Doure recognizes himself for the first time as fully distinct from
his surroundings. His experience reflects the traditional breach between

mind and matter in Western thought. While his familiarity with "the wealth of Hebraic and mediaeval imagery" sustains his sense of his own continuing identity, he doubts the reality of "all sensible objects about him," including his own body. Although the incident is painful, it does not seem to be negative. As the years go by, he recalls it with increasing clarity as one of his "first promptings towards that struggle for detachment" which is to shape the rest of his life.

Waugh's parachute training took place some seventeen years after he wrote "The Balance," and these passages in which he dealt with it imaginatively were not written for another fourteen and sixteen years respectively. Despite these intervals, when he came to write of his free-fall, it prompted reflections remarkably similar to those occasioned by the boyhood spill of his early story, but expressed in terms that unmistakably call attention to the antinomy of the loudly embattled ear and the serenely detached eye. In both parachute passages, the protagonist takes an unsettling fall through space. First, he passes out. Then, having "regained consciousness," he experiences a "moment of liberation" from the "crowded" world of "deafening noise" filled with the "smell and throb of the machine." In this moment, "his senses purged," he enters "a private, delicious universe" in which he is "absolutely isolated" in a "silent sunlit heaven" that "envelops him in a golden light." Then the moment passes; the sensible world rushes in upon him once more as he feels the pain of returning to earth.

Waugh makes sure that his readers recognize the importance of these passages and the wartime incident that gave rise to them. Without any trace of irony, the autobiographical Pinfold is said to treasure the episode "as the most serene and exalted experience of his life." The experience is, in fact, replete with religious significance for Waugh, its metaphysical implications unmistakable. It is presented as a foretaste of Elysium and Waugh even quotes from the Latin mass to describe it as a version of the "place of comfort, light and peace" *(locum refrigerii, lucis et pacis)* to which the deceased are commended by the living. This is a Platonist's model of salvation: free-fall as an intimation of one's final release from the complexities of the sensible world into the uncluttered, changeless realm of the mind, finally delivered from the gravity and noise of material existence. To be really free one must escape the enveloping treachery of the physical world. Short of that, the pain, the din, the confusion always return.

In accord with the extreme dualism of his vision, Waugh insisted upon detachment not only as the way to salvation, but also as the prudent course to take in one's daily dealings with the world. "The secret of happiness," he had written, was "to make an interior act of renunciation and to become a stranger in the world."[9] Like Pinfold, he frequently and extravagantly de-

fied his own counsel, but he seems to have believed in its wisdom nevertheless. This put him seriously at odds with early twentieth-century
modernism whose leading champions looked for deliverance from what
they considered the artificial strictures of Western culture with its narrow
emphasis on the detached analytical intelligence as the only way to truth.
By the time Waugh had begun to publish, literary and artistic fashion had
turned to a romantic existentialism that sought fulfillment by means of an
ecstatic union of subject and object, self and world, a sort of secular mysticism frequently founded upon a rediscovery of an animistic interpretation of experience closer to primitive than to modern Western
consciousness. The important goal was to get rid of the cultural assumptions that had been blocking one's unmediated intuition of reality. Against
this movement, Waugh stood squarely and unashamedly for the Western
essentialist tradition that distinguished between the unreliable world of
the senses and the incorruptible region of pure ideas, between sensation
and perception, between the random flow of material existence and the
purposefully organizing power of mind, between the confused roaring and
the wisdom of the eye.

XI

FANATICAL EXISTENCE VS. AESTHETIC EDUCATION

This study began by asserting that Waugh resisted what he thought to be the fashionable relativism that characterized the literature and philosophy of his day. To do this, he devised an alternative to mainstream modernist fiction. As we have seen, he achieved his aim by borrowing the strategies of contemporary art and film in order to parody what had become the standard themes of modernism in the first decades of the twentieth century. The point of his early novels was to illustrate the bankruptcy of a world view divested of absolutes, and dependent upon subjective sincerity and emotional conviction for its sense of values. For all their humor, these works invariably return to the sense of overriding futility that Waugh felt to be the inescapable condition of a society that had abandoned the fixed coordinates of its essentialist tradition. In his later fiction, however, Waugh attempted to break this circle of futility with realistic novels that offered plausible responses to what he considered the bleak assumptions of the modern world.

These works—the unfinished *Work Suspended, Brideshead Revisited, Helena,* and *Sword of Honour*—are, of course, quite different from his satires, yet they share with these the same philosophical premises. In their own way they continue Waugh's resistance to conventional modernist pieties concerning the nature and function of art. To illustrate this point, we need only compare a representative passage from a writer like Virginia Woolf with one from Waugh. I have chosen the particular passages presented below for two reasons: they seem to me to typify each writer's manner, and they display these respective manners as applied to similar subjects—each excerpt describes the interior of a house. The first passage appears in Woolf's *The Waves.*

> The sun fell in sharp wedges inside the room. Whatever the light touched became dowered with a fanatical existence. A plate was like a white lake. A knife looked like a dagger of ice. Suddenly tumblers revealed themselves upheld by streaks of light. Tables and chairs rose to the surface as if they had

169

been sunk under water and rose, filmed with red, orange, purple like the bloom on the skin of ripe fruit. The veins of the glaze of the china, the grain of the wood, the fibres of the matting became more and more finely engraved. Everything was without shadow. A jar was so green that the eye seemed sucked up through a funnel by its intensity and stuck to it like a limpet.[1]

The second passage appears in *Brideshead Revisited*.

It was an aesthetic education to live within those walls, to wander from room to room, from the Soanesque library to the Chinese drawing-room, adazzle with gilt pagodas and nodding mandarins, painted paper and Chippendale fret-work, from the Pompeian parlour to the great tapestry-hung hall which stood unchanged, as it had been designed two hundred fifty years before; to sit, hour after hour, in the pillared shade looking out on the terrace. (p. 80)

The passage taken from *The Waves* exemplifies conventional modernism's attempt to raise ordinary experience to an occasion of extraordinary revelation. Woolf clearly wants us to see this room stripped of any preconceptions, as though dinnerware, chairs, and tables had never existed before. Her language seeks to defamiliarize the setting. To do so, it deliberately undermines our conventional mode of perceiving light and objects. She has attempted to create a moment of pure, unconditioned sensation in which the naive eye—as though untutored by previous experience of the physical world—perceives light that is as tangible as it is visual. Sunlight has the solidity of wedges and its reflection forms columnar streaks that support glass tumblers where they stand. We do not merely see this light, we *feel* the "fanatical existence" it radiates on everything it touches in this particular moment. This is all that seems to matter. There are no references either to the style or the period of the furniture, no attempts to place this room in its historical context. In fact, the language enforces the sense of a world without duration at all. The tables and chairs have just risen to the surface as if from under water and now shimmer iridescently, newborn, in the sunlight. Everything has just arrived and continues to pulse with the process of its birth; the sun has just fallen into the room; the tumblers "suddenly" reveal themselves; the wood grain and matting fibres are becoming "more and more finely engraved." What this room was before and what it will be afterward are for this moment irrelevant questions. There is only the all-consuming immediacy of the room itself.

As discussed in chapter IX, John Maynard Keynes wrote about such experiences in his essay on G.E. Moore's influence on the Bloomsbury circle. They constituted for his friends what really mattered in life. These were the occasions for cultivating "timeless, passionate states of contemplation and communion, largely unattached to 'before' and 'after.'"[2] In order to recreate this passionate state of mind, Woolf strives to fill the void between the perceiving self and the external world, reconnect mind with matter, and, in short, return to the edenic harmony between the individual and his environment. The result should ideally be a condition that precedes linguistic conceptualization and historical categories. As the eye, captivated by the jar's intense green, becomes "stuck to it like a limpet," so subject and object become sealed in a timeless moment of blissful union. This is what Bergson meant by *durée*, the unreflective experience in which one feels oneself indisputably engaged with the very life of things and overcomes the alienation that exists intellectually between perceiver and perceived. The experience is intuitive rather than cognitive. One *feels* the truth of existence in the eternal now of Becoming. It cannot be intellectually conceptualized and linguistically packaged for ready verbal communication to others, at least not with conventional discourse. Artists, however, wielding the defamiliarizing strategies of poetic language, can sometimes recreate the conditions in which such an experience becomes available, even though they cannot rationally explain it. Obviously, neither the analytical nor the historical imagination is of any use here. Accordingly, neither enters into Woolf's description.

In contrast to Woolf's timeless room, Waugh's is thoroughly historical. He *places* each part, each object according to its style and period: the Soanesque library, the Chinese drawing room, the Chippendale fret-work, the Pompeian parlor. We are meant to see this suite of rooms through the categories of the historical imagination. However charming its immediate dazzle, it is, as Charles Ryder says of architecture elsewhere in the novel, more important in its duration beyond the moment of his perception. Its significance is in its continuity, which we are invited to contemplate as Ryder has done "hour after hour, in the pillared shade looking out on the terrace." This is no occasion for metaphysical transcendence of the interval that separates the perceiver from the perceived. Instead the beholder is led to meditate on the tradition the building represents. He is asked to reflect on the significance of its structure, designed 250 years earlier so that it would provide him views of the surrounding parklands as they appear in their present fullness. On these terms, architecture is an "aesthetic education" in the original sense of the word: it leads one out of the darkness of self-absorption and subjectivity into the awareness of the external world one shares with others, a world which requires a clear understanding of the division between subject and object. With this awareness, the individual can achieve a proportionate sense of his worth and limits. For Waugh there was no salvation to be had in this world through art or any other secular means. The modern return to a type of animistic union between mind and matter was, of course, anathema to him. This is why he insisted upon keeping clear the distinction between subject and object.]

[Waugh's resistance to the modern attempt to make art a substitute for religion is nowhere more apparent than in *Brideshead Revisited*. This resistance is not only evident in the novel's themes but also in its style. While his earlier fiction uses figurative language sparingly, *Brideshead Revisited* is remarkable for its persistent, almost obsessive use of simile. The frequency and elaborate nature of these similes have led a number of critics to complain of the novel's ornate style and express their disappointment that Waugh had given up the spare, direct prose that had suited his ironic vision so well. But there is another way to look at this departure from the earlier style: in *Brideshead Revisited* the simile becomes the device with which Waugh opposes the assumptions that underlie conventional modernist writing.] To illustrate, I have chosen five of these similes using no principle of selection other than to list them in the order they appear in the novel.

> There is no candour in a story of early manhood which leaves out of account the home-sickness for nursery morality, the regrets and resolutions of amendment, the black hours which, like zero on the roulette table, turn up with roughly calculable regularity. (p. 62)

> I knew him well in that mood of alertness and suspicion, like a deer suddenly lifting his head at the far notes of the hunt. (p. 127)

> The subject was everywhere in the house like a fire deep in the hold of a ship, below the water-line, black and red in the darkness, coming to light in acrid wisps of smoke that curled up the ladders, crept between decks, oozed under hatches, hung in wreaths on the flats, billowed suddenly from the scuttles and air pipes. (p. 163)

> Up, down and round the argument circled and swooped like a gull, now out to sea, out of sight, cloud-bound, among irrelevancies and repetitions, now right on the patch where the offal floated. (pp. 196–97)

> The indiscriminate chatter of praise all that crowded day had worked on me like a succession of advertisement hoardings on a long road, kilometre after kilometre between the poplars, commanding one to stay at some new hotel, so that when at the end of the drive, stiff and dusty, one arrives at the destination, it seems inevitable to turn into the yard under the name that had first bored, then angered one, and finally become an inseparable part of one's fatigue. (p. 270)

These selections constitute only a small sampling of the similes that appear throughout the novel. Allowing for individual variations, these figures tend to become more elaborate and extended as the narrative progresses. Two questions arise: first, why does Waugh return to the simile as his favored trope throughout this novel, and second, why does he seem to be intent upon calling our attention to this esthetic decision by making these similes so strikingly complex? The answer to both questions lies, I think, in his reaction to the modernism of his immediate predecessors.

To illustrate, let us compare Waugh's similes to Woolf's. In *The Waves* Woolf's figurative language does not point outward to the external world but rather inward to the subjective experience the external environment occasions. This I take to be what she meant when she wrote of the "luminous halo," the "semitransparent envelope surrounding us from the beginning of consciousness to the end." It was "the task of the novelist to convey" this inward experience "with as little mixture of the alien and the external as possible."[3] Accordingly, in these figures, the first terms, the objects that provoke comparisons, are not nearly as important as the second terms—the wedges of sunlight, the white lake, the dagger of ice. As we have seen, the point of this language is to appropriate externals in an ecstatic embrace of the imagination that cancels the distinction between the image and what it represents, between mind and object.

Waugh's similes have the opposite effect. They never lead to any confusion between subject and object, nor is there ever any doubt that the second term in these comparisons is subordinate to the first. However elaborately developed, the second term's purpose is always clearly illustrative. We are never in danger of fusing the two sides of the comparison in an instant of imaginative transcendence. Rather than transforming a familiar concrete object into some new and arresting sensation, the second term in these comparisons usually visualizes either a particular idea or the sequence of a character's reflections. They are not meant to defamiliarize the first term of the comparison, but rather simply to clarify it. Just as we could never mistake a statue of a blindfolded, scale-carrying woman for Justice itself, so, in the fifth simile above, we would never mistake the image of successive roadside advertising hoardings for the indiscriminate chatter of superficial praise that exhausts Charles Ryder. Waugh's similes are in the classic tradition; their second terms make public and accessible what is essentially private and unique. They are openly artificial, their function only to elucidate and elaborate.

But Waugh's use of figurative language has more than an illustrative function; it testifies to his conviction that this is an irremediably fallen world and that the only way to make it bearable is to participate in the civilized endeavor to impose order on the "anarchic raw materials of life." He thought of this endeavor as the ongoing cumulative effort of generations, the results of which could be best discerned in art which endures beyond the individual even as it shapes his life with the historical perspective it uniquely affords. This is why his similes have been constructed with Homeric elaboration, beginning with a simple comparison and then driving it through one permutation after another. They are thoroughly traditional, taking up the classical attempt to make sense of things in a way that will be communicable not only to one's contemporaries but also to future generations. Typically Waugh's simile suggests the deliberation of architecture, his favored art; it holds the two poles of its comparison in plain view, clearly separated from one another, and invites detached contemplation of its poised artifice. Their verbal construction allows for the silent space between object and figure necessary for intellectual rather than intuitive apprehension. Beyond their illustrative and decorative functions, these similes speak of Waugh's belief in the civilizing power of the word that discovers rational order in the confused roaring of our experience.

NOTES

Introduction

1. Critics representative of those who think Waugh's work lacks a consistent rationale are Donat O'Donnell (Conor Cruise O'Brien), *Maria Cross: Imaginative Patterns in a Group of Modern Catholic Writers*; Sean O'Faolain, *The Vanishing Hero: Studies in Novelists of the Twenties*; Frederick J. Stopp, *Evelyn Waugh: Portrait of an Artist*; Malcolm Bradbury, *Evelyn Waugh*; and David Lodge, *Evelyn Waugh*. With varying degrees of success, moral interpretations have been provided by Stephen Jay Greenblatt, *Three Modern Satirists: Waugh, Orwell, and Huxley*, and William J. Cook, *Masks, Modes, and Morals: The Art of Evelyn Waugh*. While all these commentators have provided important insights, it seems to me that those who have addressed both Waugh's metaphysical concerns and his personal contradictions have come closest to what makes him relevant today. Alvin B. Kernan, *The Plot of Satire*, and James F. Carens, *The Satiric Art of Evelyn Waugh*, have revealed the subtlety and complexity of Waugh's enterprise. More recently, Jeffrey M. Heath, *The Picturesque Prison: Evelyn Waugh and His Writing*, has given us an especially sensitive appraisal of how Waugh projected his personal conflicts into his fiction.

2. "Fan-Fare," *Life*, 8 April 1946, collected in *The Essays, Articles, and Reviews of Evelyn Waugh*, p. 304. In subsequent references this collection will be identified as *Essays*.

3. "The War and the Younger Generation," *Essays*, p. 62.

4. "Tolerance," *Essays*, p. 128.

5. *Decline and Fall*, pp. 1–2. Subsequent references to the Little, Brown republication edition of Waugh's works will appear parenthetically in the text.

6. Waugh subtitled this novel a conversation piece and explained in a prefatory note that Pinfold was modeled on himself.

7. O'Faolain, pp. 68–69.

8. *Labels: A Mediterranean Journal*, pp. 11–12.

9. Christopher Sykes, *Evelyn Waugh: A Biography*, p. 308. See *Evelyn Waugh and His World*, ed. David Pryce-Jones (London: Weidenfeld & Nicolson, 1973), p. 209, for a photograph of Eurich's painting.

10. "Felix Culpa," *Commonweal*, 16 July 1948, *Essays*, p. 360.

11. "Felix Culpa," p. 360.

12. "The War and the Younger Generation," *Essays*, p. 62.

I. Confused Roaring

1. This confrontation between the barbarous aristocracy and the temperate middle class seems much indebted to Matthew Arnold's *Culture and Anarchy*, from which Waugh may have also taken the title of his second novel. In discussing middle-class philistinism, Arnold declares himself "a sort of *corpus vile* to serve for illustration."

2. See Kernan, *Plot of Satire*, pp. 152–55, for a persuasive demonstration that satire naturally tends toward a circular plot because the satirist generally portrays a futile world in which progress and change are impossible.

3. Friedrich Nietzsche, *The Birth of Tragedy and The Genealogy of Morals*, trans. Francis Golffing (New York: Doubleday, 1956), pp. 34–35.

4. See Evelyn Waugh, "Come Inside," in *The Road to Damascus*, ed. John A. O'Brien (New York: Doubleday, 1949), and now collected in *Essays*, p. 367, in which Waugh recalls undertaking "an unguided and half-comprehended study of metaphysics" while at Lancing. *The Diaries of Evelyn Waugh*, include a number of brief references to his philosophical interests; the entry of 26 August 1925, p. 218, mentions he was "reading a little Bergson."

5. *Birth of Tragedy*, pp. 97, 108–9. Here and elsewhere, Nietzsche argues that the individuating categories of the intellect impose an Apollonian illusion of order and stability on the flux of existence.

6. *Birth of Tragedy*, pp. 101–2.

7. "Converted to Rome: Why It Has Happened to Me," *Essays*, p. 104.

8. *Birth of Tragedy*, p. 81.

9. Edmund Wilson, "'Never Apologize, Never Explain': The Art of Evelyn Waugh," *Classics and Commercials*, p. 146.

10. Carens, *Satiric Art*, p. 73.

11. *Labels*, p. 11.

12. Oswald Spengler, *The Decline of the West: Form and Actuality*, pp. 382, 377–428.

13. "Fan-Fare," *Essays*, p. 304.

II. Desire, Doubt, and the Superb Mean

1. "The Balance," *Georgian Stories 1926*, pp. 253–91.

2. Harold Acton, *Memoirs of an Aesthete*, p. 126.

3. Kernan, *Plot of Satire*, p. 167, considers this point but does not arrive at a definite conclusion.

4. Ronald Knox, *God and the Atom*, p. 93.

5. "The War and the Younger Generation," *Essays*, p. 62.

6. *When the Going Was Good* (Middlesex: Penguin, 1951, 1946), pp. 8, 187. In the first quotation Waugh refers to his character Charles Ryder of *Brideshead Revisited*, concluding, "Thus 'Charles Ryder'; thus myself."

7. "Half in Love with Easeful Death: An Examination of Californian Burial Customs," *Essays*, p. 336.

8. "Come Inside," *Essays*, p. 368.

9. Sykes, p. 287.

10. Sykes, p. 334.

11. "The War and the Younger Generation," *Essays*, p. 62.

12. *Diaries*, pp. 437, 443.

13. Waugh's Preface to Ronald Knox, *A Spiritual Aeneid*, p. vi.

14. "Fan-Fare," *Essays*, p. 304.

15. "Conservative Manifesto," *Essays*, pp. 161–62.

16. Martin C. D'Arcy, *The Nature of Belief* (St. Louis: Herder, 1958, 1931), pp. 65–66.

17. *Labels*, pp. 8–12; "Converted to Rome," *Essays*, pp. 103–5; and "Come Inside," *Essays*, pp. 366–68, are notable examples.

III. An Unguided and Half-Comprehended Study of Metaphysics

1. "A Modern Credo," *Oxford Broom*, 1923, I, unpaginated. A copy is held by the Humanities Research Center, University of Texas at Austin.

2. "Come Inside," *Essays*, p. 367.

3. "Come Inside," *Essays*, p. 367.

4. *Diaries*, p. 218.

5. Filippo Tommaso Marinetti, "The New Religion-Morality of Speed," *Marinetti: Selected Writing*, p. 96.

6. "Satire and Fiction," *Essays*, p. 102.

7. *The Letters of Evelyn Waugh*, ed. Mark Amory, p. 30. This is an undated note to Waugh's agent, A.D. Peters. Amory places it between October 1928 and February 1929.

8. Wyndham Lewis, "Winn and Waugh," *The Doom of Youth*, pp. 99, 106–7.

9. Wyndham Lewis, *Satire and Fiction*, p. 51.

10. "Satire and Fiction," *Essays*, p. 102. Fredric Jameson, *Fables of Aggression: Wyndham Lewis, the Modernist as Fascist*, p. 2, suggests that Lewis is read today as "a more scandalous and explosive Waugh." Put this way, Jameson's remark seems to slight Waugh for not being as ideologically extreme as Lewis. Aside from its implied devaluation, however, the assessment is a fair one. Waugh had a good deal in common with Lewis. They were especially alike in their ambivalent response to modernism. Jameson argues that Lewis fashioned his esthetic in reaction to mainstream modernism. As I argue in this and the next two chapters, Waugh also wrote in reaction to modernist fashions. He was never as systematically rigorous as Lewis, but this does not preclude the very likely possibility that Lewis served him as a model. Certainly his review of *Satire and Fiction* suggests this.

11. Henri Bergson, *Creative Evolution*, pp. 330–87.

12. Norman Mailer, "The White Negro," *Advertisements for Myself* (London: Andre Deutsch, 1961, 1957), p. 298.

13. Lewis argues throughout *Time and Western Man* against Bergson's tenets but considers his thought most closely in Book II, "An Analysis of the Philosophy of Time," pp. 131–463, which also includes discussions of Samuel Alexander, Alfred North Whitehead, and Oswald Spengler among other "time-philosophers," as Lewis called them.

14. *Satire and Fiction*, pp. 51–53.

15. *Time and Western Man*, pp. 162–259.

16. Marinetti, "The New Religion-Morality of Speed," *Marinetti: Selected Writings*, p. 96.

17. Marinetti, "The Founding and Manifesto of Futurism," *Marinetti: Selected Writings*, p. 41.

18. "Fan-Fare," p. 302.

19. Marinetti, "The Birth of a Futurist Aesthetic," *Marinetti: Selected Writings*, p. 81.

IV. A Pure Aesthete

1. Reported in Martin Stannard's review of Waugh's diaries, *New Review*, December 1976, collected in Stannard's *Evelyn Waugh: The Critical Heritage*, p. 493. The interview was conducted by John Freeman on *Face to Face*, a BBC program.

2. *Work Suspended*, in *Tactical Exercise*, p. 140.

3. "A Call to Orders," *Essays*, p. 216.

4. "The Death of Painting," *Essays*, pp. 504–5.

5. "In Defense of Cubism," *Essays*, p. 8.

6. "A Neglected Masterpiece," *Essays*, p. 82.

7. "Felix Culpa," *Essays*, p. 360.

8. *Labels*, pp. 173–82.

9. "The Death of Painting," *Essays*, pp. 503–7.

10. "A Modern Credo," I, unpaginated.

11. The exhibit was reviewed by Charensol, "Les Expositions," *L'Art Vivant*, February 1929, with some general comments about the artists included.

12. *Labels*, p. 20.

13. See reproductions in William Camfield's *Francis Picabia* (Milan: Galleria Schwarz, 1972), unpaginated.

14. See reproductions in Pamela Pritzker, *Ernst* (New York: Leon Amiel, 1975), unpaginated.
15. *Labels*, p. 14.
16. "Felix Culpa," *Essays*, p. 360.
17. Gertrude Stein, *Picasso* (London, 1939), as quoted in Wylie Sypher, *Rococo to Cubism in Art and Literature* (New York: Macmillan, 1960), pp. 310–11.
18. *Letters*, p. 215.
19. "The Balance," p. 262.

V. Smashing and Crashing: Waugh on the Modernist Esthetic

1. *Letters*, p. 270.
2. *Diaries*, p. 29.
3. *Letters*, p. 622.
4. "Fan-Fare," *Essays*, p. 302.
5. "Ronald Firbank," *Essays*, p. 59.
6. Virginia Woolf, "Modern Fiction," *Collected Essays* (New York: Harcourt, 1967), II, p. 106.
7. *Labels*, p. 181.
8. *Rossetti: His Life and Works* (New York: Dodd, Mead, 1928), p. 52.
9. *Labels*, pp. 181–82.
10. Irving Howe, *The Idea of the Modern in Literature and the Arts*, p. 14.
11. Woolf, "Mr. Bennett and Mrs. Brown," *Collected Essays*, I, p. 330.
12. Woolf, "Modern Fiction," p. 108.
13. Woolf, "Mr. Bennett and Mrs. Brown," p. 321.
14. Woolf, "Mr. Bennett and Mrs. Brown," pp. 333–34.
15. "Ronald Firbank," *Essays*, p. 57.
16. "Ronald Firbank," pp. 57–59.
17. Woolf, "How It Strikes a Contemporary," *Collected Essays*, II, p. 159.
18. "Fan-Fare," *Essays*, p. 303.
19. *When the Going Was Good*, p. 8. In the preface to this collection of his travel writings, Waugh quotes Charles Ryder at some length and then explicitly identifies Ryder's point of view with his own.
20. "Fan-Fare," p. 304.

VI. Becoming Characters: The Shameless Blonde and the Mysteriously Disappearing Self

1. Graham Martin, "Novelists of Three Decades: Evelyn Waugh, Graham Greene, C. P. Snow," in *The Modern Age*, VII of *The Pelican Guide to English Literature*, ed. Boris Ford (Middlesex: Penguin, 1961), p. 400.
2. See Waugh's review, "Satire and Fiction," p. 102.
3. "Tolerance," *Essays*, p. 128.
4. "Fan-Fare," p. 304.
5. "Felix Culpa," p. 360.
6. "Fan-Fare," p. 304.
7. *When the Going Was Good*, p. 8.
8. Kernan, *Plot of Satire*, pp. 90–103, 152–55.
9. "Fan-Fare," p. 302.
10. *Work Suspended*, as quoted by Christopher Hollis, *Evelyn Waugh*, p. 8. Hollis used the unrevised text published by Chapman & Hall, London, in 1942 in a limited edition of 500 copies. Martin Stannard, "*Work Suspended*: Waugh's Climacteric," pp. 312–13, compares the original 1942 text with the 1949 version and

finds that a good deal has been eliminated in revision, including the passage Hollis quotes.

11. "Fan-Fare," p. 302.

12. In *Diaries*, pp. 413, 418, Waugh describes the film plot he is supposed to be working on as "vulgar" and the film he watches as "appalling"; also see "Why Hollywood Is a Term of Disparagement," *Essays*, pp. 325–31.

VII. Film: The Glaring Lens of Satire

1. *Letters*, p. 2.

2. *Letters*, p. 464.

3. Sykes, pp. 55–56; *Diaries*, p. 169; The Humanities Research Center, University of Texas at Austin, kindly allowed me to screen their print.

4. "The Balance," pp. 253–91.

5. "Excursion in Reality," *Tactical Exercise*, pp. 53–69; Sykes, p. 171, discusses Waugh's work for Alexander Korda, the film producer.

6. *Labels*, p. 11.

7. "Felix Culpa," p. 360.

8. "Ronald Firbank," p. 58.

9. "Felix Culpa," pp. 362–63.

10. See Arnold Hauser, "The Film Age," in *The Idea of the Modern in Literature and the Arts*, pp. 225–35; Marshall McLuhan, *Understanding Media*, pp. 284–96.

11. "Fan-Fare," p. 303.

12. Hauser, pp. 226–34.

13. Bergson, pp. 330–35.

14. "The Balance," p. 287.

VIII. The Satirist of the Film World

1. "Felix Culpa," p. 362.

2. Martin Price, "The Irrelevant Detail and the Emergence of Form," in *Aspects of Narrative: Selected Papers from the English Institute*, ed. J. Hillis Miller (New York: Columbia University Press, 1971), p. 81.

3. Alan Spiegel, *Fiction and the Camera Eye*, pp. 92–93.

4. "Fan-Fare," p. 302; "Felix Culpa," p. 362.

5. "Ronald Firbank," p. 59.

6. "Felix Culpa," p. 362.

7. "Fan-Fare," p. 303.

8. *Labels*, p. 20.

9. Brian Wicker, "Waugh and the Narrator as Dandy," *The Story Shaped World*, pp. 155–58.

10. "Why Hollywood Is a Term of Disparagement," p. 328.

11. Virginia Woolf, "The Cinema," *Collected Essays*, II, pp. 268–72.

12. "Why Hollywood Is a Term of Disparagement," p. 329.

13. "Fan-Fare," p. 302.

14. "Why Hollywood Is a Term of Disparagement," p. 328.

15. Hauser, pp. 233–35; Spiegel, p. 32.

16. "The Balance," p. 278.

17. Woolf, "The Cinema," pp. 268–72.

IX. Chromium Plating and Natural Sheepskin: The New Barbarians

1. *Helena*, p. 47. This 1950 novel has not been republished with the others,

which is unfortunate. Whatever one makes of its apologetics, it is an entertaining historical romance with a good deal of colorful legend thrown in.

2. Alvin B. Kernan, "The Wall and the Jungle," pp. 199–202.

3. *When the Going Was Good*, p. 8.

4. *Diaries*, p. 787.

5. *Diaries*, p. 791.

6. Heath, *Picturesque Prison*, p. 381.

7. Paul Johnson, *Modern Times: The World from the Twenties to the Eighties* (New York: Harper, 1983), pp. 1–12, 697–98.

8. Claud Cockburn, "Evelyn Waugh's Lost Rabbit," p. 57, recalls that Waugh's xenophobia was so pronounced that he could not believe that Cockburn, who was his second cousin, had Hungarian relatives.

9. *Work Suspended*, in *Tactical Exercise*, pp. 157–58.

10. John Maynard Keynes, "My Early Beliefs," in *Two Memoirs* (New York: Augustus M. Kelley, 1949), pp. 83–84, 95–100.

11. Cockburn, p. 57.

12. Sykes, p. 267.

13. Cyril Connolly, *The Unquiet Grave: A Word Cycle by Palinurus* (London: Horizon, 1944), pp. 19, 49. Waugh's copy with his marginalia is in the collection of the Humanities Research Center, University of Texas at Austin.

X. The Wisdom of the Eye

1. *Diaries*, p. 788.

2. Cockburn, p. 59.

3. Sykes, p. 106; Acton, p. 127.

4. Paul Johnson, *Enemies of Society* (New York: Atheneum, 1977), pp. 149–50, argues the case against McLuhan forcefully. Like many others, however, he mistakes the media theorist's purpose. McLuhan did not intend to approve the technologically induced return to aural space; he only meant to describe it.

5. McLuhan, pp. 22–55, 77–88.

6. Lewis, *Satire and Fiction*, p. 53. Certainly Waugh's review of Lewis's book ("Satire and Fiction," *Essays*, p. 102) displays an enthusiastically admiring tone uncharacteristic of the urbane pose his other pieces cultivate.

7. "The Balance," p. 287.

8. *Letters*, p. 181.

9. *Diaries*, p. 787.

XI. Fanatical Existence vs. Aesthetic Education

1. Virginia Woolf, *The Waves* (1931; rpt. New York: Harcourt, 1959), pp. 109–10.

2. Keynes, p. 83.

3. Woolf, "Modern Fiction," p. 106.

SELECTED BIBLIOGRAPHY

Novels by Evelyn Waugh

The following works by Evelyn Waugh were republished by Little, Brown & Co., Boston, between 1977 and 1982. Each title appears with the date of its original publication.

Decline and Fall, 1928.
Vile Bodies, 1930.
Black Mischief, 1932.
A Handful of Dust, 1934.
Scoop, 1938.
Put Out More Flags, 1942.
Brideshead Revisited, 1945.
The Loved One, 1948.
Men at Arms, 1952.
Officers and Gentlemen, 1955.
The Ordeal of Gilbert Pinfold, 1957.
The End of the Battle (Unconditional Surrender), 1961.
Charles Ryder's Schooldays and Other Stories, 1982.

Other Works by Waugh

"The Balance." In *Georgian Stories 1926*. Volume 4. Ed. Alec Waugh. London: Chapman & Hall, 1926, pp. 253–91.
The Diaries of Evelyn Waugh. Ed. Michael Davies. London: Weidenfeld & Nicolson, 1976.
Edmund Campion. New York: Doubleday, 1946, 1956.
The Essays, Articles, and Reviews of Evelyn Waugh. Ed. Donat Gallagher. Boston: Little, Brown, 1983.
Helena. Boston: Little, Brown, 1951, 1950.
Labels: A Mediterranean Journal. London: Duckworth, 1930.
The Letters of Evelyn Waugh. Ed. Mark Amory. New York: Ticknor & Fields, 1980.
A Little Learning: An Autobiography. Boston: Little, Brown, 1964.
A Little Order. Ed. Donat Gallagher. London: Eyre Methuen, 1977.
Mr. Loveday's Little Outing and Other Sad Stories. London: Chapman & Hall, 1936.
Monsignor Ronald Knox. Boston: Little, Brown, 1959.
Ninety-Two Days. New York: Farrar & Rinehart, 1934.
Preface to Ronald Knox. *A Spiritual Aeneid*. 1948. Rpt. London: Burns, Oates, 1958.
Remote People. London: Duckworth, 1931.
Robbery under the Law: The Mexican Object-Lesson. London: Chapman & Hall, 1939.
"Ronald Firbank." In *Life and Letters*. Volume 2. March 1929, pp. 192–94.
Rossetti: His Life and Works. London: Duckworth, 1930.
Scott-King's Modern Europe. Boston: Little, Brown, 1949.
Sword of Honour. One-volume edition. London: Chapman & Hall, 1965.
Tactical Exercise. Boston: Little, Brown, 1954. (Includes *Work Suspended*.)
Tourist in Africa. Boston: Little, Brown, 1960.
Waugh in Abyssinia. London: Longmans, Green, 1936.
When the Going Was Good. London: Duckworth, 1946

Secondary Sources

Acton, Harold. *Memoirs of an Aesthete*. London: Methuen, 1948.
Bergonzi, Bernard. "Evelyn Waugh's Gentlemen." *Critical Quarterly* 5 (1963), pp. 23–36.
Bergson, Henri. *Creative Evolution*. Trans. Arthur Mitchell. New York: Random House, 1944, 1911.
Blazac, Alain. "Technique and Meaning in *Scoop:* Is *Scoop* a Modern Fairy-Tale?" *Evelyn Waugh Newsletter* 6 (1972), pp. 1–8.
Bradbury, Malcolm. *Evelyn Waugh*. Edinburgh and London: Oliver & Boyd, 1964.
Burgess, Anthony. *The Novel Now: A Guide to Contemporary Fiction*. New York: Norton, 1967.
Carens, James F. *The Satiric Art of Evelyn Waugh*. Seattle: University of Washington Press, 1966.
Cevasco, George A. "Huysmans and Waugh." *Evelyn Waugh Newsletter* 17 (1983), pp. 5–7.
Churchill, Thomas. "The Trouble with *Brideshead Revisited*." *Modern Language Quarterly* 28 (1967), pp. 213–28.
Cockburn, Claud. "Evelyn Waugh's Lost Rabbit." *Atlantic* 232 (December 1973), pp. 53–59.
Cook, William J. *Masks, Modes, and Morals: The Art of Evelyn Waugh*. Rutherford: Fairleigh Dickinson University Press, 1971.
Coxe, Louis O. "The Protracted Sneer." *New Republic* 8 (November 1954), pp. 20–21.
Davis, Robert M. *Evelyn Waugh*. St. Louis: Herder, 1969.
_____. "Evelyn Waugh on the Art of Fiction." *Papers on Language and Literature* 2 (1966), pp. 243–52.
_____. *Evelyn Waugh, Writer*. Norman: Pilgrim Books, 1981.
_____. "*Harper's Bazaar* and *A Handful of Dust*." *Philological Quarterly* 48 (1969), pp. 508–16.
_____. "The Mind and Art of Evelyn Waugh." *Papers on Language and Literature* 3 (1967), pp. 270–87.
_____. "Notes towards Waugh's Aesthetic." *Evelyn Waugh Newsletter* 18 (1984), pp. 1–2.
_____. "Title and Theme in *A Handful of Dust*." *Evelyn Waugh Newsletter* 6 (1972), p. 1.
Delbaere-Farant, J. "'Who Shall Inherit England?': A Comparison between *Howards End, Parade's End*, and *Unconditional Surrender*." *English Studies* 50 (1969), pp. 101–5.
Dennis, Nigel. "Evelyn Waugh: The Pillar of Anchorage House." *Partisan Review* 10 (July-August 1943), pp. 350–61.
DeVitis, A.A. *Roman Holiday: The Catholic Novels of Evelyn Waugh*. New York: Bookman, 1956.
Dooley, D.J. "Waugh and Black Humor." *Evelyn Waugh Newsletter* 2 (1968), pp. 1–3.
Doyle, Paul A. *Evelyn Waugh: A Critical Essay*. Grand Rapids: Eerdmans, 1969.
_____. "Waugh's *Brideshead Revisited*." *Explicator* 24 (1966), Item 57.
Dyson, A.E. "Evelyn Waugh and the Mysteriously Disappearing Hero." *Critical Quarterly* 2 (1960), pp. 72–79.
Eagleton, Terry. *Exiles and Emigres*. New York: Schocken, 1970.
Farr, D. Paul. "Evelyn Waugh: Tradition and a Modern Talent." *South Atlantic Quarterly* 68 (1969), pp. 506–19.
_____. "Waugh's Conservative Stance: Defending 'The Standards of Civilization'." *Philological Quarterly* 51 (1972), pp. 471–84.

Frank, Joseph. "Spatial Form in Modern Literature: and "The Dehumanization of Art." In *The Widening Gyre: Crisis and Mastery in Modern Literature.* New Brunswick: Rutgers University Press, 1963.

Frye, Northrop. *Anatomy of Criticism.* Princeton: Princeton University Press, 1973, 1957.

Fussell, Paul. "Evelyn Waugh's Moral Entertainments." In *Abroad.* New York: Oxford University Press, 1980.

Gill, Richard. *Happy Rural Seat: The English Country House and the Literary Imagination.* New Haven: Yale University Press, 1972.

Greenblatt, Stephen Jay. *Three Modern Satirists: Waugh, Orwell, and Huxley.* New Haven: Yale University Press, 1965.

Greene, Donald. "Evelyn Waugh's Hollywood." *Evelyn Waugh Newsletter* 16 (1982), pp. 1–4.

Hauser, Arnold. "The Film Age." In *The Social History of Art.* Collected in *The Idea of the Modern in Literature and the Arts.* Ed. Irving Howe. New York: Horizon, 1967, pp. 225–35.

Heath, Jeffrey M. *The Picturesque Prison: Evelyn Waugh and His Writing.* Montreal: McGill-Queen's University Press, 1982.

Hollis, Christopher. *Evelyn Waugh.* London: Longmans, Green, 1954.

Howarth, Herbert. "Quelling the Riot: Evelyn Waugh's Progress." In *The Shapeless God: Essays of Modern Fiction.* Ed. Harry J. Mooney and Thomas F. Staley. Pittsburgh: University of Pittsburgh Press, 1968, pp. 67–69.

Howe, Irving. *The Idea of the Modern in Literature and the Arts.* New York: Horizon, 1967.

Hynes, Joseph. "Varieties of Death Wish: Evelyn Waugh's Central Theme." *Criticism* 14 (1972), pp. 65–77.

Hynes, Samuel. *The Auden Generation: Literature and Politics in the 1930s.* New York: Viking, 1977.

Jameson, Fredric. *Fables of Aggression: Wyndham Lewis, the Modernist as Fascist.* Berkeley: University of California Press, 1979.

Jebb, Julian. "Evelyn Waugh: An Interview." *Paris Review* 8 (1963), pp. 73–85.

Jervis, Steven A. "Evelyn Waugh, *Vile Bodies,* and the Younger Generation." *South Atlantic Quarterly* 66 (1967), pp. 440–48.

Kaplan, Stanley R. "Circularity and Futility in *Black Mischief.*" *Evelyn Waugh Newsletter* 15 (1981) pp. 1–4.

Kenner, Hugh. *The Pound Era.* Berkeley: University of California Press, 1971.

Kermode, Frank. "Mr. Waugh's Cities." In *Puzzles and Epiphanies.* London: Routledge & Kegan Paul, 1962, pp. 164–75.

Kernan, Alvin B. *The Plot of Satire.* New Haven: Yale University Press, 1965.

————. "A Theory of Satire." In *The Cankered Muse: Satire of the English Renaissance.* New Haven: Yale University Press, 1962, 1959, pp. 1–36, 192—246.

————. "The Wall and the Jungle." *Yale Review* 53 (Winter 1963), pp. 199–220.

Knox, Ronald. *God and the Atom.* London: Sheed & Ward, 1945.

Kosok, Heinz. "The Film World of *Vile Bodies.*" *Evelyn Waugh Newsletter* 4 (1970), pp. 1–2.

Lane, Calvin W. *Evelyn Waugh.* Boston: Twayne, 1981.

————. "Waugh Incunabula." *Evelyn Waugh Newsletter* 17 (1983), p. 4.

Lewis, Wyndham. *Satire and Fiction.* London: Arthur Press, 1930.

————. *Time and Western Man.* 1927. Rpt. Boston: Beacon, 1957.

————. "The Vorticist." *Vogue* (September 1956). Collected in *Wyndham Lewis on Art: Collected Writings 1913–1956.* Ed. Walter Michel and C.J. Fix. New York: Funk & Wagnalls, 1969.

————. "Vortices and Notes." In *Wyndham Lewis on Art: Collected Writings 1913–1956.*

———. "Winn and Waugh." In *The Doom of Youth.* New York: Robert McBride, 1932.

Linck, Charles E., Jr., and Robert M. Davis. "The Bright Young People in *Vile Bodies." Papers on Language and Literature* 5 (1969), pp. 80–90.

———. "Waugh-Greenidge Film—*The Scarlet Woman." Evelyn Waugh Newsletter* 3 (1969), pp. 1–7.

Linklater, Eric. "Evelyn Waugh." In *The Art of Adventure.* London: Macmillan, 1948, pp. 44–58.

Littlewood, Ian. *The Writings of Evelyn Waugh.* Oxford: Basil Blackwell, 1983.

Lodge, David. *Evelyn Waugh.* New York: Columbia University Press, 1971.

Marcus, Steven. "Evelyn Waugh and the Art of Entertainment." *Partisan Review* 23 (Summer 1956), pp. 348–57.

Marinetti, Filippo Tommaso. *Marinetti: Selected Writings.* Ed. R.W. Flint. Trans. R.W. Flint and Arthur A. Coppotelli. New York: Farrar, Straus, 1971.

McCaffrey, Donald W. *"The Loved One:* An Irreverent, Invective, Dark Film Comedy." *Literature/Film Quarterly* 11 (1983) pp. 83–87.

McLuhan, Marshall, *Understanding Media: The Extensions of Man.* New York: McGraw-Hill, 1964.

Mikes, George. "Evelyn Waugh." In *Eight Humorists.* London: Wingate, 1954, pp. 131–46.

Nichols, James W. "Romantic and Realistic: The Tone of Evelyn Waugh's Early Novels." *College English* (October 1962), pp. 45–56.

O'Donnell, Donat (Conor Cruise O'Brien). *Maria Cross: Imaginative Patterns in a Group of Modern Catholic Writers.* London: Oxford University Press, 1952.

O'Faolain, Sean. *The Vanishing Hero: Studies in Novelists of the Twenties.* London: Eyre & Spottiswoode, 1956.

Phillips, Gene D. *Evelyn Waugh's Officers, Gentlemen and Rogues.* Chicago: Nelson-Hall, 1975.

Pritchett, V.S. "Cleverest English Novelist Alive." *New Statesman and Nation* (May 7, 1949), p. 473.

Pryce-Jones, David, ed. *Evelyn Waugh and His World.* Boston: Little, Brown, 1973.

Slater, Ann Pasternak. "Waugh's *A Handful of Dust:* Right Things in Wrong Places." *Essays in Criticism* 32 (1982), pp. 48–68.

Spengler, Oswald. *The Decline of the West: Form and Actuality.* New York: Knopf 1976, 1926.

Spiegel, Alan. *Fiction and the Camera Eye: Visual Consciousness in Film and the Modern Novel.* Charlottesville: University Press of Virginia, 1976.

Stannard, Martin. "Debunking the Jungle: The Context of Evelyn Waugh's Travel Books." *Prose Studies* 5 (1982), pp. 101–26.

———. *Evelyn Waugh: The Critical Heritage.* London: Routledge & Kegan Paul, 1984.

———. *"Work Suspended:* Waugh's Climacteric." *Essays in Criticism* 28 (October 1978), pp. 312–26.

Stopp, Frederick J. *Evelyn Waugh: Portrait of an Artist.* Boston: Little, Brown, 1958.

Sykes, Christopher. *Evelyn Waugh: A Biography.* Boston: Little Brown, 1975.

Ulanov, Barry. "The Ordeal of Evelyn Waugh." In *The Vision Obscured: Perceptions of Some Twentieth-Century Catholic Novelists.* Ed. Melvin J. Friedman. New York: Fordham University Press, 1970, pp. 79–93.

Wasson, Richard. *"A Handful of Dust:* Critique of Victorianism." *Modern Fiction Studies* 7 (1961–62), pp. 327–37.

Waugh, Alec. *My Brother Evelyn and Other Profiles.* London: Cassell, 1967.

Wicker, Brian. "Waugh and the Narrator as Dandy." In *The Story Shaped World*. Notre Dame: University of Notre Dame Press, 1975.
Wilson, Edmund. "'Never Apologize, Never Explain': The Art of Evelyn Waugh" and "Splendors and Miseries of Evelyn Waugh." In *Classics and Commercials*. New York: Farrar, Straus, 1950, pp. 140–46, 298–305.
Woolf, Virginia. "The Movies and Reality." *New Republic* (4 August 1926).
Worcester, David. *The Art of Satire*. New York: Russell & Russell, 1960, 1940.

INDEX